THE 50 GREATEST PLAYERS IN NEW YORK METS HISTORY

ALSO AVAILABLE IN THE 50 GREATEST PLAYERS SERIES

The 50 Greatest Players in Boston Celtics History
The 50 Greatest Players in Boston Red Sox History
The 50 Greatest Players in Braves History
The 50 Greatest Players in Buffalo Bills History
The 50 Greatest Players in Chicago Bears History
The 50 Greatest Players in Cincinnati Bengals History
The 50 Greatest Players in Cleveland Browns History
The 50 Greatest Players in Dallas Cowboys History
The 50 Greatest Players in Denver Broncos History
The 50 Greatest Players in Detroit Lions History
The 50 Greatest Players in Detroit Tigers History
The 50 Greatest Players in Green Bay Packers History
The 50 Greatest Players in Houston Astros History
The 50 Greatest Players in Kansas City Chiefs History
The 50 Greatest Players in Minnesota Vikings History
The 50 Greatest Players in New England Patriots History
The 50 Greatest Players in New York Giants History
The 50 Greatest Players in New York Yankees History
The 50 Greatest Players in Philadelphia Eagles History
The 50 Greatest Players in Philadelphia Phillies History
The 50 Greatest Players in Pittsburgh Pirates History
The 50 Greatest Players in Pittsburgh Steelers History
The 50 Greatest Players in San Francisco 49ers History
The 50 Greatest Players in St. Louis Cardinals History

THE 50 GREATEST PLAYERS IN NEW YORK METS HISTORY

ROBERT W. COHEN

LYONS PRESS

ESSEX, CONNECTICUT

An imprint of The Globe Pequot Publishing Group, Inc.
64 South Main Street
Essex, CT 06426
LyonsPress.com

Copyright © 2026 by Robert W. Cohen
All photos in the public domain unless otherwise noted

All rights reserved. No part of this book may be reproduced in any form or by any electronic or mechanical means, including information storage and retrieval systems, without written permission from the publisher, except by a reviewer who may quote passages in a review.

British Library Cataloguing in Publication Information available

Library of Congress Cataloging-in-Publication Data available

ISBN 978-1-4930-9162-1 (paper)
ISBN 978-1-4930-9163-8 (electronic)

CONTENTS

ACKNOWLEDGMENTS		vii
INTRODUCTION		ix
The Mets Legacy		ix
Factors Used to Determine Rankings		xvii
1	Tom Seaver	1
2	Mike Piazza	11
3	David Wright	19
4	Keith Hernandez	26
5	Dwight Gooden	34
6	Darryl Strawberry	42
7	Jacob deGrom	50
8	José Reyes	57
9	Jerry Koosman	63
10	Carlos Beltrán	72
11	Pete Alonso	79
12	Gary Carter	85
13	Edgardo Alfonzo	93
14	John Franco	99
15	Howard Johnson	106
16	Cleon Jones	112
17	Francisco Lindor	119
18	Jon Matlack	126
19	Mookie Wilson	132
20	Lee Mazzilli	138
21	David Cone	144
22	Tommie Agee	152

23	Rusty Staub	159
24	Ed Kranepool	166
25	Daniel Murphy	173
26	Al Leiter	179
27	Billy Wagner	185
28	John Olerud	192
29	Tug McGraw	199
30	Sid Fernandez	206
31	Ron Darling	212
32	Todd Hundley	217
33	Jesse Orosco	222
34	Kevin McReynolds	228
35	Carlos Delgado	235
36	Cliff Floyd	241
37	John Stearns	247
38	Robin Ventura	253
39	Félix Millán	259
40	Dave Kingman	265
41	Johan Santana	271
42	Jerry Grote	276
43	Bud Harrelson	282
44	Brandon Nimmo	289
45	Jeff McNeil	294
46	Bob Ojeda	299
47	Edwin Díaz	305
48	Lenny Dykstra	310
49	Wally Backman	316
50	Donn Clendenon	322

SUMMARY	328
GLOSSARY: ABBREVIATIONS AND STATISTICAL TERMS	329
BIBLIOGRAPHY	331

ACKNOWLEDGMENTS

I would like to thank Kate Yeakley of RMYauctions.com, George A. Kitrinos, Keith Allison, All-Pro Reels Photography, Kenji Takabayashi, D. Benjamin Miller, Andrew J. Klein, and Arturo Pardavila, each of whom generously contributed to the photographic content of this work.

INTRODUCTION

THE METS LEGACY

Left without a National League team after the Dodgers and Giants departed for California following the conclusion of the 1957 campaign, the city of New York finally received a reprieve in 1962, when the senior circuit added to its fraternity of ballclubs the expansion New York Mets and Houston Colt .45s. Founded largely through the efforts of New York based attorney William Shea, who earlier attempted to create a third major baseball league, the Mets took their name from the New York Metropolitans, a late 19th century team that competed in the American Association from 1880 to 1887.

With former Giants minority owners Joan Whitney Payson and Charles Shipman Payson holding majority interest in the Mets, they named part owner George Herbert Walker Jr. vice president and treasurer. Meanwhile, former Giants director M. Donald Grant assumed the position of chairman of the board.

Stocked primarily with aging veterans and undistinguished players selected off the rosters of other teams in an expansion draft held in October 1961, the Mets began play some six months later in New York's Polo Grounds, the longtime home of the Giants. Managed by the legendary Casey Stengel, who had been fired by the Yankees two years earlier, the Mets performed miserably in their inaugural season, compiling a record of just 40-120, before posting a mark of 51-111 the following year.

Leaving the Polo Grounds in 1964, the Mets moved into newly constructed Shea Stadium, a 55,300-seat multipurpose facility built in the Queens neighborhood of Flushing Meadows that remained home to them for the next 45 years. Showing only slight improvement over the course of the next few seasons, the Mets continued to flounder under managers Stengel (1962–1965) and Wes Westrum (1965–1967), earning the moniker "lovable losers" by finishing last in the 10-team NL all but once (they finished ninth in 1966). Yet despite their overall ineptitude, the Mets fielded some notable players during their formative years, with future Hall of Famers Gil Hodges, Duke Snider, Richie Ashburn, and Warren Spahn all gracing their roster at various times, second baseman Ron Hunt earning multiple All-Star nominations, and slugging outfielder Frank Thomas setting a single-season franchise home-run record that stood for 13 years by reaching the seats 34 times in 1962.

Although the Mets concluded the 1968 campaign with a record of 73-89 that landed them in ninth place, optimism began to grow for the first time under new manager Gil Hodges, who replaced Westrum at the helm prior to the start of the season. A firm but extremely fair man who possessed great inner strength, Hodges quickly earned the respect of his players with his honesty and forthrightness. Meanwhile, the Mets' roster featured a core of good young players that included outfielders Cleon Jones and Tommie Agee, shortstop Bud Harrelson, and pitchers Tom Seaver and Jerry Koosman.

With both the AL and NL expanding to 12 teams in 1969, MLB adopted a new two-division setup in each league that placed the Mets in the NL East with the Chicago Cubs, Pittsburgh Pirates, Philadelphia Phillies, St. Louis Cardinals, and expansion Montreal Expos. Beginning the campaign in typical fashion, the Mets lost 23 of their first 41 games. However, after improving their play dramatically during the summer months, the Mets emerged as baseball's hottest team down the stretch, winning 38 of their final 49 contests, to finish the season with a record of 100-62 that left them eight games ahead of the second-place Cubs in the division. The Mets subsequently swept the hard-hitting Atlanta Braves in three straight games in the first National League Championship Series, before upsetting the heavily favored Baltimore Orioles in five games in the World Series, completing in the process one of the most miraculous seasons in MLB history.

While the 1969 Mets, who the New York newspapers often referred to as the "Miracle" or "Amazin'" Mets, lacked star power at most positions, manager Hodges got the most out of his personnel by employing a platoon system previously made popular by Casey Stengel during his stint as Yankees skipper. Although left fielder Cleon Jones, who finished third in the league with a .340 batting average, center fielder Tommie Agee, shortstop Bud Harrelson, and catcher Jerry Grote played most every day, the rest of the lineup varied according to the opposing team's pitcher. The true strength of the team, though, lay in its pitching staff, which posted a composite ERA of 2.99 and threw a league-leading 28 shutouts. Staff ace Tom Seaver earned NL Cy Young honors by compiling a record of 25-7 and an ERA of 2.21. Jerry Koosman proved to be nearly as effective, going 17-9 with a 2.28 ERA. The Mets also received strong pitching from third starter Gary Gentry, swingman Nolan Ryan, and relievers Tug McGraw and Ron Taylor.

Unfortunately, the Mets failed to perform at nearly the same level in any of the next three seasons, posting identical 83-79 records under Hodges in 1970 and 1971, before compiling a mark of 83-73 in 1972 under Yogi Berra, who assumed managerial duties following the untimely passing of Hodges just prior to the start of the regular season. But while the magic that surrounded the 1969 squad lasted just that one season, the Mets also found themselves being hampered by poor decisions made by the front office, with the most egregious of those being the trading of top outfield prospect and future star Amos Otis to Kansas City for troubled third baseman Joe Foy and the dealing of Nolan Ryan to California for aging infielder Jim Fregosi.

Nevertheless, the Mets nearly experienced another fairy-tale ending in 1973, when a late-season surge enabled them to win the NL East title with a record of just 82-79. Using "Ya gotta believe!" as their rallying cry, the Mets subsequently stunned the powerful Cincinnati Reds in the NLCS, defeating them in five games, and then taking the Oakland Athletics to the seven-game limit in the World Series, before finally losing to the defending world champions.

Coming back down to earth in 1974, the Mets finished fifth in the six-team NL East with a record of 71-91. Although the Mets rebounded somewhat the following year to post a mark of 82-80, their mediocre showing led to the firing of Yogi Berra, who the front office replaced with coach Roy McMillan four months into the campaign. Undergoing further changes following the passing of Joan Payson at the end of the year, the Mets fell under the control of her husband Charles, who ceded much of his authority to his three daughters, the youngest of whom, Lorinda Payson de Roulet, became team president. Payson de Roulet subsequently left baseball matters in the hands of club chairman M. Donald Grant, whose penurious ways, caustic personality, and lack of baseball acumen ran the Mets into the ground.

After the Mets finished 86-76 under new manager Joe Frazier in 1976, Grant engaged in contract disputes with Tom Seaver and slugging outfielder/first baseman Dave Kingman the following year that prompted him to trade away his team's two most recognizable players on June 15, 1977, in what the New York tabloids dubbed "The Midnight Massacre." Although the Mets received a total of six players in return, none of them ended up making much of an impact, leading to the dismissal of Grant following the conclusion of the 1978 campaign. Meanwhile, the Mets began a horrific period in franchise history during which they failed to finish any higher than fifth or post more than 68 victories in any of the next seven seasons, as Frazier (1977), Joe Torre (1977–1981), George Bamberger (1982–1983), and Frank Howard (1983) all took turns managing the team. And with home attendance falling to all-time lows, Shea Stadium became known as "Grant's Tomb."

The Mets continued to play uninspired ball until well after the Payson heirs sold the team to the Doubleday publishing company for $21.1 million in January 1980, Nelson Doubleday Jr. named himself chairman of the board, minority shareholder Fred Wilpon assumed the role of club president, and longtime Baltimore Orioles executive Frank Cashen became general manager—a position he held for the next 11 years. However, things started to turn around shortly after the Mets acquired former NL MVP Keith Hernandez from the Cardinals and New York's farm system began producing talented young players such as Darryl Strawberry and Dwight Gooden.

After winning only 68 games in 1983, the Mets posted a mark of 90-72 the following year under new skipper Davey Johnson, who had previously managed in the organization's farm system. Further strengthened by the trade acquisitions of All-Star catcher Gary Carter, infielders Ray Knight and Howard Johnson, and starting pitchers Ron Darling and Sid Fernandez in 1985, the Mets finished a close second in the division to the Cardinals with a mark of 98-64. New York subsequently ran away with the NL East in 1986 by compiling a franchise-best regular-season record of 108-54, before winning a hard-fought six-game NLCS with the Astros in which the series finale lasted 16 innings. The Mets then laid claim to their second world championship by defeating the Red Sox in seven games in the World Series, winning a memorable Game 6 by scoring three times in the bottom of the 10th inning after the first two batters failed to reach base.

Like the franchise's first world championship ballclub, the 1986 Mets had an outstanding pitching staff that proved to be their greatest strength. Featuring a starting rotation that included Dwight Gooden, Ron Darling, Sid Fernandez, Bob Ojeda, and Rick Aguilera, and a bullpen headed by southpaw Jesse Orosco and right-hander Roger McDowell, the Mets had the ability to shut down the opposition on any given night, with their team ERA of 3.11 representing the lowest mark in the senior circuit. But while the 1969 Mets lacked offensive firepower, the same could not be said of the 1986 squad, which also led the NL with 783 runs scored. Speedsters Lenny Dykstra, Wally Backman, and Mookie Wilson did an excellent job of setting the table for middle-of-the-order RBI men Keith Hernandez, Gary Carter, and Darryl Strawberry. And Ray Knight, Howard Johnson, and Kevin Mitchell also offered solid run-production from the back end of the lineup.

A raucous and rowdy bunch that became known for their drug and alcohol usage, womanizing, and all-night partying, the Mets of the mid-1980s also possessed tremendous self-confidence, carrying themselves with a certain swagger that suggested to the opposition that they expected to win every time they took the field. But that same cockiness and arrogance ultimately contributed to their inability to win more than one championship.

Despite outstanding seasons from third baseman Howard Johnson and newly acquired left fielder Kevin McReynolds in 1987, the Mets finished three games behind the first-place Cardinals in the NL East with a record of 92-70. Re-establishing themselves as the team to beat in the NL the following year, the Mets compiled a league-best mark of 100-60 that left them 15 games ahead of the second-place Pirates in the division. But after winning 10 of their 11 meetings with the Dodgers during the regular season, the Mets suffered a stunning seven-game defeat at the hands of the Western Division champions in the NLCS.

The Mets subsequently traded away offensive catalysts Lenny Dykstra and Wally Backman the following offseason, contributing to a slow start from which they never fully recovered. Further troubled by clubhouse turmoil following an infamous Picture Day brawl between Darryl Strawberry and Keith Hernandez, the Mets finished the season with a record of just 87-75 that left them six games behind the first-place Cubs in the NL East. With the Mets struggling during the early stages of the ensuing campaign as well, they fired Davey Johnson and replaced him with Bud Harrelson, who guided them to an overall record of 91-71 and another second-place finish in the division.

Choosing to adopt a different approach the next few seasons, the Mets attempted to build their team around veteran players who had experienced success elsewhere, signing Vince Coleman, Eddie Murray, and Bobby Bonilla as free agents, while trading for pitchers Frank Tanana and Bret Saberhagen. However, New York's experiment failed miserably, with Coleman and Saberhagen spending much of their time on the disabled list, Bonilla exhibiting unprofessional behavior toward members of the local media, and Tanana showing his age. And with Darryl Strawberry departing via free agency at the end of 1990, staff ace David Cone being dealt to the

Toronto Blue Jays in August 1992, and Dwight Gooden succumbing to his addictions to drugs and alcohol that had plagued him for years, the Mets experienced a precipitous fall from grace, finishing well under .500 six straight times from 1991 to 1996, as Bud Harrelson (1991), Jeff Torborg (1992–1993), and Dallas Green (1993–1996) took turns managing the ballclub.

Meanwhile, although the Mets remained in the NL East after further expansion caused the league to adopt a new three-division alignment in 1993, they found themselves competing directly against a different set of teams, with the Phillies, Braves, Expos, and expansion Marlins being their fellow Eastern Division occupants and the Cardinals, Pirates, and Cubs shifting to the new NL Central.

After winning only 71 games the previous season, the Mets began to show signs of life under the new manager/GM tandem of Bobby Valentine and Steve Phillips in 1997, compiling a record of 88-74 that earned them a third-place finish in the NL East. Strengthened by the trade acquisitions of star catcher Mike Piazza and left-handed pitcher Al Leiter the following year, the Mets barely missed making the playoffs. However, they advanced to the postseason tournament in 1999, when, led by Piazza and a stellar infield that featured first baseman John Olerud, second baseman Edgardo Alfonzo, third baseman Robin Ventura, and shortstop Rey Ordóñez, they posted a mark of 96-66 during the regular season and then won a one-game playoff against the Cincinnati Reds to determine the NL wild-card representative. The Mets subsequently defeated the Arizona Diamondbacks 3–1 in the NLDS, with backup catcher Todd Pratt clinching the series with a walkoff homer. But the Mets fell victim to the Braves in the NLCS, losing to them in six exciting games after dropping the first three contests.

Advancing to the playoffs again as a wild card in 2000 after finishing one game behind the Braves in the NL East with a record of 94-68, the Mets needed only four games to dispose of the Giants in the NLDS, before earning their fourth trip to the World Series by defeating the Cardinals in five games in the NLCS. However, the Mets had the tables turned on them in the Fall Classic, losing to the Yankees in five games in the first Subway Series played in more than four decades.

Hampered by a series of poor moves made by Steve Phillips that included acquiring aging and ineffective players such as Mo Vaughn, Roberto Alomar, and Mike Bordick, the Mets labored in mediocrity the next three seasons, finishing well under .500 twice. Dissatisfied with his team's performance, Fred Wilpon, who became sole owner of the Mets when he bought out partner Nelson Doubleday on August 23, 2002, relieved Phillips of his duties midway through the 2003 campaign, just a few months after he fired manager Bobby Valentine.

Faring no better under GM Jim Duquette and manager Art Howe, the Mets finished well out of contention in both 2003 and 2004, leading to the replacement of Duquette with Omar Minaya, who had previously achieved success in Montreal by making bold player moves on a limited budget. Minaya, in turn, hired as manager longtime Yankees third base coach Willie Randolph, who, aided by the arrivals in New York of top prospects David Wright and José Reyes, guided the Mets to a record of 83-79 and a third-place finish his first year in charge.

With both Wright and Reyes establishing themselves as stars, center fielder Carlos Beltrán bouncing back from a difficult first year in the Big Apple, and slugging first baseman Carlos Delgado being acquired in a trade with the Florida Marlins, the Mets proved to be the class of the NL during the 2006 regular season, posting a league-best record of 97-65 that left them 12 games ahead of the second-place Phillies in the Eastern Division. But after sweeping the Dodgers in three straight games in the NLDS, the Mets came up short against the Cardinals in the NLCS, losing to the eventual world champions in seven games.

The Mets appeared to be on the verge of winning the NL East again in 2007, holding a seven-game lead over the second-place Phillies with just 17 games remaining in the regular season. But they lost 12 of their final 17 contests, enabling the Phillies to edge them out for the division title by one game. The Mets subsequently got off to a slow start in 2008, causing Omar Minaya to replace Willie Randolph with bench coach Jerry Manuel in mid-June. Gathering themselves under Manuel, the Mets built up a 3½-game lead over the Phillies with only 17 games remaining on the schedule. But they again faltered down the stretch, losing 10 of their final 17 contests, to finish three games behind Philadelphia.

After occupying Shea Stadium for 45 years, the Mets moved into the newly constructed Citi Field in 2009. Located adjacent to the site of the Mets' former home, Citi Field, which has a seating capacity of 41,922, very much resembles from the outside Brooklyn's old Ebbets Field, the longtime home of the Dodgers.

But while the opening of their new home ballpark created excitement around the organization, the Mets struggled terribly their first few years at Citi Field, failing to post a winning record six straight times from 2009 to 2014 under managers Jerry Manuel (2009–2010) and Terry Collins (2011–2014) and general managers Omar Minaya (2009–2010) and Sandy Alderson (2011–2014).

Run very much like a small-market team after owners Fred Wilpon and Saul Katz agreed to pay $162 million to the victims of the Bernie Madoff Ponzi scheme in 2012, the Mets chose not to pursue any top-tier players when they became available, instead seeking bargain-basement deals on the free agent market. Nevertheless, several players distinguished themselves during this period of mediocrity. Third baseman David Wright continued to put up excellent numbers year after year. José Reyes became the first Mets player to win a batting title when he led the league with an average of .337 in 2011. Right-handed knuckleballer R. A. Dickey earned NL Cy Young honors in 2012. And that same season, Johan Santana became the first pitcher in franchise history to throw a no-hitter.

Finally emerging as contenders again following the July 31, 2015, acquisition of All-Star outfielder Yoenis Céspedes and the development of an outstanding young starting rotation that included hard-throwing right-handers Jacob deGrom, Matt Harvey, and Noah Syndergaard, the Mets captured the NL East title in 2015 by winning 38 of their final 60 games. But while Céspedes proved to be the Mets' most dynamic hitter down the stretch, hitting 17 homers and driving in 44 runs over the final two months of the regular season, it was second baseman Daniel Murphy who stepped to the forefront during the postseason. After leading the Mets to a five-game victory over the Dodgers in the NLDS by homering three times, Murphy reached the seats another four times during their four-game sweep of the Cubs in the NLCS. However, the Mets subsequently suffered a five-game defeat at the hands of the Kansas City Royals in the World Series.

Although Jacob deGrom established himself as arguably the finest pitcher in the game over the course of the next few seasons, winning two Cy Young Awards, the Mets failed to advance to the postseason, coming closest in 2016, when they lost the NL Wild Card Game to the Giants. After the Mets posted a disappointing record of 70-92 in 2017, Terry Collins retired as manager, leading to the hiring of former Cleveland Indians coach Mickey Callaway. Callaway remained skipper for the next two years, presiding over the 2019 team that featured NL Rookie of the Year Pete Alonso, who set a new record for first-year players by hitting 53 homers, before being replaced, first by Carlos Beltrán and, later, by Mets quality control coach Luis Rojas following the conclusion of the campaign.

After failing to make the playoffs their first year under Rojas, the Mets fell under new ownership on October 30, 2020, when Steve Cohen purchased controlling interest in the team (95 percent) from the Wilpons. Dissatisfied with his new ballclub's 77-85 showing in 2021, Cohen replaced Rojas with Buck Showalter, who guided the Mets to a 101-61 record and a wild-card playoff berth his first year in charge. However, the Mets exited the postseason tournament quickly, losing the NL Wild Card Series to the San Diego Padres in three games. With the Mets failing to perform at the same level in 2023, Showalter received his walking papers, with new GM David Stearns hiring former Yankees bench coach Carlos Mendoza as his replacement.

After getting off to a slow start their first year under Mendoza, the Mets ended up advancing to the playoffs as a wild card by finishing the season with a record of 89-73. They subsequently defeated the Brewers in three games in the NL Wild Card Series and the Phillies in four games in the NLDS, before falling to the Dodgers in six games in the NLCS. Hoping to get his team to the next level, Steve Cohen pried superstar outfielder Juan Soto away from the Yankees by signing him to a 15-year, $765 million free agent contract on December 8, 2024.

Although Soto posted excellent numbers his first year in Flushing, concluding the 2025 campaign with 43 homers, 105 RBIs, 120 runs scored, and an NL-leading 38 stolen bases, 126 walks, and .396 on-base percentage, the Mets struggled terribly the final few months of the season, relegating them to an overall record of just 83-79 that left them one game short of advancing to the playoffs. Nevertheless, with talented players such as Soto, Francisco Lindor, Pete Alonso (if he does not opt out of his contract), Brandon Nimmo, and Edwin Díaz, and an owner who appears willing to do whatever it takes to win, the Mets figure to remain serious contenders in the NL East for the foreseeable future. Their next division title will be their seventh. They have also won five pennants and two world championships.

In addition to their accomplishments as a team, the Mets have featured several players who have attained notable individual honors during their time in Queens, with the organization boasting seven Cy Young Award winners, three home-run champions, and two batting champions. A Mets pitcher has also led the NL in wins three times, ERA seven times, and strikeouts on 12 separate occasions. Furthermore, the Mets have inducted 22 players into their Hall of Fame, eight of whom have had their numbers retired by the organization. Meanwhile, 15 members of the Baseball Hall of Fame spent at least one full season playing for the Mets.

FACTORS USED TO DETERMINE RANKINGS

With the Mets having been in existence for more than six decades, it should come as no surprise that selecting the 50 greatest players in franchise history presented a difficult task. Even after settling on my top 50 players, I found myself faced with the challenge of ranking the players that remained. Certainly, the names of Tom Seaver, Keith Hernandez, Dwight Gooden, Darryl Strawberry, Mike Piazza, and David Wright would appear at, or near, the top of virtually everyone's list, although the order might vary somewhat from one person to the next. Several other outstanding performers have gained general recognition as being among the greatest players ever to don the team's colors, with Jerry Koosman, Gary Carter, Jacob deGrom, Carlos Beltrán, and José Reyes heading the list of other Mets icons. But how does one differentiate between the all-around excellence of Wright and the offensive dominance of Piazza; or the superior pitching of Seaver and the extraordinary fielding and leadership of Hernandez? After initially deciding whom to include on my list, I then needed to determine what criteria I should use to formulate my final rankings.

The first thing I decided to examine was the level of dominance a player attained during his time in Flushing. How often did he lead the league in a major offensive or pitching statistical category? How did he fare in the annual MVP and/or Cy Young voting? How many times did he make the All-Star team?

I also needed to weigh the level of statistical compilation a player achieved while wearing a Mets uniform. Where does a batter rank in team annals in the major offensive categories? How high on the all-time list of Mets hurlers does a pitcher rank in wins, ERA, complete games, innings pitched, shutouts, and saves? Of course, I also needed to consider the era in which the player performed when evaluating his overall numbers. For example, current and recent starting pitchers such as Jacob deGrom and Johan Santana are not likely to throw nearly as many complete games or shutouts as Tom Seaver, who anchored New York's starting rotation during the 1960s and 1970s.

Other important factors I needed to consider were the overall contributions a player made to the success of the team, the degree to which he improved the fortunes of the ballclub during his time in Queens, and the manner in which he impacted the team, both on and off the field. While the number of pennants or division titles the Mets won during a particular player's years with the ballclub certainly entered into the equation, I chose not to deny a top performer his rightful place on the list if his years in Flushing happened to coincide with a lack of overall success by the team. As a result, the names of players such as John Stearns and Todd Hundley will appear in these rankings.

One other thing I should mention is that I considered a player's performance only while playing for the Mets when formulating my rankings. That being the case, the names of outstanding players such as Billy Wagner and Carlos Delgado, both of whom had most of their best years while playing for other teams, may appear lower on this list than one might expect. Meanwhile, the names of Hall of Fame players such as Willie Mays and Nolan Ryan are nowhere to be found.

Having established the guidelines to be used throughout this book, we are ready to take a look at the 50 greatest players in Mets history, starting with number 1 and working our way to number 50.

1
TOM SEAVER

Although Mike Piazza also merited brief consideration, Tom Seaver ultimately represented the only possible choice for the top spot on this list. Identified by legendary broadcaster Vin Scully as "the best right-handed pitcher I ever saw," Seaver gained general recognition as the finest hurler of his generation over the course of a 20-year Hall of Fame career that included stints with four different teams. Most closely associated with the Mets, who he led to two pennants and one world championship, Seaver became known simply as "The Franchise" during his time in New York for the level of respectability he brought to an organization that previously experienced very little success. The winner of at least 20 games four times, Seaver also compiled an ERA under 3.00, recorded more than 200 strikeouts, and threw more than 250 innings nine times each, earning in the process nine All-Star selections, three Cy Young Awards, and four top-10 finishes in the NL Cy Young voting. The Mets career leader in wins, strikeouts, shutouts, complete games, and innings pitched, "Tom Terrific," as he came to be known, later received the additional honors of having his number retired by the organization, being accorded a number 32 ranking by the *Sporting News* on that publication's 1999 list of Baseball's 100 Greatest Players, and gaining induction into the Baseball Hall of Fame in resounding fashion the first time his name appeared on the ballot.

Born in Fresno, California, on November 17, 1944, George Thomas Seaver developed a love for the game of baseball at an early age, recalling that when he tried unsuccessfully to sign up for Little League ball one year before he became eligible, "I went home and cried."

Developing into an outstanding all-around athlete during his teenage years, Seaver starred in baseball and basketball at Fresno High School, earning All-City honors in both sports. Following his graduation in 1962, Seaver enrolled at Fresno City College, where he performed well enough on the diamond the next two seasons to draw interest from University of Southern California head baseball coach Rod Dedeaux, who recruited him

Tom Seaver is generally recognized as one of the greatest right-handed pitchers in the history of the game.

for the Trojans. After proving himself worthy of a scholarship by excelling on the mound for the semiprofessional Alaska Goldpanners in the summer of 1964, Seaver posted a record of 10-2 as a sophomore at USC, prompting the Dodgers to select him in the 10th round of the June 1965 MLB Amateur Draft. But with the Dodgers offering him just $2,000 to sign with them, Seaver chose instead to return to school.

Although the Braves selected Seaver seven months later in the first round of the January 1966 MLB Draft, with the 20th overall pick, they violated MLB rules by not signing him until after USC began its season. His contract subsequently voided by MLB commissioner William Eckert, Seaver became the prize in a lottery held among teams willing to match

Atlanta's signing bonus of $51,000. Beating out two other teams for his services, the Mets inked Seaver to a deal, after which he joined the organization's top farm club in Jacksonville.

Excelling in his first year of pro ball, Seaver compiled a record of 12-12 and an ERA of 3.13, threw four shutouts, and struck out 188 batters in 210 innings pitched. Displaying at a very young age the maturity and professionalism that he exhibited throughout his career, Seaver drew praise from Suns manager Solly Hemus, who insisted that his "35-year-old head attached to a 21-year-old body" made him ready for prime time. Agreeing with his rival manager's assessment after watching Seaver from the opposing dugout one afternoon, then-Rochester and future Orioles skipper Earl Weaver later said, "It was apparent in Tom Seaver's pro debut that he was ready for the majors. He had an excellent fastball and slider, and he put them precisely where he wanted to, in and out on the black of the plate, mostly knee-high. After Jacksonville beat us, I phoned [Baltimore general manager] Harry Dalton and said that Seaver was going to be sensational, and the Orioles could give up a piece of the franchise and do well to get him."

Promoted to the parent club after just one year in the minors, Seaver performed exceptionally well in his first big-league season, earning NL Rookie of the Year honors and the first of his seven consecutive All-Star nominations by going 16-13 with an ERA of 2.76, 170 strikeouts, 18 complete games, and 251 innings pitched for a team that won only 61 games.

Recalling his early thoughts on Seaver, Mets catcher Jerry Grote said, "I didn't feel there was any way he could miss. I mean, here was a guy who was throwing gas, the mid-90s, on the corners."

Seaver also made a strong impression on Reds Hall of Fame receiver Johnny Bench, who stated, "I remember the first time I faced him. 'Here it is, hit it. That's what I got. It's probably better than what you got, and here it is, hit it.' The Mets were the buffoons of baseball. He gave them respect. All of a sudden, credibility was there."

Meanwhile, longtime Mets broadcaster Howie Rose claimed that Seaver brought a sense of hope to the fans at Shea Stadium his first year in Queens, saying, "There had always been this inescapable culture of losing, and at least among their fans, a growing sense of losing was going to be something permanent. . . . People who watched Seaver as a rookie got the sense that they had finally developed a player who was capable of doing special things, and, therefore, capable of helping the Mets achieve some pretty good things of their own along the way."

Even better in 1968, Seaver compiled a record of 16-12 and ranked among the league leaders with a 2.20 ERA, a WHIP of 0.978, 205 strikeouts, five shutouts, and 278 innings pitched, before establishing himself as arguably the finest pitcher in the game over the course of the next five seasons by posting the following numbers:

	W-L	ERA	SO	SHO	CG	IP	WHIP
1969	**25-7**	2.21	208	5	18	273.1	1.039
1970	18-12	**2.82**	**283**	2	19	290.2	1.077
1971	20-10	**1.76**	**289**	4	21	286.1	**0.946**
1972	21-12	2.92	249	3	13	262	1.115
1973	19-10	**2.08**	251	3	18	290	**0.976**

*Please note that any numbers printed in bold throughout this book signify that the player led the NL in that statistical category that year.

Consistently ranking among the league leaders in every major statistical category for pitchers, Seaver, in addition to gaining All-Star recognition each season, earned Cy Young honors twice (1969 and 1973), three top-10 finishes in the NL MVP voting, and a pair of *Sporting News* NL All-Star nominations. More importantly, Seaver led the Mets to their first pennant and world championship in 1969, before serving as the central figure on a team that won the pennant again in 1973, with Hall of Fame slugger and legendary Mets announcer Ralph Kiner later saying, "Tom Seaver was the driving force behind the players, always pushing the team to be better than they were, never letting them settle."

The 6'1", 200-pound Seaver, whose repertoire of pitches included a mid-90s fastball, an excellent curve, and an outstanding slider, employed near-perfect pitching mechanics on the mound that thousands of Little Leaguers during the 1960s and 1970s tried to imitate. A classic power pitcher, Seaver used a drop-and-drive delivery that caused his back (right) knee to scrape the dirt on the mound as he released the ball.

Expressing his admiration for the league's top pitcher, Pirates starter Steve Blass stated, "Tom Seaver is the perfect example of a power pitcher that can pitch to spots, and that's an unbeatable combination."

In addition to his natural ability and superior mechanics, Seaver possessed a tremendous intellect that helped set him apart from other hurlers. A student of pitching, Seaver received high praise for his knowledge of his craft from Johnny Bench, who said, "I never knew a pitcher with such knowledge of pitching. He had such a great mind, he could out-think the hitters."

Bothered by a sore hip in 1974, Seaver finished the season with a record of just 11-11 and an ERA of 3.20, although he still managed to throw

236 innings and rank among the league leaders with 201 strikeouts and five shutouts. Fully healthy by the start of the ensuing campaign, Seaver returned to top form, earning Cy Young honors for the third time, his eighth All-Star nomination, and another top-10 finish in the NL MVP balloting by leading the league with 22 victories (against nine losses) and 243 strikeouts, while also ranking among the leaders with a 2.38 ERA, a WHIP of 1.088, five shutouts, 15 complete games, and 280⅓ innings pitched.

Although Seaver gained All-Star recognition again in 1976 by finishing third in the league with a 2.59 ERA, a WHIP of 1.063, five shutouts, and 271 innings pitched, throwing 13 complete games, and setting a major-league record by striking out more than 200 batters (235) for the ninth straight time, the Mets' feeble offense relegated him to a record of just 14-11. Continuing to perform well in 1977, Seaver won seven of his first 10 decisions despite receiving very little run-support from his teammates. But with contract squabbles and philosophical differences with general manager M. Donald Grant creating an adversarial relationship between the two parties, the Mets completed a trade with the Reds on June 15, 1977, that sent Seaver to Cincinnati for pitcher Pat Zachry, second baseman Doug Flynn, and young outfielders Steve Henderson and Dan Norman in a deal that the New York newspapers subsequently referred to as "The Midnight Massacre."

While some members of the local media, particularly Dick Young of the *New York Daily News*, spread misinformation about the reasons behind the trade, Seaver told Kent Hannon of *Sports Illustrated* later in 1977, "The money was always secondary to my loyalty to the Mets. The people who think I was bitter about not making more money or who think I was trying to force a trade by asking that my contract be renegotiated won't believe me. But for the record, my loyalty to the Mets and my desire to make them competitive always came first. I don't think I've shown myself to be a greedy person."

Four years later, looking back at the events that transpired at the time, Seaver's wife, Nancy, told Frank Deford of that same publication, "With him, it was a matter of loyalty. And his loyalty was thrown into his face. Tom was hurt badly. I don't think, even now, he'd like to admit how much. He wanted to live and die at Shea Stadium. And they jilted him."

While news of the deal broke the hearts of Mets fans and destroyed the morale of the team, which subsequently entered an extended period of futility that lasted nearly a decade, Reds manager Sparky Anderson exulted, "This gives us the premier pitcher in baseball. Seaver just keeps climbing, and he may be the all-time all-timer before he is through."

Expressing concern over the addition of Seaver to his team's chief rival, Dodgers second baseman Davey Lopes said, "This has to be one of the biggest steals since the Babe Ruth trade. A trade is supposed to help both teams. But I don't think the Mets are as good a club as they were before. I can't see how they improved their team one iota."

Making an extremely favorable impression on his new teammates the rest of the year, Seaver, who posted a record of 14-3 following his arrival in Cincinnati that gave him an overall mark of 21-6, drew high praise from Joe Morgan, who stated, "It is something to watch him pitch. I always marveled at him when I was on the other team. But now, seeing him all the time, I say to myself, 'How did you ever get a hit off him?'"

Commenting years later on Seaver's intelligence and knowledge of opposing hitters, Johnny Bench said, "Some pitchers I could put on autopilot. Tom Seaver knew what he wanted to do and how he wanted to do it. When he pitched, I called the pitches he wanted to throw, not the ones I wanted him to throw."

Seaver ended up spending parts of six seasons in Cincinnati, compiling an overall record of 75-46 and a composite ERA of 3.18, en route to earning three more All-Star selections and another three top-five finishes in the Cy Young voting. But with an aging and often-injured Seaver going just 5-13 with a 5.50 ERA in 1982, the Reds traded him back to the Mets at the end of the year for three undistinguished players.

Unfortunately, Seaver's second tour of duty in New York lasted just one season since the Mets left him unprotected in the free agent compensation pool after he went just 9-14 with a 3.55 ERA for them in 1983. Subsequently claimed by the Chicago White Sox, Seaver split the next three seasons between the White Sox and Red Sox, posting a total of 33 victories during his time in Chicago, before announcing his retirement following the conclusion of the 1986 campaign.

Over 20 big-league seasons, Seaver compiled a record of 311-205, an ERA of 2.86, and a WHIP of 1.121, threw 231 complete games and 61 shutouts, and struck out 3,640 batters in 4,783 total innings of work. As a member of the Mets, Seaver posted an overall mark of 198-124, an ERA of 2.57, and a WHIP of 1.076, tossed 171 complete games and 44 shutouts, and recorded 2,541 strikeouts in 3,045⅔ innings pitched. A decent hitter, Seaver also homered 12 times, knocked in 86 runs, and batted .154 in a total of 1,552 plate appearances over the course of his career.

Elected to the Baseball Hall of Fame the first time his name appeared on the ballot, Seaver, who Hank Aaron identified as the toughest pitcher he ever faced, and Bob Gibson, Juan Marichal, Jim Palmer, Nolan Ryan, Steve Carlton, Bert Blyleven, and Don Sutton all named as the best pitcher of their generation in an ESPN poll, entered Cooperstown having received the highest percentage of votes ever accorded any player up until that time (98.84 percent).

Following his playing days, Seaver spent five seasons serving as a broadcaster on Yankees telecasts and another seven announcing Mets games, while also working as a public relations representative for the Chase Manhattan Bank. Eventually leaving his home in Connecticut and returning to his native California with his wife, Nancy, Seaver established a winery in the city of Calistoga, which he continued to operate until the dementia he developed some six years earlier forced him to retire from public life in 2019. The man once known as "The Franchise" and "Tom Terrific" lived until August 31, 2020, when he died in his sleep at the age of 75 from complications of Lewy body dementia and COVID-19.

Upon learning of his passing, Ed Kranepool said of his longtime Mets teammate, "He turned the organization around from a laughingstock ballclub into a complete team instantly. You knew every time out you were going to be a competitive team . . . It's a sad day in Metsville. We lost our star and our leader."

Ron Swoboda, another former Mets teammate, stated, "You put a bunch of guys together of varying abilities and you know who the great ones are. When you played behind Tom Seaver, you were playing behind greatness. And you saw it almost every game."

Recalling the influence that Seaver had on him, former Mets pitcher Jon Matlack said, "He was the consummate pro. He pitched the right way because he did everything in his life the right way. He worked hard. He studied the game. He treated people with respect. You couldn't ask for a better teammate or a better guy to work with and work alongside. You couldn't ask for a better role model."

Fellow Mets great Mike Piazza said of Seaver, "He will always be the heart and soul of the Mets, the standard which all Mets aspire to."

Meanwhile, Mets owner Fred Wilpon put Seaver's career in its proper perspective when he issued a statement that read: "He was simply the greatest Mets player of all-time and among the best to ever play the game."

METS CAREER HIGHLIGHTS

Best Season

With the Mets winning the World Series and Seaver earning a runner-up finish to Willie McCovey in the NL MVP voting, being named the winner of the Cy Young Award, and being presented with the Hickok Belt as the top professional athlete of the year, the 1969 campaign is generally considered to be his signature season. However, even though Seaver finished second in the Cy Young balloting to Ferguson Jenkins in 1971, he posted the best overall numbers of his career, concluding the campaign with a record of 20-10, 18 complete games, 286⅓ innings pitched, and a league-leading 1.76 ERA, 0.946 WHIP, and 289 strikeouts.

Memorable Moments/Greatest Performances

Seaver came within two outs of throwing a perfect game on July 9, 1969, when he recorded 11 strikeouts and yielded just a one-out single to center field by outfielder Jim Qualls in the top of the ninth inning of a 4–0 shutout of the Cubs.

Seaver turned in another dominant performance on April 22, 1970, when, in addition to allowing just two hits and two walks during a 2–1 win over the Padres, he tied Steve Carlton's then-major-league record for a nine-inning game by registering 19 strikeouts, punctuating his extraordinary effort by fanning the last 10 batters he faced.

Seaver registered 15 strikeouts and surrendered just one hit and three walks during a 4–0 shutout of the Phillies on May 15, 1970, yielding only a third-inning single by catcher Mike Compton.

In addition to allowing just three hits and three walks during a 7–1 complete-game victory over the Montreal Expos on July 9, 1970, Seaver hit the first home run of his career.

Seaver threw 27 consecutive scoreless innings from April 6 to April 21, 1971, highlighting his streak with a three-hit, 1–0 shutout of the Pirates on April 16 during which he fanned 14 batters.

Seaver helped his own cause on June 24, 1971, when he delivered the decisive blow of a 2–1 victory over Montreal by homering with no one on base in the top of the eighth inning.

Seaver threw another 31⅔ consecutive scoreless frames from August 6 to August 21, 1971.

Seaver tossed a two-hit shutout against Montreal on September 6, 1971, recording 12 strikeouts, issuing two walks, and yielding only a pair of harmless singles by third baseman Ron Hunt and second baseman Gary Sutherland during a 7–0 Mets win.

Seaver held the hard-hitting Pirates to just one hit and one walk during a 3–1 Mets win on September 26, 1971, allowing just a seventh-inning walk by second baseman Dave Cash and a single by right fielder Vic Davalillo in the same frame.

In addition to surrendering just five hits during a complete-game 2–1 victory over the eventual NL champion Reds on June 18, 1972, Seaver knocked in the game's decisive run with a solo homer in the top of the seventh inning.

Although Seaver issued four walks during a 2–0 shutout of San Diego on July 4, 1972, he held the Padres hitless until left fielder Leron Lee delivered their only safety of the contest when he singled to center field with one man out in the top of the ninth inning.

Seaver dominated Pittsburgh's lineup on September 29, 1972, recording 13 strikeouts, issuing two walks, and surrendering just a fourth-inning single by Al Oliver and a seventh-inning single by Richie Hebner during a 1–0 shutout.

Seaver again shut out the Pirates on just two hits on May 12, 1973, yielding only a pair of harmless singles by Willie Stargell and opposing pitcher Bob Moose during a 6–0 Mets win.

Seaver recorded 16 strikeouts and allowed just three hits during a complete-game 5–2 victory over the Giants on May 29, 1973.

Seaver surrendered just two hits and one walk during a 7–0 shutout of the Padres on August 15, 1973, yielding only a fifth-inning single by shortstop Derrell Thomas and a sixth-inning single by left fielder Jerry Morales.

Although he didn't figure in the decision, Seaver displayed his mettle on May 1, 1974, by working the first 12 frames of a 2–1, 14-inning loss to the Dodgers, allowing just three hits and one run, while recording 16 strikeouts.

Seaver fashioned another lengthy scoreless innings streak from June 5 to June 20, 1975, going 28⅔ straight frames without allowing a run, with the highlight of the streak coming on the 15th of the month, when he surrendered just three hits during a 6–0 shutout of the Padres.

Seaver threw the last of his five career one-hitters on April 17, 1977, when he issued four walks and yielded only a fifth-inning single by third baseman Steve Ontiveros during a 6–0 shutout of the Cubs.

Notable Achievements

- Won at least 20 games four times, surpassing 18 victories two other times.
- Compiled ERA under 3.00 nine times, posting mark under 2.00 once.
- Posted WHIP under 1.000 three times.

- Struck out more than 200 batters nine times.
- Threw more than 250 innings nine times.
- Threw at least 18 complete games five times.
- Led NL pitchers in wins twice, ERA three times, WHIP twice, strikeouts five times, complete games once, and strikeouts-to-walks ratio twice.
- Finished second in NL in wins three times, winning percentage once, WHIP twice, strikeouts once, and complete games twice.
- Holds Mets single-season records for most wins (25 in 1969), strikeouts (289 in 1971), complete games (21 in 1971), and innings pitched (290⅔ in 1970).
- Holds Mets career records for most wins (198), strikeouts (2,541), shutouts (44), complete games (171), innings pitched (3,045⅔), and starts (395).
- Ranks among Mets career leaders with 2.57 ERA (2nd), 1.076 WHIP (2nd), .615 winning percentage (3rd), and 401 pitching appearances (4th).
- Two-time division champion (1969 and 1973).
- Two-time NL champion (1969 and 1973).
- 1969 world champion.
- 1967 NL Rookie of the Year.
- Three-time NL Player of the Week.
- Two-time NL Pitcher of the Month.
- 1969 winner of Hickok Belt as top professional athlete of the year.
- Three-time NL Cy Young Award winner (1969, 1973, and 1975).
- Finished second in 1971 NL Cy Young voting.
- Finished in top 10 of NL MVP voting four times, placing as high as second in 1969.
- Nine-time NL All-Star selection (1967, 1968, 1969, 1970, 1971, 1972, 1973, 1975, and 1976).
- Three-time *Sporting News* NL All-Star selection (1969, 1973, and 1975).
- Two-time *Sporting News* NL Pitcher of the Year (1969 and 1975).
- #41 retired by Mets.
- Inducted into Mets Hall of Fame in 1988.
- Number 32 on the *Sporting News* 1999 list of Baseball's 100 Greatest Players.
- Elected to Baseball Hall of Fame by members of BBWAA in 1992.

2
MIKE PIAZZA

Regarded by many as the greatest-hitting catcher in MLB history, Mike Piazza compiled some truly exceptional offensive numbers during his 16-year Hall of Fame career that included stints with five different teams. Having most of his finest seasons for the Dodgers and Mets, Piazza, who hit more homers than any other receiver in the history of the game, earned five All-Star nominations and five top-10 finishes in the NL MVP voting during his time in Los Angeles, before gaining All-Star recognition another seven times and garnering two more top-10 finishes in the league MVP balloting as a member of the Mets by hitting more than 30 homers and batting over .300 four times each, while also driving in more than 100 runs and posting an OPS over 1.000 twice each. Along the way, Piazza helped revive a franchise that had compiled a winning record in just one of the previous seven seasons, with his many contributions to the organization prompting the Mets to retire his #31 and induct him into their Hall of Fame.

Born in Norristown, Pennsylvania, on September 4, 1968, Michael Joseph Piazza grew up in nearby Phoenixville rooting for the Philadelphia Phillies and his favorite player, Mike Schmidt. A huge baseball fan, Piazza had the opportunity to serve as the Dodgers batboy when they played in Philadelphia one summer due to his father's friendship with Los Angeles manager Tommy Lasorda. Although only 13 years old at the time, Piazza gave an early indication of his hitting prowess one day when he drove a ball into the seats at Veterans Stadium during batting practice.

Eventually establishing himself as a star on the diamond at Phoenixville High School, Piazza batted .442 and hit 11 home runs his senior year. Nevertheless, he received little interest from college scouts, forcing him to enroll at Miami-Dade Community College. Piazza subsequently spent two seasons playing first base for the Sharks, before entering the 1988 MLB Amateur Draft after batting .364 as a sophomore. Finally selected by the Dodgers in the 62nd round as a favor to Tommy Lasorda, Piazza heeded

Mike Piazza helped restore the Mets to prominence during the late 1990s.

the advice of his dad's close friend and traded in his first baseman's glove for a catcher's mitt, believing that doing so would give him his best chance of making it to the majors. Yet, while Piazza acquiesced to Lasorda's wishes, he began his professional career with a huge chip on his shoulder, recalling years later, "Nobody wanted me. Scouts told me to go to school, to forget baseball. Coaches said, 'You're never going to make it.' I appreciated their honesty because I think when someone tells you something you may not like you have to use that as fuel for motivation."

Piazza ended up spending almost four full seasons in the minor leagues, struggling defensively behind the plate but eventually developing into a solid hitter, before joining the parent club in September 1992. Named the Dodgers' starting catcher prior to the start of the ensuing campaign, Piazza began an exceptional five-year run during which he averaged 34 homers and 105 RBIs, while also batting well over .300 each season and posting an OPS over 1.000 twice. An All-Star and Silver Slugger winner each year, Piazza performed especially well in 1997, when he earned a runner-up finish in the NL MVP voting by placing near the top of the league rankings with 40 homers, 124 RBIs, 201 hits, a .362 batting average, and an OPS of 1.070.

With Piazza set to become a free agent following the conclusion of the 1998 campaign, the Dodgers offered him a six-year, $80 million contract during spring training. But Piazza rejected their offer, prompting teammate Brett Butler to comment, "Mike Piazza is the greatest hitter I have ever been around. But you can't build around Piazza because he's not a leader."

Proving to be somewhat more diplomatic, sportswriter Tim Kurkjian later wrote, "I don't think Piazza was very happy being a Dodger by then. If he was, he would have been thrilled to take that deal. So, I think he was ready to move on. I don't blame him for that. I don't blame the Dodgers, either. It was time for some new chemistry on that club."

Although Piazza began the 1998 season in Los Angeles, the Dodgers included him in a seven-player trade they completed with the Marlins on May 14 that also sent Todd Zeile to Florida in exchange for Gary Sheffield, Bobby Bonilla, Charles Johnson, Jim Eisenreich, and Manuel Barrios. However, just eight days later, the Marlins dealt Piazza to the Mets for promising young outfielder Preston Wilson, pitcher Ed Yarnall, and minor-league hurler Geoff Goetz.

Performing extremely well the rest of the year, Piazza hit 23 homers, knocked in 76 runs, batted .348, and posted an OPS of 1.024 in 109 games with the Mets, enabling him to finish the season with 32 home runs, 111 RBIs, a .328 batting average, and an OPS of .960. Piazza followed that up with four more excellent seasons, posting the following numbers from 1999 to 2002:

	HR	RBI	RUNS	AVG	OBP	SLG	OPS
1999	40	124	100	.303	.361	.575	.936
2000	38	113	90	.324	.398	.614	1.012
2001	36	94	81	.300	.384	.573	.957
2002	33	98	69	.280	.359	.544	.903

The Mets' top power threat throughout the period, Piazza led the team in homers, RBIs, slugging percentage, and OPS all four years, setting a new franchise record (since broken) in 1999 by driving in 124 runs, before establishing another franchise mark the following year by registering at least one RBI in 15 straight games. An All-Star and Silver Slugger winner each season, Piazza also earned two top-10 finishes in the NL MVP voting, placing third in the balloting in 2000, when he led the Mets to their second consecutive postseason appearance and a trip to the World Series.

Extremely strong, the right-handed hitting Piazza, who stood 6'3" and weighed 225 pounds, possessed tremendous power to all fields, hitting many of his homers to center and right-center. Piazza also did not strike out as often as most sluggers, fanning more than 90 times in a season just once his entire career. Meanwhile, Piazza's ability to hit for both power and average made him one of the finest all-around batsmen in either league.

Nevertheless, Piazza's mere presence in the middle of the lineup may well have been his greatest contribution to the Mets. The team's first true superstar since the glory days of the 1980s, Piazza helped bring credibility back to the organization, as former Met Rusty Staub suggested when he said, "Piazza immediately changed the culture around the team almost single-handedly. After a decade of malaise, they became relevant again."

Still, Piazza had his detractors, with fans and the media often criticizing him for his defensive shortcomings, which included a weak throwing arm that enabled him to throw out only 23 percent of attempted base-stealers over the course of his career. However, pitchers who worked with Piazza viewed him far more favorably, claiming that his weak arm overshadowed everything else he did on defense. Speaking on behalf of his former teammate, Hall of Fame pitcher Tom Glavine, who spent three years in New York throwing to Piazza, told NJ Advanced Media in 2014, "He did a lot of things well behind the plate. Yeah, he wasn't the greatest thrower. That unfortunately translated into people thinking that some of his other game wasn't as good as it was. He called a good game. He received the ball fine. He blocked balls fine. But so often catchers are defined defensively on how well they throw, and there's much more that goes into just being a good defensive catcher than being able to throw."

Meanwhile, former Dodgers teammate and catcher extraordinaire Mike Scioscia said of his onetime protégé, "You had to see Mike from the early days to appreciate how far he came. He made himself into a guy who could go out and catch."

There were also those who found fault with Piazza for his laid-back personality and what they perceived to be his lack of fire, finding particularly objectionable his response to the overly aggressive behavior exhibited toward him by Yankees pitcher Roger Clemens in Game 2 of the 2000

World Series. After being hit in the head by a Clemens fastball the last time the two players faced each other at Yankee Stadium some three months earlier, Piazza fouled off a pitch in his first plate appearance against him, breaking his bat in the process. As Piazza began to jog toward first base, Clemens picked up the splintered bat, which had rolled out toward the mound, and threw it in his direction, later claiming that he thought it was the ball. Although Piazza took two or three steps toward Clemens, yelling at him, "What is your problem?" he returned peacefully to his place in the batter's box when he failed to get a response. While some felt that Piazza showed great restraint by choosing not to sink to his antagonist's level, others believed that he should have responded in kind.

Piazza remained in New York for three more years, serving as the Mets' primary catcher most of that time, although he also saw a significant amount of action at first base in 2004. Experiencing a precipitous decline in offensive productions as age and injuries began to take their toll on him, Piazza failed to hit more than 20 homers, drive in more than 62 runs, or bat any higher than .286 from 2003 to 2005. Nevertheless, he received another two All-Star nominations, before signing with the San Diego Padres as a free agent at the end of 2005 when the Mets showed little interest in retaining his services.

Piazza, who hit 220 homers, knocked in 655 runs, scored 532 times, recorded 1,028 hits, 193 doubles, and two triples, batted .296, compiled an on-base percentage of .373, and posted a slugging percentage of .542 in his eight years with the Mets, subsequently split the next two seasons between the Padres and Oakland Athletics, before announcing his retirement on May 20, 2008, in a press release, which read: "Los Angeles, San Diego, Oakland and Miami—whether it was at home or on the road, you were all so supportive over the years. But I have to say that my time with the Mets wouldn't have been the same without the greatest fans in the world. One of the hardest moments of my career was walking off the field at Shea Stadium and saying goodbye. My relationship with you made my time in New York the happiest of my career, and for that, I will always be grateful. So today, I walk away with no regrets. I knew this day was coming, and over the last two years I started to make my peace with it."

Although Piazza ended his career with Hall of Fame numbers that included 427 homers (396 of which came as a catcher), 1,335 RBIs, 1,048 runs scored, 2,127 hits, 344 doubles, a .308 batting average, a .377 on-base percentage, and a .545 slugging percentage, he failed to gain admittance to Cooperstown the first three times his name appeared on the ballot due to rumors surrounding his purported use of steroids. While Piazza denied using performance-enhancing drugs on multiple occasions, an except from author Jeff Pearlman's 2010 book, *The Rocket That Fell to Earth: Roger Clemens and the Rage for Baseball Immortality*, suggested otherwise, revealing: "According to several sources, when the subject of performance-enhancing was broached with reporters he especially trusted, Piazza fessed up. 'Sure, I use,' he told one. 'But in limited doses, and not all that often.'"

The excerpt also quoted an anonymous player who competed against Piazza for years as saying, "There was nothing more obvious than Mike on steroids. Everyone talked about it, everyone knew it. Guys on my team, guys on the Mets. A lot of us came up playing against Mike, so we knew what he looked like back in the day. Frankly, he sucked on the field. Just sucked. After his body changed, he was entirely different. 'Power from nowhere,' we called it."

Nevertheless, Tom Glavine called his former Mets teammate a "first-ballot Hall of Famer, certainly the best-hitting catcher of our era, and arguably the best-hitting catcher of all time." The members of the BBWAA finally chose to take a similar stance in 2016, voting Piazza into Cooperstown by placing his name on 83 percent of the ballots they cast.

METS CAREER HIGHLIGHTS

Best Season

Although Piazza hit more homers (40), knocked in more runs (124), and scored more times (100) the previous year, he had a slightly more impactful season in 2000, when he helped lead the Mets to the NL pennant by hitting 38 homers, driving in 113 runs, scoring 90 times, batting .324, compiling an on-base percentage of .398, and posting a slugging percentage of .614, earning in the process a third-place finish in the league MVP voting.

Memorable Moments/Greatest Performances

Piazza hit safely in 24 straight games from May 25 to June 22, 1999, going 36-for-102 (.353) with eight homers, 10 doubles, five walks, 18 RBIs, and 18 runs scored.

Although the Mets ended up being eliminated from the 1999 postseason tournament by losing Game 6 of the NLCS to the Braves, 10–9, in 11 innings, Piazza delivered a huge blow in the top of the seventh inning when he put the finishing touches on a four-run rally that evened the score at 7–7 by hitting an opposite field two-run homer off John Smoltz.

Piazza led the Mets to an 8–5 win over the Pirates on April 14, 2000, by going 5-for-6 with two homers, a double, and four RBIs, with his two-out, two-run homer in the top of the 12th inning punctuating a four-run rally.

Piazza fashioned another lengthy hitting streak from June 7 to July 3, 2000, hitting safely in 21 consecutive games, going 31-for-86 (.360) with 10 homers, four doubles, seven walks, 33 RBIs, and 21 runs scored. The highlight of the streak came on June 30, when Piazza put the finishing touches on a 10-run, eighth-inning rally by hitting a two-out, three-run homer that enabled the Mets to defeat the Braves, 11–8.

Piazza contributed to a 9–4 victory over the Braves on April 9, 2001, by homering twice and knocking in five runs.

Piazza experienced his most memorable moment as a member of the Mets on September 21, 2001, when, in the first game played at Shea Stadium following the terrorist attacks on the World Trade Center, he hit a mammoth two-run homer to dead center field off reliever Steve Karsay in the bottom of the eighth inning that provided the winning margin in a 3–2 victory over the Braves.

Piazza helped lead the Mets to a 10–1 win over Arizona on April 30, 2022, by homering twice and driving in six runs.

Piazza delivered the decisive blow of a 6–4 win over the Phillies on September 9, 2002, when he homered with the bases loaded in the top of the seventh inning.

Piazza starred in defeat on April 7, 2004, going a perfect 5-for-5 at the plate with two homers, a double, and four RBIs during an 18–10 loss to the Braves.

Notable Achievements

- Hit more than 20 home runs six times, topping 30 homers four times and 40 homers once.
- Knocked in more than 100 runs twice.
- Scored 100 runs once.
- Batted .300 or better four times.
- Compiled on-base percentage over .400 once.
- Posted slugging percentage over .500 five times, topping the .600-mark twice.
- Posted OPS over .900 five times, topping the 1.000-mark twice.

- Led NL catchers in putouts, assists, and fielding percentage once each.
- Holds Mets single-season record for highest OPS (1.012 in 2000).
- Holds Mets career record for highest slugging percentage (.542).
- Ranks among Mets career leaders in home runs (4th), RBIs (4th), batting average (tied for 3rd), on-base percentage (5th), OPS (2nd), hits (8th), extra-base hits (6th), total bases (6th), and doubles (tied for 8th).
- 2000 NL champion.
- Three-time NL Player of the Week.
- Five-time Silver Slugger Award winner (1998, 1999, 2000, 2001, and 2002).
- Finished in top 10 of NL MVP voting twice, placing as high as third in 2000.
- Seven-time NL All-Star selection (1998, 1999, 2000, 2001, 2002, 2004, and 2005).
- Five-time *Sporting News* NL All-Star selection (1998, 1999, 2000, 2001, and 2002).
- #31 retired by Mets.
- Inducted into Mets Hall of Fame in 2013.
- Elected to Baseball Hall of Fame by members of BBWAA in 2016.

3
DAVID WRIGHT

The heart and soul of the Mets for more than a decade, David Wright spent parts of 14 seasons in New York providing outstanding offense, solid defense, and superior leadership to teams that won two division titles and one league championship. One of the few players to have his number retired by the organization, Wright excelled at the bat, hitting more than 20 homers six times, knocking in more than 100 runs five times, and batting over .300 on seven separate occasions, en route to establishing himself as one of the Mets' career leaders in each of those categories. A strong defender as well, Wright led all NL third sackers in putouts and assists three times each, with his exceptional all-around play earning him seven All-Star nominations and four top-10 finishes in the league MVP voting. Meanwhile, Wright, who Jacob deGrom identified as "the best teammate I've ever been around," served as captain of the Mets his last five seasons in Flushing, before the back, neck, and shoulder problems that plagued him during the second half of his career finally forced him to retire.

Born in Norfolk, Virginia, on December 20, 1982, David Allen Wright grew up with his three younger brothers in nearby Chesapeake, where he acquired his love of baseball from his father, Rhon, a former athlete who worked as a police officer in the Norfolk Police Department. Eventually developing into a star on the diamond at Chesapeake's Hickory High School, Wright earned All-State honors in each of his final three seasons and gained recognition as the Gatorade Virginia High School Player of the Year as a senior in 2001 by batting .538. Although Wright signed a letter of intent prior to the start of his senior year to play baseball at Georgia Tech following his graduation, his outstanding performance in his final season at Hickory High convinced him to enter the 2001 MLB Amateur Draft, where the Mets selected him in the first round, with the 38th overall pick.

Wright subsequently spent most of the next four seasons advancing through New York's farm system, performing well at every level, before joining the parent club in late July 2004 after posting a composite batting

David Wright hit more than 20 homers six times and batted over .300 seven times for the Mets.

average of .341 and an OPS of 1.046 in 91 games with Double-A Binghamton and Triple-A Norfolk. Named the Mets' starting third baseman immediately upon his arrival in Queens, Wright acquitted himself extremely well over the final 10 weeks of the campaign, hitting 14 homers, driving in 40 runs, scoring 41 times, batting .293, and posting an OPS of .857 in 69 games and 283 total plate appearances. Establishing himself as one of the finest players at his position the following season, Wright began an outstanding six-year run during which he posted the following numbers:

	HR	RBI	RUNS	AVG	OBP	SLG	OPS
2005	27	102	99	.306	.388	.523	.912
2006	26	116	96	.311	.381	.531	.912
2007	30	107	113	.325	.416	.546	.963
2008	33	124	115	.302	.390	.534	.924
2009	10	72	88	.307	.390	.447	.837
2010	29	103	87	.283	.354	.503	.856

In addition to those figures, Wright amassed at least 40 doubles and 300 total bases four straight times from 2005 to 2008 and stole at least 20 bases on three separate occasions, becoming the third player in team annals to surpass 30 homers and 30 steals in the same season in 2007, when he reached the seats 30 times and swiped 34 bags. The first Mets player to drive in at least 100 runs in a season as many as five times, Wright tied Mike Piazza's then single-season franchise record by amassing 124 RBIs in 2008. Two years earlier, Wright homered 20 times and set a single-season franchise mark by knocking in 74 runs by the All-Star break, before seeing his power and run-production fall off dramatically during the season's second half after advancing to the final round of the Home Run Derby. Wright also experienced a decline in offensive production during the latter stages of the 2009 campaign after Giants pitcher Matt Cain hit him in the head with a 93-mph fastball on August 15 that left him concussed. An NL All-Star in five of those six seasons, Wright also earned three *Sporting News* NL All-Star nominations, three top-10 finishes in the league MVP balloting, and Silver Slugger and Gold Glove honors twice each. Meanwhile, the Mets won one division title and finished a close second in the NL East two other times.

Although New York's lineup also featured José Reyes, Carlos Beltrán, Carlos Delgado, and Daniel Murphy at different times, Wright proved to be the team's most consistent and reliable hitter throughout the period, performing well even during the Mets' consecutive late-season collapses of 2007 and 2008. Making good use of the entire field, the right-handed-swinging Wright, who stood 6 feet and weighed 205 pounds, often reached the seats at Citi Field in right and right-center and drove the ball well to the power alleys, as evidenced by his five seasons with at least 40 doubles. And even though Wright struck out fairly frequently, fanning more than 100 times in a season eight times, he hit for a high batting average and displayed good patience at the plate, drawing more than 90 bases on balls twice. A good baserunner and solid defender as well, Wright stole 196 bases over the course of his career and made several spectacular plays in the field, including one memorable over-the-shoulder barehanded catch against San Diego in 2005 that garnered "This Year in Baseball Play of the Year" honors.

In addition to his outstanding play, Wright became known for his strong work ethic, unpretentious nature, leadership ability, and willingness to give back to the community. Always one of the first players to arrive at the ballpark and one of the last to leave, Wright proved to be extremely accommodating to fans and reporters, who often came to him for quotes long after many of his teammates left the locker room following difficult losses. Meanwhile, shortly after Wright joined the Mets, he started the David Wright Foundation, which is dedicated to increasing awareness about multiple sclerosis and raising money for organizations that fight the disease.

After missing more than five games in just two of the previous six seasons, Wright spent more than two months on the disabled list in 2011 with a stress fracture in his lower back that he sustained when he attempted to make a diving tag on Houston's Carlos Lee. Limited to only 102 games and 447 total plate appearances, Wright concluded the campaign with just 14 homers, 61 RBIs, and 60 runs scored, a batting average of only .254, and an OPS of just .771. Rebounding in a big way the following year, Wright earned All-Star honors and a sixth-place finish in the NL MVP voting by hitting 21 homers, driving in 93 runs, scoring 91 times, batting .306, and posting an OPS of .883.

However, even though Wright made the All-Star team again in 2013, problems with his back, neck, shoulder, and hamstrings prevented him from ever again playing a full schedule. After hitting 18 homers, knocking in 58 runs, batting .307, and compiling an OPS of .904 in 112 games in 2013, Wright suffered a torn rotator cuff early the following year that limited him to just eight homers, 63 RBIs, and a batting average of .269 over 134 contests. Diagnosed with lumbar spinal stenosis in 2015 and a herniated disc in his neck in 2016, Wright appeared in a total of just 75 games from 2015 to 2017, before making an emotional return to the Mets' lineup for the final two games of the 2018 season.

Having already announced that he planned to retire at the end of the year, Wright told the fans in attendance at Citi Field following the conclusion of the contest:

> It's been a long road to get to that goal, but the love and the support I've received from inside the organization, outside the organization has been first class, and words can't express the gratitude

I have for everybody. I said it when I was a younger player and I'll say it again: I truly bleed orange and blue, and throughout this process, the love and the support and the respect from inside and outside the organization have meant the world to me. Thank you to everybody involved, and you'll never have any idea how much it means to me. . . . To the fans, words can't express my gratitude and appreciation for always having my back. You've accepted me as one of your own, and that right there is a tremendous honor. . . . This is love. I can't say anything else. This is love.

Wright, who ended his career with 242 homers, 970 RBIs, 949 runs scored, 1,777 hits, 390 doubles, 26 triples, 196 stolen bases, a .296 batting average, a .376 on-base percentage, and a .491 slugging percentage, currently holds franchise records in eight different offensive categories, including RBIs, runs scored, hits, and extra-base hits. He also ranks third in home runs and is tied for third in batting average. Since retiring as an active player, Wright has worked in the Mets' front office as a special advisor.

CAREER HIGHLIGHTS

Best Season

Although Wright reached career highs in homers (33), RBIs (124), runs scored (115), and total bases (334) in 2008, he proved to be a bit more consistent the previous season, when he earned his lone top-five finish in the NL MVP voting by hitting 30 homers, driving in 107 runs, scoring 113 times, and establishing career-high marks with 196 hits, 34 stolen bases, a .325 batting average, a .416 on-base percentage, and a .546 slugging percentage.

Memorable Moments/Greatest Performances

Wright led the Mets to an 11–6 win over the Brewers on August 5, 2004, by knocking in six runs with a homer and a pair of doubles.

Wright helped lead the Mets to a lopsided 9–1 victory over the Padres on August 10, 2005, by going 4-for-5 with a homer, double, stolen base, six RBIs, and three runs scored.

Wright contributed to an 18–4 spanking of the Diamondbacks on August 24, 2005, by going 4-for-5 with two homers, a double, two RBIs, and four runs scored.

Wright led the Mets to a 5–2 win over the Braves on April 28, 2006, by driving in three runs with a pair of homers.

Wright proved to be the difference in a 6–2 win over the Reds on June 22, 2006, homering twice and knocking in four runs.

Wright provided much of the offensive firepower during a 6–0 win over the Nationals on April 15, 2008, driving in five runs with a homer and a pair of doubles.

Wright gave the Mets a 5–3 win over the Padres on August 7, 2008, when he homered off reliever Heath Bell with one man on and two men out in the bottom of the ninth inning.

Wright led the Mets to a 10–9 win over the Phillies on September 12, 2009, by hitting two homers, driving in six runs, and scoring three times, plating New York's final four runs of the contest with a pair of two-run homers in the eighth and ninth innings.

Wright contributed to a 12–2 win over the Braves on September 16, 2011, by homering twice and driving in five runs.

Wright again homered twice and knocked in five runs during a 9–5 win over the Nationals on July 19, 2012.

Notable Achievements

- Hit more than 20 home runs six times, topping 30 homers twice.
- Knocked in more than 100 runs five times.
- Scored more than 100 runs twice.
- Batted over .300 seven times.
- Compiled on-base percentage over .400 once.
- Posted slugging percentage over .500 seven times.
- Posted OPS over .900 five times.
- Recorded at least 40 doubles five times.
- Stole at least 20 bases three times, topping 30 thefts once.
- Led NL in sacrifice flies twice.
- Finished second in NL in RBIs once and hits once.
- Led NL third basemen in putouts three times, assists three times, and double plays turned once.

- Holds Mets career records for most RBIs, runs scored, hits, extra-base hits, doubles, total bases, bases on balls, sacrifice flies, plate appearances, and at-bats.
- Ranks among Mets career leaders in home runs (3rd), batting average (tied for 3rd), on-base percentage (4th), slugging percentage (8th), OPS (5th), triples (tied for 9th), stolen bases (4th), and games played (2nd).
- Two-time division champion (2006 and 2015).
- 2015 NL champion.
- Three-time NL Player of the Week.
- Two-time NL Player of the Month.
- Two-time Silver Slugger Award winner (2007 and 2008).
- Two-time Gold Glove Award winner (2007 and 2008).
- 2012 NL Wilson Defensive Third Baseman of the Year.
- Finished in top 10 of NL MVP voting four times, placing as high as fourth in 2007.
- Seven-time NL All-Star selection (2006, 2007, 2008, 2009, 2010, 2012, and 2013).
- Three-time *Sporting News* NL All-Star selection (2006, 2007, and 2008).
- #5 retired by Mets.
- Inducted into Mets Hall of Fame in 2025.

4
KEITH HERNANDEZ

Obtained from the St. Louis Cardinals in a 1983 trade that ranks as arguably the finest in franchise history, Keith Hernandez spent parts of seven seasons in New York serving as the unquestioned leader of Mets teams that won two division titles, one pennant, and one World Series. Arriving in Queens with a resume that already included two All-Star nominations, one league MVP trophy, one Silver Slugger, and five Gold Gloves, Hernandez, who many baseball experts consider the greatest fielding first baseman in the history of the game, continued to add to his legacy during his time in Flushing, earning three more All-Star selections, another three top-10 finishes in the MVP voting, his second Silver Slugger, and six more Gold Gloves with his clutch hitting, exceptional defense, and superior leadership ability. A .300 hitter for the Mets on four separate occasions, Hernandez also compiled an on-base percentage over .400 three times, knocked in more than 90 runs twice, and led all NL first sackers in every major defensive category at least once, with his total body of work leading to the eventual retirement of his uniform number 17 and induction into the Mets Hall of Fame.

Born in San Francisco, California, on October 20, 1953, Keith Hernandez grew up some 10 miles south, in the town of San Bruno, where he acquired a love of baseball at an early age from his father, John Hernandez, a former Brooklyn Dodgers farmhand. But while the half-Mexican, half-Scots-Irish Hernandez enjoyed playing the game very much, he received an undue amount of pressure from his dad, with Chris Smith writing in a 1994 *New York* magazine article, "Hernandez loved the game, but one reason he played it with such fury was that his father never stopped hounding him. Beginning when Keith was 6, John Hernandez—a former minor-leaguer whose promising career ended when he was hit in the head by a pitch—tutored, drilled and badgered his son into greatness. Even after Keith became a pro, John Hernandez was monitoring every swing via a satellite dish in the backyard of the suburban San Francisco home where Keith had grown up."

Eventually developing into a standout first baseman at Capuchino High School, Hernandez played for the varsity squad for two seasons, before a dispute with his head coach prompted him to sit out his senior year. With Hernandez subsequently receiving very few scholarship offers, he enrolled at the College of San Mateo, a local community college, where he manned first base for one season. Selected by the Cardinals in the 42nd round of the 1971 MLB Amateur Draft, Hernandez spent most of the next four seasons advancing through the St. Louis farm system, making a brief

Keith Hernandez earned six of his 11 Gold Gloves as a member of the Mets.

appearance with the parent club in 1974, before arriving in the big leagues to stay midway through the 1975 campaign.

After gradually establishing himself as the Cardinals' full-time starter at first base over the course of the next two seasons, Hernandez emerged as one the league's top players at his position in 1977, when, in addition to hitting 15 homers, driving in 91 runs, scoring 90 times, batting .291, and posting an OPS of .837, he led all NL first sackers in double plays turned for the first of six times, while also ranking second in putouts and third in assists. Though somewhat less productive at the plate the following year, Hernandez began a record string of 11 straight seasons in which he won the Gold Glove Award for his outstanding defensive work at first base.

Taking his game up a notch in 1979, Hernandez earned his first All-Star nomination and a first-place tie with Pittsburgh's Willie Stargell in the NL MVP voting by driving in a career-high 105 runs, finishing second in the league with 210 hits and a .417 on-base percentage, and topping the circuit with a .344 batting average, 116 runs scored, and 48 doubles. Continuing to perform well for the Cardinals the next three seasons, Hernandez batted over .300, compiled an on-base percentage over .400, knocked in more than 90 runs, and led all NL first basemen in putouts twice each, earning in the process his second All-Star selection and first Silver Slugger.

Despite his excellent all-around play, Hernandez shared a contentious relationship with Cardinals manager Whitey Herzog, which grew increasingly hostile during the early 1980s, a period during which the star first baseman developed an addiction to cocaine. With Herzog eventually coming to view the free-spirited Hernandez as a cancer to his team, he traded him to the last-place Mets on June 15, 1983, for pitchers Neil Allen and Rick Ownbey. Subsequently criticized for accepting less-than-equal value for his team's best player, Herzog attempted to defend the deal by hinting at Hernandez's use of drugs, which prompted the latter to threaten a libel suit. However, the Pittsburgh drug trials held two years later substantiated Herzog's remarks.

Initially upset over the idea of joining a team with a recent history of losing, Hernandez later described his feelings at the time, saying, "The Mets deserved and received no respect. And here I was, coming over from the world champions to a team with four last-place finishes in six years, and the other two next-to-last. Banished. Shipped to the Siberia of baseball."

Although the almost 30-year-old Hernandez performed well for the Mets over the final three months of the season, hitting nine homers, driving in 37 runs, scoring 43 times, batting .306, and posting an OPS of .858, his age and status as a pending free agent made his return to a team that once again finished last in the NL East far from certain. However, the Mets' front office allayed many of Hernandez's fears when it revealed to him the names of several outstanding young players it had coming up through its farm system. Assured by team management that exceptional young talents such as Dwight Gooden and Darryl Strawberry would soon be joining him in New York, Hernandez chose to adopt a wait-and-see attitude.

Claiming years later that he made the right decision, Hernandez said, "Whitey thought he was going to bury my ass in New York when he traded me here. He had no idea what the minor-league system was like. He thought he was going to stick me here to suffer for two years. Didn't happen. There was such a wealth of talent."

With Gooden, Strawberry, and others arriving in Queens in short order, the Mets soon became perennial contenders, winning two division titles, one pennant, and one world championship from 1984 to 1988. Meanwhile, Hernandez contributed to the success of the team by posting the following numbers over the course of his first four full seasons in New York:

	HR	RBI	RUNS	AVG	OBP	SLG	OPS
1984	15	94	83	.311	.409	.449	.859
1985	10	91	87	.309	.384	.430	.814
1986	13	83	94	.310	.413	.446	.859
1987	18	89	87	.290	.377	.436	.813

An All-Star in three of those four seasons, Hernandez also earned three top-10 finishes in the NL MVP voting, placing as high as second in 1984 after leading the Mets to a regular-season record of 90-72 that represented their first winning mark in nearly a decade. Hernandez also continued his string of consecutive Gold Glove nominations, winning the award each year. Meanwhile, the Mets won the World Series in 1986 and finished second in the NL East the other three years.

Although the left-handed-swinging Hernandez, who stood 6-foot and weighed a few pounds under 200, possessed occasional home-run power, he proved to be more of a line-drive hitter than a slugger. Doing an excellent job of driving the ball to the outfield gaps, Hernandez amassed more than 30 doubles in a season eight times during his career, doing so three times as a member of the Mets. Typically hitting third in the Mets' lineup, just ahead of sluggers Gary Carter and Darryl Strawberry, Hernandez excelled in the clutch, setting a single-season major-league record by collecting 24 game-winning RBIs in 1985. Blessed with a keen batting eye and tremendous patience at the plate, Hernandez also knew how to work the opposing pitcher, enabling him to consistently rank among the NL leaders in walks and on-base percentage.

Even better in the field, Hernandez used his outstanding range, catlike reflexes, superb instincts, and accurate throwing arm to gain widespread acclaim as the finest defensive first baseman in the game. Totally fearless, Hernandez charged attempted sacrifice bunts with abandon, completely taking away from the batter the entire right side of the infield in such situations, with Pete Rose once comparing bunting against him to "driving the lane against Bill Russell."

Astros skipper Hal Lanier said that the combination of Hernandez at first and any one of three Mets pitchers—Ron Darling, Roger McDowell, or Jesse Orosco—made bunting against the Mets "near impossible."

Expressing similar sentiments, Cubs manager Jim Frey revealed that he rarely asked his pitchers to bunt against the Mets, stating, "You're just asking for a force out at second, and now you've got your pitcher running the bases."

Praising Hernandez for his overall defensive brilliance, Larry Bowa suggested, "He was as good a first baseman as I've ever seen for doing everything. Bunt plays . . . his bunt plays were unbelievable! First and second, he'd charge and throw to third. Man on first, he'd charge and throw to second—he could do it with anybody."

In addition to his outstanding hitting and extraordinary defense, Hernandez served as the Mets' on-field leader virtually his entire time in New York, teaching his younger teammates how to win and play the game the right way. Also displaying a level of intensity his detractors in St. Louis often accused him of lacking, Hernandez drew praise from longtime Mets broadcaster Tim McCarver, who stated, "I've never seen a man 'in the game' as much as Keith Hernandez."

In discussing the leadership ability of Hernandez, who Mets manager Davey Johnson named team captain prior to the start of the 1987 season, Larry Bowa said, "You watch the things that this guy did in the field, it was amazing. This guy could go to the mound . . . he was like a pitching coach out there. Talk about leadership qualities . . . he was probably as good a leader as anybody I've ever seen. He would settle a pitcher down, tell him the situation, what to do."

With Hernandez being arguably the most recognizable figure on a Mets team that gradually displaced the Yankees as the number one sports attraction in New York, he came to greatly appreciate the many perks of playing in the Big Apple. A regular at Manhattan's most popular nightclubs, Hernandez dated celebrities and appeared on television shows. Meanwhile, Hernandez, whose past transgressions became public knowledge by the time the Mets established themselves as a National League powerhouse, became the poster-boy for the team's often raucous behavior, even though he discontinued his use of cocaine shortly after he arrived in Queens.

That being the case, the Mets' inability to win more than one championship caused many a finger to be pointed in the direction of Hernandez, whose position as team leader became increasingly tenuous when hamstring problems limited him to just 95 games, 55 RBIs, and a .276 batting average in 1988, and a bad knee forced him to sit out more than half of the ensuing campaign. A well-publicized confrontation with Darryl Strawberry, who perhaps admired him more than anyone else on the team at one point, further damaged Hernandez's standing within the organization, prompting the Mets to allow him to leave via free agency at the end of 1989.

Hernandez, who, during his time in New York, hit 80 homers, knocked in 468 runs, scored 455 times, collected 939 hits, 159 doubles, and 10 triples, stole 17 bases, batted .297, compiled a .387 on-base percentage, and posted a .429 slugging percentage, subsequently signed with the Cleveland Indians, with whom he appeared in just 43 games in 1990, before announcing his retirement. Over parts of 17 big-league seasons, Hernandez hit 162 homers, knocked in 1,071 runs, scored 1,124 times, amassed 2,182 hits, 426 doubles, and 60 triples, stole 98 bases, batted .296, compiled an on-base percentage of .384, posted a slugging percentage of .436, and recorded 1,682 assists in the field, which represents the fifth-highest total of any first baseman in MLB history.

Following his playing days, Hernandez spent a few years tutoring Mets first basemen during spring training, before joining Gary Cohen and former teammate Ron Darling in the broadcast booth for telecasts of Mets game on SNY in 2006.

His uniform number 17 was retired by the Mets on July 9, 2022, Hernandez said during his acceptance speech, "I realized that I had to set an example of how I conducted myself on and off the field, and I embraced that . . . It's a team. I always thought of myself as just a player, one of 25. Nothing special about me, just one of the guys, having a great time and working hard for a championship."

METS CAREER HIGHLIGHTS

Best Season

Although Hernandez posted extremely comparable numbers during the championship campaign of 1986, he made his greatest overall impact on the fortunes of the Mets in 1984, when he helped lead them to their best record in 15 years by hitting 15 homers, driving in 94 runs, scoring 83 times, and ranking among the league leaders with 97 walks, a .311 batting average, a .409 on-base percentage, and an OPS of .859, earning in the process a runner-up finish to Chicago's Ryne Sandberg in the NL MVP voting.

Memorable Moments/Greatest Performances

Hernandez came back to haunt his former team on July 24, 1984, when he collected three hits and knocked in four runs during a 9–8 victory over the Cardinals, with his two-out single in the bottom of the 10th inning plating the game's winning run.

Hernandez hit for the cycle during a 19-inning, 16–13 win over the Braves on July 4, 1985, going 4-for-10 with three RBIs and three walks, while also recording 20 putouts at first base.

Hernandez contributed to a 14–7 victory over the Expos on August 8, 1985, by going 5-for-6 with a double, three RBIs, and three runs scored.

Hernandez helped lead the Mets to a 12–4 win over the Padres on September 2, 1985, by going a perfect 5-for-5 at the plate with a homer, three RBIs, and four runs scored.

Hernandez again hit safely in all five of his trips to the plate during a 4–3 loss to the Cardinals on October 3, 1985, finishing the game with two doubles and two RBIs.

Hernandez led the Mets to a 13–2 rout of the Cubs on June 10, 1987, by homering twice and driving in three runs.

Hernandez delivered the big blow of a 5–4 win over the Pirates on September 19, 1987, when he homered with the bases loaded in the top of the fifth inning.

Hernandez helped lead the Mets to a lopsided 13–4 victory over the Braves on April 26, 1988, by homering twice and knocking in a career-high seven runs, with his second round-tripper coming with the bags full.

Notable Achievements

- Batted over .300 four times.
- Compiled on-base percentage over .400 three times.
- Hit for the cycle vs Atlanta Braves on July 4, 1985.
- Led NL with 94 bases on balls in 1986.
- Finished second in NL in on-base percentage twice, bases on balls once, and sacrifice flies once.
- Led NL first basemen in putouts once, assists three times, double plays turned twice, and fielding percentage twice.
- Ranks among Mets career leaders in batting average (2nd), on-base percentage (3rd), and bases on balls (7th).
- Two-time division champion (1986 and 1988).
- 1986 NL champion.
- 1986 world champion.
- Three-time NL Player of the Week.
- July 1985 NL Player of the Month.
- 1984 Silver Slugger Award winner.
- Six-time Gold Glove Award winner (1983, 1984, 1985, 1986, 1987, and 1988).
- Finished in top 10 of NL MVP voting three times, placing second in 1984 and fourth in 1986.
- Three-time NL All-Star selection (1984, 1986, and 1987).
- Three-time *Sporting News* NL All-Star selection (1984, 1985, and 1986).
- #17 retired by Mets.
- Inducted into Mets Hall of Fame in 1997.

5
DWIGHT GOODEN

An extraordinarily gifted pitcher who appeared destined for the Hall of Fame early in his career, Dwight Gooden ranked among the finest hurlers in the game his first few years in New York. The 1984 NL Rookie of the Year and 1985 NL Cy Young Award winner, Gooden also earned four All-Star nominations and three other top-five finishes in the Cy Young voting between 1984 and 1990 by winning at least 17 games five times, compiling an ERA under 3.00 four times, throwing more than 250 innings twice, and recording more than 200 strikeouts on four separate occasions. One of the central figures on teams that won two division titles, one pennant, and one World Series during his time in Flushing, Gooden amassed the second-most victories and posted the best winning percentage of any pitcher in franchise history, with his many contributions to the Mets prompting them to eventually retire his #16 and induct him into their Hall of Fame. Nevertheless, Gooden's addictions to cocaine and alcohol, which have haunted him for most of his adult life, ended up bringing his period of dominance to a premature end, leaving us all to wonder what might have been.

Born in Tampa, Florida, on November 16, 1964, Dwight Eugene Gooden experienced a considerable amount of turmoil early in life, once witnessing his older sister being shot five times by her husband, while also being exposed to his father's excessive drinking, womanizing, and violent behavior. Yet, despite the flaws in his father's character, young Dwight bonded with him through baseball, spending countless hours discussing, practicing, and watching the game with him.

Proving to be quite proficient in his favorite sport at a very young age, Gooden, who grew up idolizing Tom Seaver and Nolan Ryan, first learned how to throw the overhand curveball that later became a staple of his pitching arsenal at the age of seven. Often competing against boys much older than himself on the local sandlots, Gooden more than held his own, before eventually establishing himself as a standout on the diamond

Dwight Gooden recorded the second-most victories of any pitcher in franchise history.
Courtesy of RMYAuctions.com

at Hillsborough High School, where he performed so well that the Mets selected him with the fifth overall pick of the 1982 MLB Amateur Draft.

After beginning his pro career with Kingsport in the Appalachian League in 1982, Gooden spent the ensuing campaign with the Lynchburg Mets of the Class A Carolina League, for whom he went 19-4 with a 2.50 ERA and 300 strikeouts in 191 innings of work. Yet even as Gooden excelled on the mound, he began to struggle with addiction, spending much of his time off the field consuming alcohol since he believed that doing so came with the territory of being a young professional athlete.

Promoted to the parent club after just one full season in the minors, Gooden joined the Mets in the spring of 1984 at the tender age of 19. Quickly establishing himself as one of the foremost pitchers in the game, Gooden gained All-Star recognition, earned a runner-up finish to Chicago's Rick Sutcliffe in the Cy Young voting, and garnered NL Rookie of the Year honors by compiling a record of 17-9, finishing second in the circuit with a 2.60 ERA, and leading the league with 276 strikeouts and a WHIP of 1.073.

Impressed with the control and tremendous poise that Gooden displayed at such a young age, Milwaukee Brewers manager and former Baltimore Orioles pitching coach George Bamberger stated, "Eighty percent of the veteran pitchers in the league can't throw a breaking ball for a strike when they're behind in the count. Yet here's a 20-year-old kid who can. There are other young guys with as much ability, but they don't have his command. He's got a 30-year-old head on a 20-year-old body. He should be another Tom Seaver or Jim Palmer."

Rusty Staub also spoke highly of his young teammate, saying, "Dwight doesn't throw as hard as J.R. Richard or Nolan Ryan did, but he's close. And he may still develop more speed. But that's not important. His curveball is the pitch. It's virtually unhittable when it's on—an overmatch. And he'll develop a changeup. He has a chance to be as good a pitcher as there is. As long as he keeps working, keeps his mind on the game. That's what's been amazing to me: the way he's handled all the attention."

Even better in 1985, Gooden led all NL hurlers with 24 victories (against just four losses), an ERA of 1.53, 268 strikeouts, 276⅔ innings pitched, and 16 complete games, earning in the process his second All-Star nomination, NL Cy Young honors, and a fourth-place finish in the league MVP voting.

Blessed with an overpowering fastball that typically registered somewhere between 95 and 98 mph on the radar gun and a devastating curveball that buckled the knees of opposing batters, the right-handed-throwing Gooden, who stood 6'2" and weighed close to 195 pounds, dominated the opposition, with former teammate Ron Darling recalling, "The only thing I can compare it to is like in Little League, occasionally you get the kid that's almost shaving, that's better than everyone else, that strikes everyone out. That's what he was like. He was just bigger, stronger, better. No one had a chance."

Fanning the opposition with such regularity that he became known before long as "Doctor K," or just "Doc," Gooden attracted a rooting section at Shea Stadium that called itself "The K Korner," which amused itself during contests by hanging up cards with a red *K* after each of his strikeouts. Meanwhile, the Mets' home ballpark became the place to be on nights when Gooden pitched, with each of his starts being viewed very much as an event.

Continuing to perform extremely well for the Mets the next three seasons, Gooden posted the following numbers from 1986 to 1988:

	W-L	ERA	SO	IP	WHIP
1986	17-6	2.84	200	250	1.108
1987	15-7	3.21	148	179.2	1.197
1988	18-9	3.19	175	248.1	1.204

Consistently ranking among the league leaders in wins and ERA, Gooden earned two more All-Star selections and another top-five finish in the NL Cy Young voting, although he later revealed that he lost some of the zip on his fastball in the first of those campaigns, saying, "That impossible-to-track, impossible-to-time movement deserted me in 1986, and it never returned."

Gooden also disclosed that he remained one of the league's most effective pitchers even though he adopted a lifestyle that ultimately proved to be his undoing. Admitting that he began using cocaine in 1986, Gooden recalled the pressures he faced that led to his addiction when he said, "Unfortunately, in '86 is when the expectations became more than I could really handle. . . . If I only had three strikeouts, the first question after the game would be, 'What happened?' So, my next game, I would go out there and try to get 10 strikeouts, pitch a complete game, and pitch a shutout."

Claiming that he often went on three-day binges, one of which prevented him from attending the Mets' victory parade following the 1986 World Series, Gooden added, "Luckily, my heart didn't explode."

While Gooden's erratic behavior remained hidden from the public for most of 1986, it became highly publicized in December of that year when police charged him, nephew Gary Sheffield, and former high school teammate Vance Lovelace with violently resisting arrest, battery on a police officer, and disorderly conduct during a traffic stop in Tampa. After pleading no contest and being sentenced to three years' probation and 160 hours of community service, Gooden ran into further trouble during 1987 spring training when he tested positive for cocaine. Forced to miss the first two months of the regular season while undergoing counseling at the Smithers Alcoholism and Rehabilitation Center in New York, Gooden nonetheless performed well for the Mets when he returned to action in early June. But even though Gooden remained off drugs for the next few seasons, he continued to drink regularly.

After winning 18 games for a Mets team that ended up losing to the Dodgers in the 1988 NLCS, Gooden suffered a shoulder injury the following year that limited him to just 17 starts. Nevertheless, he pitched effectively whenever he took the mound, going 9-4 with a 2.89 ERA. Gooden subsequently earned a fourth-place finish in the NL Cy Young voting in 1990 by ranking among the league leaders with 19 victories (against seven losses), 223 strikeouts, and 232⅔ innings pitched, despite posting an inordinately high ERA of 3.83.

Experiencing a precipitous fall from grace the next three seasons, Gooden compiled an overall record of just 35-35, before resuming his use of cocaine in 1994. Suspended by MLB for 60 days, Gooden entered the rehabilitation program at the Betty Ford Center but began using cocaine again just two days after he left the facility. Subsequently suspended for the entire 1995 season, Gooden became so dejected that his wife, Monica, found him in his bedroom one day with a loaded gun to his head.

After receiving help from Narcotics Anonymous, Gooden mounted a comeback with the Yankees, with whom he signed as a free agent prior to the start of the 1996 campaign. A member of the Yankees for two seasons, Gooden threw a no-hitter for their 1996 world championship ballclub, before splitting his final three years in the big leagues between the Indians, Astros, Devil Rays, and Yankees. Choosing to announce his retirement in the spring of 2001, Gooden left the game with a career record of 194-112, an ERA of 3.51, a WHIP of 1.256, 68 complete games, 24 shutouts, and 2,293 strikeouts in 2,800⅔ innings pitched. As a member of the Mets, Gooden compiled a record of 157-85, an ERA of 3.10, and a WHIP of 1.175, threw 67 complete games and 23 shutouts, and struck out 1,875 batters in 2,169⅔ innings of work.

Following his retirement as an active player, Gooden briefly worked for the Yankees as a front-office assistant, before relapsing into drug and alcohol addiction multiple times from 2002 to 2019. Continuing to be plagued by his inner demons, Gooden at different times was arrested for driving while intoxicated, driving under the influence, cocaine possession, domestic abuse, child endangerment, and violating parole, resulting in him spending one year at a maximum-security state prison in Lake Butler, Florida.

Sober since 2019, Gooden now lives a middle-class life with his family in Glen Cove, Long Island.

Inducted into the Mets Hall of Fame in 2010, Gooden later received the additional honor of having his #16 retired by the team, saying at the time, "I appreciate what the Yankees did for me, but I'll always be a Met at heart."

Looking back on his playing career, Gooden says, "Not to blow smoke, but I won just about every award a pitcher can win. I won the World Series with both New York teams, had my number retired . . . got inducted into the Negro League Hall of Fame. I have a lot to be thankful for."

METS CAREER HIGHLIGHTS

Best Season

Gooden had the greatest season of his career in 1985, when he earned NL Cy Young and *Sporting News* NL Pitcher of the Year honors by leading all NL hurlers with 24 victories, a 1.53 ERA, 268 strikeouts, 16 complete games, and 276⅔ innings pitched, while also finishing second in WHIP (0.965) and shutouts (eight), with his 1.53 ERA and eight shutouts setting single-season franchise records that still stand.

Memorable Moments/Greatest Performances

Gooden recorded the first shutout of his career on May 11, 1984, when he struck out 11 batters and allowed just four hits and two walks during a 2–0 win over the Dodgers.

Gooden tossed a one-hitter on September 7, 1984, registering 11 strikeouts, issuing four walks, and yielding just a fifth-inning single to right fielder Keith Moreland during a 10–0 win over the Cubs.

Gooden dominated the Pirates in his next start, allowing just five hits and recording a career-high 16 strikeouts during a 2–0 Mets win on September 12.

Gooden turned in another dominant performance on May 10, 1985, striking out 13 batters and yielding just three hits and three walks during a 5–0 shutout of the Phillies.

Gooden matched his career-high strikeout total on August 20, 1985, when he fanned 16 batters during a 3–0 shutout of the Giants in which he surrendered seven hits and three walks.

Gooden threw 31⅔ consecutive scoreless innings from August 31 to September 21, 1985, highlighting his streak with a two-hit shutout of the

Phillies on September 16 and a 12–1 win over the Pirates five days later in which he allowed just four hits and one unearned run, while also going 3-for-4 at the plate with a homer and four RBIs.

In addition to yielding just two hits and two walks during a 4–0 shutout of the Astros on May 6, 1986, Gooden knocked in a pair of runs with a triple.

Gooden allowed just two men to reach base during a 3–0 shutout of the Cardinals on April 15, 1988, yielding only a pair of harmless singles to Tommy Herr and Ozzie Smith.

Gooden tossed another two-hit shutout on June 23, 1990, surrendering only two walks and a double and single to John Kruk during a 3–0 win over the Phillies.

Gooden hurled another gem on June 15, 1991, allowing just three hits and recording five strikeouts during a 6–0 shutout of the Astros.

Notable Achievements

- Won at least 17 games five times, topping 20 victories twice.
- Posted a winning percentage of .857 in 1985.
- Compiled ERA under 3.00 four times, posting mark under 2.00 once.
- Posted WHIP under 1.000 once.
- Struck out at least 200 batters four times.
- Threw eight shutouts in 1985.
- Threw more than 200 innings seven times, tossing more than 250 frames twice.
- Won pitching triple crown in 1985.
- Led NL pitchers in wins once, ERA once, WHIP once, strikeouts twice, complete games once, innings pitched once, and putouts twice.
- Finished second in NL in winning percentage three times, ERA once, WHIP once, strikeouts once, shutouts once, complete games once, and sacrifice hits once.
- Holds Mets single-season records for lowest ERA (1.53 in 1985) and most shutouts (eight in 1985).
- Holds Mets career record for highest winning percentage (.649).
- Ranks among Mets career leaders in wins (2nd), ERA (tied for 7th), WHIP (8th), strikeouts (2nd), shutouts (4th), complete games (3rd), innings pitched (3rd), pitching appearances (tied for 10th), and starts (3rd).
- Two-time division champion (1986 and 1988).
- 1986 NL champion.

- 1986 world champion.
- 1984 NL Rookie of the Year.
- Five-time NL Player of the Week.
- Four-time NL Pitcher of the Month.
- 1992 Silver Slugger Award winner.
- 1985 NL Cy Young Award winner.
- Finished in top five of NL Cy Young voting three other times, placing second in 1984.
- Finished fourth in 1985 NL MVP voting.
- Four-time NL All-Star selection (1984, 1985, 1986, and 1988).
- 1985 *Sporting News* NL All-Star selection.
- 1985 *Sporting News* NL Pitcher of the Year.
- #16 retired by Mets.
- Inducted into Mets Hall of Fame in 2010.

6

DARRYL STRAWBERRY

Once likened to Ted Williams for his body type and long, looping left-handed swing, Darryl Strawberry arrived in New York in 1983 as the most highly touted position player ever to come through the Mets' farm system. Blessed with a world of natural ability, Strawberry possessed all the physical tools required to excel at the major-league level. Unfortunately, drugs and alcohol ultimately prevented Strawberry from fully realizing his enormous potential. Nevertheless, "Straw," as he came to be known, ended up carving out an extremely successful 17-year career during which he totaled 335 home runs and 1,000 RBIs for four different teams. Having most of his finest seasons for the Mets, Strawberry earned seven All-Star nominations and three top-10 finishes in the NL MVP voting during his time in Flushing by hitting more than 25 homers eight times, driving in more than 100 runs three times, and posting a slugging percentage over .500 on six separate occasions. The starting right fielder on Mets teams that won two division titles, one pennant, and one World Series, Strawberry, who ranks among the franchise's career leaders in most offensive categories, later received the additional honors of having his #18 retired by the organization and gaining induction into the Mets Hall of Fame.

Born in Los Angeles, California, on March 12, 1962, Darryl Eugene Strawberry experienced a difficult childhood while growing up with his four siblings in the Crenshaw district of South Central LA, often being physically abused by his alcoholic father, who also frequently assaulted his mother. Recalling his dad, who left the family shortly after he turned 10 years of age, Strawberry said, "It's sad. I never had a real relationship with him. He never sat me down and talked to me kindly, never gave me a word of fatherly advice or counsel, never taught me to tie my shoe or hit a baseball. None of those things a father and son are supposed to do; he either ignored me or beat me."

Turning to sports as his refuge, Strawberry developed into an outstanding all-around athlete, remembering, "I was very good at every sport I tried.

Darryl Strawberry finished second in the 1988 NL MVP voting.
Courtesy of George A. Kitrinos

I'm not bragging. It was just in me. I loved it. It was pure joy for me to play baseball, basketball, and football. While I was playing, I could almost forget my anger and my troubles. Almost."

Although Strawberry excelled in both baseball and basketball at predominantly African-American Crenshaw High School, he claimed that the former came most naturally to him, saying, "Right from the start, I could pitch, I could hit home runs, I could steal bases, I could field. I didn't think much about it. I didn't study the game. I just went out there and did it."

Despite his immense talent, Strawberry suffered the indignity of being suspended from the varsity baseball team by head coach Brooks Hurst during his sophomore year for his lack of discipline, with Hurst recalling, "I had to sit him down and talk to him a lot. I had him run laps. I would tell him, 'The scouts come in here with assumptions about inner-city ball players. You have to counteract that. Don't give them the ammunition.' But finally, I just ran out of patience. . . . I just said to him, 'This isn't working out. I hope you want to come back next year.' Darryl took it pretty well. He still came to games. He helped lug the equipment."

With Strawberry rejoining the squad the following year, Crenshaw became a gathering place for major-league scouts, one of whom wrote of the lean but muscular 6'3" outfielder, "He has the body of a basketball forward and the natural baseball swing, a powerful, looping uppercut, of a historic home run hitter."

Sports Illustrated also sang Strawberry's praises in an article it published late in his senior year, posting a caption that read, "Darryl, 18, is likened to Ted Williams," after quoting scout Phil Pote as saying, "He's got a Williams-type physical makeup—tall, rangy, good leverage. He's got bat quickness. He can drive the ball. The ball just jumps off his bat."

Selected by the Mets with the first overall pick of the 1980 MLB Amateur Draft, Strawberry subsequently spent the next two-and-a-half years in the minors, before joining the parent club in May 1983. Performing well in his first big-league season, Strawberry, who stood 6'6" and weighed 190 pounds at the time, earned NL Rookie of the Year honors by hitting 26 homers, driving in 74 runs, scoring 63 times, stealing 19 bases, batting .257, and posting an OPS of .848 in 122 games and 473 total plate appearances. Despite missing a significant amount of playing time due to injury in two of the next three seasons, Strawberry gained All-Star recognition each year by averaging 27 homers, 90 RBIs, 76 runs scored, and 27 stolen bases, while also consistently ranking among the league leaders in slugging percentage. Meanwhile, the Mets rose from the depths of the NL East to a close second-place finish in both 1984 and 1985, before capturing the division title and the world championship in 1986.

However, as Strawberry emerged as one of the most prominent figures on the NL's foremost team, he began to fall prey to the temptations of living in New York. After experimenting with cocaine for the first time toward the end of his rookie season, Strawberry began using amphetamines and drinking regularly the following year. Strawberry also later admitted to routinely having sex between innings of games in which he played.

Claiming that the pressure of playing for the demanding fans at Shea Stadium contributed to his illicit behavior, Strawberry stated, "The drinking and drugging, that was a way of punishing myself and the fans, too. I figured, 'If you want to get negative on me, you won't get the best out of me.'"

A heavy drug user and drinker by 1986, Strawberry became increasingly difficult to deal with as his ego grew to monumental proportions, alienating many of his teammates with his selfish behavior and vicious reprisals. Struggling with his relationships outside of baseball as well, Strawberry received a petition for legal separation from his wife, Lisa, in January 1987 after he broke her nose with a punch the previous year.

Yet, despite the outside distractions, Strawberry continued to deliver on the playing field, having arguably the two finest seasons of his career in 1987 and 1988, when he posted the following numbers:

	HR	RBI	RUNS	AVG	OBP	SLG	OPS
1987	39	104	108	.284	.398	.583	.981
1988	**39**	101	101	.269	.366	**.545**	**.911**

Placing at, or near, the top of the league rankings in homers, RBIs, runs scored, slugging percentage, and OPS both years, Strawberry earned his fourth and fifth consecutive All-Star nominations and a pair of top-10 finishes in the NL MVP voting, placing second in the balloting in 1988, when he helped lead the Mets to their second division title in three seasons.

The most feared hitter in New York's lineup, Strawberry, who gradually added some 30 pounds of muscle onto his frame, possessed tremendous power to all fields. Employing a distinctive high leg kick, Strawberry delivered several mammoth home runs, once driving a ball off the roof of Olympic Stadium in Montreal that would have traveled an estimated 525 feet had its flight not been interrupted. On another occasion, Strawberry hit a homer that struck the clock on the scoreboard in the right field stands of Busch Stadium in St. Louis.

Blessed with outstanding speed as well, Strawberry stole more than 25 bases five times, combining with Howard Johnson in 1987 to become the first pair of teammates to surpass 30 homers and 30 steals in the same season.

Nevertheless, Strawberry's perceived lackadaisical attitude caused him to occasionally draw the ire of his teammates and Mets fans, with manager Davey Johnson suggesting that he had the ability to accomplish much more than he did when he stated, "He had the swing, the grace, the power. When he wanted to be, he was as good as it gets."

However, Lloyd McClendon, who played with Strawberry in the minors, defended his former teammate when he said, "Straw was so blessed and so graceful on the baseball field that a lot of times it looked as if he wasn't trying. But he was so talented that his talent came out and the game was so easy for him at that level that people didn't quite understand what he was quite all about. But he was a tremendous competitor."

Following a subpar 1989 campaign during which he hit 29 homers, knocked in 77 runs, batted just .225, and posted an OPS of only .779, Strawberry rebounded the following year to rank among the league leaders with 37 homers and 108 RBIs, score 92 runs, bat .277, and compile an OPS of .879, earning in the process his seventh straight All-Star selection. But with Strawberry experiencing differences with Mets management and seeking to escape the turmoil that had developed in the Mets' clubhouse, he decided to leave New York when he became a free agent at the end of the year and sign with his hometown Dodgers for five years and $20.25 million.

Strawberry, who hit 252 homers, knocked in 733 runs, scored 662 times, collected 1,025 hits, 187 doubles, and 30 triples, stole 191 bases, batted .263, compiled an on-base percentage of .359, and posted a slugging percentage of .520 as a member of the Mets, performed well for the Dodgers his first year in Los Angeles, gaining All-Star recognition by hitting 28 homers, driving in 99 runs, batting .265, and compiling an OPS of .852. However, after injuring his back early in 1992, Strawberry spent most of the next two seasons on the disabled list, during which time he divorced his first wife, Lisa, and remained addicted to drugs and alcohol.

Released by the Dodgers after spending time at the Betty Ford Clinic, Strawberry played briefly for the Giants, before nearly going to jail for tax evasion. Ultimately let off with probation and community service, Strawberry ended up signing in 1995 with the Yankees, with whom he spent parts of the next five seasons playing for teams that won three World Series. Yet Strawberry continued to be plagued by troubles off the playing field. After surviving a bout with colon cancer in 1998, Strawberry served a 140-day MLB-mandated suspension for possessing cocaine and soliciting an undercover police officer for sex the following year, before announcing his retirement at season's end with career totals of 335 homers, 1,000 RBIs, 898 runs scored, 1,401 hits, 256 doubles, 38 triples, and 221 stolen bases, a lifetime batting average of .259, a .357 on-base percentage, and a .505 slugging percentage.

Following his playing days, Strawberry, who MLB suspended for substance abuse three times, continued to struggle with addiction and run-ins with the law for the next few years, spending a considerable amount of time in treatment centers and prison on drug-related charges. Strawberry also had to undergo surgery twice to remove cancerous tissue from his colon. Finally straightening out his life with the help of his third wife, Tracy, whom he met at a drug recovery convention, Strawberry now lives in St. Peters, Missouri, where, as a born-again Christian and an ordained minister, he helps others struggling with addiction and devotes a great deal of his time to his family, church, and his charity work for those affected by autism.

After suffering a heart attack less than three months earlier that forced him to undergo a stent procedure, Strawberry attended a ceremony at Citi Field on June 1, 2024, during which the Mets retired his #18. Expressing his loyalty to the organization during the festivities, Strawberry stated, "My eight seasons here were the greatest of my career, and I will always be a Met. No matter how anybody wants to look at it or chop it up, I'm a Met. I'm a homegrown from the organization, and I'm proud of that."

METS CAREER HIGHLIGHTS

Best Season

Strawberry had a big year for the Mets in 1988, when he earned a runner-up finish in the NL MVP voting by leading the league with 39 homers, a .545 slugging percentage, and an OPS of .911, while also stealing 29 bases, batting .269, and ranking among the circuit leaders with 101 RBI and 101 runs scored. But Strawberry posted slightly better overall numbers the previous season, when, en route to earning a sixth-place finish in the MVP balloting, he homered 39 times, knocked in 104 runs, and established career-high marks with 108 runs scored, 151 hits, 32 doubles, 36 stolen bases, 97 walks, a .284 batting average, a .398 on-base percentage, and a .583 slugging percentage.

Memorable Moments/Greatest Performances

Strawberry contributed to a lopsided 10–1 victory over the Cardinals on June 28, 1983, by homering twice and driving in five runs.

Strawberry delivered the decisive blow of an 8–5 win over the Phillies on September 18, 1984, when he homered off reliever Al Holland with two men out and two men on base in the top of the ninth inning.

Strawberry led the Mets to a 16–4 rout of the Braves on July 20, 1985, by driving in seven runs with a triple and two homers, reaching the seats once with the bases loaded and once with two men on.

Strawberry provided most of the offensive firepower during a 7–2 win over the Cubs on August 5, 1985, going 4-for-4 with three homers, five RBIs, and four runs scored.

Strawberry went a perfect 5-for-5 at the plate during an 8–1 win over the Braves on April 30, 1986, concluding the contest with a homer, double, three RBIs, and two runs scored.

Strawberry homered twice, doubled, singled, and knocked in four runs during a 6–5 victory over the Astros on July 3, 1986, tying the score in the bottom of the 10th inning with a two-run blast, before Ray Knight hit a game-winning solo homer two outs later.

Strawberry delivered the decisive blow of a 4–1 win over the Pirates on September 28, 1986, when he homered with two men out and two men on base in the top of the 11th inning.

Strawberry led the Mets to a 23–10 pasting of the Cubs on August 16, 1987, by going 4-for-5 with a homer, triple, two doubles, walk, stolen base, five RBIs, and five runs scored.

Strawberry gave the Mets a dramatic 4–3 victory over the Reds on May 6, 1988, by homering off John Franco with two men out and one man on base in the bottom of the 10th inning.

Strawberry provided further heroics on September 11, 1990, when he gave the Mets a 10–8 win over the Cardinals by homering off ace reliever Lee Smith with one man aboard in the bottom of the ninth inning.

Notable Achievements

- Hit more than 25 home runs eight times, topping 30 homers three times.
- Knocked in more than 100 runs three times.
- Scored more than 100 runs twice.
- Posted slugging percentage over .500 six times.
- Posted OPS over .900 three times.
- Stole more than 20 bases five times, topping 30 thefts once.
- Hit three home runs in one game vs Chicago Cubs on August 5, 1985.
- Led NL in home runs, slugging percentage, and OPS once each.

- Finished second in NL in home runs, RBIs, and slugging percentage once each.
- Holds franchise record for most intentional bases on balls (108).
- Ranks among Mets career leaders in home runs (2nd), RBIs (2nd), runs scored (3rd), hits (9th), extra-base hits (3rd), triples (7th), total bases (4th), bases on balls (2nd), stolen bases (5th), slugging percentage (2nd), OPS (3rd), sacrifice flies (6th), games played (9th), plate appearances (7th), and at-bats (8th).
- Two-time division champion (1986 and 1988).
- 1986 NL champion.
- 1986 world champion.
- 1983 NL Rookie of the Year.
- Four-time NL Player of the Week.
- September 1987 NL Player of the Month.
- Two-time Silver Slugger Award winner (1988 and 1990).
- Finished in top 10 of NL MVP voting three times, placing second in 1988 and third in 1990.
- Seven-time NL All-Star selection (1984, 1985, 1986, 1987, 1988, 1989, and 1990).
- Two-time *Sporting News* NL All-Star selection (1988 and 1990).
- #18 retired by Mets.
- Inducted into Mets Hall of Fame in 2010.

7
JACOB DEGROM

A dominant pitcher whose won-lost record fails to do him justice, Jacob deGrom spent parts of nine seasons in New York, performing at a level rarely seen much of that time. Despite receiving poor run support and very little help from the Mets' bullpen, deGrom managed to win two Cy Young Awards, earn two top-10 finishes in the NL MVP voting, and gain All-Star recognition four times by compiling an ERA under 2.00 twice, posting a WHIP under 1.000 six times, and recording more than 200 strikeouts on four separate occasions. The winner of at least 14 games twice, deGrom, who holds several franchise records, including lowest career ERA and WHIP, helped lead the Mets to three playoff appearances and one NL pennant, before departing for Texas following the conclusion of the 2022 campaign.

Born in DeLand, Florida, on June 19, 1988, Jacob Anthony deGrom grew up with his two sisters some 25 miles southwest of Daytona Beach, where he acquired his love of baseball from his father, Tony, an AT&T lineman, who built him a batting cage in the family's backyard to help him develop his swing. Eventually emerging as a standout in multiple sports at Calvary Christian Academy, a small school located in nearby Ormond Beach, deGrom starred in both baseball and basketball, gaining recognition from the Florida Athletic Coaches Association as District 9 Class 1A Player of the Year for his excellence on the court, while also earning First-Team All-Conference honors on the diamond.

After being bypassed by all 30 teams in the 2007 MLB Draft, deGrom enrolled at Stetson University, a private college in DeLand, where he spent his first two seasons playing both shortstop and third base, before gradually transitioning to the mound during his junior year. Selected by the Mets in the ninth round of the 2010 MLB Draft after compiling a record of 4-5 and an ERA of 4.48 in 17 pitching appearances at Stetson, deGrom received a $95,000 signing bonus, after which he began his pro career with the rookie-level Kingsport Mets.

Jacob deGrom earned NL Cy Young honors twice during his time in Flushing.
Courtesy of All-Pro Reels Photography

His progression slowed by a partial tear of the ulnar collateral ligament in his right (pitching) elbow that required Tommy John surgery to repair, deGrom ended up spending parts of four seasons in the minor leagues, before finally being called up to the majors in May 2014 after going 4-0 with a 2.58 ERA at Triple-A Las Vegas. Starting 22 games for the Mets the rest of the year, deGrom acquitted himself extremely well, earning NL Rookie of the Year honors by compiling a record of 9-6 and an ERA of 2.69, while also registering 144 strikeouts in 140$\frac{1}{3}$ innings pitched.

Part of an outstanding young starting rotation that also included Matt Harvey and Noah Syndergaard, deGrom helped the Mets win the division title and advance to the World Series in 2015 by posting a regular-season mark of 14-8, ranking among the league leaders with an ERA of 2.54 and a WHIP of 0.979, and striking out 205 batters in 191 innings of work, earning in the process his first All-Star selection. Although the Mets ultimately suffered a five-game defeat at the hands of the Kansas City Royals in the World Series, with deGrom getting hit hard in his lone start, he performed very well against the Dodgers and Cubs in the playoffs, allowing a total of just four earned runs in 20 innings pitched, en route to winning all three of his starts.

Troubled by discomfort in his elbow and numbness in his fingers that caused him to undergo a second surgery on his ulnar nerve during the latter stages of the campaign, deGrom experienced something of a setback in 2016, going just 7-8 with a 3.04 ERA and 143 strikeouts over 148 innings. But he rebounded the following year to compile a record of 15-10 and finish second in the league with 239 strikeouts, although he posted a career-high ERA of 3.53.

DeGrom subsequently established himself as arguably the finest pitcher in the game over the course of the next two seasons, going 10-9 with 269 strikeouts, a WHIP of 0.912, and a major-league leading 1.70 ERA in 2018, before leading all NL hurlers with 255 strikeouts and compiling a record of 11-8, an ERA of 2.43, and a WHIP of 0.971 the following year. Named to the NL All-Star team both years, deGrom also earned consecutive Cy Young nominations, with voters taking into consideration his lack of support from his teammates, who failed to hit for him and squandered many late leads he turned over to the bullpen.

Having developed a diverse pitching repertoire that included a mid-to-upper-90s fastball, an 87-mph slider, a 79-mph curveball, and an 84-mph changeup that he learned from Johan Santana early in his career, the 6'4", 190-pound deGrom mixed his pitches well and worked to both sides of the plate, making him extremely effective against both right-handed and left-handed batters. Employing outstanding mechanics and an exceptional work ethic, deGrom earned the respect and admiration of his fellow hurlers, with teammate Marcus Stroman saying, "DeGrom's got the best mechanics, I tell anybody, and a lot of it's his body; how much of an athlete he is. A lot of it is also physical and what he was born with."

When asked who he enjoyed watching the most, former NL Cy Young Award winner Jake Arrieta said without hesitation, "It's such an easy question. If everybody on the planet doesn't say 'Jacob deGrom' they're not . . .

know what I'm saying? I've told people this for a couple of years. I think he's the best starting pitcher to ever put on the uniform."

Arrieta continued, "When he came into the big leagues, his average fastball velocity was around 93, or maybe a tick over. It's gone steadily up since then, and now he's sitting at 99 mph, averaging. It blows you away to see what he can do as a starting pitcher."

In discussing his mindset on the mound, deGrom stated, "I think my job is to keep the ball down. I always say I try to go out there and get early contact, and strikeouts just seem to happen."

As a former infielder, deGrom also proved to be an excellent hitting pitcher, homering three times, knocking in 29 runs, and batting .204 in 423 total plate appearances and 383 official at-bats. An outstanding fielder as well, deGrom received a Wilson Defensive Player of the Year Award at the end of 2015 as the best defensive player statistically at his position in the majors.

After being named New York Athlete of the Decade by the *New York Post* in December 2019, deGrom performed extremely well for the Mets again during the pandemic-shortened 2020 campaign, earning a third-place finish in the Cy Young voting by winning four of his six decisions, compiling an ERA of 2.38 and a WHIP of 0.956, and recording a league-high 104 strikeouts in only 68 innings of work. DeGrom subsequently got off to a tremendous start in 2021, setting a major-league record by compiling an ERA of 0.56 through his first 10 starts of the season. But after experiencing tightness in his forearm and soreness in his elbow, deGrom ended up spending most of the season's second half on the disabled list. Yet even though deGrom made just 15 starts and threw only 92 innings, his 7-2 record, 1.08 ERA, and 146 strikeouts earned him All-Star honors and a ninth-place finish in the Cy Young balloting. Unfortunately, deGrom continued to be plagued by arm problems in 2022, when, limited to just 11 starts and 64⅓ innings, he struck out 102 batters and compiled a record of 5-4 and an ERA of 3.08.

Choosing to sign with the Texas Rangers for five years and $185 million when he became a free agent at the end of the year, deGrom elected to leave New York when the Mets refused to offer a 34-year-old pitcher with a history of arm problems such a lengthy contract.

In discussing his decision, deGrom stated, "It was never that I wanted to leave New York. It's not like I wanted out of there. I enjoyed my time there. I have great friends still from there. And it was just that the Rangers pursued me and came after me, and when you sit down and try to go over the places you can see yourself playing, the Rangers were definitely atop that list."

In attempting to shed further light on deGrom's departure, former Mets manager Buck Showalter suggested, "He didn't want to leave. He would've liked to stay and finish it. Jake's a pleaser. He wants to bring what people want. He didn't want to leave, but the way it was all put to him . . . it wasn't like he wanted to go to some tax-free state like Texas. It wasn't like he preordained this. . . . People think there was this cloak and dagger behind the scenes. Jake's a simple guy who wants to pitch and feel right when he pitches. . . . Understand that he loved the Mets. He loved being there. There's always more than just one reason why things happen. Trust me."

Initially, the Mets' decision to let deGrom go elsewhere appeared to be a wise one. Plagued by recurring arm problems that forced him to undergo a second Tommy John surgery in 2023, deGrom started just nine games for the Rangers his first two seasons in Texas. But deGrom, who compiled a record of 82-57, an ERA of 2.52, and a WHIP of 0.998, threw four complete games and two shutouts, and struck out 1,607 batters in 1,326 total innings of work as a member of the Mets, experienced a bounce-back year with the Rangers this past season, posting a mark of 12-8 and an ERA of 2.97, while striking out 185 batters over 172⅔ innings.

METS CAREER HIGHLIGHTS

Best Season

Although deGrom won more games in three other seasons, he pitched his best ball for the Mets in 2018, when he earned a fifth-place finish in the league MVP voting and both Cy Young and NL *Sporting News* Pitcher of the Year honors for the first time by leading the majors with a 1.70 ERA and finishing second in the NL with a WHIP of 0.912, 269 strikeouts, 217 innings pitched, and a strikeouts-to-walks ratio of 5.848. DeGrom's ERA of 1.70 represented the third-lowest mark posted by any pitcher with at least 30 starts in a season since the lowering of the pitching mound in 1969. Meanwhile, deGrom tied a major-league record by allowing three or fewer runs in 25 straight starts.

Memorable Moments/Greatest Performances

Although deGrom didn't figure in the decision, he performed brilliantly in his first postseason appearance, recording 13 strikeouts and allowing no runs, five hits, and one walk over the first seven innings of the Mets 3–1 win over the Dodgers in Game 1 of the 2015 NLDS.

DeGrom yielded just one walk and one hit during a 5–0 shutout of the Phillies on July 17, 2016, surrendering only a third-inning single by opposing pitcher Zach Eflin.

In addition to allowing just three hits, two walks, and one unearned run over the first eight innings of a 5–1 win over the Nationals on June 18, 2017, deGrom hit the first of his three career homers with no one aboard in the bottom of the third inning.

DeGrom again reached the seats when he homered during a 6–4 win over the Marlins on April 3, 2019, in which he struck out 14 batters and allowed just three hits over seven scoreless innings.

In addition to yielding just three hits and three unearned runs over the first six innings of a 4–3 win over the Rockies on April 17, 2021, deGrom recorded 14 strikeouts, nine of which came in succession.

DeGrom recorded a career-high 15 strikeouts and allowed just two hits during a 6–0 shutout of the Nationals on April 23, 2021, surrendering only a second-inning single to third baseman Starlin Castro and a third-inning double to right fielder Andrew Stevenson.

DeGrom threw 32⅓ consecutive scoreless innings from May 25 to June 26, 2021, winning all four of his decisions during that timeframe.

Notable Achievements

- Compiled ERA under 3.00 six times, posting mark under 2.00 twice.
- Posted WHIP under 1.000 six times.
- Struck out more than 200 batters four times.
- Threw more than 200 innings three times.
- Led NL pitchers in ERA once and strikeouts twice.
- Holds Mets single-season records for best WHIP (0.912 in 2018) and most strikeouts per nine innings pitched (13.765 in 2020).
- Holds Mets career records for lowest ERA (2.52), best WHIP (0.998), most strikeouts per nine innings pitched (10.907), and best strikeouts-to-walks ratio (5.304).
- Ranks among Mets career leaders in wins (tied for 7th), winning percentage (6th), strikeouts (4th), innings pitched (8th), and starts (7th).

- 2015 division champion.
- 2015 NL champion.
- Three-time NL Player of the Week.
- Two-time NL Pitcher of the Month.
- 2014 NL Rookie of the Year.
- 2015 Wilson Defensive Pitcher of the Year.
- Two-time NL Cy Young Award winner (2018 and 2019).
- Finished third in 2020 NL Cy Young Award voting.
- Finished in top 10 of NL MVP voting twice, placing as high as 5th in 2018.
- Four-time NL All-Star selection (2015, 2018, 2019, and 2021).
- Three-time NL *Sporting News* Pitcher of the Year (2018, 2019, and 2020).
- Two-time All-MLB First-Team selection (2019 and 2020).

8
JOSÉ REYES

The Mets' starting shortstop for nearly a decade, José Reyes spent parts of 12 seasons in New York, serving as the team's offensive catalyst much of that time. An electrifying player who became known for his speed, energy, and charismatic personality, Reyes, who holds franchise records for most triples and stolen bases, batted .300 or better three times, scored more than 100 runs four times, and swiped more than 50 bags on four separate occasions, earning in the process four All-Star nominations and one top-10 finish in the NL MVP voting. A member of Mets teams that won one division title and made two playoff appearances, Reyes led the NL in triples four times, steals three times, and batting average once, becoming in 2011 the first player in team annals to win a batting title.

Born in Santiago, Dominican Republic, on June 11, 1983, José Bernabe Reyes grew up with his younger sister in a one-bedroom home located in Palmar Arriba, a small suburb of the agricultural region of Villa González. Developing a love for baseball at an early age, Reyes received his introduction to the sport by competing in neighborhood games played on any available semi-clear surface, where old milk cartons or other bits of cardboard served as mitts and bats and balls were scarce.

Eventually making a name for himself in the local leagues, Reyes received an invitation to a tryout camp in Santiago, where Mets scouts spotted him for the first time. Signed by the Mets at the age of 16 on August 16, 1999, Reyes began his professional career the following spring with Kingsport in the Rookie League, after which he spent most of the next four seasons advancing through New York's farm system.

Excelling wherever he went, Reyes made an extremely favorable impression on everyone who watched him perform, with Mets director of pro scouting and assistant GM Carmen Fusco stating, "He's the best young player I've seen in 28 years of scouting."

Meanwhile, opposing minor-league manager and former MLB All-Star Cecil Cooper said of Reyes, "He has great hands and super range and an

In 2011, José Reyes became the first Mets player to win a batting title.
Courtesy of Arturo Pardavila

outstanding arm. His baseball instincts are terrific, and he's a plus runner. He's got all the tools to be a great one at the major league level."

Promoted to the parent club midway through the 2003 campaign, Reyes ended up starting 69 games at shortstop for the Mets, hitting five homers, driving in 32 runs, scoring 47 times, batting .307, stealing 13 bases, and committing nine errors in the field, before seeing limited duty the following year due to a strained hamstring and the free agent acquisition of Japanese infielder Kazuo Matsui. Named the Mets' starting shortstop and leadoff hitter prior to the start of the 2005 season, Reyes struggled somewhat with his plate discipline, walking only 27 times in more than 700 total plate appearances. Nevertheless, he posted solid overall numbers, finishing the year with seven homers, 58 RBIs, 99 runs scored, 190 hits, a

.273 batting average, an OPS of .687, and a league-leading 17 triples and 60 stolen bases. Meanwhile, even though Reyes led all NL shortstops with 18 errors, he displayed tremendous range in the field, prompting teammate Al Leiter to proclaim, "He can go down as one of the greatest shortstops in the game."

First-year Mets manager Willie Randolph also saw great potential in Reyes, saying, "It's so exciting to think and dream about what he can do. The ceiling's really high."

Taking his game up a notch in 2006, Reyes began an outstanding three-year run during which he posted the following numbers:

	HR	RBI	RUNS	HITS	3B	SB	AVG	OPS
2006	19	81	122	194	17	64	.300	.841
2007	12	57	119	191	12	78	.280	.775
2008	16	68	113	204	19	56	.297	.833

In addition to leading the NL in triples and stolen bases twice each, the switch-hitting Reyes ranked among the league leaders in runs scored and hits each season, topping the circuit in the last category once as well. Showing greater patience at the plate, Reyes also improved his pitch selection, allowing him to draw a career-high 77 bases on balls in 2007 and raise his on-base percentage from just .300 in 2005 to over .350 in each of the next three seasons. An All-Star in both 2006 and 2007, Reyes also earned Silver Slugger honors and a seventh-place finish in the NL MVP voting in the first of those campaigns, when he helped lead the Mets to 97 victories and their first division title in 18 years.

Blessed with exceptional speed, the 6-foot, 190-pound Reyes ran the bases extremely well, proving to be particularly effective at swiping bags, going from first to third on hits, and legging out triples. An aggressive baserunner, Reyes revealed his mentality when he stated, "When I get to first base, I start thinking about third. . . . I like triples—when I hit a ball in the gap, all I think about is a triple."

Deceptively strong, Reyes also possessed the ability to reach the seats from both sides of the plate, finishing in double digits in homers seven times during his career, including five times as a member of the Mets.

Considering it his responsibility to spark the Mets' offense, Reyes said, "I'm the leadoff hitter; it's my job to lead this team. I know people say the way I go is how the Mets go, so I'll do whatever it takes."

Claiming that he considered Reyes to be the most exciting player in the game, Yankees third baseman Alex Rodriguez stated, "They [the Mets} have the world's greatest player playing shortstop over there, and the most exciting. I turn on the TV every time I get a chance to watch him."

The excitement that Reyes generated helped make him a favorite of Mets fans, who also appreciated his outgoing personality. Known for his elaborate run-scoring celebrations, Reyes also taught the Shea faithful the Spanish language between innings on the stadium's Diamond Vision screen in his spots as "Professor Reyes."

Limited by a calf injury and a torn right hamstring to just 36 games and 166 total plate appearances in 2009, Reyes hit only two homers, knocked in just 15 runs, and scored only 18 times. But after missing the start of the ensuing campaign due to a hyperactive thyroid gland, Reyes rebounded to hit 11 homers, drive in 54 runs, score 83 times, steal 30 bases, bat .282, and post an OPS of .749, earning in the process his third All-Star nomination. An All-Star again in 2011, Reyes hit seven homers, knocked in 44 runs, compiled an OPS of .877, ranked among the league leaders with 101 runs scored, 181 hits, and 39 stolen bases, and topped the circuit with 16 triples and a batting average of .337. Yet despite winning the batting title, Reyes received a considerable amount of criticism in the media when, after leading off the final game of the regular season with a bunt single, he asked manager Terry Collins to remove him from the contest to help protect his slim lead over Milwaukee's Ryan Braun in the batting race.

A free agent at the end of the year, Reyes signed a six-year, $106 million contract with the Miami Marlins on December 7, 2011, beginning in the process a baseball odyssey that saw him play for three different teams over the course of the next four seasons. After just one year in Miami, Reyes spent the next two-and-a-half years in Toronto, before being traded to the Colorado Rockies midway through the 2015 campaign. Playing his best ball for the Marlins in 2012, Reyes batted .287, scored 86 runs, and stole 40 bases. Reyes also had a solid season for the Blue Jays in 2014, batting .287, scoring 94 times, and swiping 30 bags.

After finishing out the 2015 season in Colorado, Reyes experienced off-field problems for the first time in his career while vacationing with his wife in Hawaii during the following offseason. Arrested on charges of domestic violence, Reyes allegedly grabbed his wife by the throat and shoved her into a door, causing injuries to her side, neck, and wrist before hotel security called the police. Subsequently suspended by MLB commissioner Rob Manfred for the first two months of the 2016 campaign, Reyes ended up being designated for assignment by the Rockies on June 15, making him a free agent. Signed by the Mets to a minor-league contract less than two weeks later, Reyes returned to the city of his greatest triumphs shortly thereafter, spending the final two-and-a-half years of his career seeing a significant amount of action at shortstop, third base, and second, before announcing his retirement after batting just .189 in 110 games in 2018.

Thanking Mets fans for their support when announcing his decision on Twitter, Reyes said, "Mets fans, what can I say? We never got the ring we hoped we would get, but I can't imagine playing in front of any better fans in the whole world. Your passion and energy always lifted me higher, and for that I will always be grateful. . . ."

Over parts of 16 seasons, Reyes hit 145 homers, knocked in 719 runs, scored 1,180 times, collected 2,138 hits, 387 doubles, and 131 triples, stole 517 bases, batted .283, compiled an on-base percentage of .334, and posted a slugging percentage of .427. In his 12 years with the Mets, Reyes hit 108 homers, knocked in 521 runs, scored 885 times, amassed 1,534 hits, 272 doubles, and 113 triples, swiped 408 bags, batted .282, compiled a .334 on-base percentage, and posted a .433 slugging percentage.

After retiring from baseball, Reyes transitioned into the entertainment industry, where, under the stage name "La Melaza," he produces reggaeton and Latin music that resonates with fans from his home country and beyond.

METS CAREER HIGHLIGHTS

Best Season

Although Reyes won the batting title with a mark of .337 in 2011, he made his greatest overall impact on the fortunes of the Mets in 2006, when he helped lead them to the NL East title by batting .300, posting an OPS of .841, leading the league with 17 triples and 64 stolen bases, and reaching career-highs in homers (19), RBIs (81), and runs scored (122).

Memorable Moments/Greatest Performances

Reyes contributed to an 8–0 win over the Angels on June 15, 2003, by going 3-for-4 with a home run and five RBIs, delivering the game's big blow in the top of the second inning when he homered with the bases loaded.

Reyes knocked in all three runs the Mets scored during a 3–1 win over the Braves on August 28, 2003, with a pair of homers.

Reyes hit safely in 20 consecutive games from July 17 to August 7, 2005, going 34-for-91 (.374) with two triples, four doubles, four walks, nine RBIs, and nineteen runs scored.

Reyes collected five hits in one game for the only time in his career during a 14-inning, 8–7 victory over the Braves on May 5, 2006, going 5-for-7 with a triple, a walk, and two runs scored.

Reyes starred in defeat on June 21, 2006, when he hit for the cycle during a 6–5 loss to the Reds, going 4-for-5 with one RBI and two runs scored.

Although the Mets lost to the Phillies, 11–4, on August 15, 2006, Reyes had a huge game, knocking in all four New York runs with three homers.

Reyes contributed to a 7–2 win over Arizona on May 2, 2008, by going 4-for-5 with two triples, a double, and three runs scored.

Notable Achievements

- Batted .300 or better three times.
- Scored more than 100 runs four times.
- Recorded more than 200 hits once.
- Finished in double digits in triples six times.
- Stole more than 30 bases six times, topping 50 thefts on four occasions.
- Hit for the cycle vs Cincinnati Reds on June 21, 2006.
- Hit three home runs in one game vs Philadelphia Phillies on August 15, 2006.
- Led NL in batting average once, hits once, triples four times, and stolen bases three times.
- Holds Mets single-season record for most stolen bases (78 in 2007).
- Holds Mets career records for most triples (113) and most stolen bases (408).
- Ranks among Mets career leaders in RBIs (tied for 9th), runs scored (2nd), hits (2nd), extra-base hits (2nd), doubles (2nd), total bases (2nd), games played (3rd), plate appearances (3rd), and at-bats (2nd).
- 2006 division champion.
- Two-time NL Player of the Week.
- April 2007 NL Player of the Month.
- 2006 Silver Slugger Award winner.
- Finished seventh in 2006 NL MVP voting.
- Four-time NL All-Star selection (2006, 2007, 2010, and 2011).
- 2006 *Sporting News* NL All-Star selection.

9
JERRY KOOSMAN

The Mets' number two starter virtually his entire time in New York, Jerry Koosman spent much of his career being overshadowed by Tom Seaver. Nevertheless, Koosman, who served as a regular member of the Mets' starting rotation from 1968 to 1978, proved to be one of the NL's foremost hurlers most of his time in Queens. The winningest left-handed pitcher in team annals, Koosman won at least 17 games three times, compiled an ERA under 3.00 four times, recorded 200 strikeouts once, and threw more than 200 innings on nine separate occasions, en route to establishing himself as one of the franchise's career leaders in all four categories. An outstanding big-game pitcher, Koosman helped lead the Mets to two pennants and one world championship by winning all four of his postseason decisions, with his victory over Baltimore in Game 5 of the 1969 World Series cementing his Mets legacy. A two-time NL All-Star who also earned one runner-up finish in the Cy Young voting, Koosman later received the additional honors of having his #36 retired by the organization and gaining induction into the Mets Hall of Fame.

Born in Appleton, Minnesota, on December 23, 1942, Jerome Martin Koosman grew up with his three siblings on the family farm, where he spent his youth balancing schoolwork and chores such as cleaning barns and repairing fences with more enjoyable endeavors such as ice fishing on the nearby lake and playing baseball with his brother in the family's hayloft. Developing into a standout pitcher by the time he turned 13 years of age, Koosman began competing in various leagues, where he often faced batters much older than himself.

After further honing his skills in high school, Koosman briefly attended the Morris branch of the University of Minnesota, before transferring to the State School of Science in Wahpeton, North Dakota, where his status as a transfer student made him ineligible to play for the school's baseball team. However, after being drafted into the US Army in 1962 and assigned to Fort Bliss in El Paso, Texas, Koosman resumed his baseball career as a

Jerry Koosman won more games than any other left-handed pitcher in team annals.

member of his unit's team. Scouted by the Mets while at Fort Bliss on the recommendation of his catcher, John Luchese, who had connections to the organization, Koosman made a favorable impression on Red Murff, who signed him as an amateur free agent for $1,600 on August 27, 1964.

Following his discharge later that year, Koosman spent the 1965 season compiling an overall record of 5-13 and a composite ERA of 4.61 with two different lower-level minor-league teams, causing the Mets to seriously consider releasing him, with the team's farm director, Joe McDonald, recalling, "We didn't think he was much of a prospect. He threw hard, but he didn't have a breaking ball."

But Koosman's status within the organization changed dramatically in 1966 after he learned how to throw the slider from former big-league pitcher and then-Mets minor-league pitching instructor, Frank Lary. Armed with his new weapon, Koosman compiled a record of 12-7 and a league-leading 1.38 ERA at Class A Auburn of the New York–Penn League, earning him a promotion to Triple-A Jacksonville the following year. Performing well for the Suns in 1967, Koosman went 11-10 with a 2.43 ERA and 183 strikeouts in 178 innings pitched. However, he proved to be far less effective in his nine appearances with the parent club, losing both his decisions, posting an ERA of 6.04, and yielding 19 bases on balls in just 22⅓ innings of work.

Despite his poor showing during his brief stint in the big leagues the previous year, the 25-year-old Koosman began the 1968 season as a regular member of the Mets' starting rotation.

Establishing himself before long as the team's number two starter behind Tom Seaver, Koosman earned All-Star honors and a close second-place finish to Johnny Bench in the NL Rookie of the Year voting by compiling a record of 19-12, posting a WHIP of 1.100, registering 178 strikeouts, and ranking among the league leaders with a 2.08 ERA, seven shutouts, 17 complete games, and 263⅔ innings pitched. An All-Star again in 1969, Koosman helped lead the Mets to the NL pennant by going 17-9 with a 2.28 ERA, a WHIP of 1.058, 180 strikeouts, six shutouts, 16 complete games, and 241 innings pitched. Continuing to excel in the postseason, Koosman defeated Baltimore twice in the World Series, with his 5–3 complete-game win in Game 5 giving the Mets their first world championship. Commenting years later on Koosman's outstanding pitching, Mets coach Joe Pignatano stated, "I think Koosman was a better big-game pitcher for us that year than Seaver."

Unbeknownst to many, Koosman performed as well as he did in 1969 despite spending the entire year pitching in pain. In addition to missing three weeks in May with a knot in the teres minor muscle of his rotator cuff that bothered him all season, Koosman had to wear shoe cushions to cope with bone spurs in his heel that caused him to favor one leg over the other.

Praising his former teammate for excelling under such adverse conditions, Ron Swoboda said, "People didn't realize the physical problems the guy had. He was a wreck. His arm hurt all the time, and he pitched the entire season in pain. I would see all that, and he never complained, and I just admired the hell out of him."

The 6'2", 210-pound Koosman also earned the respect of his teammates with his willingness to stand up for them, which he exhibited one cold night at Shea Stadium in early September 1969. With the Mets having closed the gap on the Cubs in the NL East to just 2½ games, the two teams faced each other in a pivotal two-game series. Trying to make a statement with his very first pitch of the series opener, Chicago right-hander Bill Hands directed a fastball right at Tommie Agee's head, sending him sprawling to the turf. In response, Koosman opened the top of the second inning by drilling Cubs cleanup hitter Ron Santo in the arm with his best fastball.

Recalling the incident, Ron Swoboda stated, "Hands was a sinker/slider pitcher. Jerry Koosman threw a 90-plus fastball, and when he hit you, you stayed hit . . . And Koosie would *hit* ya. . . . No one moved. I think it scared the living shit out of them."

Looking back on his show of support for his teammates, Koosman remembered, "[Gil] Hodges didn't say a word. It's just something you learn. It's how the game is played. . . . I was telling them, 'Here's what happens if you throw at my hitters.'"

Claiming that Koosman's gesture achieved its desired effect, Joe Pignatano stated, "After that, nobody would intimidate us."

Plagued by injuries again in 1970 that included tightness in his left forearm and a broken jaw he sustained when a line drive off the bat of fellow Mets pitcher Gary Gentry struck him in the mouth as he ran in the outfield during batting practice in Cincinnati on June 7, Koosman ended up missing several starts. Nevertheless, he managed to compile a record of 12-7 and rank among the league leaders with an ERA of 3.14 and a WHIP of 1.226.

Koosman again spent some time on the disabled list in 1971 after tearing a muscle in his upper back during a start in San Francisco. And with Koosman receiving very little run-support from his teammates, he finished the season with a record of just 6-11, although he compiled a very respectable 3.04 ERA. Koosman subsequently suffered through a difficult 1972 campaign during which he got off to such a poor start that new Mets manager Yogi Berra sent him to the bullpen in early May to work out his problems.

Recalling his early struggles, Koosman said, "I literally forgot how to wind up. I used to use a cadence count when I pitched: it was 'one-two-three-four, then pitch,' but I had picked up a lot of bad habits."

Eventually righting himself, Koosman rejoined the starting rotation a month later, after which he went on to compile a record of 11-12 and an ERA of 4.14.

Returning to top form in 1973, Koosman helped the Mets capture their second pennant by compiling an ERA of 2.84, posting a WHIP of

1.179, throwing 12 complete games and three shutouts, and registering 156 strikeouts in 263 innings of work, although he again pitched in bad luck, finishing the season with a record of just 14-15.

Koosman's lack of run-support from his teammates proved to be a recurring theme during his time in New York, with Ron Swoboda pointing to his status as the team's number two starter as the primary reason for his misfortune, saying, "Koosman got a lot of the tough matchups. Why would you burn your number one guy against the other team's number one?"

Koosman, though, claimed that he had to deal with the same issues the other members of the Mets' pitching staff had to contend with, stating, "Our feeling was this: If you got four runs, it was a laugher. If you got three runs, you'd win. If you got two runs, you had to win half your games, and some of them you should win 1-0. We just knew we'd have to win with one, two, or three runs."

Koosman continued to pitch well for the Mets in 1974 and 1975, going 15-11 with a 3.36 ERA, 188 strikeouts, 13 complete games, and 265 innings pitched in the first of those campaigns, before compiling a record of 14-13 and an ERA of 3.42, registering 173 strikeouts, and throwing 11 complete games, four shutouts, and 239 2/3 innings in the second. Performing even better in 1976, Koosman earned a runner-up finish to San Diego's Randy Jones in the Cy Young voting by ranking among the league leaders with 21 victories (against 10 losses), an ERA of 2.69, a WHIP of 1.096, 200 strikeouts, and 17 complete games.

Claiming that the loss of his father just prior to the start of the regular season helped him focus better than ever before, Koosman recalled, "I felt the spirit of my dad was on my shoulder the whole year. My cadence count was in perfect rhythm the entire year. I was never, ever able to reach that level of concentration again. . . . That was my greatest year."

Koosman spent two more seasons in New York pitching for losing Mets teams, posting a composite record of 11-35, before the sad state of the organization prompted him to demand a trade to his hometown Minnesota Twins. Acquiescing to Koosman's directive, the Mets completed a trade with the Twins on December 8, 1978, that sent him to Minnesota for minor-league pitchers Jesse Orosco and Greg Field.

Recalling his feelings at the time, Koosman said, "I hated to leave but the front office of the Mets did not want to win, and I just couldn't stomach that."

Koosman added, "It was sad. I had my heart and soul and blood in the Mets, and I wanted to do everything I could to make them succeed. But our top form was so short-lived. Only five years, from '69 through '73. . . . Where did it all go? How could it happen so fast?"

Koosman, who left New York with an overall record of 140-137, an ERA of 3.09, a WHIP of 1.219, 108 complete games, 26 shutouts, five saves, and 1,799 strikeouts in 2,544⅔ innings pitched, ended up spending the next three seasons in Minnesota, posting 20 victories for the second and final time in his career his first year in the Twin Cities, before splitting his final four big-league seasons between the Chicago White Sox and Philadelphia Phillies. Announcing his retirement following the conclusion of the 1985 campaign, Koosman ended his 19-year major-league career with a record of 222-209, an ERA of 3.36, a WHIP of 1.259, 140 complete games, 33 shutouts, 17 saves, and 2,556 strikeouts in 3,839⅓ innings pitched.

Looking back on his playing career more than two decades later, Koosman said during a 2008 interview, "I could have had more shutouts and more strikeouts. But I always believed in throwing the least amount of pitches possible and letting them hit it."

Admired by the men who played behind him, Koosman drew praise from Ed Kranepool, who stated, "I always thought when the going got tough, I wanted Jerry Koosman on the mound. You look at all the important games we had; he was always one of the starting pitchers."

Ron Swoboda also spoke highly of his former teammate, saying, "Coming behind Seaver, we don't wear World Series rings if you don't have a guy like Koosman. Tom is the man and No. 1 in our rotation, but Koosman came behind him with the same kind of stuff."

Swoboda continued, "He was a warrior. You loved him because he was the kind of gamer that you wanted to hang out with. He played the whole game all the time and brought dominant stuff out there and a dominant attitude."

Following his playing days, Koosman initially settled in Chaska, Minnesota, where he became involved in a program designed to showcase the finest young baseball talent in the country that failed to gain steam. Koosman later spent a few seasons serving the Mets as a minor-league pitching instructor, before relocating to Osceola, Wisconsin, where he ran his own machine design business, Mesa Technology, Inc. Unfortunately, Koosman ran afoul of the law in 2009, when he pleaded guilty to misdemeanor federal tax evasion after failing to pay his income taxes for three years. Subsequently sentenced to six months in prison, Koosman, who now lives on income from Social Security and occasional appearance fees, apologized for his actions prior to accepting his punishment, telling the court, "Like most people in their 60s, I've made some bad decisions in my life. I shouldn't have listened to those people about the tax returns, but I did, and I take full responsibility."

More than a decade later, on August 28, 2021, the Mets retired Koosman's #36, making him just the third player in franchise history (after Tom Seaver and Mike Piazza) to be so honored. Acknowledging the many contributions that Koosman made to the organization through the years, Jeff Wilpon, Mets CEO at the time, said, "Jerry is one of the most iconic Mets of all time, and this forever honor is a tremendous representation of what he meant to this organization."

In response, Koosman stated, "This honor isn't only for me and my family, it's for the legions of fans I grew to love. To know that my number will be retired and sit alongside other team legends is one of the greatest tributes I could ever be granted. I was always proud to be a Met. Today, I am even prouder."

METS CAREER HIGHLIGHTS

Best Season

Although Koosman also performed brilliantly for the Mets in 1968 and 1969, he had the finest season of his career in 1976, when, in addition to throwing 247⅓ innings and three shutouts, he placed near the top of the league rankings with 21 wins (second), 17 complete games (second), 200 strikeouts (third), a strikeouts-to-walks ratio of 3.030 (third), a 2.69 ERA (fourth), a .677 winning percentage (fourth), and a WHIP of 1.096 (fifth), earning in the process a second-place finish in the Cy Young voting.

Memorable Moments/Greatest Performances

Koosman tossed a four-hit shutout against the Cardinals on July 21, 1968, issuing one walk and recording 12 strikeouts during a 1–0 Mets win.

Koosman yielded just three hits and three walks during a 2–0 shutout of the Pirates on September 13, 1968.

Although Koosman didn't figure in the decision, he worked the first 10 innings of a 1–0, 11-inning loss to San Diego on May 28, 1969, surrendering just four hits and two walks, while recording a career-high 15 strikeouts.

Koosman held the hard-hitting Pirates to just three hits and three walks during a 1–0 shutout on September 12, 1969, with Roberto Clemente reaching him for a pair of singles.

Koosman performed magnificently in the 1969 World Series, winning both his starts against Baltimore by allowing just four runs and seven hits in 17$\frac{2}{3}$ total innings of work. After yielding just two hits and three walks over the first 8$\frac{2}{3}$ innings of a 2–1 victory in Game 2, Koosman pitched the Mets to a 5–3 win in the Game 5 clincher by tossing a complete-game five-hitter.

Koosman allowed just two hits during a 4–1 complete-game victory over the Pirates on September 20, 1970, surrendering only a sixth-inning homer to third baseman José Pagán and an eighth-inning single to Willie Stargell.

Koosman threw 32$\frac{1}{3}$ consecutive scoreless innings from August 19 to September 17, 1973, posting a composite record of 4–0 and tossing three straight shutouts.

Koosman recorded 11 strikeouts and allowed just five hits during a 1–0 shutout of the eventual world champion Reds on August 15, 1976.

Koosman won a 1–0 pitchers' duel with San Francisco's John Montefusco on September 1, 1976, yielding just three hits and one walk, while registering six strikeouts.

Koosman tossed a complete-game two-hitter on September 11, 1976, allowing just one unearned run, a sixth-inning single by right fielder Jerry Mumphrey, and a seventh-inning single by Ted Simmons during a 4–1 win over the Cardinals.

In addition to surrendering just four hits during an 8–1 complete-game victory over the Giants on May 17, 1977, Koosman hit one of his two career homers.

Notable Achievements

- Won at least 17 games three times, topping 20 victories once.
- Compiled ERA under 3.00 four times, posting mark under 2.50 twice.
- Struck out 200 batters once.
- Threw seven shutouts in 1968.
- Threw at least 16 complete games three times.
- Threw more than 200 innings nine times, tossing more than 250 frames on three occasions.
- Finished second in NL in wins once and complete games once.

- Ranks among Mets career leaders in wins (3rd), ERA (6th), strikeouts (3rd), shutouts (tied for 2nd), complete games (2nd), innings pitched (2nd), pitching appearances (5th), and starts (2nd).
- Two-time division champion (1969 and 1973).
- Two-time NL champion (1969 and 1973).
- 1969 world champion.
- 1968 *Sporting News* NL Rookie Pitcher of the Year.
- April 1973 NL Player of the Month.
- July 1976 NL Pitcher of the Month.
- Finished second in 1976 NL Cy Young voting.
- Two-time NL All-Star selection (1968 and 1969).
- #36 retired by Mets.
- Inducted into Mets Hall of Fame in 1989.

10
CARLOS BELTRÁN

An outstanding all-around player who proved himself worthy of serious Hall of Fame consideration during a 20-year major-league career that included stints with seven different teams, Carlos Beltrán spent parts of seven seasons in Queens excelling for the Mets at the bat, in the field, and on the basepaths. A member of the Mets' starting outfield from 2005 to 2011, Beltrán, who previously made a name for himself with the Kansas City Royals, earned two Silver Sluggers, three Gold Gloves, five All-Star nominations, and one top-five finish in the NL MVP voting during his time in Flushing by hitting more than 20 homers, driving in more than 100 runs, and posting an OPS over .900 three times each, while also scoring more than 100 runs twice and leading all NL outfielders in putouts once. Named the center fielder on the Mets 50th Anniversary All-Time Team in 2012, Beltrán continues to rank extremely high in team annals in most offensive categories even though he spent much of his career playing for other teams.

Born in Manati, Puerto Rico, on April 24, 1977, Carlos Iván Beltrán spent his youth competing in several sports, with baseball and volleyball being his favorites. Choosing to focus exclusively on baseball after enrolling at Fernando Callejo High School, Beltrán eventually developed into such a standout that the Kansas City Royals selected him in the second round of the 1995 MLB Amateur Draft.

After signing with the Royals, the right-handed-swinging Beltrán spent most of the next four seasons advancing through Kansas City's farm system, during which time he taught himself how to switch-hit, with the help of minor-league batting instructor Kevin Long and New York Yankees center fielder and fellow Puerto Rican Bernie Williams. Promoted to the majors during the latter stages of the 1998 campaign, Beltrán appeared in 14 games with the Royals, before laying claim to the starting center field job the following year.

Carlos Beltrán earned five All-Star nominations as a member of the Mets.
Courtesy of Keith Allison

Performing extremely well in his first full big-league season, Beltrán earned AL Rookie of the Year honors by hitting 22 homers, driving in 108 runs, scoring 112 times, stealing 27 bases, batting .293, and posting an OPS of .791, while also leading all players at his position in putouts and assists. Following an injury-marred 2000 campaign during which he appeared in only 98 games, Beltrán established himself as one of the better all-around players in the game over the course of the next three seasons, earning one All-Star nomination and one top-10 finish in the AL MVP balloting by batting over .300 twice, averaging 26 homers, 102 RBIs, 107 runs scored, and 36 stolen bases, and leading all league center fielders in assists twice.

Nevertheless, Beltrán's status as a pending free agent prompted the Royals to trade him to the Houston Astros on June 24, 2004, in a three-team deal that also included the Oakland Athletics. Continuing to perform at an elite level in Houston, Beltrán finished the season with 38 homers, 104 RBIs, 121 runs scored, a batting average of .267, and an OPS of .915, before putting together a memorable postseason during which he hit eight homers, knocked in 14 runs, scored 21 times, batted .435, and posted an OPS of 1.539, although the Astros ended up losing to the St. Louis Cardinals in the NLCS in seven games.

Subsequently offered a seven-year, $119 million contract by the Mets, Beltrán elected to go to Queens, causing GM Omar Minaya to proclaim, "When we started to put our team together, this was not even on our radar. In New York history, the National League franchises have had great center fielders. I can't think of another player who symbolizes that vision more than Carlos Beltrán."

In response, Beltrán stated, "Of course, there will be expectations of me. I have expectations of myself. Day in and day out, I want to represent the organization with dignity and honor. And I understand that when you do well, people love you, and if you don't do well, people boo you."

Beltrán's last statement proved prophetic, as his subpar performance his first year in Flushing caused him to often incur the wrath of the fans at Shea Stadium. Bothered by a quadriceps injury for much of 2005, Beltrán concluded the campaign with just 16 homers, 78 RBIs, 83 runs scored, 17 steals, a batting average of .266, and an OPS of .744, although he still managed to gain All-Star recognition for the first of three straight times. Rebounding in a big way the following year, Beltrán helped lead the Mets to their first division title in almost two decades by placing near the top of the league rankings in homers (41), RBIs (116), runs scored (127), and OPS (.982), while also batting .275 and stealing 18 bases, earning in the process a fourth-place finish in the NL MVP voting. However, even though Beltrán hit three homers against St. Louis in the NLCS, his season ended on a sour note when he struck out looking with the bases loaded, two men out, and the Mets trailing the Cardinals by a score of 3–1 in the bottom of the ninth inning of Game 7.

Although Mets fans found it difficult to forgive Beltrán for the passivity he displayed in his final plate appearance of the 2006 season, they came to appreciate everything he brought to the team. A true five-tool player, the 6'1", 215-pound Beltrán hit the ball with authority from both sides of the plate, ran the bases well, and did an excellent job of fielding his position and throwing out baserunners, leading all league center fielders in putouts twice and assists four times over the course of his career. Meanwhile, Beltrán stole more than 20 bases in a season eight times, accomplishing the feat twice as a member of the Mets.

Beltrán had two more excellent years for the Mets, hitting 33 homers, driving in 112 runs, scoring 93 times, stealing 23 bases, batting .276, and posting an OPS of .878 in 2007, before reaching the seats 27 times, ranking among the league leaders with 112 RBIs and 116 runs scored, swiping 25 bags, batting .284, and compiling an OPS of .876 in 2008. Limited by a bad knee to just 81 games in 2009, Beltrán failed to post the same lofty totals, concluding the campaign with only 10 homers, 48 RBIs, and 50 runs scored. Nevertheless, he managed to compile a career-high batting average of .325 and an OPS of .915.

After undergoing surgery on his knee the following offseason, Beltrán remained sidelined until July 2010. Appearing a step or two slower upon his return to action, Beltrán struggled somewhat both at the plate and in the field, hitting seven homers, driving in 27 runs, and batting just .255 in 64 games, while also failing to reach some balls in center field that would have been well within his range a few years earlier. Moved to right field the following season, Beltrán started 91 games at that post for the Mets in 2011, hitting 15 homers, knocking in 66 runs, batting .289, and posting an OPS of .904, before being traded to the Giants for pitching prospect Zack Wheeler on July 28.

Beltrán, who hit 149 homers, knocked in 559 runs, scored 551 times, collected 878 hits, 208 doubles, and 17 triples, stole 100 bases, batted .280, compiled an on-base percentage of .369, and posted a slugging percentage of .500 as a member of the Mets, ended up finishing out the year in San Francisco, before splitting the next six seasons between the Cardinals (2012–2013), Yankees (2014–2016), Rangers (2016), and Astros (2017). An All-Star another three times, Beltrán played his best ball for the Cardinals, hitting 32 homers, driving in 97 runs, batting .269, and posting an OPS of .842 in 2012, before hitting 24 homers, knocking in 84 runs, batting. 296, and compiling an OPS of .830 the following year. Beltrán also performed well for the Yankees and Rangers in 2016, hitting a total of 29 homers, driving in 93 runs, batting .295, and posting an OPS of .850.

Choosing to announce his retirement after assuming the role of DH for the world champion Astros in 2017, Beltrán ended his career with 435 homers, 1,587 RBIs, 1,582 runs scored, 2,725 hits, 565 doubles, 78 triples, 312 stolen bases (in 361 attempts), a .279 batting average, a .350 on-base percentage, and a .486 slugging percentage. Just the fourth switch-hitter to reach the 400-homer plateau, Beltrán also has the highest stolen base success rate (88.3 percent) of any major-league player with at least 300 career attempts.

Following his playing days, Beltrán briefly worked for the Yankees as a special advisor to general manager Brian Cashman, before being named manager of the Mets on November 1, 2019. However, a little over two months later, Beltrán and the Mets mutually agreed to part ways when he became the only player implicated by name for his role in the Astros sign-stealing scandal. Subsequently hired by the YES Network to serve as an analyst on Yankees telecasts, Beltrán ended up spending one year in the broadcast booth, before once again being lured away by the Mets, this time as a front office executive.

METS CAREER HIGHLIGHTS

Best Season

Although Beltrán also posted impressive numbers in 2007 and 2008, he had his finest all-around season for the Mets in 2006, when, in addition to batting .275 and compiling an on-base percentage of .388, he established career-high marks with 41 homers, 116 RBIs, 127 runs scored, and an OPS of .982, with his 127 runs scored setting a single-season franchise record that still stands. Excelling in the field as well, Beltrán earned Gold Glove honors by committing just two errors in 372 chances and leading all NL center fielders with 13 assists and six double plays.

Memorable Moments/Greatest Performances

Beltrán gave the Mets a 9–8 win over the Phillies on May 23, 2006, when he led off the bottom of the 16th inning with a home run off right-handed reliever Ryan Madson.

Beltrán led the Mets to a 10–6 win over the Diamondbacks on June 9, 2006, by going 4-for-5 with two homers, a double, three RBIs, and four runs scored.

After homering twice and knocking in five runs during an 11–3 win over the Braves the previous day, Beltrán duplicated that effort during a 10–6 victory over Atlanta on July 30, 2006, hitting one of his homers with the bases loaded.

Beltrán gave the Mets an 8–7 win over the Cardinals on August 22, 2006, when he homered off closer Jason Isringhausen with one man out and one man on base in the bottom of the ninth inning.

Beltrán contributed to an 8–3 win over the Phillies on June 30, 2007, by going 4-for-5 with two homers, three RBIs, and three runs scored.

After driving in a pair of runs earlier in the contest, Beltrán gave the Mets a 5–3 win over Arizona on June 11, 2008, by homering with one man aboard in the bottom of the 13th inning.

Beltrán knocked in all five runs the Mets scored during a 5–4 win over the Marlins on August 29, 2008, with a homer and single, delivering the game's decisive blow in the top of the ninth inning, when he reached the seats with the bases loaded.

Beltrán led the Mets to a 9–5 win over the Rockies on May 12, 2011, by hitting three homers and knocking in six runs.

Notable Achievements

- Hit more than 20 home runs three times, topping 30 homers twice and 40 homers once.
- Knocked in more than 100 runs three times.
- Scored more than 100 runs twice.
- Batted over .300 once.
- Compiled on-base percentage over .400 once.
- Posted slugging percentage of .500 or better five times.
- Posted OPS over .900 three times.
- Recorded 40 doubles once.
- Stole more than 20 bases twice.
- Hit three home runs in one game vs Colorado Rockies on May 12, 2011.
- Finished second in NL in runs scored twice.
- Led NL outfielders in putouts once.
- Led NL center fielders in assists and double plays once each.
- Holds Mets single-season record for most runs scored (127 in 2006).
- Ranks among Mets career leaders in home runs (7th), RBIs (7th), runs scored (10th), on-base percentage (6th), slugging percentage (6th), OPS (4th), doubles (7th), extra-base hits (7th), bases on balls (10th), and sacrifice flies (7th).
- 2006 division champion.
- Four-time NL Player of the Week.
- Two-time Silver Slugger Award winner (2006 and 2007).

- Three-time Gold Glove Award winner (2006, 2007, and 2008).
- Finished fourth in 2006 NL MVP voting.
- Five-time NL All-Star selection (2005, 2006, 2007, 2009, and 2011).
- 2006 *Sporting News* NL All-Star selection.

11
PETE ALONSO

The most prolific home run hitter in franchise history, Pete Alonso has spent the last seven seasons in Flushing contributing significantly to teams that have advanced to the playoffs twice and the NLCS once with his prodigious slugging. The only Mets player to surpass 40 homers three times, Alonso established a new MLB record for first-year players when he reached the seats 53 times as a rookie in 2019. Alonso has also driven in more than 100 runs four times and posted a slugging percentage over .500 on five separate occasions, earning in the process five All-Star selections, one All-MLB First-Team nomination, two top-10 finishes in the NL MVP voting, and the favor of Mets fans, who rejoiced when he re-signed with the team prior to the start of the 2025 campaign after it appeared he might go elsewhere.

Born in Tampa, Florida, on December 7, 1994, Peter Morgan Alonso grew up in the South but feels a special connection to the city of New York. The great-grandson of Spanish refugees who fled Barcelona during the Spanish Civil War, migrated to Queens, and later settled in Lancaster, Ohio, Alonso recounted, "My great grandpa moved his family to Queens in the '30s when things were getting unstable and dangerous in his home country of Spain. But the bonds between my family and this city go so much deeper than just that. My grandpa grew up in Queens and graduated from NYU after serving in World War II. . . . My grandma delivered my dad at a hospital in—where else?—Queens."

Revealing that he developed a love for baseball at an early age, Alonso remembered, "As a kid, I just loved the game, and playing catch with my dad and hitting in the front yard wasn't enough. He signed me up for T-ball when I was three years old. It was a little early because the minimum age was four, but my dad was like, 'I've got to get him on a team somehow.'"

Alonso continued, "Growing up, I played pretty much everywhere around the diamond, but my best positions were catcher and first baseman. I also played football, lacrosse, soccer, and basketball. I loved all sports, and

Pete Alonso's 53 homers in 2019 established a new MLB record for rookies.
Courtesy of D. Benjamin Miller

I played just about everything except hockey. In high school, I knew that I couldn't play them all, so I had to make a very tough decision."

After attending Jesuit High School in Tampa for two years, Alonso transferred to Henry B. Plant High School, where he chose to focus exclusively on baseball. Proving that he made the right decision, Alonso performed so well that he received an athletic scholarship to the University of Florida. Continuing to excel at the collegiate level, Alonso gained All–Southeastern Conference recognition as a freshman, before batting .374, posting an OPS of 1.128, hitting 14 homers, and driving in 60 runs in just 58 games his junior year.

Subsequently selected by the Mets in the second round of the 2016 MLB Amateur Draft in what he considers to be the fulfillment of some sort of prophecy, Alonso stated, "When the Mets drafted me, it was like destiny or something. When they brought me to town to sign my contract, I couldn't stop looking around and thinking about how my grandpa might have driven down the same streets back in the day or walked past the same buildings. And now, every time I put on my uniform, there's real, genuine significance there. I feel it deeply. I absolutely cherish the fact that the name ALONSO is what's on the back of my jersey. It's not my name, as an individual. It doesn't say PETE back there. It's my family's name. My family's history! And I feel truly blessed by all the connections there."

Alonso added, "My grandpa passed away before I made it to the bigs, but in so many ways I feel like he's out there with me when I pull that jersey on and head out to first. He loved baseball—he'd tell me stories all the time about listening to Brooklyn Dodgers games on the radio back in the day—and I know he'd be so proud. Not just because his grandson made it to the show. But also because he made it to the show here. In this particular place."

After signing with the Mets for $909,200, Alonso spent the next three seasons in the minors, before joining the parent club in 2019 after hitting 36 homers, knocking in 119 runs, and batting .285 with Double-A Binghamton and Triple-A Las Vegas the previous year. Performing magnificently in his first big-league season after being named the Mets' starting first baseman, Alonso earned All-Star and NL Rookie of the Year honors by leading the majors with 53 homers, driving in 120 runs, scoring 103 times, batting .260, compiling an on-base percentage of .358, and posting a slugging percentage of .583. Although not nearly as productive during the pandemic-shortened 2020 campaign, Alonso hit 16 homers and knocked in 35 runs in only 57 games, before finishing third in the league with 37 homers, driving in 94 runs, batting .262, and posting an OPS of .863 the following year.

Nicknamed the "Polar Bear" for his size and great physical strength, the right-handed-hitting Alonso, who stands 6'3" and weighs 245 pounds, is a slugger in the truest sense of the word. Blessed with tremendous power to all fields, Alonso has the ability to drive the ball well over 400 feet to either left, center, or right, with several of his longest homers going to the opposite field. Extremely popular with the hometown fans largely because of his home-run-hitting prowess, Alonso has also endeared himself to the "Flushing Faithful" with his friendly demeanor, engaging personality, and generous nature, which prompted him and his wife, Haley, to form The

Alonso Foundation, a charitable organization that supports youth, veteran, and animal causes.

Still, Alonso does have his shortcomings. Like most sluggers, he strikes out frequently and doesn't hit for a particularly high batting average, fanning at least 127 times in each of his six full big-league seasons, while never batting any higher than .272. Alonso is also slow afoot, doesn't run the bases well, and proved to be something of a liability in the field early in his career, although his defensive play has improved dramatically the last few seasons.

Returning to top form in 2022, Alonso earned his second All-Star nomination and an eighth-place finish in the NL MVP voting by finishing second in the league with 40 homers, topping the circuit with a franchise-record 131 RBIs, scoring 95 times, batting .271, and posting an OPS of .869, with his 40 homers making him the first player in team annals to reach that mark twice. Alonso followed that up by ranking among the league leaders with 46 homers and 118 RBIs in 2023, although his batting average and OPS slipped to .217 and .821, respectively.

After turning down a seven-year, $158 million contract extension the Mets offered him during the early stages of the 2024 campaign, Alonso ended up having an off year, hitting just 34 homers, driving in only 88 runs, batting .240, and posting a career-low OPS of .788. Alonso subsequently spent much of the following offseason engaging in lengthy contract negotiations with the Mets, before finally agreeing with them on a two-year $54 million deal that included a player opt-out after the 2025 season.

Proving his worth this past season, Alonso earned All-Star honors by hitting 38 homers, driving in 126 runs, scoring 87 times, posting an OPS of .871, and establishing career-high marks in batting average (.272), hits (170), and doubles (41), leading the league in the last category. Heading into the 2026 campaign, Alonso boasts career totals of 264 home runs, 712 RBIs, 580 runs scored, 951 hits, and 183 doubles, a lifetime batting average of .253, a .341 on-base percentage, and a .516 slugging percentage.

CAREER HIGHLIGHTS

Best Season

Alonso had a big year for the Mets in 2022, when, in addition to setting a single-season franchise record by driving in 131 runs, he hit 40 homers, scored 95 times, amassed 309 total bases, batted .271, and compiled an OPS of .869. However, he posted slightly better overall numbers in 2019, when he earned a seventh-place finish in the NL MVP voting by establishing a new rookie record for homers (53), finishing third in the league with 120 RBIs, placing second in the circuit with 348 total bases, scoring 103 times, batting .260, and posting an OPS of .941.

Memorable Moments/Greatest Performances

Alonso broke Aaron Judge's record for most home runs by a rookie when he reached the seats for the 53rd time during a 3–0 victory over the Braves on September 28, 2019.

Alonso led the Mets to a 10–8 win over the Braves on August 15, 2019, by going a perfect 5-for-5 at the plate with a homer and six RBIs.

Alonso knocked in two of the three runs the Mets scored during a 3–1 win over the Diamondbacks on September 9, 2019, with a pair of solo homers.

Alonso gave the Mets a 9–7 win over the Yankees on September 3, 2020, when he hit a two-run homer off reliever Albert Abreu in the bottom of the 10th inning.

Alonso provided most of the offensive firepower during a 3–0 victory over the Blue Jays on July 23, 2021, driving in all three runs with a pair of homers.

Alonso proved to be the difference in a 6–1 win over the Phillies on May 8, 2022, going 3-for-5 with two homers and five RBIs.

Alonso gave the Mets a 7–6 win over the Cardinals on May 19, 2022, when he homered with one man aboard in the bottom of the 10th inning.

Alonso knocked in all five runs the Mets scored during a 5–1 win over the Nationals on July 28, 2023, with a pair of homers.

Alonso led the Mets to a lopsided 11–2 victory over the Cubs on August 7, 2023, by homering twice and driving in six runs.

Alonso experienced the most memorable moment of his career in the top of the ninth inning of Game 3 of the 2024 NL Wild Card Series, when he hit an opposite field three-run homer off Milwaukee closer Devin Williams that proved to be the decisive blow of a series-clinching 4–2 Mets win.

Alonso helped lead the Mets to a 6–1 win over the Dodgers on June 4, 2025, by driving in five runs with a pair of homers.

Alonso gave the Mets a 5–2 victory over Texas on September 14, 2025, that ended their eight-game losing streak by hitting a three-run homer off right-handed reliever Luis Curvelo in the bottom of the 10th inning.

Notable Achievements
- Has hit more than 30 home runs six times, topping 40 homers three times and 50 homers once.
- Has knocked in more than 100 runs four times.
- Has scored more than 100 runs once.
- Has posted slugging percentage over .500 five times.
- Has posted OPS over .900 once.
- Has led NL in home runs, RBIs, doubles, and extra-base hits once each.
- Has finished second in NL in home runs once, RBIs twice, and total bases once.
- Holds MLB home run record for rookies (53 in 2019).
- Holds Mets single-season records for most home runs (53), RBIs (131), total bases (348), and extra-base hits (85).
- Holds Mets career record for most home runs (264).
- Ranks among Mets career leaders in RBIs (3rd), runs scored (8th), extra-base hits (4th), total bases (5th), slugging percentage (3rd), and OPS (tied for 6th).
- Five-time NL Player of the Week.
- April 2025 NL Player of the Month.
- 2019 NL Rookie of the Year.
- 2025 Silver Slugger Award winner.
- Has finished in top 10 of NL MVP voting twice.
- Five-time NL All-Star selection (2019, 2022, 2023, 2024, and 2025).
- 2019 All-MLB First-Team selection.

12
GARY CARTER

Already recognized as the finest catcher in the game by the time he arrived in New York in 1985, Gary Carter proved to be the final piece of the puzzle for a Mets team with championship aspirations. After earning seven All-Star selections, two top-10 finishes in the NL MVP voting, three Silver Sluggers, and three Gold Gloves with the Montreal Expos from 1974 to 1984, Carter made a huge impact on the Mets over the course of the next few seasons, helping them win two division titles, one pennant, and one world championship by hitting at least 20 homers three times and driving in at least 100 runs twice, while also providing outstanding defense behind the plate and superior on-field leadership. A four-time All-Star during his time in Queens, Carter also earned two more Silver Sluggers and another pair of top-10 finishes in the league MVP balloting, further enhancing in the process a resume that eventually gained him induction into the Baseball Hall of Fame.

Born in Culver City, California, on April 8, 1954, Gary Edmund Carter grew up just outside of Los Angeles, where his father assumed the role of both parents after young Gary's 37-year-old mother died of leukemia one month after he turned 12 years of age. Developing a love of sports early in life, Carter played Little League baseball and won the seven-year-old national division of the NFL's first Punt, Pass & Kick skills competition in 1961.

An outstanding all-around athlete, Carter starred in multiple sports at Sunny Hills High School, excelling as a quarterback in football and an infielder in baseball. Offered nearly 100 scholarships to play football in college, Carter initially signed a letter of intent to attend UCLA, before choosing instead to pursue a career in baseball after suffering torn knee ligaments in his senior year that forced him to sit out the football season.

Selected by the Montreal Expos in the third round of the 1972 MLB Amateur Draft, Carter spent most of the next three seasons in the minor leagues polishing his receiving skills after being moved to catcher, before

Gary Carter helped lead the Mets to two division titles, one pennant, and one world championship.

joining the parent club during the latter stages of the 1974 campaign. A regular member of the Expos' lineup in 1975, Carter earned All-Star honors and a runner-up finish in the NL Rookie of the Year voting by hitting 17 homers, driving in 68 runs, and batting .270, while splitting his time between catcher and right field. Used in a similar fashion the following year, Carter missed a significant amount of time due to injury, later saying, "I was out of position. I was running into walls [in the outfield] and hurting myself."

Named Montreal's everyday starting catcher prior to the start of the 1977 season, Carter soon established himself as the finest all-around receiver in the game, hitting at least 20 homers six times and driving in more than 100 runs twice from 1977 to 1984, while also leading all players at his position in fielding percentage twice, putouts six times, and assists on five separate occasions. Particularly outstanding in 1980, 1982, and 1984, Carter earned a runner-up finish in the NL MVP voting in the first of those campaigns by ranking among the league leaders with 29 homers and 101 RBIs, before hitting 29 homers, knocking in 97 runs, scoring 91 times, batting .293, and posting an OPS of .890 in the second, and reaching the seats 27 times, leading the league with 106 RBIs, batting .294, and compiling an OPS of .853 in the third.

Nevertheless, Carter, whose youthful exuberance and ever-present smile earned him the nickname "The Kid," rubbed several of his Montreal teammates the wrong way with his unabashed enthusiasm, preoccupation with his image, and fondness for being in the spotlight, which caused some of them to derisively refer to him as "Camera Carter." Expressing his dissatisfaction with Carter on one occasion, Expos star center fielder Andre Dawson stated that he considered him "more of a glory hound than a team player."

Ultimately deciding to part ways with Carter, the Expos completed a trade with the rapidly improving Mets on December 10, 1984, that sent him to New York for infielder Hubie Brooks, catcher Mike Fitzgerald, outfielder Herm Winningham, and pitcher Floyd Youmans. Expressing his elation after completing the deal, Mets GM Frank Cashen said, "This is a banner day for the New York Mets. Everyone is aware of our need for a right-handed power hitter, and they don't come any better than Gary Carter."

Inserted into the cleanup spot in the batting order upon his arrival in Queens, Carter lived up to all of Cashen's expectations his first year with the Mets, leading them to a regular-season record of 98-64 and a close second-place finish to the Cardinals in the NL East by hitting 32 homers, driving in 100 runs, batting .281, and posting an OPS of .853. Excelling behind the plate as well, Carter led all NL catchers in putouts and did a superb job of handling a young starting rotation that included Dwight Gooden, Ron Darling, and Sid Fernandez, with his outstanding all-around play earning him All-Star honors and a sixth-place finish in the league MVP voting. Carter followed that up by hitting 24 homers, knocking in 105 runs, scoring 81 times, batting .255, and compiling an OPS of .776 for the Mets' 1986 world championship ballclub, earning in the process his ninth All-Star nomination and a third-place finish in the NL MVP balloting.

Extremely strong, the 6'2", 210-pound Carter possessed a burly frame that made him an imposing figure at the plate. Employing an almost straight-up stance in which he bent his knees slightly and held the bat vertical, Carter made excellent use of his powerful shoulders and forearms when he swung, chopping at the ball with a horizontal stroke, like a lumberjack attacking a tree. Primarily a pull-hitter, Carter hit almost all his homers to left field, although he also had the ability to drive the ball to the outfield gaps.

In discussing his former Mets teammate, Tim Teufel said, "I remember him being a clutch hitter with such tremendous pop in his bat. To be able to hit home runs and doubles the way he did, as well as calling a great game each time out, that was amazing."

An outstanding defender as well, Carter possessed a strong throwing arm and did an excellent job of framing pitches, blocking the plate, calling a game, and tracking the tendencies of opposing batters, with Mets manager Davey Johnson calling him "a one-man scouting system."

Carter also drew praise for his defense and dedication to his profession from Keith Hernandez, who said, "He was a human backstop back there. Early, before his knees went bad, you couldn't steal on him in Montreal. When he wasn't able to throw because of his knees, that never affected his performance. He was running on and off the field after three outs. This guy played in some pain, and it was hustle, hustle, hustle."

Meanwhile, Larry Bowa, who stole more than 300 bases during his career, said of Carter, "This guy put a little fear in you when you were on first base even if you got a good jump . . . A lot of catchers were on ego trips; they didn't want you to steal, so they would call just fastballs . . . I respect Gary Carter because he would call breaking balls. He was not intimidated by any base stealer. He would call his game."

Although Carter, who embraced Christianity during his time in Montreal as a way of better accepting the premature passing of his mother, carried himself with far more decorum than many of his Mets teammates, he came to be viewed as one of the team's foremost leaders, with Tim Teufel saying, "Gary was one of the leaders in the clubhouse. . . . He wasn't afraid to speak up, but he wasn't critical of anyone. He always talked to the player he needed to in a very encouraging manner."

Yet, as had been the case in Montreal, there were some who doubted Carter's sincerity, interpreting his effervescent personality and friendliness toward the media as ways of drawing attention to himself. Still others considered him to be something of a prude. However, those closest to Carter felt differently, with Ira Berkow of the *New York Times* writing upon his induction into the Baseball Hall of Fame, "He delighted in relationships."

Meanwhile, Ed Lynch said of his former Mets teammate, "I remember when he came to New York with all the pressure on him. We were expected to win, and he was expected to lead us, and both came through. He loved the media, loved the expectations, and lived up to all of them."

After being named team co-captain prior to the start of the 1987 campaign, the 33-year-old Carter earned his third consecutive All-Star nomination as a member of the Mets by hitting 20 homers and driving in 83 runs, despite being hampered by numerous injuries that caused him to score just 55 runs, compile a batting average of only .235, and post an OPS of just .682. Elaborating on the physical problems that Carter encountered over the course of the season, an article appearing in the *Palm Beach Sun-Sentinel* the following spring revealed, "It took six cortisone shots for Carter to get through last season—to sustain a troublesome ankle, knee, shoulder, back, and elbow. No wonder his offensive production slipped."

When asked about his injury-marred campaign, Carter said, "I was hurting every day last year. I should have been put on the disabled list several times, but they weren't disabling injuries. In my early- to mid-20s, a lot of the type of injuries I have today were easier to shake off. You learn to appreciate the good days in which you feel like a human being."

Plagued by injuries again in 1988, Carter finished the season with just 11 homers, 46 RBIs, 39 runs scored, and a .242 batting average, before being limited by knee problems that forced him to undergo arthroscopic surgery to only 50 games, two homers, and a .183 batting average the following year. Released by the Mets at the end of the 1989 season, Carter, who, during his time in New York, hit 89 homers, knocked in 349 runs, scored 272 times, amassed 542 hits, 73 doubles, and seven triples, batted .249, compiled an on-base percentage of .319, and posted a slugging percentage of .412, signed with the San Francisco Giants, with whom he spent one year assuming a part-time role. Carter subsequently split the next two seasons between the Dodgers and Expos, before announcing his retirement following the conclusion of the 1992 campaign with career totals of 324 homers, 1,225 RBIs, 1,025 runs scored, 2,092 hits, 371 doubles, and 31 triples, a .262 batting average, a .335 on-base percentage, and a .439 slugging percentage.

Following his playing days, Carter spent seven years working as a television color commentator, first for the Florida Marlins (1993–1996) and then for the Expos (1997–1999), before returning to the Mets in 2001. After assuming various roles within the organization for the next six years, including roving minor-league catching instructor, minor-league catching coordinator, and minor-league manager, Carter spent two years managing in the independent leagues, before accepting the position of head coach at Palm Beach Atlantic University. All the while, Carter remained active in the

Gary Carter Foundation he established in 2000 to help support the physical, mental, and spiritual well-being of children. Carter also championed causes that fought leukemia and illiteracy.

Carter continued to coach at Palm Beach Atlantic until 2011, when he received a diagnosis of multiple brain tumors after complaining of headaches and memory loss. Forced to undergo aggressive chemotherapy after surgery at the Duke University Medical Center proved unsuccessful, Carter responded well at first, before developing several new tumors. Carter lived until February 16, 2012, when he died in West Palm Beach, Florida, at only 57 years of age. Nine days later, the Mets announced their plans to add a memorial patch to their uniforms that season, which would feature a black home plate with Carter's #8 and "KID" inscribed on it.

Reminiscing about Carter following his passing, Tom Verducci of *Sports Illustrated* wrote, "I cannot conjure a single image of Gary Carter with anything but a smile on his face. I have no recollection of a gloomy Carter, not even as his knees began to announce a slow surrender . . . Carter played every day with the joy as if it were the opening day of Little League. . . . Gary actually took a lot of grief from his teammates for being a straight arrow. It wasn't the cool thing to do but on the same token, I think he actually served as a role model for a lot of these guys as they aged. He was the ballast of that team [the Mets]. They did have a lot of fun, there's no question about that, but they were also one of the fiercest, most competitive teams I've ever seen, and obviously their comebacks from the '86 postseason defines that team. Carter was a huge part of that."

METS CAREER HIGHLIGHTS

Best Season

Carter's first year in New York proved to be his finest as a member of the Mets. In addition to doing an expert job of handling a pitching staff that allowed the fewest runs of any in the league, Carter ranked among the NL leaders with 32 homers and 100 RBIs, scored 83 runs, batted .281, and posted an OPS of .853, earning in the process a sixth-place finish in the NL MVP balloting and his fourth Silver Slugger.

Memorable Moments/Greatest Performances

Carter made his Mets debut a memorable one, giving his new team a 6–5 win over the Cardinals in the 1985 regular-season opener by hitting a solo homer off Neil Allen in the bottom of the 10th inning.

Carter delivered the decisive blow of a 5–3 win over the Braves on May 7, 1985, when he homered off Bruce Sutter with the bases loaded in the bottom of the eighth inning.

Carter led the Mets to a 6–2 victory over the Cubs on August 11, 1985, by knocking in four runs with a pair of two-run homers.

Carter had a huge game against San Diego on September 3, 1985, hitting three homers and knocking in six runs during an 8–3 Mets win.

Carter followed that up by homering twice, driving in three runs, and scoring three times during a 9–2 win over the Padres the very next day.

Carter helped lead the Mets to an 11–0 rout of the Braves on July 11, 1986, by driving in a career-high seven runs with a three-run homer in the first inning and a second-inning grand slam.

Carter gave the Mets a 2–1 victory over Houston in Game 5 of the 1986 NLCS when he singled home Wally Backman from second base with one man out in the bottom of the 12th inning.

Carter helped the Mets even the 1986 World Series at two games apiece by knocking in three runs with a double and a pair of homers during a 6–2 win over Boston in Game 4.

Carter subsequently ignited the Mets' improbable three-run rally in the bottom of the 10th inning of Game 6 of that year's Fall Classic that resulted in a 6–5 win over the Red Sox by delivering the first of three consecutive two-out singles.

Carter reached a milestone on August 11, 1988, when he hit the 300th home run of his career with no one aboard in the top of the second inning of a 9–6 win over the Cubs.

Notable Achievements

- Hit at least 20 home runs three times, topping 30 homers once.
- Knocked in at least 100 runs twice.
- Led NL with 15 sacrifice flies in 1986.
- Finished third in NL with 105 RBIs in 1986.
- Led NL catchers in putouts twice and double plays turned once.
- Two-time division champion (1986 and 1988).
- 1986 NL champion.

- 1986 world champion.
- September 8, 1985, NL Player of the Week.
- September 1985 NL Player of the Month.
- Two-time Silver Slugger Award winner (1985 and 1986).
- 1989 Roberto Clemente Award winner.
- Finished in top 10 of NL MVP voting twice, placing as high as third in 1986.
- Four-time NL All-Star selection (1985, 1986, 1987, and 1988).
- Two-time *Sporting News* NL All-Star selection (1985 and 1986).
- Inducted into Mets Hall of Fame in 2001.
- Elected to Baseball Hall of Fame by members of BBWAA in 2003.

13
EDGARDO ALFONZO

Once described by the *New York Times* as "a versatile and dependable player whose combination of a robust batting average, solid power, and flawless defense could make him the premier second baseman in the major leagues," Edgardo Alfonzo spent eight years in New York ingratiating himself to the hometown fans with his consistently excellent hitting and strong defensive play at both second base and third. Considered by many to be the most complete player on Mets teams that advanced to the playoffs twice and the World Series once, Alfonzo hit more than 20 homers twice, knocked in more than 100 runs once, scored more than 100 runs twice, and batted over .300 on four separate occasions, while also annually ranking among the top players at his position in putouts, assists, and fielding percentage. A onetime All-Star, Alfonzo also won one Silver Slugger and earned one top-10 finish in the NL MVP voting, before being further honored by gaining induction into the Mets Hall of Fame.

Born in Santa Teresa del Tuy, Venezuela, on November 8, 1973, Edgardo Antonio Alfonzo grew up some 40 miles southeast of Caracas, where he lived the simple life, later describing his youth as "Go to school, play ball, nothing else." The youngest of four children, Edgardo, whose father worked as a truck driver for a medical supply company and mother taught preschool, learned how to play baseball from his brother, Edgar, who later played, coached, and managed in the minor leagues. After honing his skills on the local sandlots and briefly attending Cecilio Acosto High School in Caracas, Alfonzo received tryouts with a pair of the Mets' top Latin American scouts, the second of whom signed him as an international free agent in February 1991 for $10,000.

Recalling the difficulties he subsequently faced, Alfonzo said, "It's a lot to think about. 17 years old, you come from a Latin country to the United States, one of the biggest countries in the world, and you have to learn everything from the beginning. The culture, how to act, how you're going to play baseball. . . . You have to walk away from your family—we're

Edgardo Alfonzo proved to be arguably the most complete player on Mets teams that advanced to the playoffs twice and the World Series once.

not talking about two weeks; we're talking about months. Then you have to learn stuff that you don't have. I mean, you don't think before that it's going to happen. . . . It is a tough time. Sometimes you go to sleep without anything in your stomach because, instead of eating something, you're saving money to take home or to send to your parents."

Alfonzo ended up spending four years in the minor leagues, hitting well wherever he went while playing mostly second base and shortstop, before joining the parent club in 1995. Manning multiple positions in the Mets infield his first year in New York, Alfonzo shared playing time at third base with Bobby Bonilla and Tim Bogar, while also occasionally filling in at second for Jeff Kent. Appearing in a total of 101 games, 79 of which he started, Alfonzo hit four homers, knocked in 41 runs, batted .278, and posted an OPS of .683. Used in a similar role the following year, Alfonzo saw a significant amount of action at second, short, and third, committing a total of 11 errors in 117 games in the field, while homering four times, driving in 40 runs, batting .261, and compiling an OPS of .649.

Inserted at third base full-time in 1997, Alfonzo had the best season of his young career, earning a 13th-place finish in the NL MVP voting by hitting 10 homers, driving in 72 runs, scoring 84 times, batting .315, and compiling an OPS of .823 for a Mets team that posted its first winning record in seven seasons. Alfonzo followed that up with another strong showing in 1998, concluding the campaign with 17 homers, 78 RBIs, 94 runs scored, a batting average of .278, and an OPS of .782.

With the Mets signing veteran third sacker Robin Ventura as a free agent the following offseason, they moved Alfonzo to second base, where he established himself as arguably the league's finest all-around player at his position over the course of the next two seasons, posting the following numbers on offense:

	HR	RBI	RUNS	AVG	OBP	SLG	OPS
1999	27	108	123	.304	.385	.502	.886
2000	25	94	109	.324	.425	.542	.967

In addition to tying for the team lead in batting average in the second of those campaigns, Alfonzo led the Mets in hits, doubles, and runs scored both years, earning in the process one All-Star nomination, one Silver Slugger, and one top-10 finish in the NL MVP voting. Excelling in the field as well, Alfonzo committed just five errors and led all NL second basemen with a .993 fielding percentage in 1999, with *Sports Illustrated* publishing an article at one point during the campaign that identified the Mets' quartet of Alfonzo, John Olerud, Robin Ventura, and Rey Ordóñez as the "greatest defensive infield in baseball history." More importantly, the Mets advanced to the playoffs both years and won the NL pennant in 2000.

One of the more underrated hitters of his era, the right-handed-swinging Alfonzo, who stood 5'11" and weighed 210 pounds, possessed good power to all fields, a keen batting eye, and the ability to work the count. Primarily a line-drive hitter, Alfonzo drove the ball well from foul line to foul line, amassing at least 40 doubles in a season twice. In describing his approach at the plate, Alfonzo said, "My mentality was, try to go the other way . . . let the ball come to me and explode to it."

An excellent clutch hitter, Alfonzo, who usually hit out of either the second or third spot in the batting order, drew praise for his ability to perform well under pressure from Mets manager Bobby Valentine, who stated, "He gets in an RBI situation and doesn't worry about it. He just hits."

A *New York Times* article written during the 2000 playoffs quoted teammate Darryl Hamilton as saying, "When we get in a situation where we need a hit . . . everybody on this team wants Fonzie at the plate."

Mets infielder Matt Franco also held Alfonzo in high esteem, stating, "He's just a model of consistency. He is a great teammate. He is on an even keel. He plays immaculate defense. He is a tremendous, tremendous hitter. He's just the best player we have."

Meanwhile, in comparing Alfonzo to the other top second basemen of the day, an article that appeared in the *New York Times* in 1999 suggested, "Roberto Alomar is slicker. Craig Biggio is grittier. Jeff Kent possesses more power, and Jay Bell is having a special season. However, Alfonzo might be the most complete player at his position this year."

Hampered by a variety of injuries that included a bad back that forced him to spend three weeks on the disabled list, Alfonzo failed to perform at the same elite level in 2001, hitting 17 homers, driving in only 49 runs, and batting just .243. Rebounding somewhat the following year, Alfonzo batted .308 and posted an OPS of .851. But he again missed playing time due to an injured left hand and a strained oblique muscle, limiting him to just 16 homers and 56 RBIs.

A free agent at the end of the year, Alfonzo very much wanted to remain in New York. But with the Mets offering him a two-year deal worth only $11 million, Alfonzo chose instead to sign with the San Francisco Giants for four years and $26 million. Before leaving New York, though, Alfonzo showed his love for Mets fans by buying ad space on top of 30 New York City cabs for 30 days that displayed a message which read: "Fonzie ♥ NY / Edgardo Thanks You!"

Alfonzo, who hit 120 homers, knocked in 538 runs, scored 614 times, collected 1,136 hits, 212 doubles, and 14 triples, stole 45 bases, batted .292, compiled a .367 on-base percentage, and posted a .445 slugging percentage in his eight years with the Mets, ended up spending three seasons in San Francisco starting for the Giants at third base, failing to regain his earlier form, before assuming a backup role with both the Los Angeles Angels of Anaheim and the Toronto Blue Jays in 2006. Released by Toronto in mid-June, Alfonzo subsequently spent the next several seasons playing winter ball in Venezuela and trying to mount a comeback with different minor-league teams, before officially retiring as an active player in 2012 with major-league totals of 146 homers, 744 RBIs, 777 runs scored, 1,532 hits, 282 doubles, and 18 triples, a lifetime batting average of .284, and an OPS of .782.

Following his playing days, Alfonzo returned to the Mets, first as a club ambassador and, later, as a minor-league coach and manager. Alfonzo remained with the organization until 2019, when he received his walking papers after spending the previous three seasons managing the Brooklyn Cyclones of the New York–Penn League. Alfonzo later became manager of the Staten Island FerryHawks of the independent Atlantic League.

METS CAREER HIGHLIGHTS

Best Season

Alfonzo had a tremendous year for the Mets in 2000, earning his lone All-Star nomination by hitting 25 homers, driving in 94 runs, scoring 109 times, collecting 176 hits and 40 doubles, batting .324, compiling an on-base percentage of .425, and posting a slugging percentage of .542. However, he made a slightly greater overall impact in 1999, when he earned an eighth-place finish in the league MVP voting and a spot on the *Sporting News* NL All-Star Team by establishing career-high marks in homers (27), RBIs (108), runs scored (123), hits (191), and doubles (41), while also batting .304, compiling a .385 on-base percentage, posting a .502 slugging percentage, and leading all NL second basemen with a .993 fielding percentage.

Memorable Moments/Greatest Performances

Alfonzo hit safely in 20 straight games from June 10 to July 10, 1997, going 32-for-77 (.416) with three homers, seven doubles, eight walks, 16 RBIs, and 12 runs scored.

Alfonzo contributed to a 15–6 win over the Giants on August 27, 1997, by going 4-for-5 with five RBIs and three runs scored.

Alfonzo helped lead the Mets to a 12–5 win over the Padres on August 11, 1999, by scoring three times and knocking in five runs with a homer and double.

Alfonzo had the greatest offensive day of his career on August 30, 1999, when he went a perfect 6-for-6 at the plate, with three homers, five RBIs, and six runs scored during a 17–1 rout of the Astros.

Although Alfonzo batted just .250 during the Mets' four-game victory over the Diamondbacks in the 1999 NLDS, he slugged three homers, knocked in six runs, scored six times, and posted an OPS of 1.243. Particularly outstanding in Game 1, Alfonzo homered twice and knocked in five runs during New York's 8–4 win, with one of his round-trippers coming in the top of the ninth inning with the bases loaded.

Alfonzo helped lead the Mets to a five-game win over the Cardinals in the 2000 NLCS by batting .444, posting an OPS of 1.176, driving in four runs, and scoring five times.

Notable Achievements

- Hit more than 20 home runs twice.
- Knocked in more than 100 runs once.
- Scored more than 100 runs twice.
- Batted over .300 four times.
- Compiled on-base percentage over .400 once.
- Posted slugging percentage over .500 twice.
- Posted OPS over .900 once.
- Topped 40 doubles twice.
- Had six hits and three home runs in one game versus Houston Astros on August 30, 1999.
- Finished third in NL with 123 runs scored in 1999.
- Led NL second basemen with a .993 fielding percentage in 1999.
- Ranks among Mets career leaders in batting average (tied for 5th), on-base percentage (7th), RBIs (8th), runs scored (5th), doubles (6th), hits (5th), extra-base hits (10th), total bases (8th), bases on balls (8th), sacrifice flies (5th), games played (10th), plate appearances (8th), and at-bats (9th).
- 2000 NL champion.
- 1999 Silver Slugger Award winner.
- Finished eighth in 1999 NL MVP voting.
- 1999 *Sporting News* NL All-Star selection.
- 2000 NL All-Star selection.
- Inducted into Mets Hall of Fame in 2021.

14
JOHN FRANCO

The most accomplished reliever in Mets history, John Franco spent 14 seasons in New York excelling on the mound for his hometown team. One of the premier closers of his era, Franco, who gained All-Star recognition three times with the Cincinnati Reds prior to joining the Mets, saved at least 30 games five times following his arrival in Queens, en route to amassing more saves than anyone else in team annals. A member of the Mets' 2000 NL championship ballclub, Franco earned *Sporting News* NL Fireman of the Year honors twice and his final All-Star nomination during his time in Flushing, before being further honored by gaining induction into the Mets Hall of Fame.

Born in Brooklyn, New York, on September 17, 1960, John Anthony Franco grew up with his older brother, James Jr., in the Gravesend section of South Brooklyn, in a 28-building project called the Marlboro Houses. The son of a city sanitation worker who switched his allegiance from the Dodgers to the Mets when the former relocated to California in 1958, John spent his youth rooting for the Mets as well, with his dad recalling, "They [John and brother James] would roam their neighborhood looking for Borden's milk cartons. Twenty cartons meant a free ticket in the upper deck at Shea Stadium, so they would go through garbage cans and pester their relatives."

After learning how to play the game on the sandlots of Marine Park, Bay Eighth Street, Erasmus Field, and the Parade Grounds, Franco developed into a standout pitcher at nearby Lafayette High School, performing especially well in his senior year, when he compiled a record of 14-1 and averaged 17 strikeouts a game. But with Franco standing only 5'7" and weighing just 140 pounds at the time, no team selected him in the annual MLB Draft, prompting him to enroll at St. John's University in Queens, where he combined with future AL Cy Young Award winner Frank Viola for three years to give the Red Storm a formidable pitching tandem.

John Franco amassed more saves than anyone else in team annals.

Looking back on his college days, Franco, who tossed multiple no-hitters despite missing part of his sophomore year with an arm injury, said, "I had a great experience at St. John's. We ruled the East back then. One of my big regrets was that I hurt my arm and didn't get a chance to pitch in the College World Series. I think if I was healthy, we'd have had a really good chance to win that year."

Choosing to forgo his final year of college, Franco entered the June 1981 MLB Amateur Draft, where the Dodgers selected him in the fifth round. Franco subsequently spent two years advancing through the Los Angeles farm system, during which time he learned his signature pitch—the changeup—from fellow southpaw Sandy Koufax, a roving minor-league instructor for the organization at the time.

Traded to the Reds during the early stages of the 1983 campaign, Franco, who had previously worked exclusively as a starter, spent the rest of the year struggling terribly in the minors while splitting his time between starting and relieving. However, after being moved to the bullpen full-time the following year, Franco performed well enough to earn an in-season promotion to the parent club.

Franco subsequently spent his first two seasons in Cincinnati serving as a setup man and left-handed complement to righty closer Ted Power, compiling an overall record of 18-5 and collecting a total of 16 saves, before displacing Power as the team's primary closer in 1986. Excelling in his new role, Franco earned All-Star honors in three of the next four seasons by posting a composite record of 24-25 and amassing 132 saves, while also compiling an ERA under 3.00 three times. Especially outstanding in 1988, Franco gained recognition as the NL Rolaids Reliever of the Year by going 6-6 with a 1.57 ERA and a league-leading 39 saves.

Expressing his admiration for Franco at one point during the 1989 campaign, Mets manager Davey Johnson called him "the most consistent reliever we've got in our league."

Padres Hall of Fame outfielder Tony Gwynn also had high praise for Franco, saying, "He's good, real good. He can throw anything for a strike."

Although Franco earned his third All-Star nomination in 1989 by compiling an ERA of 3.12 and finishing third in the league with 32 saves, his impending free agency and alleged involvement in the gambling scandal surrounding manager Pete Rose prompted the Reds to trade him to the Mets for hard-throwing reliever Randy Myers at the end of the year.

Commenting on the deal afterward, Mets assistant general manager Joe McIlvaine said, "It's really a judgment call. They're both good, and it's a tough thing to give up a younger pitcher. But we felt like a change of scenery might be coming at the right time."

Meanwhile, Franco recalled thinking how much he welcomed a return to New York and playing for the team he had always loved, stating, "When I heard the news, I felt like my head went through the ceiling."

Excelling in his first season with the Mets, Franco helped lead them to a close second-place finish to the Pirates in the NL East by winning five of his eight decisions, compiling an ERA of 2.53, striking out 56 batters in 67⅔ innings of work, and leading the league with 33 saves, earning in the process the last of his four All-Star selections and his second NL Rolaids Reliever of the Year award. Franco followed that up with two more outstanding seasons, posting an ERA of 2.93 and ranking among the league leaders with 30 saves in 1991, before going 6-2 with a 1.64 ERA and 15 saves in 1992, despite missing two months with an inflamed elbow that eventually forced him to undergo surgery.

Though small in stature, the 5'10", 170-pound Franco possessed a good fastball that typically registered somewhere in the low 90s on the radar gun. However, Franco considered his "out pitch" to be his changeup, which many likened to a screwball since it tended to break away from right-handed batters.

In discussing his former college teammate, Frank Viola, who also spent three seasons pitching with Franco in New York, stated, "Here's this little guy, but he was a power pitcher—90-plus fastball, real good breaking ball, incredible poise on the mound. But his style had to change after he blew his arm out in college and hurt it again in the pros. So, he went from a power pitcher to a control pitcher—a guy with great location and a devastating changeup. And that's all he really needs. Two pitches."

Adding that Franco's streetwise personality and use of psychology made him valuable in the clubhouse and more effective on the mound, Viola said, "We both have good heads. . . . What we do best is think ahead of the hitters, set them up, and make them crazy."

With Franco having grown up in the area, he also possessed the perfect temperament to succeed in New York, once saying, "You have to have some thick skin to play here. It's hard. Especially as a relief pitcher, you have to be able to turn the page quite a bit. Some guys could handle it, some couldn't."

Plagued by elbow problems again in 1993, Franco saved just 10 games and compiled an inordinately high ERA of 5.20. But he rebounded the following year to lead all NL relievers with 30 saves, before amassing a total of 131 saves over the course of the next four seasons.

Forced to surrender his role as closer to Armando Benítez due to an injury to the middle finger of his pitching hand in 1999, Franco nevertheless finished the season with a 2.88 ERA and 19 saves. Although fully recovered by the start of the ensuing campaign, Franco spent the 2000 season working as a setup man for the harder-throwing Benítez, saving only four games, before seriously considering signing with the Phillies as a free agent at the end of the year. However, Franco ultimately chose to return to the Mets, saying, "I got opinions from family and friends on what I should do. The only opinion that mattered was what was in my heart. This is what I wanted. Going to the Hall of Fame, I can't worry about that now. I'm worrying about next year and winning. Five or 10 years down the road, there's no guarantee in anything. This is the decision I made."

Remaining a setup man the rest of his time in New York, Franco saved a total of just four games. Nevertheless, he continued to maintain a strong presence in the clubhouse and the community, particularly following the terrorist attacks on the World Trade Center on September 11, 2001. Deeply affected by the events that transpired, Franco, who the Mets named team captain earlier in the year, later said, "I lost friends who were firemen, policemen, people who worked for Cantor Fitzgerald (the investment bank). That stuff stays with you forever."

Named that year's recipient of the Lou Gehrig Memorial Award, which is presented annually to the player who "best demonstrates his character and integrity both on and off the field," Franco later received high praise from former New York City fire commissioner Sal Cassano, who said, "He helped us get through a very difficult time. It hit home because his uncle was a firefighter, and his dad worked for the city. He did so much, bringing players to meet with kids who'd lost their parents."

Having undergone Tommy John surgery the previous offseason, Franco sat out the entire 2002 campaign, before going a combined 2-10 with just two saves over the course of the next two seasons. With the Mets showing no interest in bringing him back at the end of 2004, Franco signed as a free agent with the Houston Astros, ending in the process his 14-year stint in Queens.

Franco, who compiled a record of 48-56, an ERA of 3.10, and a WHIP of 1.365, amassed 276 saves, and recorded 592 strikeouts in 702⅔ innings of work as a member of the Mets, ended up appearing in only 31 games with the Astros, before announcing his retirement midway through the 2005 campaign. Over parts of 21 big-league seasons, Franco posted a record of 90-87, an ERA of 2.89, and a WHIP of 1.333, collected 424 saves, and struck out 975 batters in 1,245⅔ innings pitched. Currently seventh on MLB's all-time saves list, Franco saved more games than any other left-hander in the history of the game.

Since retiring as an active player, Franco has remained heavily involved with youth baseball in New York City and has served as an ambassador and guest instructor for the Mets at various times.

Inducted into the Mets Hall of Fame in 2012, Franco received high praise at the time from team COO Jeff Wilpon, who said in a statement, "John set a very high standard during his career, both on and off the field. It's great that during our 50th anniversary season we can have John—a true New Yorker in every sense—inducted into the Mets Hall of Fame."

Looking back on his playing career, Franco said, "You can't judge a person by his size, but you could judge 'em by the heart he has. And I have always had a big heart. Every time I went out there, I gave 150 percent. It wasn't pretty at times, but I was under control, and I knew what I was doing. And I enjoyed every minute of it, through the good times and the bad times."

METS CAREER HIGHLIGHTS

Best Season

Franco earned his lone All-Star selection as a member of the Mets in 1990, when he went 5-3 with a 2.53 ERA, 1.286 WHIP, and league-leading 33 saves. He also performed extremely well in 1994 and 1996, earning a seventh-place finish in the Cy Young voting in the first of those campaigns by compiling an ERA of 2.70, posting a WHIP of 1.320, and leading the NL with 30 saves, before going 4-3 with an ERA of 1.83, a WHIP of 1.389, and 28 saves in the second. But Franco posted his best overall numbers for the Mets in 1997, when, in addition to winning five of his eight decisions, he compiled an ERA of 2.55 and a WHIP of 1.150, recorded 36 saves, and struck out 53 batters in 60 innings pitched.

Memorable Moments/Greatest Performances

Franco reached several milestones during his time in New York, with the first of those coming on July 6, 1991, when he recorded the 200th save of his career by retiring the final batter of a 2–1 victory over the Phillies.

Franco registered his 300th career save on April 29, 1996, when he worked a scoreless ninth inning during a 3–2 win over the Expos, becoming in the process the first southpaw to reach that mark.

Franco broke Tom Seaver's franchise record for most mound appearances on June 19, 1998, when he appeared in his 402nd game as a member of the Mets.

Franco recorded the 400th save of his career on April 14, 1999, when he struck out three of the four batters he faced in the ninth inning of a 4–1 win over the Marlins

Franco acquitted himself extremely well against the Diamondbacks in the 1999 NLDS. Appearing in three of the four contests, Franco allowed no runs and just one hit in 3⅔ innings of work, earning a victory in the series finale (a 4–3 Mets win) by retiring all three batters he faced in the top of the 10th inning.

Franco posted the lone Mets victory of the 2000 World Series by working one scoreless inning of relief during their 4–2 win over the Yankees in Game 3.

Notable Achievements

- Saved at least 30 games five times.
- Compiled ERA under 3.00 nine times, posting mark under 2.00 twice.
- Led NL in saves twice.
- Holds franchise records for most saves and most pitching appearances.
- Ranks among Mets career leaders in ERA (tied for 7th).
- 2000 NL champion.
- Two-time *Sporting News* NL Fireman of the Year (1990 and 1994).
- 1990 NL Rolaids Relief Man of the Year.
- 1990 NL All-Star selection.
- Inducted into Mets Hall of Fame in 2012.

15
HOWARD JOHNSON

A hard-hitting third baseman who became just the second player in MLB history to surpass 30 homers and 30 steals in the same season more than twice, Howard Johnson spent nine years in New York, starting for the Mets at the hot corner most of that time. Combining outstanding power with excellent speed, the switch-hitting Johnson hit more than 30 homers three times and knocked in more than 100 runs twice, while also stealing at least 30 bases on four separate occasions. A member of Mets teams that won two division titles and one world championship, Johnson earned two All-Star selections and three top-10 finishes in the NL MVP voting, before being further honored by gaining induction into the Mets Hall of Fame in 2023.

Born in Clearwater, Florida, on November 29, 1960, Howard Michael Johnson grew up with his two younger siblings in a family known for its kindness and generosity, saying years later after donating money to a home for abused children, "My father and mother worked with abused children when I was growing up, so I heard about those things."

Acquiring his love of baseball from his father, who taught him how to switch-hit at a very young age, Johnson, a natural left-hander, also learned how to throw right-handed from his dad. Eventually establishing himself as a star on the diamond at Clearwater High School, Johnson excelled as both an infielder and pitcher, compiling an ERA of 0.91 and recording 110 strikeouts in 91 innings pitched during his senior year.

Selected by the Yankees in the 23rd round of the 1978 MLB Amateur Draft, Johnson chose to continue his education and improve his draft stock when he failed to receive an offer of a signing bonus. After spending one year at St. Petersburg Junior College, Johnson decided to turn pro when the Detroit Tigers claimed him with the 12th overall pick of the following year's draft. Johnson subsequently spent most of the next five seasons advancing through Detroit's farm system, although he also appeared in a limited number of games with the parent club in both 1982 and 1983. Arriving in the

Howard Johnson surpassed 30 homers and 30 steals in the same season three times as a member of the Mets.

majors to stay in 1984, Johnson saw a significant amount of action at third base for a Tigers team that ended up winning the World Series, hitting 12 homers, driving in 50 runs, and batting .248 in 116 games and 402 total plate appearances. But with the Tigers seeking to add another pitcher to their rotation, they traded Johnson to the Mets for right-handed starter Walt Terrell at the end of the year.

Platooned with the right-handed-hitting Ray Knight his first year in New York, Johnson appeared in 126 games, 93 of which he started at third base. Garnering 428 total plate appearances, Johnson hit 11 homers, knocked in 46 runs, batted .242, and posted an OPS of .693.

Johnson subsequently assumed the role of a utility infielder during the championship campaign of 1986, hitting 10 homers, driving in 39 runs, batting .245, and posting an OPS of .787, while splitting his time between third base and shortstop.

With Knight signing with the Baltimore Orioles as a free agent at the end of the year, Johnson laid claim to the starting third base job. Excelling in his first season as a full-time starter, Johnson earned a 10th-place finish in the NL MVP voting by hitting 36 homers, driving in 99 runs, scoring 93 times, stealing 32 bases, batting .265, compiling an on-base percentage of .364, and posting a slugging percentage of .504, with his 36 round-trippers setting a new league record for most home runs by a switch-hitter in a season.

Attributing his improved performance to his opportunity to play every day, Johnson, who struggled from the right side of the plate early in his career, said that, once Knight left the Mets, he spent hours in the batting cage every day hitting right-handed to prepare himself for the full-time job. But with the 5'11", 180-pound Johnson also exhibiting the ability to drive the ball much farther than he ever did before, he found himself being accused by opposing managers more than once of corking his bat. Addressing those accusations long after his playing career ended, Johnson said, "All I've ever said is that when they X-rayed my bats, they came up clean."

Meanwhile, former Mets skipper Davey Johnson commented, "If it was corked, he had a carpenter who could do just about anything with wood. Did I see the cork? No. Did he probably cork his bat? Yes."

Bothered by a sore right shoulder that forced him to undergo arthroscopic surgery at the end of the year, Johnson posted far less impressive numbers in 1988, finishing the season with just 24 homers, 68 RBIs, 85 runs scored, 23 steals, a .230 batting average, and an OPS of .765. But with Johnson fully healthy by the start of the 1989 campaign, he rebounded to bat .287, compile an on-base percentage of .369, lead the league with 104 runs scored, and ranked among the leaders in seven other offensive categories, including homers (36), RBIs (101), stolen bases (41), and slugging percentage (.559), earning in the process his first All-Star selection and a fifth-place finish in the NL MVP balloting.

Commenting on his outstanding performance at the end of the year, Johnson said, "I always had that rap of being a dead fastball hitter who couldn't hit anything else. I learned how to hit the curveball this year."

Always an excellent fastball hitter, Johnson possessed an extremely quick bat that enabled him to turn on the heater perhaps better than anyone else in the Mets' lineup. Quite strong for someone his size, Johnson, who teammate Ron Darling called, "Pound for pound, the strongest player I ever played with," had outstanding power from both sides of the plate. But as Johnson matured as a hitter, he also gained a better command of the strike zone and became more adept at hitting the breaking ball. An outstanding baserunner as well, Johnson used his speed and aggressiveness to swipe more than 20 bags six straight times and regularly take out opposing infielders attempting to turn the double play.

Impressed with his former teammate's grit and aggressive style of play, Bob Ojeda said, "I think of a dirty uniform when I think of HoJo's playing days."

Though not an elite defender, Johnson also did a solid job in the field, once saying, "I'm not the best defensive player in the world. I'm not the worst, either. My dad always told me, 'If you hit, they'll find a place for you in the field.' But I know I make my living driving in runs."

Moved to shortstop for part of the 1990 season by new Mets manager Bud Harrelson, Johnson slumped somewhat at the plate, batting just .244 and posting an OPS of only .753, although he still managed to hit 23 homers, drive in 90 runs, score 89 times, and steal 34 bases. Despite seeing a considerable amount of action at multiple positions (third base, shortstop, and right field) again in 1991, Johnson returned to top form, earning All-Star honors and a fifth-place finish in the NL MVP voting for the second time by leading the league with 38 homers and 117 RBIs, while also scoring 108 runs, stealing 30 bases, batting .259, and posting an OPS of .877.

Plagued by injuries in each of the next two seasons, Johnson experienced a precipitous decline in offensive production. Limited by shoulder and knee problems to just 100 games and 410 total plate appearances in 1992, Johnson hit seven homers, knocked in 43 runs, scored 48 times, stole 22 bases, batted .223, and posted an OPS of .666. Johnson subsequently appeared in only 72 games in 1993 after sustaining a season-ending injury to his right thumb while sliding into second base in mid-July. A free agent at the end of the year, Johnson signed with the Colorado Rockies when the Mets failed to make him a significant offer.

During his nine seasons in New York, Johnson hit 192 homers, knocked in 629 runs, scored 627 times, collected 997 hits, 214 doubles, and 18 triples, stole 202 bases, batted .251, compiled an on-base percentage of .341, and posted a slugging percentage of .459. He ended up spending one year with the Rockies and another with the Chicago Cubs, serving both teams as a part-time player, before announcing his retirement at the end of 1995. Although Johnson attempted a comeback with the Mets one year later, he retired for good when he failed to make their roster during spring training. Over parts of 14 big-league seasons, Johnson hit 228 homers, knocked in 760 runs, scored 760 times, amassed 1,229 hits, 247 doubles, and 22 triples, stole 231 bases, batted .249, compiled an on-base percentage of .340, and posted a slugging percentage of .446.

Following his playing days, Johnson returned to the Mets, with whom he spent more than a decade assuming various roles within the organization, including scout, minor-league manager, first base coach, and hitting coach. Johnson also later served as a hitting coach in the farm systems of the Texas Rangers and Seattle Mariners, before assuming the same post with the Toros de Tijuana of the Mexican League in 2020.

Inducted into the Mets Hall of Fame in 2023, Johnson received high praise at the time from Mets announcer and fellow inductee, Gary Cohen, who said, "There are very few players in the history of the game who have been switch hitters with the power and speed that HoJo brought to the table, and to be a three-time 30-30 player is an extraordinary feat. His time in this Hall of Fame should have started a long time ago."

METS CAREER HIGHLIGHTS

Best Season

Johnson had a big year for the Mets in 1991, leading the NL with 38 homers, 117 RBIs, 76 extra-base hits, and 15 sacrifice flies, while also placing second in the circuit with 108 runs scored and a .535 slugging percentage, amassing 302 total bases, compiling an OPS of .877, stealing 30 bases, and batting .259, with his 38 homers and 30 steals making him just the second player to reach the 30 mark in both categories in the same season as many as three times (with Bobby Bonds being the other). But Johnson posted slightly better overall numbers in 1989, when, in addition to hitting 36 homers, driving in 101 runs, batting .287, and leading the league with 104 runs scored, he established career-high marks in slugging percentage (.559), OPS (.928), hits (164), doubles (41), total bases (319), stolen bases (41), and extra-base hits (80).

Memorable Moments/Greatest Performances

After hitting safely in three of his four previous trips to the plate, Johnson delivered the decisive blow of a 6–4 win over the Cardinals on July 29, 1987, when he homered with one man on base in the top of the 10th inning.

Johnson gave the Mets a 2–1 win over the Cubs on June 2, 1988, when he led off the bottom of the 13th inning with a home run to center field off left-handed reliever Frank DiPino.

Johnson contributed to a 13–6 win over the Cubs on September 8, 1988, by going a perfect 5-for-5 at the plate with a homer, double, and four RBIs.

Johnson led the Mets to a 5–3 win over the Expos on June 19, 1989, by knocking in four runs with a pair of two-run homers.

Johnson helped lead the Mets to a 15–10 win over the Cubs on June 13, 1990, by driving in five runs, with his grand slam homer in the top of the ninth inning, putting the game out of reach.

Notable Achievements

- Hit more than 20 home runs five times, topping 30 homers on three occasions.
- Knocked in more than 100 runs twice.
- Scored more than 100 runs twice.
- Posted slugging percentage over .500 three times.
- Posted OPS over .900 once.
- Surpassed 40 doubles once.
- Stole more than 20 bases six times, topping 30 thefts four times and 40 thefts once.
- Led NL in home runs, RBIs, runs scored, and sacrifice flies once each.
- Finished second in NL in home runs once, runs scored once, and slugging percentage twice.
- Ranks among Mets career leaders in home runs (5th), RBIs (5th), runs scored (4th), hits (10th), extra-base hits (5th), doubles (5th), total bases (7th), stolen bases (3rd), bases on balls (4th), intentional bases on balls (2nd), sacrifice flies (3rd), games played (7th), plate appearances (6th), and at-bats (7th).
- Two-time division champion (1986 and 1988).
- 1986 NL champion.
- 1986 world champion.
- June 25, 1989, NL Player of the Week.
- Two-time NL Player of the Month.
- Two-time Silver Slugger Award winner (1989 and 1991).
- Finished in top 10 of NL MVP voting three times, placing 5th in balloting twice.
- Two-time NL All-Star selection (1989 and 1991).
- 1989 *Sporting News* NL All-Star selection.
- Inducted into Mets Hall of Fame in 2023.

16
CLEON JONES

The Mets' most consistent hitter during the first decade of their existence, Cleon Jones established himself as the first legitimate offensive threat in team annals over parts of 12 seasons. An excellent line-drive hitter with occasional home-run power, Jones batted over .300 twice, with his .340 average in 1969 representing the second-highest single-season mark ever posted by a member of the team. A good baserunner and solid defender as well, Jones helped lead the Mets to two pennants and one world championship with his strong all-around play, earning in the process one All-Star selection, one top-10 finish in the NL MVP voting, and a place in the Mets Hall of Fame. Yet Jones, who a panel of sportswriters and broadcasters named the Mets' "All-Time Leftfielder" in 2012, will always be remembered as much as anything for his involvement in some of the most significant moments in franchise history.

Born in Plateau, Alabama, on August 4, 1942, Cleon Joseph Jones grew up just north of downtown Mobile in an area known for its ever-present smell from the local paper mills. Raised by his mother and grandmother in the segregated South after his father relocated to Chicago to escape persecution following an altercation with a white man, Jones lost his mom at the age of 10 when she died suddenly.

Finding comfort in sports, Jones often played baseball and football on the streets and vacant lots of Mobile, where, despite being a natural left-hander, he transformed himself into a right-handed batter, recalling years later, "There was this one field that we put some old shirts down for bases. Behind right field there was this little creek, and behind left field, well, man, it just went on and on for miles. We played our games there, and after a couple of games, I had lost four or five balls when I hit them left-handed into the water. We didn't have too many real baseballs, so when the other guys came to me and said, 'You better stop doing that or we ain't got no more baseballs here,' I just turned around. That's how I became a right-handed hitter. I just wanted to save those balls."

Cleon Jones finished third in the NL batting race in 1969 with a career-high mark of .340.

An excellent all-around athlete, Jones went on to star alongside childhood friend and future Mets teammate Tommie Agee in both baseball and football at Mobile County High School, before spending one year at Grambling State University and another at Alabama A&M University, continuing to compete in both sports the entire time. Recruited by the Mets while in college, Jones signed with them as an amateur free agent on July 5, 1962, after which he spent most of the next three seasons in the minors, appearing in a total of just 36 games with the parent club.

Arriving in New York to stay in 1966, Jones spent most of the year starting in center field for the Mets and hitting anywhere from first to fifth in the batting order. Although somewhat out of place in center, the 6-foot, 190-pound Jones, who possessed above-average speed and an adequate throwing arm, earned a fourth-place finish in the NL Rookie of the Year voting by hitting eight homers, driving in 57 runs, batting .275, posting an OPS of .689, and leading the team with 74 runs scored and 16 stolen bases. Playing all over the outfield in 1967, Jones suffered through a dismal campaign during which he hit only five homers, knocked in just 30 runs, scored only 46 times, and batted just .246.

Moved to left field full-time in 1968 following the hiring of Gil Hodges as manager and the acquisition of Tommie Agee during the offseason, Jones responded well to manning just one position and playing alongside his longtime friend in the outfield. In addition to ranking second among all players at his post in fielding percentage, Jones, who spent the year hitting almost exclusively out of the number three spot in the lineup, homered 14 times, knocked in 55 runs, scored 63 others, posted career-high marks in doubles (29) and steals (23), and compiled a batting average of .297 that placed him sixth in the league rankings. Even better in 1969, Jones earned his lone All-Star nomination and a seventh-place finish in the NL MVP voting by hitting 12 homers, driving in 75 runs, scoring 92 times, swiping 16 bags, finishing third in the league with a .340 batting average, placing fifth in the circuit with a .422 on-base percentage, and posting an OPS of .904, while also leading all NL left fielders with a .991 fielding percentage. In the middle of his finest season, though, Jones became embroiled in controversy when Hodges, in the view of many, sent a message to the rest of the team by removing his best hitter from a contest for not hustling.

The incident occurred during a one-sided loss to Houston at a soggy Shea Stadium on July 30, 1969, when Jones allowed Astros catcher Johnny Edwards to reach second base with a double by failing to get to the ball as quickly as Hodges would have liked. Once Edwards reached second, Hodges left the Mets' dugout, walked slowly out to left field, and, according to Jones, said, "If you're not running good, why don't you just come out of the ball game?" Jones added, "Then he turned around and headed toward the dugout. I knew he had something more than my leg in mind, and I followed him in."

While some newspaper accounts claimed that Jones left the game due to a leg injury, others speculated that Hodges removed him from the contest as a way of sending a message to the entire team that he would not tolerate a lack of effort from anyone.

Years later, Jones provided further insight during an interview with SportsNet New York, revealing that, once he arrived in left field, Hodges asked him why he did not look good going after the flyball. Jones then pointed down to the wet turf, reminded his manager of his leg injury, and told him that the conditions made it difficult for him to play his best. The two men subsequently agreed that he should not be playing, and they walked off the field together. Although Jones added that Hodges would never publicly embarrass any player, he also claimed that his removal from the game instilled a fear in the other members of the team that made the incident the turning point of the season.

After the Mets laid claim to the division title, Jones helped lead them to a three-game sweep of Atlanta in the NLCS by homering once, knocking in four runs, scoring four times, batting .429, and posting an OPS of 1.252. Although Jones subsequently batted just .158 against Baltimore in the World Series, his involvement in two crucial plays during the Game 5 clincher helped him earn a permanent place in Mets history.

With the Orioles holding a 3–0 lead in the bottom of the sixth inning, Baltimore starter Dave McNally delivered a pitch to Jones that hit the dirt and bounced into the Mets dugout. While home plate umpire Lou DiMuro called the offering a ball, Jones started toward first base believing that the pitch had hit him. However, DiMuro changed his ruling after Gil Hodges emerged from the dugout with the ball and pointed to a small smudge of shoe polish. DiMuro sent Jones to first, after which Donn Clendenon began a Mets comeback that resulted in a 5–3 Series-clinching win by hitting a two-run homer. And three innings later, Jones sealed the victory when he caught Davey Johnson's two-out flyball to deep left field on the edge of the warning track, taking a knee as the ball settled into his glove.

Jones followed up his stellar 1969 campaign with two more solid seasons, hitting 10 homers, driving in 63 runs, scoring 71 times, batting .277, and posting an OPS of .769 in 1970, before tying his career high with 14 homers, knocking in 69 runs, scoring 63 times, batting .319, and compiling an OPS of .856 in 1971.

Injured for much of the next two seasons, Jones missed a significant amount of playing time each year, greatly limiting his offensive production. Nevertheless, he emerged as the Mets' hottest hitter down the stretch in 1973, helping to lead them to their second NL pennant by hitting six homers and driving in 14 runs in the final 10 games of the regular season, before batting an even .300 against Cincinnati in the NLCS.

And once again, Jones proved to be a central figure in an extraordinarily important play, which occurred against the Pirates at Shea Stadium on September 20. With the Mets trailing Pittsburgh by 1½ games in the NL East and less than 10 games left in the regular season, the two teams entered the 13th inning with the scored tied at 3–3. With two men out and Pittsburgh's Richie Zisk on at first in the top of the frame, Dave Augustine hit a long flyball to left field that, if not a home run, appeared certain to drive in Zisk with the go-ahead run. But the ball hit the corner of the top edge of the wall and bounced directly to Jones. Jones then turned and delivered an accurate relay throw to Wayne Garrett, who nailed Zisk at the plate with a perfect peg to catcher Ron Hodges. The Mets subsequently pushed across a run in the bottom of the inning to come away with a 4–3 win that proved critical in their successful run to the division title and NL pennant.

Despite appearing in only 124 games in 1974, Jones posted solid numbers, finishing the season with 13 homers, 60 RBIs, 62 runs scored, a batting average of .282, and an OPS of .763. But a pair of ugly incidents the following season ultimately led to his departure from New York.

Left behind in Florida at the end of spring training to rehabilitate his surgically repaired knee, Jones engaged in illicit behavior with a woman in the back of a van that caused police to arrest him for indecent exposure. Though never prosecuted, Jones subsequently suffered the public humiliation of being ordered by Mets chairman of the board M. Donald Grant to attend a press conference in New York, where, with his wife, Angela, at his side, he had to apologize to her and Mets fans for his actions.

Some two months later, during the eighth inning of a July 18, 1975, meeting with the Braves at Shea Stadium, Mets manager Yogi Berra sent Jones in to pinch-hit for Ed Kranepool. After Jones lined out to shortstop, Berra told him to play left field in the top of the ninth inning. But Jones refused to do so, saying that he still had to wrap his knee, and yelling to his skipper, "Get someone else out there!" According to the *Sporting News*, a shouting match ensued between the two men that ended with "Jones flinging his glove down, pulling towels off the rack, and storming up the runway to the clubhouse."

Berra, who called the incident "the most embarrassing thing that's happened to me since I became a manager," and added, "I had to change my whole lineup around because of him," subsequently delivered a "Him or Me" ultimatum to the Mets. Unable to find a suitable trade partner, the Mets released Jones on July 27, ending his lengthy association with the organization. Over parts of 12 seasons in New York, Jones hit 93 homers, knocked in 521 runs, scored 563 times, collected 1,188 hits, 182 doubles, and 33 triples, stole 91 bases, batted .281, compiled an on-base percentage of .340, and posted a slugging percentage of .406, with his totals in each of the first four categories placing him first in team annals at the time of his departure.

After being released by the Mets, Jones signed as a free agent with the Chicago White Sox just prior to the start of the 1976 campaign. However, he ended up appearing in only 12 games with the Pale Hose, before being released again and subsequently announcing his retirement.

Following his playing days, Jones coached for a time at Bishop State Community College in Mobile, where he worked with both the women's softball team and the men's baseball team. Jones also ran a fast-food business, worked for a maintenance company, and spent several years doing community service work in Mobile, once telling *New York Post* sportswriter Maury Allen, "I work for the city, work with kids, work with the elderly. I enjoy it." The now-retired, 83-year-old Jones currently resides with his wife, Angela, in his native Mobile.

METS CAREER HIGHLIGHTS

Best Season

Jones had easily his finest season in 1969, when, in addition to hitting 12 homers, he posted career-high marks in RBIs (75), runs scored (92), hits (164), walks (64), batting average (.340), on-base percentage (.422), and slugging percentage (.482).

Memorable Moments/Greatest Performances

Jones gave the Mets a 3–0 win in the second game of their doubleheader split with the Cubs on April 27, 1969, when he homered with two men aboard in the bottom of the ninth inning.

Jones performed exceptionally well during the Mets' three-game sweep of the Braves in the 1969 NLCS, going 6-for-14 (.429) with a homer, two doubles, two stolen bases, four RBIs, four runs scored, and an OPS of 1.252.

Jones fashioned a 23-game hitting streak from August 25 to September 15, 1970, going 40-for-98 (.408) with two homers, three triples, six doubles, eleven walks, 16 RBIs, and 20 runs scored.

Jones gave the Mets a 2–1 victory over the Padres on August 21, 1971, by hitting a two-out solo home run off starter Dave Roberts in the bottom of the ninth inning.

Jones provided further heroics one week later, when he again homered with two men out and no one on in the bottom of the ninth inning to give the Mets a 2–1 win over the Dodgers on August 28.

After homering and driving in two runs earlier in the contest, Jones ended an 18-inning marathon with the Phillies on August 1, 1972, by delivering a two-out bases loaded single to right field that gave the Mets a 3–2 victory over their Eastern Division rivals.

Jones proved to be the difference in a 3–0 Opening Day win over the Phillies in 1973, knocking in all three runs with a pair of homers off Steve Carlton.

After hitting a two-run homer earlier in the game, Jones delivered the big blow of a 7–3 win over the Pirates on September 19, 1973, when he homered off ace reliever Dave Giusti with two men aboard in the bottom of the eighth inning.

Jones helped lead the Mets to a 10–7 win over Oakland in Game 2 of the 1973 World Series by going 3-for-5 with a homer and three runs scored, reaching the seats against Vida Blue in the top of the second inning.

Notable Achievements

- Batted over .300 twice.
- Compiled on-base percentage over .400 once.
- Posted OPS over .900 once.
- Stole more than 20 bases once.
- Finished third in NL with .340 batting average in 1969.
- Led all NL left fielders with .991 fielding percentage in 1969.
- Ranks among Mets career leaders in RBIs (tied for 9th), runs scored (9th), hits (4th), triples (4th), total bases (9th), sacrifice flies (4th), games played (6th), plate appearances (5th), and at-bats (5th).
- Two-time division champion (1969 and 1973).
- Two-time NL champion (1969 and 1973).
- 1969 world champion.
- Finished seventh in 1969 NL MVP voting.
- 1969 NL All-Star selection.
- 1969 *Sporting News* NL All-Star selection.
- Inducted into Mets Hall of Fame in 1991.

17
FRANCISCO LINDOR

The emotional leader of Mets teams that have advanced to the playoffs in two of the last four seasons, Francisco Lindor has experienced several highs and lows during his time in New York. After being acquired in a trade with the Cleveland Indians (Guardians), with whom he earned four All-Star selections and three top-10 finishes in the AL MVP voting, and subsequently signed to an exorbitant long-term contract by new Mets owner Steve Cohen just prior to the start of the 2021 campaign, Lindor struggled terribly his first year in Flushing, causing him to often incur the wrath of the hometown fans. However, since that time, Lindor has turned the boos into cheers by excelling for the Mets both at the bat and in the field. In addition to hitting more than 30 homers three times and driving in more than 100 runs once, Lindor has led all NL shortstops in putouts and assists once each, earning in the process four top-10 finishes in the league MVP voting, three All-MLB Second-Team nominations, and one All-Star selection. Meanwhile, Lindor's fiery temperament and charismatic personality have helped make him the leader of a Mets ballclub that has gradually established itself as a force to be reckoned with in the NL East.

Born in Caguas, Puerto Rico, on November 14, 1993, Francisco Miguel Lindor grew up with his three siblings in a close-knit family that valued hard work and dedication. Exhibiting a fondness for baseball at a young age, Lindor learned how to play the game from his father, an accomplished softball player, who helped him develop his fielding skills by hitting groundballs to him from the top of a hill while the younger Lindor stood partway down the slope.

After moving with his family at the age of 12 to central Florida, Lindor enrolled at Montverde Academy Prep School, where he performed well both in the classroom and on the diamond, maintaining a high grade-point average, while also earning a spot on the *USA Today* All-USA high school baseball team. Selected by Cleveland with the eighth overall pick of the

Francisco Lindor finished runner-up in the 2024 NL MVP voting. Courtesy of All-Pro Reels Photography

2011 MLB Amateur Draft, Lindor decided to sign with the Indians for $2.9 million rather than accept a full baseball scholarship to Florida State University.

Lindor subsequently spent the next three-and-a-half years advancing through Cleveland's farm system, before arriving in the majors to stay midway through the 2015 campaign. Acquitting himself extremely well in his first tour of duty at the big-league level, Lindor earned a runner-up finish in the AL Rookie of the Year voting by hitting 12 homers, driving in 51 runs, scoring 50 times, batting .313, and posting an OPS of .835 in 99 games and 438 total plate appearances. Following another strong showing in 2016, Lindor established himself as arguably the finest all-around shortstop in the American League over the course of the next three seasons, averaging 34 homers, 85 RBIs, and 110 runs scored from 2017 to 2019, while also compiling a composite batting average of .278, posting an OPS of better than .840 each year, and winning two Silver Sluggers and two Gold Gloves.

Somewhat less productive during the pandemic-shortened 2020 campaign, Lindor hit just eight homers, knocked in only 27 runs, and batted .258 in 60 games and 266 total plate appearances. Nevertheless, with Lindor approaching free agency, the Indians knew that a big payday awaited him, prompting them to complete a trade with the Mets on January 7, 2021, that sent the star shortstop and pitcher Carlos Carrasco to New York for infielders Amed Rosario and Andrés Giménez, and minor leaguers Josh Wolf and Isaiah Greene. The Mets and Lindor subsequently spent nearly three long months haggling over a new contract, before the two sides finally agreed to a $10-year, $341 million deal on March 31 that promised to keep him in Queens through 2031.

While Mets fans initially rejoiced over the signing of Lindor, they soon came to view it as another case of the organization acquiring someone who lacked the ability to excel under the bright lights of New York. With the 27-year-old Lindor immersed in an 0-for-23 slump during the early stages of the campaign, he heard boos in his home ballpark for the first time in his career that only grew worse as the season progressed. Frustrated by his own performance and the lack of support he received from the fans at Citi Field, Lindor responded on one occasion with a thumbs-down gesture toward the crowd that further incensed the team's fanbase. To his credit, though, Lindor later took accountability for his actions and apologized, saying, "As a man, you grow. As my wife [Katia] likes to say, 'Your brain finally fully develops.' I believe my brain has finally fully developed, so I've learned. I've grown. I'm more mature. I know how to deal with certain things a lot more now."

After finishing his first season in Flushing with just 20 homers, 63 RBIs, 73 runs scored, a .230 batting average, and a .734 OPS, Lindor began to win over Mets fans in 2022 by hitting 26 homers, driving in 107 runs, scoring 98 times, batting .270, and posting an OPS of .788 for a team that advanced to the playoffs with a record of 101-61. In addition to setting new single-season franchise records for most home runs and RBIs by a shortstop, Lindor led all players at his position in putouts, earning in the process All-MLB Second-Team honors and a ninth-place finish in the league MVP voting for the first of two straight times. Although the Mets won only 75 games the following year, Lindor had another solid season, hitting 31 homers, knocking in 98 runs, scoring 108 times, stealing a career-high

31 bases, batting .254, and posting an OPS of .806, while also leading all league shortstops in assists.

Perhaps the finest switch-hitter in the game today, the 5'11", 190-pound Lindor swings the bat well from both sides of the plate, although he drives the ball a bit more as a left-handed batter. An excellent baserunner as well, Lindor has scored more than 100 runs and swiped more than 20 bags five times each during his career, successfully converting more than 80 percent of his stolen base attempts. Also an outstanding fielder, Lindor's quickness, exceptional range, sure hands, and strong throwing arm have allowed him to consistently rank among the top players at his position in putouts, assists, and fielding percentage.

In addition to the aforementioned qualities, Lindor possesses superior leadership ability, which he exhibited in many ways over the course of the 2024 campaign. Agreeing to move to the leadoff spot in the batting order on May 18 after getting off to his usual slow start, Lindor helped breathe life into the Mets' struggling offense the rest of the year by providing a spark at the top of the lineup. Eventually coming to embrace his new role, Lindor, who ended up earning a runner-up finish in the NL MVP voting by hitting 33 homers, driving in 91 runs, scoring 107 times, stealing 29 bases, batting .273, and posting an OPS of .844, stated, "I just love getting things started. I think it's kind of cool to be able to get a base hit, steal a base or hit a home run or a double. And you just get the crowd and team going."

Lindor also helped greatly alter the fortunes of a Mets ballclub that ultimately advanced to the NLCS by calling a players-only meeting following a three-game sweep by the Dodgers in late May that left their record at a disappointing 22-33.

Expressing his admiration for his teammate at one point during the campaign, Brandon Nimmo said, "With Francisco starting off a little slow, obviously, he was disappointed with it, but he never lets it affect him. He always knows that it takes a long time to have a good season. He's an unbelievable player, and I'm glad to have him on my team. He just shows up and is very professional every single day."

In discussing the influence that Lindor had on him in his first season as a regular member of the Mets' starting lineup, third baseman Mark Vientos stated, "I'm an observer. I just watch. I watch what he does, and I pick up things, and I'm like, 'OK, I need to do this. I need to get better at this.' The cheat sheet is right in front of me. If I want to be an MVP-type of player, it's right in front of me to see what it takes."

Pete Alonso added, "He's [Lindor's] been a jack of all trades this year. Hitting for power, hitting for average, great defense. From a performance aspect, that's exactly what you want to see. He's checked pretty much every box."

Meanwhile, Jesse Winker, who joined the Mets just prior to the trade deadline, said of his new teammate, "He cares about everybody, and he cares about winning. I feel like, as a guy who represents the organization, it's exactly what you want. And on top of that, he does something every night to help the team win."

Revealing the source of his inspiration, Lindor stated, "I owe it to the fans, I owe it to my teammates, I owe it to this organization, and I owe it to myself. I will go every day and give everything I have, no matter what. There is always a reason to play the game—whether it's to be better, be in the playoffs, for your numbers, or for the young kid that saved money to come watch you play. So, no matter what, you have to give it everything you got."

Lindor continued, "I play for the fans. I play for this organization and this city, for the people here. Whenever I feel the same love that I give them, it's special. I love it. It's easier to come to work whenever you feel like you have a whole city behind you."

Batting leadoff for the Mets again in 2025, Lindor had another excellent year, gaining All-Star recognition by hitting 31 homers, driving in 86 runs, finishing third in the league with 117 runs scored, swiping 31 bases, batting .267, and posting an OPS of .811. Lindor, who will enter the 2026 campaign with career totals of 279 homers, 856 RBIs, 1,011 runs scored, 1,664 hits, 339 doubles, 26 triples, and 216 stolen bases, a lifetime batting average of .273, a .342 on-base percentage, and a .475 slugging percentage, has hit 141 homers, driven in 445 runs, scored 503 times, collected 768 hits, 148 doubles, and 11 triples, stolen 117 bases, batted .261, compiled an on-base percentage of .338, and posted a slugging percentage of .462 as a member of the Mets.

METS CAREER HIGHLIGHTS

Best Season

Although Lindor recorded a career-high 107 RBIs two years earlier, he posted his best overall numbers as a member of the Mets in 2024, when, in addition to driving in 91 runs, stealing 29 bases, and batting .273, he placed in the league's top 10 in seven different offensive categories, including home runs (33) runs scored (107), doubles (39), total bases (309), slugging percentage (.500), and OPS (.844), with his 33 homers and 29 steals making him the first shortstop in MLB history to surpass the 25-mark in both categories in the same season three times.

Memorable Moments/Greatest Performances

Lindor knocked in all five runs the Mets scored during a 5–1 win over the Nationals on June 19, 2021, with two homers and a single.

Lindor led the Mets to a 7–6 win over the Yankees on September 12, 2021, by hitting three homers and driving in five runs.

Lindor helped lead the Mets to a 17–6 victory over Oakland on April 14, 2023, by knocking in seven runs with a homer and double, reaching the seats with the bases loaded in the top of the second inning.

Lindor contributed to a 9–0 rout of the Diamondbacks on July 6, 2023, by going 5-for-5 at the plate, with a homer, two triples, and three runs scored.

Lindor led the Mets to an 8–2 win over the Giants on April 24, 2024, by going 4-for-5 with two homers and four RBIs.

Lindor helped lead the Mets to a lopsided 12–3 victory over the Yankees on July 24, 2024, by knocking in five runs with a pair of homers.

Lindor provided most of the offensive firepower during a 7–1 win over the Padres on August 24, 2024, driving in five runs with a pair of homers, one of which came with the bases loaded.

Lindor hit a huge home run on the final day of the 2024 regular season, when, with the Mets trailing the Braves, 7–6, in the top of the ninth inning, he delivered what proved to be the game-winning blow of an 8–7 victory by reaching the seats with one man aboard, helping his team clinch a playoff berth in the process.

Lindor subsequently hit another memorable home run in Game 4 of the 2024 NLDS, when he delivered the decisive blow of a series-clinching 4–1 win over the Phillies by homering with the bases loaded in the bottom of the sixth inning.

Lindor gave the Mets a 5–4 victory over the Cardinals on April 18, 2025, when he led off the bottom of the ninth inning with a home run off right-handed reliever Ryan Fernandez.

Lindor led the Mets to a 5–4 win over the Phillies on April 21, 2025, by driving in four runs with a pair of homers.

Notable Achievements

- Has hit at least 20 home runs five times, topping 30 homers on three occasions.
- Has knocked in more than 100 runs once.
- Has scored more than 100 runs three times.
- Has stolen more than 20 bases three times, topping 30 thefts twice.
- Has led NL shortstops in putouts and assists once each.
- Ranks among Mets career leaders in home runs (8th) and stolen bases (7th).
- Three-time NL Player of the Week.
- Two-time Silver Slugger Award winner (2023 and 2024).
- Has finished in top 10 of NL MVP voting four times, placing as high as second in 2024.
- 2025 All-Star selection.
- Three-time All-MLB Second-Team selection (2022, 2023, and 2024).

18
JON MATLACK

An outstanding left-handed pitcher who served as a key member of the Mets' 1973 pennant-winning ballclub, Jon Matlack spent parts of seven seasons in New York, establishing himself as one of the finest southpaws in franchise history. A three-time NL All-Star who later received the additional honor of gaining induction into the Mets Hall of Fame, Matlack won at least 15 games three times, recorded more than 200 strikeouts once, threw more than 250 innings twice, and compiled an ERA under 3.00 on three separate occasions, accomplishing most of those feats after being involved in a terrible on-field incident that nearly ended his playing career.

Born in West Chester, Pennsylvania, on January 19, 1950, Jonathan Trumpbour Matlack got his rather unusual middle name from his mother, Marcella Trumpbour, whose maiden name came from her Dutch ancestors, who first arrived in this country in Saugerties, New York, during the 1700s. The eldest of eight children, Matlack began playing baseball in Little League, starting out as an outfielder, before being converted into a pitcher following a growth spurt that made him one of his team's biggest players.

Eventually developing into a standout hurler at West Chester High School, which was renamed Henderson High School during his senior year, Matlack performed so well on the mound that the Mets selected him with the fourth overall pick of the 1967 MLB Amateur Draft, before he even turned 18 years of age. Matlack subsequently spent most of the next five seasons advancing through New York's farm system, making a brief appearance with the parent club in 1971, before joining the Mets for good the following year.

Inserted into the starting rotation as a replacement for Nolan Ryan, whom the Mets had dealt to the California Angels during the offseason, the 22-year-old Matlack excelled in his first big-league season, earning NL

Jon Matlack earned NL Rookie of the Year honors in 1972.

Rookie of the Year honors by compiling a record of 15-10, ranking among the league leaders with a 2.32 ERA, posting a WHIP of 1.172, tossing eight complete games and four shutouts, and striking out 169 batters in 244 innings of work.

The fact that Matlack had the good fortune of joining a pitching staff that also included elite starters Tom Seaver and Jerry Koosman certainly helped him immensely during his first year in New York. While Seaver shared with Matlack his thoughts on conditioning, getting the proper amount of rest, and preparing himself mentally for each start, fellow southpaw Koosman provided him with a scouting report on each hitter. But the

6'3", 205-pound Matlack also deserved much of the credit for the success he experienced as a rookie. Matlack, whose pitching repertoire included a good, hard fastball and a wide variety of breaking pitches, possessed outstanding "stuff" that gave him the ability to navigate his way through opposing lineups in any number of ways. Blessed with a resilient arm, Matlack also proved himself capable of working deep into games, taking much of the pressure off the Mets bullpen.

Somewhat less successful in 1973, Matlack won just 14 of his 30 decisions, although he compiled a very respectable 3.20 ERA, finished third in the league with a career-high 205 strikeouts, and threw 242 innings, 14 complete games, and three shutouts, posting most of those numbers after surviving a near career-ending injury during the early stages of the campaign. Facing the Braves at Shea Stadium on May 8, Matlack suffered a hairline fracture of the skull when a line drive off the bat of Atlanta shortstop Marty Perez struck him on the forehead.

Recalling the incident years later, Matlack said, "They came out and checked me on the mound. I thought I got hit in the mouth because it really hurt. I'm reaching to see if I've got any teeth left and [catcher] Jerry Grote grabs my hand and says, 'Wait for the trainer.' As I'm looking up, I could see my forehead. That's when I realized I got hit there, because it was swollen."

Carried off the field on a stretcher, Matlack, some thought at the time, had thrown his last pitch. But he amazingly returned to the mound just 11 days later and ended up playing an important role in the Mets' improbable run to the NL pennant, winning five of his final six decisions during the regular season, before shutting out the Cincinnati Reds on just two hits in Game 2 of the NLCS.

Hampered by poor run support in 1974, Matlack finished the season with a record of just 13-15. Nevertheless, he proved to be one of the NL's most effective pitchers, earning All-Star honors for the first of three straight times by ranking among the league leaders with an ERA of 2.41, a WHIP of 1.119, 195 strikeouts, 265⅓ innings pitched, and 14 complete games, while also topping the circuit with seven shutouts.

Continuing to perform extremely well for the Mets the next two seasons, Matlack went 16-12 with a 3.38 ERA, 1.233 WHIP, eight complete games, three shutouts, and 154 strikeouts in 228⅔ innings pitched in 1975, before compiling a record of 17-10 and an ERA of 2.95, posting a WHIP of 1.118, registering 153 strikeouts, leading all NL hurlers with six shutouts, and placing near the top of the league rankings with 16 complete games and 262 innings pitched the following year.

But when Matlack won just seven of his 22 decisions and compiled an ERA of 4.21 for a Mets team that finished last in the NL East in 1977, management decided to include him in a complicated four-team trade at the end of the year. In a deal that also involved the Braves, Pirates, and Texas Rangers, the Mets sent Matlack to Texas and first baseman-outfielder John Milner to Pittsburgh, essentially for first baseman Willie Montañez and outfielders Tom Grieve and Ken Henderson.

Recalling his feelings upon learning of the trade, Matlack said, "It totally shocked me because you never want to be let go. I felt like I was a real part of something."

Matlack, who left New York with an overall record of 82-81, a composite ERA of 3.03, a WHIP of 1.195, 65 complete games, 26 shutouts, and 1,023 strikeouts in 1,448 total innings of work, ended up spending the next six seasons in Texas, pitching his best ball for the Rangers in 1978, when he went 15-13 with a 2.27 ERA, 18 complete games, and 270 innings pitched. Released by the Rangers after being relegated to spot-starting duties in 1983, Matlack announced his retirement, ending his big-league career with a record of 125-126, an ERA of 3.18, a WHIP of 1.233, 97 complete games, 30 shutouts, and 1,516 strikeouts in 2,363 innings pitched.

Following his playing days, Matlack spent four years selling commercial real estate and raising horses, before beginning a lengthy career as a pitching coach and, later, as a pitching coordinator, in the farm systems of the San Diego Padres, Chicago White Sox, Detroit Tigers, and Houston Astros. Finally retiring to private life in 2013, the now 76-year-old Matlack currently resides with his wife in Johnsburg, New York.

Finding comfort these many years later in how he pitched for the Mets during his six-plus seasons in New York, Matlack says, "I'm proud of my career with the Mets. Looking back at it the way they look at stats today, I probably pitched a lot better than I thought I did."

METS CAREER HIGHLIGHTS

Best Season

Although Matlack also performed extremely well in 1972 and 1974, he had his finest all-around season as a member of the Mets in 1976, when, in addition to posting a career-high 17 victories, he compiled an ERA of 2.95, registered 153 strikeouts, ranked among the NL leaders with a WHIP of

1.118, 16 complete games, and 262 innings pitched, and topped the circuit with six shutouts.

Memorable Moments/Greatest Performances

Matlack yielded just one hit and two walks during a 1–0 shutout of the Astros on July 10, 1973, surrendering only a sixth-inning double to second baseman Tommy Helms.

Matlack hurled another gem on August 8, 1973, recording nine strikeouts and allowing just two hits and two walks during a 1–0 shutout of the Dodgers.

Matlack quieted the bats of the Big Red Machine in Game 2 of the 1973 NLCS, registering nine strikeouts and yielding just two hits and three walks during a 5–0 shutout of the Reds.

Matlack turned in another exceptional effort against Oakland in Game 4 of the 1973 World Series, evening the Fall Classic at two games apiece by allowing just three hits and one unearned run over the first eight innings of a 6–1 Mets win.

In addition to allowing just four hits during a 4–2 complete-game win over the Giants on May 8, 1974, Matlack recorded a career-high 12 strikeouts.

Matlack tossed a one-hit shutout against the Cardinals on June 29, 1974, registering seven strikeouts, issuing three walks, and surrendering only a third-inning single to opposing pitcher John Curtis during a 4–0 Mets win.

Matlack yielded just four hits and struck out 10 batters during a 2–0 shutout of the Cubs on September 3, 1974.

Matlack dominated the Dodgers' lineup on June 12, 1975, surrendering just three hits and issuing one walk during a 2–0 shutout of the defending NL champions.

Notable Achievements

- Won at least 15 games three times.
- Compiled ERA under 3.00 three times, finishing with mark under 2.50 twice.
- Recorded more than 200 strikeouts once.
- Threw more than 220 innings five times, tossing more than 250 frames twice.
- Led NL pitchers in shutouts twice.

- Ranks among Mets career leaders in wins (tied for 7th), ERA (5th), strikeouts (9th), shutouts (tied for 2nd), complete games (4th), innings pitched (6th), and starts (8th).
- 1973 division champion.
- 1973 NL champion.
- 1972 NL Rookie of the Year.
- 1975 All-Star Game MVP.
- Three-time NL All-Star selection (1974, 1975, and 1976).
- Inducted into Mets Hall of Fame in 2021.

19
MOOKIE WILSON

A speedy switch-hitting outfielder who endeared himself to the hometown fans with his tremendous hustle, positive attitude, and engaging personality, Mookie Wilson established himself as one of the most popular players in franchise history during his 10 seasons in New York. Persevering through the dark days of the early 1980s, Wilson helped lead the Mets to two division titles, one pennant, and one world championship by batting over .290 twice, scoring at least 90 runs twice, and stealing more than 20 bases seven times, with his 281 thefts representing the second-highest total in team annals. Yet, despite his many other accomplishments, Wilson, who gained induction into the Mets Hall of Fame in 1996, will always be remembered more than anything for one play that earned him a permanent place in Mets lore.

Born in Bamberg, South Carolina, on February 9, 1956, William Hayward Wilson acquired his rather unusual nickname as a small child when his inability to properly pronounce the word milk resulted in him saying "mook" instead. Raised on a farm with his 11 siblings, Wilson grew up in the segregated South, recalling years later, "They were troubling times, when you really had to be careful where you went and what you said."

The son of a sharecropper who instilled in him a love of God and baseball, Wilson developed into a star pitcher at Bamberg-Ehrhardt High School, which he led to a state championship his senior year. Offered an athletic scholarship to South Carolina State University as graduation neared, Wilson initially signed a letter of intent to attend SCSU. However, after the school discontinued its baseball program, Wilson chose instead to enroll at Spartanburg Methodist College in Spartanburg, South Carolina, where he spent two seasons playing for the Pioneers, before transferring to the University of South Carolina. After pitching and playing the outfield for the Gamecocks for one year, Wilson elected to sign with the Mets when they selected him in the second round of the 1977 MLB Amateur Draft.

Mookie Wilson ranks second in franchise history in stolen bases.

Wilson subsequently spent almost four full seasons advancing through the Mets' farm system, during which time he became a full-time outfielder. Meanwhile, Wilson experienced a life-changing event while at Double-A Jackson in 1978, when he married the mother of a four-year-old boy his brother, Richard, had fathered out of wedlock, making him both the child's uncle and stepfather.

Promoted to the Mets during the latter stages of the 1980 campaign after batting .295, scoring 92 runs, and stealing 50 bases at Triple-A Tidewater, Wilson appeared in 27 games with the parent club, batting .248, scoring 16 times, and swiping seven bags in his first tour of duty at the big-league level. Although Wilson manned all three outfield posts at one time or another the following season, he spent most of the year starting in center field for the Mets. Performing relatively well for a team that posted a record of just 41-62 during the strike-interrupted campaign, Wilson earned a seventh-place finish in the NL Rookie of the Year voting by batting .271, scoring 49 runs, and stealing 24 bases. One of the few bright spots on teams that finished last in the NL East in each of the next two seasons, Wilson batted .279, scored 90 runs, collected 178 hits, and stole 58 bases in 1982, before batting .276, scoring 91 times, amassing 176 safeties, and swiping 54 bags the following year.

Blessed with superior running speed, the 5'10", 170-pound Wilson proved to be the Mets' most exciting player his first few seasons in New York. Hitting mostly out of the leadoff spot in the batting order, Wilson created havoc on the basepaths, stealing a total of 158 bases from 1982 to 1984. Meanwhile, Wilson's great speed and tremendous hustle enabled him to consistently rank among the league leaders in triples. Although Wilson possessed very little power, hitting as many as 10 home runs in a season just once, he hit well from both sides of the plate, with his biggest weakness being his lack of selectivity, which caused him to strike out nearly three times as often as he walked over the course of his career. Wilson also did an excellent job of patrolling center field at Shea Stadium, finishing second among all NL outfielders in putouts twice, while placing third on two other occasions.

As much as anything, though, Wilson became known for his friendly, unassuming nature and strong moral fiber, which set him apart from many of his Mets teammates. A deeply religious man who retained his spirituality amid all the raucous behavior that surrounded him, Wilson later said, "I didn't really appreciate my religious faith until I got to New York. . . . You have to have that inner strength to stay humble."

Wilson remained the Mets' full-time starter in center field for one more year, hitting 10 homers, driving in 54 runs, scoring 88 times, collecting 10 triples, stealing 46 bases, batting .276, and posting an OPS of .717 in 1984, before missing nearly half of the ensuing campaign after undergoing arthroscopic surgery in early July to repair torn cartilage in his right shoulder. Wilson subsequently suffered an injury during spring training in 1986 when a ball thrown by shortstop Rafael Santana during a baserunning drill struck him in the eye, shattering the sunglasses he wore to reduce the glare in the outfield. Carted off the field on a stretcher and needing 25 stitches, Wilson ended up missing the first month of the regular season, during which time Lenny Dykstra filled in for him in center. Upon his return to action, Wilson platooned with Dykstra until early August, when he moved to left field following the release of George Foster. Appearing in 123 games and garnering 416 total plate appearances for a Mets team that ran away with the NL East, Wilson finished the season with nine homers, 45 RBIs, 61 runs scored, 25 stolen bases, a .289 batting average, and an OPS of .775.

Continuing to start in left field for the Mets during the postseason, Wilson batted just .115 against Houston in the NLCS, before rebounding somewhat to bat .269, score three runs, and steal three bases against Boston in the World Series. Making his greatest impact in Game 6, Wilson stepped to the plate in the bottom of the 10th inning with two men out, runners on first and third, and the Mets trailing by a score of 5–4. After Red Sox reliever Bob Stanley uncorked a wild pitch that sent home Kevin Mitchell from third base with the tying run, Wilson tapped a slow roller toward first baseman Bill Buckner that went through his legs, plating Ray Knight with the winning run.

Asked about the fateful play afterward, Wilson said, "I had a pitch I should've handled really well, middle in low, but kind of rolled over it. I knew the ball was hit slowly, so I gotta run, and the pitcher was slow getting there. I didn't see the ball go through Buckner. I just saw it go behind him. . . ."

With Buckner hobbled by bad knees, Wilson maintained that he would have beaten him to the bag even if he had fielded the ball cleanly. Nevertheless, Buckner became the object of scorn in Boston, while Wilson etched his name into Mets history.

Following the acquisition of Kevin McReynolds in December 1986, Wilson spent the next two seasons playing all over the outfield, although he saw the greatest amount of action in center, where he shared playing time with Lenny Dykstra. Performing well in a part-time role in both 1987 and 1988, Wilson hit nine homers, knocked in 34 runs, scored 58 times, stole 21 bases, and established career-high marks with a .299 batting average and an OPS of .814 in the first of those campaigns, before hitting eight homers, driving in 41 runs, scoring 61 times, stealing 15 bases, batting .296, and posting an OPS of .776 in the second.

Wilson continued to assume the role of a part-time player through the first two months of the 1989 season. But when the Mets traded Lenny Dykstra and Roger McDowell to Philadelphia for Juan Samuel in mid-June with the intention of making the latter their everyday center fielder, Wilson asked to be traded to another team. Granting Wilson's request, the Mets dealt him to the Toronto Blue Jays for reliever Jeff Musselman and minor-league pitcher Mike Brady on July 31, ending his lengthy association with the organization.

Wilson, who, during his time in New York, hit 60 homers, knocked in 342 runs, scored 592 times, collected 1,112 hits, 170 doubles, and 62 triples, stole 281 bases, batted .276, compiled an on-base percentage of

.318, and posted a slugging percentage of .394, ended up spending parts of three seasons in Toronto, before announcing his retirement following the conclusion of the 1991 campaign. Over the course of 12 big-league seasons, Wilson hit 67 homers, knocked in 438 runs, scored 731 times, amassed 1,397 hits, 227 doubles, and 71 triples, stole 327 bases, batted .274, compiled a .314 on-base percentage, and posted a .386 slugging percentage.

Following his playing days, Wilson earned his bachelor's degree from Mercy College in New York, after which he spent the next few years selling stocks and bonds. Eventually returning to the game he loved, Wilson rejoined the Mets in 1997; since that time he has served the organization in various capacities, including first-base coach, minor-league manager, minor-league baserunning coordinator, roving instructor, and club ambassador. Since 2014, Wilson, who in 2001 released with his family a gospel CD entitled, *Don't Worry, the Lord will Carry You Through* and later penned the book *Mookie: Life, Baseball, and the '86 Mets*, has also served as an ordained minister for Zion Mill Creek Baptist Church in Columbia, South Carolina. When not in church or working with fellow seniors, Wilson speaks to athletes of all ages across the country about baseball, health and wellness, and God.

Now 70 years of age, Wilson continues to be most closely associated with that one singular play from the 1986 World Series that has made him a Mets icon. Claiming that he has come to accept that fact, Wilson says, "Initially, it did bother me that my career was defined by one play. I think I've done more for the game than just hit a groundball—not even a hard-hit groundball. But I came to understand . . . it's part of baseball history. It's part of the Mets history, and to deny being a part of it is wrong."

METS CAREER HIGHLIGHTS

Best Season

It could be argued that Wilson played his best ball for the Mets in 1984, when, in addition to driving in 54 runs, scoring 88 times, stealing 46 bases, batting .276, and compiling an OPS of .717, he established career-high marks with 10 homers, 10 triples, and 240 total bases. But Wilson posted slightly better overall numbers in 1982, when he hit five homers, collected nine triples, scored 90 runs, batted .279, compiled an OPS of .683, and reached career highs in RBIs (55), hits (178), and steals (58), with his 58 thefts setting a then-single-season franchise record (since broken).

Memorable Moments/Greatest Performances

After hitting safely in three of his five previous trips to the plate, Wilson gave the Mets a 7–6 win over the Cardinals on September 20, 1981, when he homered off Hall of Fame reliever Bruce Sutter with two men out and one man on base in the bottom of the ninth inning.

Wilson contributed to a 9–4 victory over the Expos on September 16, 1982, by going 4-for-5 with a homer, double, stolen base, and three runs scored.

Wilson helped lead the Mets to a 14–4 rout of the Reds on July 7, 1984, by going a perfect 4-for-4 at the plate with a homer, four RBIs, and two runs scored.

Wilson starred in defeat on May 23, 1986, going 5-for-5 with a triple, double, stolen base, and two RBIs during a 7–4 loss to the Padres.

Wilson will always be remembered for his role in the Mets' improbable 10th-inning comeback against the Red Sox in Game 6 of the 1986 World Series that resulted in a 6–5 victory. With the Mets already having scored twice in the frame after the first two batters failed to reach base, Wilson hit a slow roller down the first base line that went through Bill Buckner's legs, allowing Ray Knight to score from second with the winning run.

Wilson homered twice in one game for the only time in his career during a 4–3 win over the Phillies on April 10, 1988, concluding the contest with three hits and three RBIs.

Notable Achievements

- Finished in double digits in triples once.
- Stole more than 20 bases seven times, topping 40 thefts three times and 50 thefts twice.
- Finished second in NL in triples once.
- Led NL center fielders in putouts once and double plays turned three times.
- Ranks among Mets career leaders in runs scored (7th), hits (6th), triples (2nd), stolen bases (2nd), games played (8th), and at-bats (6th).
- Two-time division champion (1986 and 1988).
- 1986 NL champion.
- 1986 world champion.
- Inducted into Mets Hall of Fame in 1996.

20
LEE MAZZILLI

Unfairly hyped by the Mets publicity department as "the next Willie Mays" upon his arrival in Queens, Lee Mazzilli never came close to living up to the unreasonable expectations set for him by a front office seeking to create interest in a ballclub that ranked among the worst in the major leagues. Nevertheless, the Brooklyn-born Mazzilli proved to be one of the few bright spots on teams that consistently finished at, or near, the bottom of the NL East standings. A solid switch-hitting outfielder who possessed decent power, good speed, and a keen batting eye, Mazzilli hit at least 15 home runs three times, stole more than 30 bases twice, and batted over .300 once from 1977 to 1980, earning in the process one All-Star nomination. And after departing from New York following the conclusion of the 1981 campaign, Mazzilli returned to the Mets five years later to help them win two division titles, one pennant, and one world championship.

Born in Brooklyn, New York, on March 25, 1955, Lee Louis Mazzilli grew up with his two older siblings in the borough's Sheepshead Bay section, just minutes from Coney Island. The son of former welterweight boxer Libero Mazzilli, whose family had immigrated to the United States from Bari, Italy, Mazzilli spent his early years living in a second-floor apartment on East 12th Street, between Avenue Y and Avenue Z, recalling, "We were what you'd call a lower-class family. My parents, my brother, my sister, and I lived in a two-bedroom house. But we were a close family. We loved each other."

An outstanding all-around athlete, Mazzilli excelled as a speed skater during his youth, winning or sharing three straight national skating championships between the ages of 12 and 16, with childhood friend Bob Fenn, who later became a top skating coaching, remembering, "Lee was very fast and had very good agility and balance. Skating short track, you've got to be a bit of a daredevil, and Lee was very confident in himself, very determined."

Ultimately forced to choose between skating and baseball when a qualifying event conflicted with his team's playoff games, Mazzilli told the

Lee Mazzilli proved to be one of the few bright spots on mostly losing Mets teams.

Baltimore Sun in 2003, "I had a passion for speedskating, did it with all my heart. But I don't know that I would have made the [1972] Olympic team. And it was a different era back then; there weren't all these other sports. Baseball was the No. 1 sport by far, and it was always my first love."

Mazzilli continued, "When I was in kindergarten, if somebody asked me what you wanted to be when you grew up, a doctor or a lawyer, I'd say a major league ballplayer. I used to go to Met games, especially when the Giants came in from San Francisco with Willie Mays and Juan Marichal. I was there when they played that 32-inning doubleheader in 1964, but I had to leave early to go home. After all, I was only 9 years old."

Adding that he had the advantage of being naturally ambidextrous, Mazzilli said, "I always could switch-hit. I always could throw with either hand. I'd just pick up a baseball and throw it, either way."

Eventually establishing himself as a star outfielder at Brooklyn's Abraham Lincoln High School, Mazzilli batted .386 over three seasons, prompting the Mets to select him with the 14th overall pick of the 1973 MLB Amateur Draft. Requesting an audience with his childhood hero, Willie Mays (then in the final season of his illustrious career), immediately after signing with the Mets for $50,000, Mazzilli recalled, "I signed the contract at Shea [Stadium]. Joe McDonald asked me if there was anything I wanted to see, and I told him, 'Yeah, Willie Mays. I'd like to meet Willie Mays.' So, they took me down to the clubhouse, the trainer's room. I walk in, and Willie Mays is on the trainer's table."

Mazzilli subsequently spent most of the next three seasons in the minors, performing well at every stop, before joining the Mets during the latter stages of the 1976 campaign after batting .292, posting an OPS of .895, and amassing a league-leading 111 bases on balls at Double-A Jackson. Appearing in 24 games with the Mets during the final month of the season, Mazzilli struggled at the plate, batting just .195, although he homered twice, knocked in seven runs, and stole five bases.

Named the Mets' starting center fielder prior to the start of the 1977 campaign, Mazzilli performed fairly well in his first full big-league season, hitting six homers, driving in 46 runs, scoring 66 times, stealing 22 bases, batting .250, and posting an OPS of .679, while also leading all NL center fielders with 391 putouts. Showing marked improvement the following year, with the help of Mets manager and fellow Brooklyn native Joe Torre, who treated him very much like an adopted son, and Mets coach Willie Mays, who helped him with his fielding and taught him how to make his signature basket catch, Mazzilli proved to be arguably the best all-around player on a team that finished last in the NL East with a record of just 66-96. In addition to hitting 16 homers and driving in 61 runs, Mazzilli scored 78 times, swiped 20 bases, batted .273, and compiled an OPS of .785.

With the Mets' on-field struggles causing attendance at Shea Stadium to plummet to historic lows, Mazzilli became the focus of a marketing campaign that sought to take advantage of his Brooklyn roots and matinée idol looks. Listed at 6'1" and 180 pounds, the athletically built Mazzilli possessed a lean but muscular physique, dark hair, dark eyes, and olive-colored skin, making him a favorite of the team's young female fans. Mazzilli also played the game with a certain flair, sliding into bases head-first and gathering in flyballs with the basket catch that he learned from his childhood idol. But while Mazzilli welcomed the adulation of the Mets' fanbase, he preferred to keep a low profile off the field and be judged more for his contributions to the team. Somewhat uncomfortable being cast as the face of the franchise, Mazzilli said during a 1980 interview, "I just want to be known as a guy who works hard and does things right. I want to be known as a ballplayer's ballplayer."

Taking his game up a notch in 1979, Mazzilli earned his lone All-Star nomination by hitting 15 homers, driving in 79 runs, scoring 78 times, stealing 34 bases, batting .303, ranking among the league leaders with 93 bases on balls and a .395 on-base percentage, and compiling a slugging percentage of .449. Mazzilli followed that up with another solid season, concluding the 1980 campaign with 16 homers, 76 RBIs, 82 runs scored, 41 stolen bases, a batting average of .280, and an OPS of .801.

Yet even though Mazzilli clearly established himself as the Mets' best all-around player by the end of the 1980 season, he failed to develop into the truly elite player the organization hoped he would eventually become. Displaying only moderate power at the plate, Mazzilli never hit more than 16 homers in a season. Furthermore, Mazzilli exhibited only average instincts, somewhat limited range, and a weak throwing arm in the outfield.

After spending some time at first base in 1980, Mazzilli moved to left field the following year to accommodate Mookie Wilson, who laid claim to the starting center field job.

Battling elbow and back problems, Mazzilli performed poorly during the strike-shortened campaign, hitting just six homers, driving in only 34 runs, and batting just .228. Subsequently made expendable with the acquisition of slugging outfielder George Foster from the Cincinnati Reds on February 10, 1982, Mazzilli headed for Texas shortly thereafter when the Mets traded him to the Rangers for minor-league pitchers Ron Darling and Walt Terrell just prior to the start of the 1982 regular season.

Mazzilli ended up splitting the 1982 campaign between the Rangers and Yankees, serving both teams as a part-time player, before assuming a similar role in Pittsburgh for the next three-and-a-half years. Released by the Pirates on July 23, 1986, the 31-year-old Mazzilli signed with the Mets as a free agent less than two weeks later, saying at the time, "I never wanted to leave the Mets. Shea Stadium was my home."

Although Mazzilli received a limited amount of playing time over the final two months of the season, he contributed to the Mets' world championship ballclub by batting .276, posting an OPS of .848, homering twice, and driving in seven runs in 72 total plate appearances, before hitting safely in two of his five trips to the plate against Boston in the World Series. Mazzilli remained with the Mets for most of the next three seasons, assuming the role of a reserve outfielder and pinch-hitter, while also providing veteran leadership on a team with several strong personalities. Released by the Mets just prior to the July 31, 1989, trade deadline, Mazzilli signed with the Toronto Blue Jays, with whom he finished out the season, before announcing his retirement at the end of the year. Over parts of 14 big-league seasons, Mazzilli hit 93 homers, knocked in 460 runs, scored 571 times, collected 1,068 hits, 191 doubles, and 24 triples, stole 197 bases, batted .259, compiled an on-base percentage of .359, and posted a slugging percentage of .385. As a member of the Mets, Mazzilli hit 68 homers, knocked in 353 runs, scored 404 times, amassed 796 hits, 148 doubles, and 22 triples, stole 152 bases, batted .264, compiled a .357 on-base percentage, and posted a .396 slugging percentage.

Following his playing days, Mazzilli briefly owned a sports bar on Manhattan's Upper West Side called Lee Mazzilli's Sports Café, worked at a mortgage bank, and served as commissioner of the independent Northeast League, before spending nearly a decade coaching and managing at both the minor- and major-league levels. After piloting the Baltimore Orioles from 2004 to 2005, Mazzilli served as bench coach under Joe Torre in New York for one season. Mazzilli then spent two years working as a studio analyst for SportsNet New York, before accepting a front office position with the Yankees.

Looking back on his playing career, Mazzilli said, "The fame . . . I couldn't understand it. I felt like everything I did had to be right, because when there's all the publicity, and when you are so recognizable, that's all people know you as."

Meanwhile, Joe Torre—perhaps hinting at some of the rumors of drug abuse that followed Mazzilli during his playing days—stated, "I don't think his talents were overtouted. He was a good-looking kid from Brooklyn who hit the ball hard and could run like a deer. And he got caught up in the hype. He had the ability to become a very good ball player. Instead, he became a superstar before his time."

METS CAREER HIGHLIGHTS

Best Season

Mazzilli played his best ball for the Mets from 1978 to 1980, having his finest all-around season in 1979, when, in addition to hitting 15 homers, scoring 78 runs, stealing 34 bases, batting .303, and posting an OPS of .844, he established career-high marks with 79 RBIs, 181 hits, 34 doubles, 268 total bases, and 93 bases on balls.

Memorable Moments/Greatest Performances

Mazzilli gave the Mets a 5–4 win over the Pirates on September 20, 1976, when he hit a two-out, two-run homer off right-handed reliever Kent Tekulve in the bottom of the ninth inning.

Mazzilli delivered the decisive blow of a 4–0 win over the Phillies on July 4, 1978, when he homered with the bases loaded off Larry Christenson in the bottom of the sixth inning.

Mazzilli became the first Mets player to homer from both sides of the plate in a game during an 8–5 win over the Dodgers on September 3, 1978, concluding the contest with four hits and three RBIs.

Mazzilli helped lead the Mets to a 9–8 win over the Cubs on June 30, 1979, by homering twice and driving in four runs.

Mazzilli again homered twice and knocked in four runs during a 7–4 win over the Cardinals on July 13, 1980.

Mazzilli led the Mets to a 10–7 win over the Cubs on September 14, 1980, by collecting three hits, homering once, driving in five runs, and scoring three times.

Notable Achievements

- Batted over .300 twice.
- Stole more than 20 bases four times, topping 40 thefts once.
- Led NL center fielders in putouts once.
- Ranks sixth in franchise history in stolen bases.
- Two-time division champion (1986 and 1988).
- 1986 NL champion.
- 1986 world champion.
- 1979 NL All-Star selection.

21
DAVID CONE

A hard-throwing right-hander who served as a key member of the Mets' starting rotation from 1988 to 1992, David Cone spent parts of seven seasons in Flushing, ranking among the finest pitchers in the senior circuit much of that time. A 20-game winner for the Mets' 1988 NL East championship ballclub, Cone recorded more than 200 strikeouts and threw more than 200 innings on four separate occasions during his time in Queens, earning in the process two All-Star selections and one third-place finish in the NL Cy Young voting. Continuing to perform at an elite level after being traded from the Mets to the Toronto Blue Jays during the latter stages of the 1992 campaign, Cone spent another decade in the big leagues, earning three more All-Star nominations, three more top-five finishes in the Cy Young balloting, and winning the award once, with his 20 victories for the Yankees in 1998 making him the only man to win at least 20 games in a season for both New York teams.

Born in Kansas City, Missouri, on January 2, 1963, as a youngster David Brian Cone acquired the toughness for which he later became known, later describing his parents as "tough, hard-nosed, blue-collar people," and adding, "They went by the sort of kick-the-bird-out-of-the-nest type of theory. You had to fly or fall to the ground. In some ways, I really appreciate that. In other ways, maybe we both regret that we haven't fostered that close, affectionate relationship that some families have. Part of my resiliency and so-called toughness, emotionally, is due to that background. Part of the problems I have emotionally, too, are due to that background."

The youngest of four children, Cone competed with his sister and two brothers in fierce Wiffle ball games in the family's backyard during his childhood, before honing his baseball skills on the local sandlots. Eventually establishing himself as a star in multiple sports at Rockhurst High, an all-boys Jesuit school, Cone quarterbacked the football team to the district championship and excelled on the court at point guard. Meanwhile, since

David Cone won 20 games for the Mets in 1988.

Rockhurst did not field a baseball team, Cone played summer ball in the Ban Johnson League, where he faced competition much older than himself.

Recruited by several colleges for both baseball and football as graduation neared, Cone initially accepted a scholarship to the University of Missouri, before changing his plans when his hometown Kansas City Royals selected him in the third round of the 1981 MLB Amateur Draft. Cone subsequently performed brilliantly during his first two minor-league seasons, compiling an overall record of 22-7 at two different levels of Kansas City's farm system. However, an injury sustained early in 1983 forced Cone to sit out the entire year, during which time he took a job working on the assembly line for a company that produced conveyor belts. Later claiming that his year away from the game proved to be a turning point in his life,

Cone said that he recalled telling himself, "Conie, you either make it happen, or this is the life in store for you."

Returning to the playing field in 1984, Cone spent the next three years in the minors performing somewhat erratically, with former Omaha teammate Jamie Quirk recalling, "David had a fastball and a slider back then. He was almost there, but he kept trying to strike everybody out. I wanted to persuade him to be in the strike zone more and set the batters up—let them hit the ball now and then, but where you wanted them to hit it. He got the idea some days."

Dealt to the Mets just prior to the start of the 1987 season for pitcher Rick Anderson, catcher Ed Hearn, and minor-league hurler Mauro Gozzo in what then-Royals owner Ewing Kauffman later called "the worst trade we ever made," Cone appeared in a few games with New York's Triple-A affiliate in Tidewater, before joining the parent club. Armed with two new pitches, a split-finger fastball and a sidearm slider he called "Laredo," Cone made a strong impression on his new teammates, remembering, "The first game I pitched with the Mets, Keith Hernandez says, 'I love the way you pitch. You keep dropping down and throwing sidearm. We love your style.'"

Claiming that the encouragement he received from Hernandez and others following his arrival in New York represented something new to him, Cone stated, "They made me feel more welcome in one day than the Royals had in six years. . . . After the first couple of weeks, they kind of embraced me and, for the first time in my career, I felt liberated. Kansas City was really a conservative organization, and I butted heads with the Royals in their minor-league system about style—'You can't throw sidearm sliders . . . You can't pitch this way.' They tried to break me and change my mechanics the whole way through. . . . It was liberating for me when I got to the Mets. I was embraced by Keith Hernandez and Gary Carter, and all those guys."

Cone ended up starting 13 games for the Mets his first year in Queens, which included a lengthy stint on the disabled list with a fractured pinky. But after going 5-6 with a 3.71 ERA in 1987, Cone helped lead the Mets to the division title the following year by compiling a record of 20-3 and finishing second in the league with an ERA of 2.22 and 213 strikeouts, earning in the process All-Star honors and a third-place finish in the NL Cy Young voting.

However, Cone erred in judgment when he agreed to collaborate with *Daily News* sportswriter Bob Klapisch on a ghostwritten column based on clubhouse interviews during the NLCS. Looking back on the series of events that transpired after he made several ill-advised comments about Dodgers reliever Jay Howell after the Mets rallied from a ninth-inning deficit to win Game 1, Cone said, "Bob Klapisch just kind of asked me some questions in the clubhouse, and things got a little crazy in the aftermath of a big win in Game 1 of the playoffs, and I never got a chance to read it before it went out, and I got credit for the byline. To this day, I still can't believe I allowed that to happen, that I wouldn't at least see the final copy before I put my name on it."

The Dodgers, who used Cone's remarks as bulletin board material, subsequently scored five runs against him in just two innings that night, to even a series they eventually won in seven games at a game apiece, with Cone later admitting, "It definitely affected how I pitched. It was the first time I felt physically inhibited by nerves. My legs felt heavy from being so nervous."

Although the Mets failed to return to the playoffs in either of the next two seasons, they remained serious contenders in the NL East, with Cone pitching well for them both years. After going 14-8 with a 3.52 ERA and 190 strikeouts in 219⅔ innings pitched in 1989, Cone compiled a record of 14-10 and an ERA of 3.23, threw 211⅔ innings, and led all NL hurlers with 233 strikeouts the following year.

Capable of dominating the opposition on any given night, the 6'1", 185-pound Cone, who once struck out 19 batters in a game, possessed a wide arsenal of pitches that included a cut fastball, a curve, a changeup, a lethal split-finger fastball, which he used as his out pitch, and the "Laredo," a nasty sidearm slider that broke six inches off the plate. And with Cone fanning batters at a steady pace, a group known as the "Coneheads" (named after the *Saturday Night Live* sketch) formed in the left field upper deck at Shea Stadium. Claiming that the group, which donned pointy rubber head coverings and raised a large *K* with every strikeout, served as an inspiration to him, Cone said, "I can tell you that the Coneheads were a motivating factor whenever I took the mound. I didn't want to let them down."

Extremely popular with the local media as well, the candid and articulate Cone chatted with writers regularly, even doing interviews with them on the days he pitched. Nevertheless, several embarrassing incidents eventually caused Cone to fall out of favor with team management, with one of those occurring during a 7–4 loss to the Braves on April 30, 1990, when he allowed two runners to circle the bases and cross the plate while he argued with an umpire with the ball in his hand. Cone again drew the ire of Mets brass the following season when he engaged in a shouting and poking match with manager Bud Harrelson after he shook off a pitchout from bench coach Doc Edwards.

Cone also became involved in several troubling incidents off the playing field. Although he never developed the addiction to cocaine that plagued some of his teammates, Cone often partied with them and stayed out until all hours of the evening. Meanwhile, Cone found himself being accused more than once of engaging in inappropriate sexual behavior, including pleasuring himself in front of three women in the bullpen area at Shea Stadium one evening in 1989 and raping another woman in 1991. Although all charges made against him proved to be baseless, Cone stated years later, "Even though both cases were cleared up and my name was completely cleared, the damage had been done. I've had to live with that. There was part of me that said, at some point, 'Be more careful, cover your ass a little better, but you can still live, you can still have fun.' I thought there was a lot of reckless journalism, but I sort of came full circle and said, 'Now, wait a minute—you did put yourself in a position to be taken advantage of a couple of times.'"

Cone spent one more full season in New York, going 14-14 with a 3.29 ERA and a league-leading 241 strikeouts in 1991, before compiling a record of 13-7 and an ERA of 2.88, tossing a league-high five shutouts, and striking out 214 batters over the first five months of the ensuing campaign. But with Cone set to become a free agent at the end of the year and ownership concerned over his off-field troubles, the Mets traded him to the Toronto Blue Jays for second baseman Jeff Kent and minor-league outfielder Ryan Thompson on August 27, 1992.

Recalling his reaction to the deal, Cone said, "The trade was a wake-up call for me. It was time to take a hard look at myself—what am I doing wrong here? Or at least, what are the perceptions of what I'm doing wrong? You're getting a reputation as a kid with great stuff, some of the best stuff in the big leagues as far as pitching goes, and also one of the biggest flakes. I kind of looked at that and said, 'Is this how I want to be remembered?' Not that I had any great revelations or made any great changes in my life, but I certainly looked at it and tried to address it."

After helping the Blue Jays win the World Series in 1992, Cone signed with the Royals as a free agent at the end of the year. Struggling somewhat in his first season back in Kansas City, Cone went just 11-14 with a 3.33 ERA, before winning the AL Cy Young Award in 1994 by compiling a record of 16-5 and an ERA of 2.94. Traded back to Toronto at season's end, Cone ended up splitting the 1995 campaign between the Blue Jays and Yankees, posting a composite record of 18-8 and an ERA of 3.57, before signing with the Yankees when he became a free agent again at the end of the year.

Cone subsequently spent five eventful seasons with the Mets' crosstown rivals, earning his final two All-Star nominations by helping the Yankees win four world championships. Particularly outstanding in 1998, Cone led all AL hurlers with 20 victories and recorded more than 200 strikeouts (209) for the seventh and final time in his career. While pitching for the Yankees, Cone also became just the 14th pitcher of the modern era to hurl a perfect game and had to undergo vein-graft surgery after doctors discovered a life-threatening aneurysm in his right shoulder, later saying, "I didn't even know what it was or what it meant. It was very scary. I just wanted to know if my career was over at that point."

While Cone continued to pitch for a few more seasons, he lost much of his velocity, forcing him to rely more on guile and finesse. In discussing his later years, Cone said, "A lot of wear and tear just took its toll, and I lost some velocity, so I had to adjust, get more creative, probably throw breaking stuff, less fastballs, change angles a bit more."

Following his five-and-a-half-year stint with the Yankees, Cone spent one season with the Red Sox, before sitting out the 2002 campaign. Cone subsequently attempted a comeback with the Mets in 2003. But after going just 1-3 with a 6.50 ERA through late May, he announced his retirement, citing a chronic hip problem.

Over parts of 17 big-league seasons, Cone compiled a record of 194-126, an ERA of 3.46, and a WHIP of 1.256, threw 56 complete games and 22 shutouts, and struck out 2,668 batters in 2,898⅔ innings pitched. As a member of the Mets, Cone went 81-51 with a 3.13 ERA, a WHIP of 1.192, 34 complete games, 15 shutouts, and 1,172 strikeouts in 1,209⅓ innings of work.

Following his playing days, Cone remained away from the game for a few years, before joining the Yankees' broadcast team on the YES Network, where he works alongside Michael Kay and former teammate Paul O'Neill. Cone, who also has served as a color analyst on ESPN's *Sunday Night Baseball* telecasts for several years, continues to contribute to several charitable causes through the David Cone Foundation, which helps fund Joe Torre's Safe at Home Foundation (against domestic violence) and various medical causes, including the ALS Association and cancer research.

METS CAREER HIGHLIGHTS

Best Season

Cone easily had his finest season as a member of the Mets in 1988, when he earned a third-place finish in the NL Cy Young voting and a 10th-place finish in the MVP balloting by compiling a record of 20-3 that gave him a league-best winning percentage of .870, posting a WHIP of 1.115, throwing 231⅓ innings and a career-high eight complete games, tossing four shutouts, and finishing second in the league with a 2.22 ERA and 213 strikeouts.

Memorable Moments/Greatest Performances

Cone came within four outs of tossing a no-hitter on June 19, 1988, when he yielded just two walks, a two-out, eighth-inning single by shortstop Steve Jeltz, and a ninth-inning single by center fielder Milt Thompson during a 6–0 shutout of the Phillies.

Cone threw a complete-game one-hitter on August 29, 1988, yielding just two walks and a fourth-inning double by Tony Gwynn during a 6–0 win over the Padres.

After faltering in Game 2 of the 1988 NLCS, Cone came up big for the Mets in Game 6, evening the series at three games apiece by recording six strikeouts and allowing just five hits and three walks during a 5–1 complete-game win over the Dodgers.

Cone became the 25th pitcher in MLB history to throw an immaculate inning when he struck out the side on just nine pitches in the fifth inning of a 3–2 victory over the Reds on August 30, 1991, during which he recorded nine strikeouts and allowed six hits and two runs in six innings of work.

Cone dominated the St. Louis lineup on September 20, 1991, registering 11 strikeouts, issuing one walk, and surrendering just an eighth-inning double to right fielder Félix José during a 1–0 one-hit shutout.

Cone turned in another dominant performance in the final game of the 1991 regular season, recording 19 strikeouts and yielding just three hits and one walk during a 7–0 shutout of the Phillies.

Cone struck out 11 batters and surrendered just two hits and four walks during a 4–0 shutout of Houston on April 28, 1992, holding the Astros hitless until the top of the eighth inning, when pinch-hitter Benny Distefano reached base on an infield single with one man out.

Notable Achievements

- Won 20 games in 1988.
- Compiled ERA under 3.00 twice, finishing with mark under 2.50 once.
- Recorded more than 200 strikeouts four times.
- Threw more than 200 innings four times.
- Recorded 19 strikeouts vs Philadelphia Phillies on October 6, 1991.
- Led NL pitchers in winning percentage once, shutouts once, strikeouts twice, and strikeouts-to-walks ratio once.
- Finished second in NL in ERA once and strikeouts twice.
- Holds Mets single-season record for highest winning percentage (.870 in 1988).
- Ranks among Mets career leaders in wins (9th), winning percentage (4th), ERA (10th), strikeouts (6th), shutouts (5th), and complete games (7th).
- 1988 division champion.
- Two-time NL Player of the Week.
- May 1988 NL Pitcher of the Month.
- Finished third in 1988 NL Cy Young voting.
- Finished 10th in 1988 NL MVP voting.
- Two-time NL All-Star selection (1988 and 1992).

22
TOMMIE AGEE

The offensive catalyst of the Mets' 1969 world championship ballclub, Tommie Agee spent five seasons in New York providing "the Amazins" with power and speed at the top of their lineup and outstanding defense in center field. Batting leadoff for the Mets most of his time in Queens, Agee slugged more than 20 homers, scored more than 95 runs, and stole more than 20 bases twice each, finishing first on the team in each of those categories on multiple occasions. An excellent defender as well, Agee led all NL outfielders in putouts once, with his strong all-around play earning him one top-10 finish in the league MVP voting and a place in the Mets Hall of Fame. Yet Agee will always be remembered more than anything by Mets fans for his brilliant performance in Game 3 of the 1969 World Series that provided much of the impetus for a stunning Series win over the heavily favored Baltimore Orioles.

Born in Magnolia, Alabama, on August 9, 1942, Tommie Lee Agee moved with his family at the age of one some 30 miles northwest, to the city of Mobile, where he grew up with his nine sisters and one brother. Raised in the segregated South, Agee spent his early years living in a low-income section of a city that became known for producing an outstanding crop of baseball players that included Hall of Famers Hank Aaron, Willie McCovey, and Billy Williams.

After first displaying his considerable athletic ability in junior high school, Agee enrolled at Mobile County High, where he excelled in football, baseball, basketball, and track, starring in the first two sports alongside lifelong friend and future Mets teammate Cleon Jones. Offered a baseball scholarship to Grambling State University, a historically Black school in Louisiana, Agee performed magnificently in his one year of college ball, compiling a batting average of .533 that represented the highest single-season mark in Southwestern Athletic Conference history at the time.

Subsequently pursued by scouts from virtually every major-league team, Agee elected to forgo his final three years of college and sign with the

Tommie Agee earned a permanent place in Mets lore with his fabulous performance in Game 3 of the 1969 World Series.

Cleveland Indians for $60,000. Recalling the frenzy that surrounded his close friend, Cleon Jones said, "I was at his house when he came back after his first year at Grambling. There were thirty or forty scouts, all of them trying to talk to him, trying to get him signed. That blew me away, man."

Agee ended up spending most of the next four seasons advancing through Cleveland's farm system, appearing in a total of only 31 games with the parent club, before being included in a three-team trade with the Chicago White Sox and Kansas City Athletics on January 20, 1965, that sent him, pitcher Tommy John, and catcher John Romano to Chicago, essentially for slugging outfielder Rocky Colavito. After one more year in the minors, Agee arrived in the big leagues to stay in 1966, when, after being named Chicago's starting center fielder during spring training, he went on to earn All-Star and AL Rookie of the Year honors by hitting 22 homers, driving in 86 runs, scoring 98 times, stealing 48 bases, batting .273, and posting an OPS of .773, while also leading all AL outfielders in putouts.

Despite being named an All-Star again in 1967, Agee experienced something of a sophomore jinx, finishing the season with just 14 homers, 52 RBIs, 73 runs scored, and a .234 batting average. Displeased with Agee's performance, the White Sox completed a trade with the Mets on December 15, 1967, that sent him and utility infielder Al Weis to New York for a package of four players that included hard-hitting outfielder Tommy Davis and pitcher Jack Fisher.

Claiming that new Mets manager Gil Hodges pushed hard for the deal, longtime team broadcaster Bob Murphy recalled, "The first thing Gil wanted to do was acquire Tommie Agee. He wanted a guy to bat leadoff with speed and that also could hit for power."

Agee's tenure in New York got off to an inauspicious start when Bob Gibson beaned him in his first spring training at-bat, causing him to spend several days in the hospital. Unfortunately, things did not improve much once the regular season began, with Agee finishing his first year in New York with just five homers, 17 RBIs, 30 runs scored, and a .217 batting average in 132 games and 368 official at-bats.

However, following an offseason of soul searching and a pep talk from Hodges, Agee rebounded in 1969 to establish himself as the key to the Mets' offense. In addition to leading the team with 26 homers, 76 RBIs, and 97 runs scored, Agee batted .271 and posted an OPS of .806 for the NL champions, earning in the process a sixth-place finish in the league MVP voting. Agee also provided outstanding defense in center field and helped Cleon Jones have the finest season of his career, with his longtime friend later saying, "I had a great year because of him. There weren't many people getting on base, but he was. And he made us a good defensive team. We didn't have a whole lot of offense, but we didn't beat ourselves. He made the difference defensively."

Carrying his strong play over to the postseason, Agee homered twice, knocked in four runs, batted .357, and compiled an OPS of 1.295 during the Mets' three-game sweep of Atlanta in the NLCS. Although Agee subsequently batted just .167 against the Orioles in the World Series, he almost singlehandedly defeated them in Game 3 by hitting a solo homer and saving five runs with a pair of superb catches in center field that enabled the Mets to come away with a 5–0 victory.

A strong defender, the 5'11", 195-pound Agee possessed outstanding range and an above-average throwing arm, although he occasionally experienced lapses in concentration in the outfield, causing him to lead all league center fielders in errors four times. The right-handed-swinging Agee also struck out fairly often, fanning more than 100 times in a season on five separate occasions, including three times as a member of the Mets. Nevertheless, Agee's combination of power and speed made him a tremendous threat at the top of the lineup. Equally capable of stealing a base or driving the ball into the seats, Agee, who hit one of the longest home runs in Shea Stadium history, became the first player in team annals to surpass 20 homers and 20 steals in the same season during his time in New York.

Agee accomplished the last feat in 1970, when, in addition to earning Gold Glove honors by leading all NL outfielders with 374 putouts, he hit 24 homers, knocked in 75 runs, scored 107 times, stole 31 bases, batted .286, and posted an OPS of .812. Limited by an injured knee to just 113 games the following year, Agee hit 14 homers, knocked in 50 runs, and scored 58 times, although he still managed to swipe 28 bases, bat .285, and post an OPS of .790. Plagued by back and knee problems in 1972, an overweight and out of shape Agee ceded much of his playing time in center field to Willie Mays, who the Mets acquired on May 11. Seeing action at all three outfield spots, Agee, who appeared in 114 games and garnered 422 official at-bats, slumped to 13 homers, 47 RBIs, 52 runs scored, and a .227 batting average.

Deciding to part ways with Agee at the end of the year, the Mets traded him to the Houston Astros on November 27, 1972, for backup outfielder Rich Chiles and minor-league pitcher Buddy Harris, neither of whom ended up making any sort of impact in New York. Expressing his unhappiness upon learning of the deal, Agee said, "I gave it all I had for five years. I'm very disappointed they thought so lowly of me to make that trade. It seems like they didn't want me anymore."

In trying to explain the Mets' rationale for trading Agee for so little, Steve Jacobson later wrote in *Newsday*, "There was a feeling in the front office that Agee and Cleon Jones, partners in the *Outfielder's Lounge* [restaurant] in Elmhurst, Queens, were too close; that they'd do better without each other."

Yet when asked about that notion, Agee told Jacobson, "I can't see that. I know when I do good, Cleon tries to do better. If I have a good year, Cleon doesn't want me to outdo him."

Agee, who, in his five seasons with the Mets, hit 82 homers, knocked in 265 runs, scored 344 times, collected 632 hits, 107 doubles, and 14 triples, stole 92 bases, batted .262, compiled an on-base percentage of .329, and posted a slugging percentage of .419, ended up splitting the 1973 campaign between the Astros and Cardinals, batting just .222 in 110 games and 288 total plate appearances, before announcing his retirement the following spring after being released by the Dodgers. Over parts of 12 big-league seasons, Agee hit 130 homers, knocked in 433 runs, scored 558 times, amassed 999 hits, 170 doubles, and 27 triples, stole 167 bases, batted .255, compiled a .320 on-base percentage, and posted a .412 slugging percentage.

Following his playing days, Agee returned to New York, where he became active in several youth programs and continued to operate his restaurant until the mid-1980s, when he took a job with a Manhattan insurance firm. While working for that company on January 22, 2001, the 58-year-old Agee suffered a massive heart attack on the sidewalk in front of his place of business that claimed his life.

Upon learning of his former teammate's passing, Ed Charles stated, "In that miraculous year of 1969, he was very special to us. I can't recall anyone who ever said a bad word about Tommie Agee, or anyone that wasn't taken by that disarming smile of his."

Ron Swoboda said, "He was a great friend, and the way he conducted himself after his playing days were over was admirable. He's gone way too soon."

Meanwhile, Cleon Jones, who briefly played center field for the Mets prior to Agee's arrival in New York, continued to marvel at how his close friend made playing the position at windy Shea Stadium look so easy, saying, "I hated it; every guy before me hated it. But Tommie never complained. I watched Willie Mays, Curt Flood, Vada Pinson—a lot of guys come into this Shea Stadium outfield. Nobody played it better than Tommie Agee."

Looking back on the Mets' improbable run to the 1969 world championship long after his playing career ended, Agee said, "When I think back, I take pride in how I was a vital part of that team the whole year. Most of the guys on that team platooned, but I played every day, and I hustled on the field. I don't think I get the credit I deserve on that particular team for what I did, but the fans remember, and they tell me about it every day as I walk the streets of New York. . . . When you win in New York, it just happens to carry on. Every day I walk around the city and people stop me and want to talk about 1969. They remember some home run I hit or the time I stole home in the 10th inning. They remember that team."

METS CAREER HIGHLIGHTS

Best Season

Despite the many contributions he made during the championship campaign of 1969, Agee had his finest all-around season for the Mets in 1970, when, in addition to leading all NL outfielders in putouts, he hit 24 homers, knocked in 75 runs, stole 31 bases, and established career-high marks with 107 runs scored, 182 hits, 30 doubles, 298 total bases, a .286 batting average, a .469 slugging percentage, and an OPS of .812.

Memorable Moments/Greatest Performances

Agee led the Mets to a 4–2 win over the Expos on April 10, 1969, by hitting a pair of solo homers, one of which landed in the left field upper deck at Shea Stadium, some 480 feet from home plate. Commenting on Agee's tremendous blow, which proved to be the only homer ever hit to that part of the ballpark, teammate Ron Swoboda said, "It would have hit the bus in the parking lot if it hadn't hit the seats."

Agee contributed to a 9–4 victory over the Giants on June 10, 1969, by going 4-for-5 with two homers, three RBIs, and three runs scored.

Agee again homered twice during a 9–7 win over the Expos on July 13, 1969, this time driving in four runs and scoring four times.

Agee gave the Mets a 1–0 win over the Giants on August 19, 1969, when he homered off starter Juan Marichal with one man out in the bottom of the 14th inning.

Agee had what *Sports Illustrated* called "the greatest day any centerfielder ever had in a World Series" in Game 3 of the 1969 Fall Classic, when he led the Mets to a 5–0 win over the Orioles by homering once and making two spectacular catches in center field that prevented five runs from scoring. After leading off the bottom of the first inning with a home run to center field off Jim Palmer, Agee saved two runs in the top of the fourth inning by making a tremendous backhand catch near the base of the wall in left-center field on a drive hit by Elrod Hendricks. Three innings later, Agee robbed Paul Blair of a three-run triple when he made a superb diving grab in deep right-center field with the bases loaded and two men out.

Agee contributed to an 8–1 win over the Braves on June 12, 1970, by going 4-for-5 at the plate with a pair of solo homers and four runs scored.

Agee hit for the cycle during a 10–3 win over the Cardinals on July 6, 1970, going 4-for-5 with four RBIs and two runs scored.

Agee gave the Mets a 2–1 win over the Dodgers on July 24, 1970, when he recorded a straight steal of home with two men out in the bottom of the 10th inning.

Agee helped lead the Mets to a 12–9 win over the Pirates on August 8, 1970, by going 5-for-6 with a triple, two doubles, a stolen base, two RBIs, and four runs scored.

Agee led the Mets to a 5–4 victory over the Reds on August 23, 1970, by going 4-for-4 with a pair of solo homers.

After singling and doubling earlier in the contest, Agee gave the Mets an 8–6 win over the Padres on May 7, 1972, when he homered with two men out and one man aboard in the bottom of the 10th inning.

Notable Achievements

- Hit more than 20 home runs twice.
- Scored more than 100 runs once.
- Stole more than 20 bases twice, topping 30 thefts once.
- Hit for the cycle vs St. Louis Cardinals on July 6, 1970.
- Led NL outfielders in putouts once.
- 1969 division champion.
- 1969 NL champion.
- 1969 world champion.
- 1969 NL Comeback Player of the Year.
- June 1970 NL Player of the Month.
- 1970 Gold Glove Award winner.
- Finished sixth in 1969 NL MVP voting.
- Inducted into Mets Hall of Fame in 2002.

23
RUSTY STAUB

Acquired from the Montreal Expos just prior to the start of the 1972 campaign for a package of three promising young players, Rusty Staub spent the next four seasons in New York patrolling right field and anchoring the middle of the Mets' batting order. The driving force behind the team's successful march to the 1973 NL pennant, Staub hit 19 homers twice, batted over .290 once, posted an OPS over .800 twice, and knocked in more than 75 runs three times, becoming in 1975 the first player in franchise history to surpass 100 RBIs in a season. Although the Mets elected to part ways with Staub following the conclusion of the 1975 campaign, he later returned to New York, where he spent the last five seasons of his career assuming the role of a part-time player and pinch-hitter deluxe, establishing himself in the process as one of the most popular players in team annals.

Born in New Orleans, Louisiana, on April 1, 1944, Daniel Joseph Staub acquired the nickname Rusty before he even left the hospital, with his mother, Alma, recalling, "I wanted to name him Daniel so I could call him Danny for short. But one of the nurses nicknamed him Rusty for the red fuzz he had all over his head, and it stuck."

Although Rusty and his older brother Chuck acquired their love of baseball from their father, Ray, a schoolteacher and former minor-league catcher, Chuck remembered in the book, *Rusty Staub of the Expos*, "He [Ray] didn't push us into sports. It was just there, and we loved it. But I'm sure if Rusty or myself wanted to play the violin, Dad would have bust a gut swinging a deal for the best violin money could buy."

After combining with his brother to help lead Jesuit High School to the 1960 American Legion national championship and the 1961 Louisiana State AAA championship, Rusty received scholarship offers from several colleges for both baseball and basketball. Ultimately choosing to sign with the newly minted Houston Colt .45s (who later changed their name to the Astros) for $100,000 in September 1961, Staub spent just one full season in the minors, before being promoted to the parent club.

Rusty Staub starred for the Mets in the 1973 postseason, homering four times and driving in 11 runs.

Barely 19 years of age when he made his major-league debut with Houston in the spring of 1963, Staub proved himself incapable of competing successfully at the big-league level, struggling terribly at the plate the next season-and-a-half while splitting his time between first base and the outfield. Demoted to the minors midway through the 1964 season, Staub spent the rest of the year rediscovering his stroke at Triple-A Oklahoma City, before returning to Houston the following year.

Far more confident in his abilities by the start of the 1965 campaign, the now 21-year-old Staub laid claim to the starting right field job, after which he gradually emerged as one of the league's better players at his position over the course of the next four seasons. A two-time All-Star during his time in Houston, Staub performed especially well for the Astros in 1967, when he homered 10 times, knocked in 74 runs, finished fifth in the league with a .333 batting average, and topped the circuit with 44 doubles.

Despite Staub's strong play, his differences with manager Harry Walker prompted the Astros to trade him to the expansion Montreal Expos prior to the start of the 1969 season. Quickly establishing himself as a fan favorite in Montreal, Staub, who became known as *Le Grand Orange* for the color of his hair, endeared himself to the locals with his willingness to learn the French language and outstanding play on the field. Having arguably the three most productive seasons of his career at Parc Jarry, whose inviting dimensions allowed him to become more of a home-run hitter and run producer, Staub earned three consecutive All-Star nominations by averaging 26 homers, 90 RBIs, and 94 runs scored from 1969 to 1971, while also compiling batting averages of .302, 274, and .311, and posting a career-high OPS of .952 in the first of those campaigns.

Nevertheless, when the Mets came calling with an offer of top outfield prospect Ken Singleton and young infielders Mike Jorgensen and Tim Foli, the Expos dealt him to New York on April 5, 1972. Unfortunately, a fractured wrist he sustained when future teammate George Stone hit him with a pitch on June 3 prevented Staub from making much of an impact his first year in Queens. Limited to only 66 games and 278 total plate appearances, Staub ended up hitting just nine homers, driving in only 38 runs, and batting .293.

Staub subsequently got off to a poor start in 1973, before rebounding to finish the season with 15 homers, 76 RBIs, 77 runs scored, 36 doubles, a .279 batting average, and an OPS of .781. Particularly outstanding down the stretch, Staub helped the Mets go on an exceptional 24-9 run that earned them the division title by batting .321 and compiling an OPS of .892. Continuing to perform well in the postseason, Staub led the Mets to a five-game victory over the powerful Cincinnati Reds in the NLCS by excelling both at the bat and in the field. In addition to hitting three homers and driving in five runs during the series, Staub made two excellent catches in right field during a 2–1 extra-inning loss in Game 4, one of which caused him to partially separate his right shoulder when he crashed into the outfield wall at Shea Stadium. Despite being unable to throw overhand because of the injury, Staub nearly led the Mets to another upset win over the Oakland Athletics in the World Series by batting .423, homering once, and knocking in six runs.

Although the lefty-swinging Staub, who stood 6'2" and weighed approximately 210 pounds when he first arrived in New York, possessed good power at the plate, he proved to be much more of a line-drive hitter than a true home-run threat. Extremely consistent, Staub generally made solid contact with the ball, striking out more than 61 times in a season just once his entire career, with Cardinals catcher Ted Simmons commenting, "If Rusty decided he wasn't going to strike out, you couldn't strike him out. I mean, it wasn't a matter of him trying to foul the ball off. He would put an at-bat on you. Every swing was critical."

Blessed with a keen batting eye and outstanding patience as well, Staub typically walked far more often than he struck out, drawing more than 100 bases on balls on two separate occasions.

Expressing his admiration for Staub as a hitter, Joe Torre, who played both with and against him at different times, stated, "He was a good hitter. He was a very studious hitter. When he was young and had a lean body, he was scary."

Although slow afoot, Staub also proved to be a capable outfielder, catching virtually everything within his reach and using his strong throwing arm to lead all NL outfielders in assists four times, including twice as a member of the Mets.

Following a slightly subpar showing in 1974 (19 homers, 78 RBIs, 65 runs, .258 average), Staub bounced back in 1975 to hit 19 homers, drive in 105 runs, score 93 times, bat .282, and post an OPS of .818, earning in the process a 14th-place finish in the NL MVP voting. But with the Mets seeking additional pitching and displeased with Staub's decision not to join the rest of the team on a trip to Japan at the end of the year, they completed a trade with the Tigers on December 12, 1975, that sent their best hitter to Detroit for veteran left-hander Mickey Lolich.

While Lolich failed miserably during his one season in Queens, Staub ended up spending three-and-a-half extremely productive years in Detroit, surpassing 20 homers and 100 RBIs twice each while serving the Tigers almost exclusively as a designated hitter. Traded back to the Expos during the latter stages of the 1979 campaign, Staub finished out the season in Montreal, before spending one year with the Texas Rangers.

A free agent at the end of 1980, a much-heavier Staub elected to return to the Mets, with whom he spent the 1981 season platooning at first base with Dave Kingman and pinch-hitting. Recalling how much not playing full-time bothered him, Staub, who, in 70 games and 186 total plate appearances, hit five homers, knocked in 21 runs, and batted .317, stated, "That was the most difficult time of my career, feeling deep down in my heart that I was the best player at my position and not being given the opportunity to play. When I agreed to come here, I told Frank Cashen I could still play regularly for a lot of teams—the money was going to be the same wherever I went—and I thought we saw eye to eye. But then they made the decision not to use me as a regular. It was the toughest adjustment I've ever made in my life."

Staub continued, "I talked with myself. I asked myself, 'What's the most important thing in my life? Should getting 3,000 hits be my predominant goal? Or should being part of the Mets, part of the community, be more important?' I needed an outside view, an analytic rather than an emotional view, so I talked to my closest friends about it. I finally decided that the best thing for my life would be to stay here."

Named a player-coach prior to the start of the 1982 campaign, Staub spent the year assuming a part-time role, before serving the Mets almost exclusively as a pinch-hitter the next three seasons. Performing brilliantly in that role, Staub, who often sported black batting gloves and choked up on the bat during the latter stages of his career, tied an NL record in 1983 by hitting safely in eight straight pinch-hitting appearances, while also equaling a single-season major-league mark by driving in 25 runs as a pinch-hitter.

Choosing to announce his retirement following the conclusion of the 1985 campaign, Staub ended his 23-year big-league career with 292 homers, 1,466 RBIs, 1,189 runs scored, 2,716 hits, 499 doubles, 47 triples, 47 stolen bases, a .279 batting average, a .362 on-base percentage, and a .431 slugging percentage. The only player to accumulate at least 500 hits for four different teams, Staub amassed 709 safeties, hit 75 homers, knocked in 399 runs, scored 296 times, collected 130 doubles and seven triples, batted .276, compiled a .358 on-base percentage, and posted a .419 slugging percentage as a member of the Mets.

In summarizing Staub's playing career some years later, Tim McCarver said, "Rusty was just a good all-around player for four different teams. He was a very good offensive player when he was older and a very good defensive player when he was younger."

Lee Mazzilli also spoke of his former Mets teammate, saying, "He was a situational-type hitter that knew what to look for, when to look for it, how to look for it in situations. When I played with Rusty, and then when I played against him, I always felt that he was going to hit the ball hard somewhere—like hard contact and be a tough out. . . . And if you needed a home run to beat you, he could do that too."

After retiring from baseball, Staub, a lifelong bachelor and gourmet cook who opened the first of his two self-named restaurants in 1977, remained in the New York area for many years, continuing to operate his eateries well into the 1990s, while also providing radio and television color commentary for Mets home games from 1986 to 1995. Staub also spent decades giving back to the community, raising millions of dollars to fight hunger, and founding the New York Police and Fire Widows' and Children's Benefit Fund, which raised money and provided additional support to families of first responders killed in the line of duty.

After surviving a heart attack in 2015, Staub passed away in a West Palm Beach, Florida, hospital on March 29, 2018, just three days before his 74th birthday, succumbing to organ failure following a month-long battle with pneumonia.

Upon learning of his former Mets teammate's passing, Ron Hodges said, "Rusty was a great hitter and leader for our team. He really studied pitchers and could accurately guess what pitch was coming. He also showed great toughness by playing through the pain of his injury when he ran into the wall in right field making that catch. Baseball lost a great friend."

Meanwhile, Keith Hernandez stated, "Obviously, this is a sad day for Met-land here. Rusty's a very dear friend. He's just been a great friend. But he was in a lot of pain. So, it's better. He's in a better place."

METS CAREER HIGHLIGHTS

Best Season

Staub had his finest all-around season as a member of the Mets in 1975, when, in addition to hitting 19 homers, driving in 105 runs, scoring 93 times, amassing 30 doubles, batting .282, and posting an OPS of .818, he led all NL outfielders with 15 assists.

Memorable Moments/Greatest Performances

Staub led the Mets to a 5–2 win over the Astros on April 25, 1973, by going 3-for-4 with a pair of solo homers.

Staub helped lead the Mets to a 12–2 rout of the Braves on July 18, 1973, by homering twice and knocking in five runs.

Staub performed exceptionally well for the Mets in the 1973 postseason, first leading them to a five-game victory over the Reds in the NLCS by hitting three homers and driving in five runs. Particularly outstanding in Game 3, Staub knocked in four runs with a pair of homers during a 9–2 Mets win. Although the Mets subsequently lost the World Series to Oakland in seven games, Staub continued his hot hitting, homering once, driving in six runs, batting .423, and posting an OPS of 1.080, with his strongest showing coming during a 6–1 win in Game 4, when he went 4-for-4 with a homer and five RBIs.

Staub helped lead the Mets to a 9–7 win over the Phillies on September 20, 1975, by going 5-for-6 at the plate with a homer and double.

Staub gave the Mets a 6–4 victory over the Phillies on September 25, 1984, when he hit a pinch-hit two-run homer off Larry Andersen with one man out in the bottom of the ninth inning, becoming in the process just the second player in major-league history (Ty Cobb being the other) to homer as both a teenager and a 40-year-old.

Notable Achievements

- Knocked in more than 100 runs once.
- Batted over .300 once.
- Compiled on-base percentage of .400 once.
- Led NL outfielders in assists and double plays turned twice each.
- Ranks among Mets career leaders in sacrifice flies (8th) and intentional bases on balls (9th).
- 1973 division champion.
- 1973 NL champion.
- Inducted into Mets Hall of Fame in 1986.

24
ED KRANEPOOL

The longest-tenured player in franchise history, Ed Kranepool spent more seasons and appeared in more games in a Mets uniform than anyone else in team annals. Signed by the organization right out of high school at the tender age of 17, Kranepool joined the Mets in their inaugural season of 1962 with huge expectations surrounding him. Although "The Krane," as he came to be known, failed to develop into the star player Mets fans hoped he would become, he ended up spending 18 years in New York, establishing himself as one of the franchise's career leaders in several statistical categories. A onetime NL All-Star who later received the additional honor of gaining induction into the Mets Hall of Fame, Kranepool persevered through many losing seasons to take part in one world championship and two pennant-winning celebrations, making him one of the most beloved figures in team annals.

Born in the Bronx, New York, on November 8, 1944, Edward Emil Kranepool III entered the world less than four months after his father lost his life while serving his country in France during World War II. Raised by his mother mostly on the money she received from a military pension, Kranepool recalled, "We were not an affluent family, obviously on a military pension, and I guess that's why my days were spent in a playground as an athlete. When I was 10 years of age, I joined Little League, and that was the start of my baseball career."

Obsessed with baseball throughout his youth, the future Mets first baseman learned the game from his Little League coach and neighbor, Jim Schiaffo, who became a father-figure to him, with Kranepool saying, "He was a good, good friend. He had two sons, and he considered me the third son he never had. He loved baseball; he loved working with the kids."

Initially a pitcher in the Little Leagues, Kranepool spent most of his time playing first base and the outfield after he broke his left elbow while running the bases, remembering, "A guy on the opposing team stuck his leg out, and I tripped over it on the concrete. Medically, they didn't set it

Ed Kranepool appeared in more games in a Mets uniform than any other player in team annals.

properly, and it just never healed properly. I performed well afterwards, but I never pitched as well as I did."

Eventually developing into a star on the diamond after experiencing a growth spurt during his sophomore year at James Monroe High School in the Bronx, Kranepool hit 19 home runs in his three seasons on the varsity squad. Particularly outstanding in his senior year, the left-handed-swinging Kranepool broke Hall of Famer Hank Greenberg's long-standing school record by homering nine times, prompting many to begin referring to him as "the gentile Hank Greenberg." Excelling in basketball as well, the 6'3", 205-pound Kranepool earned All-City honors in his final season by averaging 24 points per game, causing several schools, including St. John's and North Carolina, to offer him scholarships. But with baseball remaining his first love and major-league scouts beating down his door, Kranepool elected to forgo college and turn pro as soon as he graduated from high school.

Although Kranepool received more lucrative offers from a few other teams, including the Yankees, he decided to sign with the expansion Mets, who provided him with an opportunity to play close to home and reach the majors quickly. Inking his deal with the Mets on June 27, 1962, on the kitchen table of his family's home at Castle Hill Avenue in the Bronx, Kranepool received an $80,000 bonus and additional incentives based on how far he progressed within the organization, later saying, "Did I get the best contract? Probably not. Money wasn't the only thing—I just wanted to play somewhere. . . . Still, it was more money than I ever expected in my life."

After purchasing a white T-bird convertible and an eight-room split-level home in White Plains that he shared with his mother, Kranepool appeared in a few games with the Mets, before joining their Triple-A affiliate in Syracuse (they only had two minor-league teams at the time). Feeling very much out of place in his new surroundings, Kranepool recalled, "I had never been away from home. I didn't know what it was like staying in a hotel by myself. I couldn't go out with the guys. Most of the guys were much older than me. . . . You come of age in a hurry. You're thrown into it. I think I was force-fed into the major leagues right away, and of course into Triple-A. You don't think you belong here because you just signed. I was playing sandlot baseball and high school baseball, and these guys are much older than me. This is their livelihood. Now you're in the real world. You wake up in a hurry."

Promoted to the parent club following a strong spring training in 1963, Kranepool spent the entire season in New York, hitting a pair of homers, driving in 14 runs, and batting .209 in 86 games and 273 official at-bats, while splitting his time between first base and right field. Playing mostly first base the following year, Kranepool hit 10 homers, knocked in 45 runs, batted .257, and compiled an OPS of .703 in 119 games, establishing himself in the process as one of the better players on a team that posted only 53 victories. Off to an excellent start in 1965, Kranepool earned the distinction of being the only Mets player named to the NL All-Star team by hitting seven homers, driving in 36 runs, and batting .288 through early July. However, he finished the year with just 10 homers, 53 RBIs, and a .253 batting average after slumping during the season's second half. Although Kranepool remained the Mets' primary first sacker the next four seasons, he often found himself being platooned, preventing him from hitting more than 16 homers or driving in more than 57 runs.

With Kranepool unable to live up to the expectations Mets fans originally set for him, he came to realize that he might have made a mistake by signing with a team that offered him such an accelerated path to the big leagues, saying years later, "It might not have been to my best advantage to get to the major leagues so fast. On an expansion team like the Mets, you have [more] inexperience than on a better ball club; a kid of 17 isn't equipped to handle that pressure. If I was on a good ballclub, the pressure to handle that wouldn't be so great. With the Mets, we were a bad ballclub. They said, 'Ed's going to lead them from a bad ballclub to the pennant.' One player, even a Hall of Famer, can't do that."

Kranepool also felt that he never learned how to hit properly since he began his major-league career at such a young age, stating, "I was aggressive, very competitive. I would swing at balls I couldn't hit, being young and anxious, and I would get out."

Meanwhile, Kranepool's first wife, Carole, claimed that her former husband's outside interests slowed his development, saying, "He was consumed by baseball, but he also had a drive within him to make money. Coming out of the Bronx, he had nothing. He was very poor. And he had this tremendous desire to be successful. And it was through baseball that he would achieve that success."

With 1969 World Series hero Donn Clendenon receiving most of the playing time at first base the following year, Kranepool saw very little action, causing him to perform terribly at the plate. Demoted to Triple-A Tidewater after compiling a batting average of just .118 through June 23, Kranepool briefly considered retirement, before accepting his re-assignment. Returning to the Mets later in the year after batting .310 in 47 games at Tidewater, Kranepool finished the season with just three RBIs and a .170 batting average. But while Kranepool admitted that his demotion to the minors had been a humbling experience, he also claimed that it helped dramatically improve his relationship with Mets manager Gil Hodges, recalling, "Gil Hodges and I had a different relationship after that. I didn't like him. I didn't like Gil Hodges when I first played. When you're on a bad ballclub, you get negative vibes around you. Certain things, he didn't like what I did; I didn't like how he handled me. When I got sent down and came back—I could've quit at that point—I did very well, and he learned to respect me, and I learned to respect him."

Reclaiming his starting first base job in 1971, Kranepool had arguably the most productive season of his career, hitting 14 homers, driving in 58 runs, scoring 61 times, batting .280, and posting an OPS of .786, while also leading all players at his position with a .998 fielding percentage. After one more year at first, Kranepool spent the next few seasons splitting his time between first base and left field, although he saw a limited amount of action at both posts. Meanwhile, as Kranepool entered the latter stages of his career, he developed into a more consistent hitter, compiling batting averages of .300, .323, .292, and .281 from 1974 to 1977. Also establishing himself as one of the finest pinch-hitters in the game, Kranepool batted .377 off the bench over the course of those four seasons, with his .486 average in 1974 (17-for-35) setting a single-season mark for pinch-hitting that still stands for players with at least 30 at-bats.

In discussing his ability to perform so well in that role, Kranepool said, "I was able to motivate myself to pinch-hit and perform. I was trying to prove the managers wrong by not playing me, and I wound up very successful."

However, Kranepool's relationship with the Mets' front office gradually deteriorated following the 1975 passing of team owner Joan Payson, with whom he shared a close relationship. Unable to get along with new GM Joe McDonald, Kranepool recalled, "I didn't have a good relationship with Joe McDonald. I didn't respect him. I didn't like him; he didn't know anything about baseball. There were termites who ate away at the organization, and he was part of the termites. Donald Grant got blamed for it, but Joe McDonald was the one who made the trades."

Released by the Mets following the conclusion of the 1979 campaign after hinting that he might retire at the end of the year, Kranepool received the news in a short notice that arrived in the mail on November 1, later saying, "I never knew I retired. I went from one thing to another."

Kranepool, who ended his playing career with 118 homers, 614 RBIs, 536 runs scored, 1,418 hits, 225 doubles, 25 triples, a .261 batting average, a .316 on-base percentage, a .377 slugging percentage, and a franchise-record 1,853 games played and 90 pinch-hits, subsequently considered purchasing part ownership of the Mets when the team went up for sale. However, a group headed by Fred Wilpon and Nelson Doubleday bought the team instead, prompting Kranepool to leave baseball for good.

Kranepool, who worked as a stockbroker during his playing days, continued to make his living on Wall Street for several years following his retirement, before opening a restaurant and taking a job with a credit card processing company. Kranepool also spent six years serving as a spokesman for Pfizer, traveling the country promoting diabetes awareness after learning that he had developed the disease. Suffering from poor health in his later years, Kranepool lost his big toe and underwent a kidney transplant, before dying of cardiac arrest at the age of 79 on September 8, 2024.

Upon learning of his longtime teammate's passing, Jerry Koosman called him "the best first baseman I ever played with," and added, "We knew each other so well, and I could tell by his eyes if a runner was going or not. He saved me a lot of stolen bases."

Ron Swoboda also paid tribute to his former teammate, saying, "If there's a Mr. Met, it's Ed Kranepool. He was through and through a New Yorker, and a New York Met."

CAREER HIGHLIGHTS

Best Season

Although Kranepool compiled an OPS of .779 and established career-high marks in batting average (.323) and on-base percentage (.370) in 1975, he appeared in only 106 games and accumulated just 325 official at-bats. That being the case, Kranepool had his finest all-around season in 1971, when, in addition to hitting 14 homers and batting .280, he reached career highs in RBIs (58), runs scored (61), and OPS (.786).

Memorable Moments/Greatest Performances

Kranepool led the Mets to a 7–6 win over the Giants on April 24, 1965, by hitting a pair of solo homers off Jack Sanford.

Kranepool starred in defeat on April 23, 1966, driving in all four runs the Mets scored during a 5–4 loss to the Braves with a pair of homers.

Kranepool accounted for both Mets runs during a 2–0 win over the Expos on April 29, 1969, with a pair of solo homers off Jim "Mudcat" Grant.

Kranepool led the Mets to a 5–2 win over the Dodgers on June 3, 1969, by homering twice and knocking in three runs.

After homering off Ferguson Jenkins earlier in the contest, Kranepool gave the Mets a 4–3 victory over the Cubs on July 8, 1969, by driving in Cleon Jones from third base with a single to left-center field with two men out in the bottom of the ninth inning.

Kranepool experienced one of the most memorable moments of his career in Game 3 of the 1969 World Series, when he plated the final run of a 5–0 victory over the Orioles with a solo homer off Dave Leonhard in the bottom of the eighth inning.

Notable Achievements

- Batted .300 or better twice.
- Holds franchise records for most games played (1,853) and most pinch-hits (90).
- Ranks among Mets career leaders in RBIs (6th), hits (3rd), extra-base hits (8th), doubles (4th), total bases (3rd), bases on balls (9th), sacrifice flies (2nd), plate appearances (2nd), and at-bats (3rd).
- Two-time division champion (1969 and 1973).
- Two-time NL champion (1969 and 1973).
- 1969 world champion.
- 1965 NL All-Star selection.
- Inducted into Mets Hall of Fame in 1990.

25

DANIEL MURPHY

A solid line-drive hitter who posted one of the highest career batting averages in team annals, Daniel Murphy spent parts of seven seasons in New York, excelling at the bat but struggling somewhat in the field at multiple positions for mostly mediocre Mets teams. A .300 hitter twice during his time in Flushing, Murphy earned one All-Star nomination with his consistently excellent hitting, which helped lead the Mets to their first division title in nearly a decade. And once in the playoffs, Murphy put on a memorable hitting performance that ranks among the greatest in postseason history.

Born in Jacksonville, Florida, on April 1, 1985, Daniel Thomas Murphy displayed a fondness for hitting a baseball at a very young age, with his father recalling, "As long as you would throw the baseball to him, he would swing the bat all day long." After getting started in his favorite pastime at a nearby batting cage, Daniel began competing in neighborhood games with his younger brother, Jonathan, who remembered, "I always looked up to Daniel and how he went about his business. He always played hard, he was passionate, and he always wanted to win."

Eventually developing into a standout in multiple sports at Englewood High School, Murphy excelled in both baseball and football, performing well enough as an infielder on the diamond to receive a scholarship to Jacksonville University. Inserted into the third spot in the batting order his first year at Jacksonville after demonstrating an unusually sophisticated grasp of hitting, Murphy drove the ball from foul line to foul line, prompting Dolphins head coach Terry Alexander to later say, "He was ahead of the game. It was more of a professional approach." A three-year starter in college, Murphy compiled a career batting average of .366 for the Dolphins, performing especially well his junior year, when he earned Atlantic Sun Conference Player of the Year honors by posting a mark of .398.

Selected by the Mets in the 13th round of the 2006 MLB Amateur Draft, with the 394th overall pick, Murphy spent most of the next three

Daniel Murphy set an MLB record by homering in six consecutive postseason games in 2015.

seasons advancing through New York's farm system, hitting well wherever he went while playing mostly third base, before being summoned to the big leagues in August 2008. With David Wright manning third base, Luis Castillo stationed at second, and Carlos Delgado holding down first for the parent club, Murphy moved to left field, where he struggled with the glove but batted .313 over the final two months of the season. Inserted at first base the following year after Delgado sustained a serious injury to his hip that forced him to undergo surgery, Murphy had a solid season, batting .266, posting an OPS of .741, driving in 63 runs, amassing 38 doubles, and leading the powerless Mets with 12 homers.

Murphy subsequently missed the entire 2010 season after injuring his knee during spring training and tearing his MCL during a minor-league rehab assignment. Returning to action in 2011, Murphy performed well over the first four months of the campaign, batting .320, posting an OPS of .809, hitting six homers, and driving in 49 runs while splitting his time in the field between first base, second, and third, before suffering a season-ending injury to his MCL in a collision with Atlanta's José Constanza on August 7.

Fully recovered by the start of the 2012 campaign, Murphy established himself as the Mets' full-time starter at second base and the team's number two hitter in the everyday lineup. Having another solid offensive season, Murphy hit six homers, knocked in 65 runs, scored 62 times, batted .291, compiled a .332 on-base percentage, and posted a .403 slugging percentage. Improving upon those numbers in 2013, Murphy hit 13 homers, knocked in 78 runs, scored 92 times, finished second in the league with 188 hits, stole 23 bases, batted .286, compiled an on-base percentage of .319, and posted a slugging percentage of .415. Although Murphy proved to be somewhat less productive at the plate in 2014, hitting just nine homers and driving in only 57 runs, he earned All-Star honors by leading the Mets with 172 hits, 37 doubles, and a .289 batting average.

Primarily a gap-to-gap hitter his first several years in the league, the left-handed-swinging Murphy drove the ball well to the power alleys at spacious Citi Field, enabling him to amass more than 35 doubles on five separate occasions. But even though Murphy surpassed 10 homers in just two of his first five full seasons with the Mets, at 6'1" and 223 pounds, he had the ability to reach the seats, which he exhibited during the 2015 playoffs.

After helping the Mets win the NL East title by hitting 14 homers, driving in 73 runs, batting .281, posting an OPS of .770, and striking out just 38 times in 538 total plate appearances, Murphy began an exceptional postseason run by homering three times, driving in five runs, and batting .333 during New York's five-game NLDS win over the Dodgers. Continuing his hot hitting against the Cubs in the NLCS, Murphy led the Mets to a four-game sweep of their overmatched opponents by hitting four homers, knocking in six runs, and batting .529, earning in the process series MVP honors. Murphy's extraordinary performance put him in elite company since, not only did he become the first player in MLB history to homer in six consecutive playoff games, but he also joined the immortal Lou Gehrig on an extremely exclusive list of men to hit safely, score at least one run, and collect at least one RBI in seven straight postseason contests.

Commenting on Murphy's sudden development into a power hitter, Mets GM Sandy Alderson stated, "I think Daniel Murphy is a different hitter today than he was two, three months ago. He's looking to do damage. He's looking sort of middle of the field and pull as opposed to kind of going the other way. More selective at the plate. I think that has a lot to do with Dan applying what [hitting coaches] Kevin Long and Pat Roessler have been advocating. So, I don't think this is a phase for him. I think that in some ways he's a fundamentally different hitter than he was, as recently as three, four months ago. And the intensity that he has in the playoff situation certainly is evident, as well. He's really focused, and he's always been sound mechanically. But I think his approach is a little bit different, which has made him a more dangerous hitter."

Meanwhile, Mets manager Terry Collins discussed Murphy's ability to prepare himself for every at-bat by retaining a tremendous amount of information, saying, "The first time I met Dan Murphy, I was the field coordinator here, and he got his knee torn up in the last game of spring training (2010), and I didn't know him. On our travels, I'd go to St. Lucie to see our teams down there, and Dan Murphy's at the rookie league game in the morning and the St. Lucie game at night. And all he talks about is baseball, so I'm not shocked that Dan Murphy is aware of every single pitch that happens during the game."

Unfortunately, Murphy came back down to earth in the World Series, batting just .150 with no homers and no RBIs during the Mets' five-game loss to Kansas City. Subsequently offered a one-year, $15.8 million deal by the Mets when he became a free agent at the end of the year, Murphy chose instead to sign with the Washington Nationals for three years and $37.5 million, thereby ending his seven-year stint in New York.

Murphy, who hit 62 homers, knocked in 402 runs, scored 422 times, collected 967 hits, 228 doubles, and 20 triples, stole 57 bases, batted .288, compiled a .331 on-base percentage, and posted a .424 slugging percentage as a member of the Mets, performed at a whole different level his first two seasons in Washington. After earning a runner-up finish in the NL MVP voting in 2016 by hitting 25 homers, driving in 104 runs, batting .347, and leading the league with 47 doubles, a .595 slugging percentage, and an OPS of .985, Murphy homered 23 times, knocked in 93 runs, batted .322, and posted an OPS of .928 the following year, garnering in the process All-Star and Silver Slugger honors for the second straight time. Meanwhile, after struggling with his defense his entire time in New York, Murphy turned himself into a competent fielder, committing a total of just 20 errors over the course of those two seasons.

Although Murphy remained a productive hitter for the rest of his career, he failed to perform at the same elite level, never again hitting more than 13 homers, driving in more than 78 runs, or batting any higher than .299. Choosing to announce his retirement following the conclusion of the 2020 campaign after splitting the previous three seasons between the Nationals, Cubs, and Colorado Rockies, Murphy ended his career with 138 homers, 735 RBIs, 710 runs scored, 1,572 hits, 371 doubles, 29 triples, 68 stolen bases, a .296 batting average, a .341 on-base percentage, and a .455 slugging percentage.

After making an unsuccessful comeback attempt with the minor-league Salt Lake Bees in 2023, Murphy retired for good. He subsequently settled in Nashville, Tennessee, where he enjoys being part of the community and availing himself of the city's vibrant culture. Murphy later assumed a part-time broadcasting position with SNY, for whom he occasionally does color commentary on Mets games.

METS CAREER HIGHLIGHTS

Best Season

Despite his fabulous postseason performance in 2015, Murphy posted his best overall numbers as a member of the Mets in 2013, when he hit 13 homers, knocked in 78 runs, batted .286, compiled an OPS of .733, and finished in the league's top 10 in runs scored (92), hits (188), doubles (38), total bases (273), and steals (23).

Memorable Moments/Greatest Performances

Murphy led the Mets to a 7–4 win over the Nationals on May 27, 2009, by driving in five runs with a homer, double, and single.

Murphy knocked in all four runs the Mets scored during a 4–2 win over the Cubs on September 6, 2009, with a homer, triple, and single.

Murphy contributed to a lopsided 17–1 victory over the Cubs on June 27, 2012, by hitting a pair of homers and driving in four runs.

Murphy helped lead the Mets to an 11–0 rout of the Nationals on July 26, 2013, by going 4-for-5 with two homers, five RBIs, and three runs scored.

Murphy put on a memorable performance during the 2015 playoffs, first leading the Mets to a five-game victory over the Dodgers in the NLDS by hitting three homers, driving in five runs, scoring five times, batting .333, and posting an OPS of 1.143.

Even better in the NLCS, Murphy hit four homers, knocked in six runs, scored six times, batted .529, compiled a slugging percentage of 1.294, and posted an OPS of 1.850 during the Mets' four-game sweep of the Cubs. Especially outstanding in Game 4, Murphy went 4-for-5 with a homer, double, and two RBIs.

Notable Achievements

- Batted over .300 twice.
- Topped 40 doubles once.
- Stole more than 20 bases once.
- Finished second in NL with 188 hits in 2013.
- Ranks among Mets career leaders in batting average (7th) and doubles (3rd).
- Holds MLB record for most consecutive postseason games with a home run (6).
- 2015 division champion.
- 2015 NL champion.
- September 1, 2013, NL Player of the Week.
- 2015 NLCS MVP.
- 2014 NL All-Star selection.

26
AL LEITER

Plagued by injuries and inconsistency early in his career, Al Leiter seemed unlikely to ever amount to much after his first few years in the big leagues. However, after overcoming his various ailments and learning how to better control his emotions, Leiter developed into one of the better southpaws in the game, contributing significantly to teams that won three pennants and two World Series by posting double-digit win totals 10 straight times. Having most of his finest seasons for the Mets from 1998 to 2004, Leiter helped lead the team he followed as a youth to two playoff appearances and one NL championship by winning at least 15 games three times, while also throwing more than 200 innings on three separate occasions. Perhaps best remembered for authoring one of the finest big-game pitching performances in team annals, Leiter earned one All-Star nomination during his time in New York, before being further honored by gaining induction into the Mets Hall of Fame.

Born in Toms River, New Jersey, on October 23, 1965, Alois Terry Leiter grew up with his five brothers and two sisters in nearby Bayville, where he acquired a love of baseball at an early age even though he never developed a close relationship with his father, who divorced his mother shortly after he turned 14 years of age. A huge fan of the Mets, Leiter later described summers in New Jersey as "WOR, Bob Murphy, Lindsey Nelson, and Ralph Kiner."

Establishing himself as a star on the diamond at Central Regional High School, Leiter gradually emerged as one of the finest pitchers in the state, performing especially well his senior year, when he threw consecutive no-hitters and fanned 32 batters during a 13-inning game, en route to earning All-America honors. Selected by the Yankees in the second round of the 1984 MLB Amateur Draft following his graduation, Leiter expressed high hopes and tremendous confidence upon signing with New York's "other team," stating, "I want to be another Tom Seaver. I really think I'm going to do it, too."

Al Leiter's two-hit shutout of Cincinnati in a one-game playoff in 1999 earned the Mets a postseason berth.

However, it took Leiter several years to reach his full potential. After spending almost four full seasons toiling in the Yankees' farm system, where Ron Guidry taught him how to throw the cut fastball that eventually became his signature pitch, Leiter received brief callups to the parent club in both 1987 and 1988. Struggling terribly with his control in his 18 total mound appearances, Leiter issued 48 bases on balls in 80 innings of work. Meanwhile, Leiter displayed a lack of composure, with former Yankees teammate Tommy John later saying, "If they had named him to start on Opening Day [in 1989], he wouldn't have slept for a week. That's how highstrung he was. He was a rookie bouncing off the walls."

Having finally grown weary of waiting for Leiter to mature, the Yankees traded him to the Toronto Blue Jays for outfielder Jesse Barfield during the early stages of the 1989 campaign. Leiter subsequently missed virtually all of the next four seasons due to problems with his elbow and left shoulder, which required two arthroscopic surgeries, before beginning his major-league career in earnest in 1993, when he won nine games for the world champion Blue Jays. A regular member of Toronto's starting rotation the next two years, Leiter pitched fairly well, posting a total of 17 victories. However, Leiter didn't develop into a top-flight starter until after he signed as a free agent with the Florida Marlins, for whom he compiled an overall record of 27-21 from 1996 to 1997, earning All-Star honors in the first of those campaigns by going 16-12 with a 2.93 ERA.

But Marlins owner Wayne Huizenga chose to part ways with almost all of his team's higher priced players after Florida won the 1997 World Series, so Leiter found himself heading home to join his beloved Mets when they acquired him on February 6, 1998, for a package of three minor-league players that included outfielder Rob Stratton and pitchers A. J. Burnett and Jesús Sánchez.

Reaching new heights upon his arrival in New York, Leiter earned a sixth-place finish in the 1998 NL Cy Young voting by ranking among the league leaders with 17 wins (against six losses) and an ERA of 2.47, while also registering 174 strikeouts in 193 innings of work. Although Leiter proved to be somewhat less effective during the 1999 regular season, going just 13-12 with a 4.23 ERA, he earned a permanent place in Mets lore by shutting out the Reds on just two hits in a "winner take all" one-game playoff at Cinergy Field in Cincinnati for the NL Wild Card berth, thereby sending his team to the playoffs for the first time since 1988. Returning to top form in 2000, Leiter helped the Mets advance to the playoffs again by compiling a record of 16-8 and an ERA of 3.20, posting a WHIP of 1.212, and striking out 200 batters in 208 innings pitched, garnering in the process his second All-Star nomination.

An extremely hard thrower early in his career, the 6'2", 205-pound Leiter gradually developed into more of a finesse pitcher, although he continued to depend primarily on his cutter, sinking fastball, and sharp-breaking slider to retire opposing batters. As his career progressed, Leiter also gained better command of his pitches. Nevertheless, he became known for working deep into counts, causing him to often throw well over 100 pitches. Meanwhile, despite his maturation into a more polished pitcher, Leiter remained fidgety and nervous on the mound, exhibiting a variety of quirks that included chomping on his glove and stomping around. But while Leiter's idiosyncrasies often made his teammates chuckle, they further endeared him to Mets manager Bobby Valentine, who stated, "Everyone says you're supposed to control your emotions. Al allowed his to propel him forward. I appreciated that."

Very much enjoying his time with the Mets, Leiter particularly delighted in meeting former members of the organization, mentoring his younger teammates, and talking pitching on team flights with Tom Seaver, who served as a Mets broadcaster from 1999 to 2005. A New Yorker through-and-through, Leiter also gave back to the community through his Leiter's Landing Foundation, which he started with his wife, Lori, to raise funds for the education, health, and social awareness of children in the area. Playing a key role as well in the team's efforts to bring comfort to the families of September 11 victims, Leiter, said Bobby Valentine, "has a great way of looking into someone's eyes when talking to them. You feel like he's looking right into your brain or soul. He was able to show the compassion that was needed in a very sincere way."

Leiter remained a staple of the Mets' starting rotation for the next three seasons, going 11-11 with a 3.31 ERA in 2001 and 13-13 with an ERA of 3.48 the following year, before compiling a record of 15-9 and an ERA of 3.99 in 2003. But after Leiter won 10 of his 18 decisions and posted an ERA of 3.21 for a Mets team that finished well out of contention for the fourth straight time in 2004, management declined his $10 million option for 2005, making him a free agent.

Leiter, who compiled an overall record of 95-67, an ERA of 3.42, and a WHIP of 1.300, threw 10 complete games and seven shutouts, and struck out 1,106 batters in 1,360 total innings of work as a member of the Mets, subsequently signed with the Florida Marlins, with whom he spent the first half of the 2005 campaign, before finishing out the season back in New York with the Yankees. Choosing to retire at the end of the year, Leiter, who posted a record of 162-132, an ERA of 3.80, and a WHIP of 1.386, threw 16 complete games, tossed 10 shutouts, and registered 1,974 strikeouts in 2,391 innings pitched over parts of 19 big-league seasons, said upon making his announcement, "I love the game, but when you've been a front-end starter, that's the way you think of yourself. I think I can still get people out, but my body tells me differently."

Having previously worked as a studio analyst for ESPN during its postseason telecasts in 1998 and 1999, Leiter transitioned seamlessly into a career in broadcasting following his playing days. Joining the YES Network in 2006, Leiter spent the next 13 years doing color commentary and studio analysis of Yankees games, before becoming in 2019 a baseball operations advisor for the Mets. In that position, Leiter focuses on scouting and player development at all levels of the organization, with an emphasis on mental preparation for pitchers. Leiter and his wife also continue to manage their Leiter's Landing Foundation from their home in Summit, New Jersey.

METS CAREER HIGHLIGHTS

Best Season

Although Leiter threw more innings (208) and struck out more batters (200) in 2000, he pitched his best ball for the Mets in 1998, when he established career-best marks in wins (17), ERA (2.47), WHIP (1.150), complete games (four), and shutouts (two).

Memorable Moments/Greatest Performances

Leiter tossed his first shutout as a member of the Mets on May 23, 1998, when he allowed just four hits, issued one walk, and recorded seven strikeouts during a 3–0 win over the Brewers.

Although Leiter didn't figure in the decision, he allowed just two runs and recorded a career-high 15 strikeouts over the first seven innings of a 13-inning, 5–4 win over the Cubs on August 1, 1999.

Leiter turned in his most memorable performance as a member of the Mets on October 4, 1999, when, in a one-game playoff to determine which team advanced to the divisional round of the postseason tournament, he allowed just two hits, issued four walks, and recorded seven strikeouts during a 5–0 shutout of the Reds.

Leiter hurled another gem on August 13, 2000, when he registered 12 strikeouts and yielded just two hits and one walk over the first eight innings of a 2–0 win over the Giants.

Leiter shut out the Phillies on just five hits on September 10, 2000, issuing two walks and striking out nine batters during a 3–0 Mets win.

Leiter topped that performance on April 18, 2002, yielding just two hits and two walks during a 1–0 shutout of the Expos in which he also recorded eight strikeouts.

Leiter made history on April 30, 2002, when he became the first pitcher to defeat all 30 major-league teams by allowing just three hits and no earned runs over the first seven innings of a 10–1 win over the Diamondbacks.

Notable Achievements

- Won at least 15 games three times.
- Compiled ERA under 3.00 once.
- Recorded 200 strikeouts once.
- Threw more than 200 innings three times.
- Ranks among Mets career leaders in wins (6th), winning percentage (tied for 7th), strikeouts (8th), innings pitched (7th), and starts (6th).
- 2000 NL champion.
- 2000 Roberto Clemente Award winner.
- Two-time NL Pitcher of the Month.
- 2000 NL All-Star selection.
- Inducted into Mets Hall of Fame in 2023.

27
BILLY WAGNER

One of baseball's premier closers for more than a decade, Billy Wagner served as the ace of three different bullpens over the course of a lengthy major-league career that spanned parts of 16 seasons. A hard-throwing left-hander who depended primarily on his blazing fastball to retire opposing batters, Wagner spent 10 years closing out games for the Houston Astros and Philadelphia Phillies, earning four All-Star nominations and one top-five finish in the NL Cy Young voting by amassing a total of 284 saves, before arriving in New York in 2006. Continuing to excel on the mound for the next three seasons, Wagner gained All-Star recognition two more times by collecting another 101 saves for the Mets, in helping them capture their first division title in nearly two decades. Yet Wagner will always be remembered by Mets fans as much as anything for his outspoken nature and controversial comments that rubbed many of his teammates the wrong way.

Born to teenage parents in Marion, Virginia, on July 25, 1971, William Edward Wagner grew up in poverty, later describing a typical breakfast as "a few crackers with peanut butter and a glass of water." Raised in a toxic environment characterized by frequent domestic squabbles between his mother and father, who divorced shortly after he turned five years of age, Billy and his younger sister, Chastity, spent most of their youth being shuttled back and forth between their parents and grandparents. Finally gaining some sense of stability in his life after he moved in with his aunt, uncle, and cousins at the age of 14, Wagner spent the rest of his teenage years living some 30 miles northwest of Marion, in the Tannersville/Tazwell region of Virginia.

An outstanding all-around athlete, Wagner, a natural right-hander who, after breaking his right arm twice at the age of seven while playing football, learned to throw left-handed, starred in baseball and football at Tazewell High School. Especially proficient on the diamond, Wagner excelled as both a center fielder and pitcher, earning Virginia Region IV Player of the Year honors as a senior in 1990 by batting .451 and stealing 23 bases, while

Billy Wagner gained All-Star recognition twice as a member of the Mets.

also posting a record of 7-1, compiling an ERA of 1.52, and striking out 116 batters in only 46 innings of work. But with Wagner standing just 5'5" and weighing only 135 pounds at the time, he received very little attention from major-league scouts or Division I schools, prompting him to enroll at Ferrum College, a small Division III liberal arts college located in Ferrum, Virginia.

After playing both baseball and football during his freshman year, Wagner chose to focus exclusively on further developing his mound skills when Ferrum's defensive coordinator suggested he do so after watching him pitch in the spring. Embarking on a weightlifting program, Wagner added some

40 pounds onto his frame, allowing him to increase the velocity on his fastball from 84 to 98 mph. Developing into a dominant pitcher, Wagner struck out 327 batters in 182⅓ total innings of work and set an NCAA career record that still stands by allowing just 2.22 hits per nine innings pitched.

Creating quite a stir with his extraordinary mound work, Wagner made tiny Ferrum the place to be on days he pitched, with veteran MLB evaluator Roy Clark remembering, "Billy's junior year, you couldn't even get a seat in the stands when he started. Not only scouts, but word of mouth from all over the area. When Billy was on the mound, it was a show. . . . For all three years, he was appointment viewing. It was such an event in that little town."

Recalling the first time he saw Wagner pitch, Clark said, "I was scouting with Atlanta at the time, but I would go up to Ferrum and do the clinics. I go up there one time, and Coach Abe Naff says to me, 'Roy, I want you to see this left-hander I got.' So, the kid started throwing. I break out the radar gun—and at the time, I knew my gun was a couple ticks slow—but his first pitch was 95, which I think was the equivalent of 100 or 101."

Clark continued, "Someone said to me, 'I think your gun is broken.' Well, I got a couple more pitches, and it wasn't too broken. It was the hardest I've ever seen anybody throw."

Former North Carolina Wesleyan head coach Mike Fox also stood in awe of Wagner, remembering, "The first two years, he'd close Games 1 and 2 of a series and start Game 3. I vividly remember players coming back to the dugout with looks on their faces I'd never seen before. A left-hander throwing in the mid-90s? At that level, it seemed like 105. It was amazing. Certainly, the best I saw at my time at Wesleyan, for sure."

Unfortunately, Wagner's accuracy did not match his velocity, with Coach Naff stating, "He'd either strike 'em out or walk 'em early in his career. We always thought his wildness was a positive, instead of a negative."

Wagner himself admitted, "My mechanics at the beginning were . . . not good."

With Wagner having grown to 5'10" and 180 pounds by his junior year, the Astros selected him with the 12th overall pick of the 1993 MLB Amateur Draft. Wagner subsequently spent most of the next three seasons starting in the minor leagues, before making a brief appearance with the parent club toward the end of the 1995 campaign. Arriving in the big leagues to stay in 1996, Wagner worked exclusively out of the bullpen, going 2-2 with a 2.44 ERA, saving nine games, and recording 67 strikeouts and 30 walks in 51⅔ innings pitched.

Asked about his transition from starter to reliever, Wagner replied, "It's tough to blow three games in a row and have the courage to go back out there. But if you go through what I went through as a kid, not knowing if I was going to eat or who I was going to live with, this is nothing."

Named Houston's closer prior to the start of the 1997 campaign, Wagner struggled somewhat in that role the next two seasons, saving 53 games, but blowing several other opportunities. However, after adding a reliable curveball to his repertoire of pitches and improving his control in 1999, Wagner began an exceptional five-year run during which he earned three All-Star nominations and one top-five finish in the NL Cy Young voting by saving a total of 163 games, while also compiling an ERA under 2.00 twice.

Despite Wagner's outstanding pitching, the Astros grew weary of his frequent criticism of team management for trading away top talent to bring in less expensive players, prompting them to deal him to the Phillies for three young pitchers on November 3, 2003. In explaining his departure from Houston, Wagner later said, "How can I say this politely? They had become tired of my bluntness."

Wagner performed extremely well in Philadelphia the next two seasons, earning All-Star honors for the fourth time in 2005 by saving 38 games and compiling an ERA of 1.51. But his mouth got him into trouble again in July of that year when he said the Phillies "ain't got a chance" of making the playoffs and criticized his teammates for not having enough intensity, leading to a confrontational team meeting during which he claimed outfielder Pat Burrell called him a "rat."

Choosing to sign with the Mets for four years and $42 million when he became a free agent at the end of the year, Wagner said upon inking his deal with his new team, "The Mets are trying to win a World Series. I felt like this was the right place to be. There's a difference between winning and being competitive. In the end, I thought the Phillies were more interested in being competitive than winning."

Excelling in his first year in New York, Wagner helped lead the Mets to the NL East title by winning three of his five decisions, compiling an ERA of 2.24, posting a WHIP of 1.106, finishing second in the league with 40 saves, and striking out 94 batters in 72⅓ innings pitched. Commenting on his former teammate's exceptional pitching, Astros closer Brad Lidge stated, "He's the best there is in baseball. He dominates guys."

Wagner began the 2007 campaign in similar fashion, earning his fifth All-Star nomination by successfully converting 17 of his 18 save opportunities and compiling an ERA of 1.64 through the first week of July. However, even though Wagner finished the season with 34 saves, a 2.63 ERA, and 80 strikeouts in 68⅓ innings pitched, he failed to perform at the same elite level following the All-Star break, struggling in particular during the month of August, when he posted an ERA of 6.23.

Wagner gained All-Star recognition again in 2008 by saving 27 games, compiling an ERA of 2.30, posting a WHIP of 0.894, and recording 52 strikeouts in 47 innings of work, before missing the final month of the season after tearing the ulnar collateral ligament and the flexor pronator tendon in his left elbow. Prior to being shut down, though, Wagner created controversy by criticizing some of his teammates for what he perceived to be their lack of professionalism.

After denouncing starting pitcher Oliver Pérez for lasting just 1⅔ innings during a home loss to Pittsburgh a few weeks earlier, Wagner accused unnamed teammates—presumably Carlos Delgado and Carlos Beltrán—for not being accountable to the media following a 1–0 loss to the Washington Nationals on May 15, saying in an expletive-filled tirade, "Somebody want to tell me why the closer is being interviewed, and I didn't even play . . . and why they are over there and not being interviewed? I got it; they're gone [from the clubhouse]. Big shocker."

Continuing to air his grievances during his weekly interview with Michael Kay of ESPN a few days later, Wagner said, "I was not a participant in the game. And the guys that had participated were gone. We're all upset and we're all unhappy about the way we were playing. I hadn't even played; I had no role in the game. David Wright is always there. The same guys are always there. But there needs to be the other guys accountable."

When asked if his comments were directed toward the team's Latin players, Wagner responded, "I think it's just certain guys. I don't think it's Latin, white or black. I don't think it's a color thing. I think some guys need to stand there and take the bad with the good."

Ultimately accused by some of being racially biased, Wagner addressed those charges by saying, "I'm getting all kinds of criticism for calling out a guy [Delgado], and for being a racist. It's a little much. I didn't even say a name. Now, the fans think I'm some racist bigot who wants to go after my teammates. Like I said, it's a bit much."

While Wagner later backtracked from his comments and personally apologized to Delgado for making such negative insinuations about him that appeared in the newspapers, the Mets suggested that others not put too much stock in his remarks, with manager Willie Randolph saying, "Billy is going to be honest and straightforward. Sometimes, Billy gets a little frustrated and says what he feels. I don't try to put any gag on anyone, but you have to be smart enough to know in some cases that you're being used, and that you need to really be guarded in what you say."

After undergoing Tommy John surgery to repair his injured elbow, Wagner missed most of the 2009 season, appearing in just two games with the Mets, before being traded to the Red Sox for a pair of nondescript players in late August. Upon completion of the deal, Mets GM Omar Minaya stated, "He [Wagner] wanted to be part of a pennant race. We were able to get a couple of prospects for him. We felt it was the right thing to do."

Wagner, who compiled a record of 5-5, an ERA of 2.37, and a WHIP of 1.054, saved 101 games, and struck out 230 batters in 189⅔ innings pitched during his time in New York, finished out the season in Boston, before signing with Atlanta as a free agent at the end of the year. After earning All-Star honors for the Braves in 2010 by amassing 37 saves, winning seven of his nine decisions, and compiling an ERA of 1.43, the 39-year-old Wagner announced his retirement, ending his career with 422 saves, an overall record of 47-40, an ERA of 2.31, a WHIP of 0.998, and 1,196 strikeouts in 903 total innings of work—figures that gained him induction into the Baseball Hall of Fame the final time his name appeared on the ballot in 2025.

Following his playing days, Wagner returned home to Virginia, where he became a full-time dad to his four children, worked on the family farm, and eventually became the head baseball coach at The Miller School of Albemarle. Concerned greatly with the welfare of others, Wagner also remains heavily involved with the Second Chance Learning Center he established in 2005 to assist at-risk youth with counseling and other help.

METS CAREER HIGHLIGHTS

Best Season

Wagner posted his best overall numbers as a member of the Mets in 2006, when he earned Cy Young consideration (he finished sixth in the voting) by going 3-2 with a 2.24 ERA, a WHIP of 1.106, 40 saves, and 94 strikeouts in 72⅓ innings pitched.

Memorable Moments/Greatest Performances

Wagner earned a 7–6 victory over the Yankees on May 19, 2006, by working a perfect ninth inning during which he needed only 12 pitches to strike out the side.

Wagner recorded the 300th save of his career when he worked a scoreless ninth inning during a 7–6 win over the Pirates on July 4, 2006.

Wagner threw 21 consecutive scoreless innings from June 15 to August 8, 2007, allowing just 11 hits, winning his lone decision, and converting all 12 of his save opportunities.

Notable Achievements

- Saved more than 30 games twice, topping 40 saves once.
- Compiled ERA under 3.00 three times, posting mark under 2.50 twice.
- Posted WHIP under 1.000 once.
- Finished second in NL with 40 saves in 2006.
- Ranks sixth in franchise history in saves.
- 2006 division champion.
- Two-time NL All-Star selection (2007 and 2008).
- Elected to Baseball Hall of Fame by members of BBWAA in 2025.

28
JOHN OLERUD

One of the finest all-around first basemen of his era, John Olerud spent parts of 17 seasons in the major leagues contributing to the success of teams that won five division titles and two world championships with his consistently excellent hitting and superior defense. An outstanding contact hitter who also possessed good power at the plate, Olerud hit more than 20 homers five times, knocked in more than 100 runs four times, and batted over .300 on four separate occasions, earning in the process two All-Star nominations and one top-five finish in the league MVP voting. A member of the Mets from 1997 to 1999, Olerud help lead a resurgence that resulted in an appearance in the 1999 NLCS by surpassing 20 homers twice, while also driving in more than 90 runs and compiling an on-base percentage over .400 each season. The Mets single-season record holder for highest batting average and highest on-base percentage, Olerud also set franchise marks for highest career batting average, on-base percentage, and OPS, before departing for Seattle, where he helped lead the Mariners to an MLB-record 116 regular-season wins in 2001.

Born in Seattle, Washington, on August 5, 1968, John Garrett Olerud acquired his love of baseball from his father, John Sr., a onetime minor-league player who eventually became a dermatologist and professor of medicine at the University of Washington. Developing into a standout on the diamond himself at Interlake High School in nearby Bellevue, Olerud, who also played varsity basketball and golf, earned All-County and All-State honors his senior year by leading the Saints to the state championship with his excellent work as both a pitcher and first baseman.

Selected by the Mets in the 27th round of the 1986 MLB Amateur Draft, the 17-year-old Olerud chose instead to enroll at Washington State University, where he earned All-America honors as a freshman by batting .414, while also compiling a record of 8-2 and an ERA of 3.00. Even better his sophomore year, Olerud gained recognition from *Baseball America* as the College Player of the Year by hitting 23 homers, knocking in 81 runs,

John Olerud holds franchise records for highest career batting average, on-base percentage, and OPS.

batting .464, going a perfect 15-0 with a 2.49 ERA on the mound, and recording 113 strikeouts in 122⅔ innings pitched, becoming in the process the first player in college baseball history to win 15 games and surpass 20 home runs in the same season.

With a career in professional baseball looming on the horizon, Olerud experienced a major setback in January 1989, when he collapsed one afternoon while jogging around the Washington State athletics complex. Subsequently diagnosed with a subarachnoid hemorrhage, which caused bleeding into his spinal column, Olerud remained in the hospital for two weeks, before returning to class. However, a visit a few weeks later to Dr. Richard Winn, the head of neurosurgery at the University of Washinton, revealed a life-threatening brain aneurysm that forced Olerud to undergo six hours of extremely high-risk surgery. While the operation proved successful, Olerud began wearing a helmet on the baseball field at all times when he eventually returned to action—a practice he continued throughout his career.

After rejoining the Cougars in the spring, Olerud decided to skip the 1989 MLB Draft and return to Washington State for his senior year, telling teams not to pick him. Nevertheless, the Toronto Blue Jays selected him in the third round, after which they made him an offer he couldn't refuse. In addition to presenting Olerud with a three-year contract worth $800,000 that included a $250,000 signing bonus, the Blue Jays promised Olerud that he would start his career in the majors, prompting him to later say, "They made me an offer that was too good to pass up. I had an opportunity to be in a pennant race, and that's something a lot of great players never experience . . . I didn't think they could offer me enough to drive me away from Washington State, but what they came up with were things I couldn't have had after my senior year."

Olerud, who left Washington State as the school's career leader in batting average (.434), slugging percentage (.824), and wins for a pitcher (26), ended up appearing in six games with the Blue Jays during the month of September, before assuming the role of a part-time DH in 1990, when he earned a fourth-place finish in the AL Rookie of the Year voting by hitting 14 homers, driving in 48 runs, and batting .265. Despite those relatively modest numbers, Olerud made an extremely favorable impression on teammate Pat Borders, who commented, "He has unbelievable ability. It makes me mad because I work so hard, and I could never have a swing as nice as his. He reminds you of Wade Boggs—he has a super eye and a great swing. Everything is so compact, it's hard to make him look bad on any pitch."

Toronto's starting first baseman in each of the next three seasons, Olerud served as a key member of teams that won three straight division titles and two World Series, performing especially well in 1993, when he earned All-Star honors and a third-place finish in the AL MVP balloting by hitting 24 homers, driving in 107 runs, scoring 109 times, collecting 200 hits, and leading the league with 54 doubles, a .363 batting average, a .473 on-base percentage, and an OPS of 1.072.

Although Olerud posted decent offensive numbers the next three seasons, he failed to come close to matching his 1993 totals, causing him to fall out of favor with team management, which elected to trade him to the Mets for right-handed pitcher Robert Person following the conclusion of the 1996 campaign.

Recalling the circumstances surrounding the deal, former Blue Jays GM Gord Ash stated, "They [Olerud and Toronto's coaching staff] just weren't on the same page. John was not a pull hitter. John was a guy who liked to spray the ball around the field, with a high batting average and a good on-base percentage. . . . A lot of people like to think of first base as a power position. I don't think it's essential, but it just got to the point where it was better for him and better for us if we moved on. I don't think we got enough return for him at the time."

Feeling somewhat liberated upon being informed of the trade, Olerud said at the time, "It's been frustrating the last couple of years to not play as well as I feel I'm capable of playing. I'm looking forward to the new opportunity, turning things around, and having a good year."

Adapting well to New York, Olerud had an excellent season for the Mets in 1997, helping to lead them to their first winning record in seven years by hitting 22 homers, driving in 102 runs, scoring 90 times, batting .294, compiling an on-base percentage of .400, and posting a slugging percentage of .489. Olerud followed that up in 1998 by hitting 22 homers, knocking in 93 runs, scoring 91 times, and placing near the top of the league rankings with a .354 batting average, a .447 on-base percentage, and an OPS of .998, earning in the process praise from Mets manager Bobby Valentine, who stated, "I don't know if there is a better pure hitter there. But as far as who I want to put up there for one hit, or who hits the best, I'd have to vote for John. Maybe I'm prejudiced because he's my guy, but if I wanted to go out and watch a pure hitter in New York, I'd have to buy a ticket to see John."

Teammate Mike Piazza added, "He's so disciplined. You watch him every day, and he just does not make mistakes with his at-bats."

Meanwhile, in addressing the success he experienced during his first two seasons in Queens, the always modest and soft-spoken Olerud said in his typically understated manner, "I don't feel like I've got it all figured out just yet. But I feel like I've gotten better and more comfortable as the years go by at just knowing what I need to do to be successful, and to help a team."

Blessed with one of the sweetest swings in the game, the left-handed-hitting Olerud, who stood 6'5" and weighed 210 pounds, used the entire field, almost always put the ball in play when he swung the bat, and drove the ball well to the outfield gaps, amassing at least 30 doubles in a season 10 times during his career. An extremely patient hitter with excellent knowledge of the strike zone, Olerud, who consistently ranked among the league leaders in bases on balls, also knew how to work the count, with former Blue Jays teammate Pat Hentgen saying, "I know as a starting pitcher, facing a guy like John Olerud was a nightmare because he's going to walk, he's not a selfish hitter, and he could spray the ball over the field. He was an incredibly tough out, and he could beat you in many different ways. Even a down year for him was a great season overall."

Outstanding with the glove as well, Olerud once appeared on the cover of *Sports Illustrated* with second baseman Edgardo Alfonzo, shortstop Rey Ordóñez, and third baseman Robin Ventura when the magazine identified the quartet as the "greatest defensive infield in baseball history."

Olerud had another excellent year for the Mets in 1999, helping them advance to the playoffs as a wild card by hitting 19 homers, driving in 96 runs, scoring 107 times, drawing 125 bases on balls, batting .298, and compiling a .427 on-base percentage and a .463 slugging percentage during the regular season, before homering three times, knocking in 12 runs, and batting .349 against Arizona and Atlanta in the playoffs. But despite his fondness for the Mets and the city of New York, Olerud elected to return to his home state of Washington and sign a three-year, $20 million deal with the Seattle Mariners when he became a free agent at the end of the year.

In explaining his decision at the time, Olerud said, "This was a real difficult decision for me. There were times when I was leaning towards the Mets, definitely. I came close, but never to the point where I said, 'Let's go for it.' One of the big things was family considerations. It's definitely a tough decision. You look at the things you're going to miss with the Mets, but I think this is the right decision for me, the right decision for my family. I have a good feeling about it, a peaceful feeling about the decision."

Olerud, who, during his three years with the Mets, hit 63 homers, knocked in 291 runs, scored 288 times, collected 524 hits, 109 doubles, and five triples, batted .315, compiled an on-base percentage of .425, and posted a slugging percentage of .501, ended up spending most of the next five seasons in Seattle, helping to lead the Mariners to two playoff appearances and one division title by hitting more than 20 homers, driving in more than 100 runs, and batting over .300 twice each. Olerud also led all AL first basemen in assists three times and fielding percentage twice, with his outstanding all-around play earning him one All-Star nomination and three Gold Gloves.

However, with Olerud failing to perform at the same level in 2004, the Mariners released him in late July, after which he signed with the Yankees. After finishing out the season in New York, Olerud spent the 2005 campaign assuming a part-time role in Boston, before announcing his retirement at the end of the year with career totals of 255 homers, 1,230 RBIs, 1,139 runs scored, 2,239 hits, 500 doubles, and 13 triples, a lifetime batting average of .295, an on-base percentage of .398, and a slugging percentage of .465.

Following his playing days, Olerud settled with wife and three children in the Seattle suburb of Clyde Hill, where he and his wife, Kelly, created the Jordan Fund in honor of his daughter, Jordan, who was born with a rare chromosome abnormality known as trisomy 2p, 5p that forced her to spend her early childhood eating through a tube, unable to walk or speak. Unfortunately, after undergoing close to a dozen surgeries and other medical procedures during the first five years of her life, Jordan ultimately passed away in 2020 at the age of 19. But the Jordan Fund continues to help pay for the treatments of other special needs children.

METS CAREER HIGHLIGHTS

Best Season

Although Olerud posted outstanding numbers in each of his three years in New York, he had his finest season as a member of the Mets in 1998, when, in addition to hitting 22 homers, knocking in 93 runs, and scoring 91 times, he amassed 197 hits and 307 total bases, drew 96 bases on balls, compiled an OPS of .998, and finished second in the league with a .354 batting average and a .447 on-base percentage, setting in the process single-season franchise records in each of the last two categories.

Memorable Moments/Greatest Performances

Olerud gave the Mets a 4–3 win over the Rockies on May 19, 1997, when he hit a two-run homer with one man out in the bottom of the ninth inning.

After homering with one man aboard earlier in the contest, Olerud delivered the decisive blow of a 10–8 win over the Pirates on June 29, 1997, when he reached the seats again with a man on base in the top of the ninth inning.

Olerud hit for the cycle during a 9–5 win over the Expos on September 11, 1997, going 4-for-5 with five RBIs and two runs scored.

Olerud delivered the big blow of a 7–5 victory over the Pirates on September 24, 1997, when he homered with the bases loaded in the bottom of the sixth inning.

Olerud hit safely in 23 consecutive games from July 19 to August 9, 1998, going a combined 40-for-89 (.450) with five homers, 10 doubles, 10 walks, 19 RBIs, and 14 runs scored.

Notable Achievements

- Hit more than 20 home runs twice.
- Knocked in more than 100 runs once.
- Scored more than 100 runs once.
- Batted over .300 once.
- Compiled on-base percentage of at least .400 three times.
- Posted slugging percentage over .500 once.
- Posted OPS over .900 once.
- Hit for the cycle vs Montreal Expos on September 11, 1997.
- Finished second in NL in batting average once and on-base percentage once.
- Holds Mets single-season records for highest batting average (.354 in 1998) and highest on-base percentage (.447 in 1998).
- Holds Mets career records for highest batting average, on-base percentage, and OPS.
- Ranks fifth in franchise history in slugging percentage.
- Three-time NL Player of the Week.

29
TUG MCGRAW

A quirky southpaw who, when asked if he preferred natural grass to AstroTurf, replied, "I don't know. I never smoked any AstroTurf," Tug McGraw spent parts of nine seasons in New York, serving as the ace of the Mets' bullpen much of that time. The first true closer in franchise history, McGraw amassed more than 20 saves twice for teams that won two pennants and one World Series, earning in the process one All-Star nomination and a place in the Mets Hall of Fame. Yet McGraw will always be remembered more than anything for coining the phrase "Ya Gotta Believe" that became the Mets' battle cry during their improbable run to the 1973 NL pennant.

Born in Martinez, California, on August 30, 1944, Frank Edwin McGraw grew up with his two brothers some 25 miles northeast of San Francisco. Revealing how he got his rather unusual nickname, McGraw told author Stanley Cohen in *A Magic Summer: The Amazin' Story of the 1969 New York Mets*, "My mother started calling me Tug when I was an infant because of the way I nursed. 'He's a real Tugger,' she said. I never answered to another name."

Raised by his father, Frank Sr., after his bipolar mother abandoned the family following a stay at Napa State Mental Hospital, McGraw had mostly bad memories of his mom, who often physically and verbally abused him and his brothers. Finding solace in sports, McGraw eventually developed into a standout pitcher at St. Vincent Ferrer High School in nearby Vallejo.

Enrolling in Vallejo Junior College following his graduation in 1962, McGraw spent one season pitching for the Falcons, before the Mets signed him as an amateur free agent at the insistence of his older brother, Hank—already a member of the organization. Recalling the circumstances surrounding his signing, McGraw said in *A Magic Summer*, "He [Hank] said, 'If there isn't room in this game for my brother, then I don't want to play either.' He threatened to quit. The Mets weren't really pleased about it, but

Tug McGraw served as closer for Mets teams that won two pennants and one World Series.

Hank was a good prospect, so they offered me a $7,000 bonus and sent me to their rookie league."

McGraw spent less than one full year in the minors, before his status as a "bonus baby" forced the Mets to summon him to New York in 1965. Still only 20 years old when he made his big-league debut, McGraw pitched fairly well for the last-place Mets over the course of the season, winning just two of his nine decisions, but compiling a very respectable ERA of 3.32, while working as both a starter and a reliever.

McGraw subsequently split the next two seasons between the Mets and their Triple-A affiliate in Jacksonville, posting an overall record of just 2-12 as a starter for the parent club, before pitching exclusively for the Suns in

1968. While in the minors, though, McGraw learned from veteran hurler Ralph Terry what would become his signature pitch, the screwball.

Left unprotected for the first three rounds of the 1968 MLB Expansion Draft, McGraw went undrafted by both the San Diego Padres and Montreal Expos, allowing him to remain with the Mets. And with McGraw pitching well in the spring, he earned a spot on the major-league roster, beginning the season as a spot-starter/middle-inning reliever, before being moved to the bullpen full-time by manager Gil Hodges in early June.

Recalling his career-altering conversation with Hodges years later, McGraw said, "By June, I was still pitching well and Gil called me into his office. He said, 'Tug, I have three pieces of advice for you. One, I think you should think about staying in the bullpen permanently. You could be a great reliever and at best an average starter. Two, this team needs a late-inning stopper, and I want you to be my stopper. Three, I think you'll make a lot more money as a reliever than as a starter. Now, it's up to you.' I said, 'Gil, if you think that's the way for me to go, I'm there already.' The rest is history."

With McGraw assuming the role of closer, the Mets won 38 of their final 49 regular-season contests, overcoming in the process the first-place Chicago Cubs, who ended up finishing second to them in the division, eight games back. Meanwhile, McGraw, who concluded the campaign with a record of 9-3, 12 saves, and an ERA of 2.24, excelled down the stretch, surrendering just two runs in his final 29⅔ innings of work.

Somewhat less effective in 1970, McGraw went 4-6 with 10 saves and a 3.28 ERA, before reaching the apex of his career the next two seasons. After going 11-4, saving eight games, and compiling an ERA of 1.70 in 1971, McGraw earned All-Star honors the following year by posting a record of 8-6, finishing second in the league with 27 saves, and once again compiling an ERA of 1.70.

Although the 6-foot, 185-pound McGraw possessed a good fastball and effective curve, he relied most heavily on his screwball to retire opposing batters. In discussing the effectiveness of his favorite offering, which darted in on right-handed batters and away from lefties, McGraw stated, "The only other pitcher with a screwball was Jim Brewer of the Dodgers, so the hitters weren't used to seeing it."

A bit of a screwball himself, McGraw became known for his colorful quotes and distinctive gestures that made him a fan favorite in New York, with Frank Litsky of the *New York Times* writing, "He wore his sandy hair long, and with his little-boy face and boyish enthusiasm, he was a crowd favorite. After a third out, he would run off the mound, slapping his glove against a thigh. After a close call, he would pat his heart."

McGraw subsequently got off to a terrible start in 1973, surrendering many big hits and blowing several leads, with his poor pitching contributing to an equally unimpressive showing by the Mets, who remained 12 games off the pace in the NL East at the midway point of the season. However, everything turned around for both McGraw and the Mets shortly after he had lunch one day that summer with Joe Badamano, a motivational speaker who had been close to Gil Hodges. Recalling his meeting with Badamano, McGraw stated, "Joe kept saying, 'You've got to believe in yourself.' If I didn't *believe*, I could never do it. I had to stop worrying, start thinking positively. 'You gotta *believe*, Tug,' he said. 'That's it, I guess, you gotta *believe*.'"

Adopting the phrase as his own personal mantra, McGraw began repeating it to fans and teammates, uttering it for the first time at the end of a long and tiresome speech delivered by Mets executive M. Donald Grant during a July 9 team meeting. Claiming that Grant "took 20 minutes for him to say what should have taken five," McGraw finally burst into his refrain after the team chairman stated, "We still believe in you," remembering, "I stopped the speech in its tracks. I jumped and ran around to a couple of lockers, grabbing guys and yelling, 'Do you believe? Ya gotta believe!'"

Before long, "Ya Gotta Believe" became the rallying cry for a Mets team that ended up winning the NL pennant. Meanwhile, McGraw performed magnificently over the final month of the campaign, winning four games and saving 10 others, to finish the season with a record of 5-6, 25 saves, and an ERA of 3.87.

Unfortunately, neither the Mets nor McGraw experienced the same level of success in 1974. Plagued by pain in his shoulder throughout the season, McGraw went just 6-11 with a 4.16 ERA and three saves for a Mets team that finished next-to-last in the NL East with a record of 71-91. Asked to start a few games during the latter stages of the campaign, McGraw later wrote in his autobiography, *Ya Gotta Believe!* "They just put me on display. By starting, it made me look like I was healthy, which was important because the word had started to spread around the league that I wasn't. So, they put me on display as a starter after being a reliever all those years."

With the Mets feeling that the 30-year-old McGraw had seen his best days, they included him in a trade with the Phillies at the end of the year that sent him and outfielders Don Hahn and Dave Schneck to Philadelphia for catcher John Stearns, pitcher Mac Scarce, and outfielder Del Unser. Over parts of nine seasons in New York, McGraw posted an overall record of 47-55, compiled an ERA of 3.17 and a WHIP of 1.306, registered 86 saves, threw five complete games and one shutout, and struck out 618 batters in 792⅔ innings pitched.

Proving that he still had a lot left in the tank after undergoing a minor surgical procedure on his shoulder, McGraw ended up spending 10 seasons in Philadelphia, earning his second All-Star nomination and one top-five finish in the NL Cy Young voting by winning another 49 games and recording 94 more saves. Particularly outstanding in 1980, McGraw helped the Phillies win their first world championship by going 5-4 with a 1.46 ERA and 20 saves.

Choosing to announce his retirement following the conclusion of the 1984 campaign, McGraw, who ended his 19-year major-league career with a record of 96-92, 180 saves, an ERA of 3.14, a WHIP of 1.254, and 1,109 strikeouts in 1,514⅔ innings pitched, subsequently spent more than a decade working as a sports anchor and reporter for *Action News* on WPVI, the ABC affiliate in Philadelphia. McGraw also wrote three children's books, rejoined the Phillies organization as a special spring training instructor, and reconciled with his son, country singing star Tim McGraw, whom he had fathered out of wedlock while pitching in the minor leagues many years earlier.

Diagnosed with an inoperable brain tumor in March 2003, McGraw staved off his inevitable fate longer than expected by undergoing chemotherapy and taking experimental drugs paid for by his famous son. After battling his illness for 10 months, McGraw passed away at the age of 59 on January 5, 2004, with Tim at his bedside. The 2004 Mets subsequently honored McGraw by wearing his name and the three words "Ya Gotta Believe" on their sleeve.

Following McGraw's passing, Mets owner Fred Wilpon issued a statement that read: "Tug was a battler on and off the field. I know he fought the disease with every ounce of energy he had. We'll all miss him dearly."

In discussing his former teammate, who established The Tug McGraw Foundation in 2003 to enhance the quality of life of children and adults stricken with brain tumors, Tom Seaver said, "Tug McGraw was one of the great characters of the game of baseball. He just had a joy for life and living. But what people sometimes overlook because he was always happy-go-lucky was what kind of competitor he was on the mound. No one competed with more intensity than he did."

Former Phillies catcher Bob Boone also spoke of his longtime teammate and close friend, saying, "I was real pleased I was able to be with him a little bit the last couple of months. All of a sudden, it hit, and he went real quick, which probably is a blessing. . . . I know he got more living out of his 59 years than anybody. What you saw was what Tug was. There was no phoniness at all. He loved people and loved life."

METS CAREER HIGHLIGHTS

Best Season

Although McGraw also performed extremely well in 1969 and 1971, he had his finest all-around season for the Mets in 1972, when, in addition to compiling an ERA of 1.70 for the second straight year, he went 8-6 with a WHIP of 1.047, recorded 92 strikeouts in 106 innings pitched, and registered a career-high 27 saves, earning in the process his lone All-Star selection as a member of the team.

Memorable Moments/Greatest Performances

Before being moved to the bullpen full-time earlier in the year, McGraw surrendered just two runs over the first 7⅔ innings of a 5–2 victory over Sandy Koufax and the Dodgers on August 26, 1965, ending in the process the Hall of Fame southpaw's 13-game unbeaten streak against the league's worst team.

McGraw allowed just two hits during a 5–1 complete-game victory over the Phillies on August 21, 1966, yielding only singles to Harvey Kuenn and opposing pitcher Jim Bunning.

McGraw earned a victory on July 15, 1971, by working six scoreless innings of relief during a 9–4 win over the Astros, yielding just one hit and two walks, while striking out eight.

Although the Mets lost to the Expos, 10–2, on September 8, 1971, McGraw worked 2⅓ scoreless innings of relief and hit the only home run of his career.

In addition to allowing just one run in 5⅓ innings of relief, McGraw knocked in the decisive runs of a 4–2 win over the Expos on September 7, 1973, with a two-run single in the top of the 15th inning.

Making a rare start on September 1, 1974, McGraw performed brilliantly, giving the Mets a 3–0 victory over the Braves by tossing a 5-hit shutout.

Notable Achievements

- Won 11 games in 1971.
- Saved more than 20 games twice.
- Compiled ERA under 2.50 three times, posting mark under 2.00 twice.
- Threw more than 100 innings four times.
- Recorded more than 100 strikeouts once.
- Finished second in NL in saves twice.
- Ranks among Mets career leaders in saves (7th) and pitching appearances (7th).
- Two-time division champion (1969 and 1973).
- Two-time NL champion (1969 and 1973).
- 1969 world champion.
- September 1, 1974, NL Player of the Week.
- 1972 NL All-Star selection.
- Inducted into Mets Hall of Fame in 1993.

30
SID FERNANDEZ

Although Sid Fernandez often found himself being overlooked and underappreciated by Mets fans because he spent his entire time in New York pitching in the shadow of Dwight Gooden, he proved to be one of the finest hurlers in team annals. A left-handed strikeout pitcher against whom opposing batters had a difficult time squaring up the baseball, "El Sid," as he came to be known, twice led the majors in fewest hits allowed per nine innings pitched, posting the third-lowest mark in MLB history over the course of his career. A member of the Mets from 1984 to 1993, Fernandez won at least 14 games three times and compiled an ERA under 3.00 on five separate occasions, earning in the process two All-Star selections, before splitting his final four big-league seasons between three different teams.

Born in Honolulu, Hawaii, on October 12, 1962, Charles Sidney Fernandez IV grew up on the southeast end of the island of Oahu, where his father worked as a civilian foreman at the Pearl Harbor Shipyards and his mother worked as a teller in the credit union on the Marine base. Of mostly Portuguese heritage, Fernandez began playing tee-ball at the age of six, before eventually graduating to baseball. A fan of the San Francisco Giants during his youth, Fernandez recalled, "They had the Dodger and Giant games on the radio every day in Hawaii, so most of the people are either Dodger fans or Giant fans. I listened to the Giants every day on the radio. Willie McCovey, Jim Ray Hart."

After leading his Little League team to the state championship and his Colt League squad to the national title, Fernandez enrolled at Honolulu's Kaiser High School, where he threw a no-hitter in his very first start as a junior in 1980. Fernandez followed that up by leading Kaiser High to the state championship in his senior year, prompting the Dodgers to select him in the third round of the 1981 MLB Amateur Draft. Fernandez subsequently spent three seasons advancing through the Los Angeles farm system, tossing another two no-hitters and recording 21 strikeouts

Sid Fernandez twice led the majors in fewest hits allowed per nine innings pitched.

in a game, before joining the Dodgers during the latter stages of the 1983 campaign. But after Fernandez appeared in only two games with them, the pitching-rich Dodgers traded him and minor-league infielder Ross Jones to the Mets on December 8, 1983, for infielder-outfielder Bob Bailor and left-handed reliever Carlos Díaz.

Although Fernandez eventually came to enjoy his time in New York, he initially expressed disappointment upon learning of the deal, saying at the time, "Let's face it, I come from paradise, and I've come to a concrete city."

Plagued by control problems, Fernandez spent much of the 1984 and 1985 campaigns shuttling back and forth between the Mets and their Triple-A affiliate in Tidewater, compiling an overall record of 15-15 with the parent club. Yet even though Fernandez walked a total of 114 batters in 260 innings pitched, he displayed a great deal of potential, performing especially well in 1985, when, en route to posting a record of 9-9, he compiled an ERA of 2.80, recorded 180 strikeouts in 170⅓ innings pitched, and led all NL hurlers in fewest hits allowed per nine innings pitched (5.706) and most strikeouts per nine innings of work (9.511).

Joining the Mets for good in 1986, Fernandez contributed to their world championship ballclub by compiling a record of 16-6 and an ERA of 3.52, posting a WHIP of 1.233, and striking out 200 batters in 204⅓ innings pitched, earning in the process the first of his two All-Star nominations and a seventh-place finish in the NL Cy Young voting. Despite missing three weeks in 1987 with an injured knee, Fernandez again gained All-Star recognition by going 12-8 with a 3.81 ERA, a WHIP of 1.263, and 134 strikeouts in 156 innings of work. Fernandez followed that up with two more excellent seasons, compiling a record of 12-10 and an ERA of 3.03, posting a WHIP of 1.053, and ranking among the league leaders with 189 strikeouts in 1988, before going 14-5 with a 2.83 ERA, a WHIP of 1.058, and 198 strikeouts in 1989.

Although officially listed at 6'1" and 220 pounds, Fernandez, who wore uniform number 50 in honor of his home state and favorite TV show, *Hawaii Five-O*, weighed more than 250 pounds most of his career. Yet despite his hefty frame, Fernandez proved to be one of the most difficult pitchers in the game for opposing players to hit. Often described as "sneaky-fast," Fernandez possessed an unorthodox pitching motion that included a hesitation at the end, followed by a sudden slingshot sidearm delivery. And with Fernandez hiding the ball behind his body prior to delivering it to home plate, his pitches seemed to come out of his uniform. This deceptive motion, coupled with a rising fastball and sweeping slow curve that made him particularly tough on left-handed batters, allowed Fernandez to consistently rank among the NL leaders in strikeouts during his time in New York.

Despite his excellent work on the mound, Fernandez, who admitted to being shy, timid, and naïve in the ways of the world when he first arrived in Queens, often found himself being derided for his gullibility and excessive weight, with John Harper and Bob Klapisch portraying him in their book, *The Worst Team Money Could Buy*, as "The Big Pineapple" who believed that professional wrestling was real.

Bothered by a sore knee for much of 1990, Fernandez went just 9-14 with a 3.46 ERA, although he still managed to finish fifth among NL hurlers with 181 strikeouts and lead the league in fewest hits allowed per nine innings pitched for the third time. Fernandez subsequently missed most of the 1991 campaign with a broken wrist he sustained during spring training and a knee injury he suffered shortly after he returned to action. But after undergoing surgery to repair his knee at the end of the year, Fernandez, who at the time of the procedure weighed 261 pounds, attended the Duke University clinic, where he got into the best shape of his career. Having shed more than 40 pounds, Fernandez returned to top form in 1992, compiling a record of 14-11 and an ERA of 2.73, posting a WHIP of 1.067, and registering 193 strikeouts in 214⅔ innings pitched.

Unfortunately, the 1992 campaign ended up being the last truly productive season of Fernandez's career. After being limited by another knee injury to just 18 starts and five wins in 1993, Fernandez signed with the Orioles as a free agent at the end of the year. The oft-injured Fernandez subsequently split the next four seasons between the Orioles, Phillies, and Astros, never again appearing in more than 19 games or posting more than six victories, before announcing his retirement on August 1, 1997, due to elbow problems.

Over parts of 15 big-league seasons, Fernandez compiled a record of 114-96, an ERA of 3.36, and a WHIP of 1.144, threw 25 complete games and nine shutouts, and struck out 1,743 batters in 1,866⅔ innings pitched. As a member of the Mets, Fernandez posted a record of 98-78, an ERA of 3.14, and a WHIP of 1.113, tossed 23 complete games and nine shutouts, registered 1,449 strikeouts in 1,584⅔ innings of work, and held opposing hitters to a composite batting average of just .204, with his career-mark of 6.85 hits allowed per nine innings pitched placing him third all-time, behind only Nolan Ryan and Sandy Koufax.

Following his playing days, Fernandez returned to his native Hawaii, where he briefly worked as an executive assistant to Honolulu mayor Jeremy Harris in an effort to find sponsors and users for sporting facilities of the island of Oahu. Fernandez also later served as Honolulu sports industry development director and assumed the position of pitching coach for the semipro Alaska Baseball League's Hawaii Island Movers. Now retired, Fernandez, who spends much of his time playing golf, continues to award college scholarships to seniors from his alma mater, Kaiser High School, through the Sid Fernandez Foundation that he established with his wife, Noelani, several years ago.

METS CAREER HIGHLIGHTS

Best Season

Fernandez pitched his best ball for the Mets in 1989, when, in addition to posting a record of 14-5 that gave him an NL-best .737 winning percentage, he compiled an ERA of 2.83, ranked among the league leaders with a WHIP of 1.058 and 198 strikeouts, and established career-high marks with 219⅓ innings pitched, six complete games, and two shutouts.

Memorable Moments/Greatest Performances

Fernandez turned in a tremendous all-around effort during an 11–0 shutout of Atlanta on July 11, 1986, holding the Braves to just two hits, issuing three walks, and recording nine strikeouts, while also going 3-for-4 at the plate with a pair of doubles.

Fernandez turned in a similarly impressive performance on July 3, 1988, allowing just two hits, issuing two bases on balls, and registering 12 strikeouts during a 5–0 shutout of the Astros, while also hitting safely twice and driving in one run.

Although Fernandez suffered a 3–2 defeat at the hands of the Braves on July 14, 1989, he recorded a career-high 16 strikeouts.

In addition to yielding just two hits and registering 13 strikeouts during a 6–1 complete-game win over the Cardinals on September 21, 1989, Fernandez went 3-for-4 at the plate and hit the only home run of his career.

Fernandez followed that up with another brilliant outing, allowing just three hits, issuing three walks, and striking out nine batters during a 3–0 shutout of the Phillies on September 26, 1989.

Fernandez dominated Montreal's lineup on April 22, 1990, yielding just two hits and two walks during a 5–0 shutout.

Fernandez scattered three hits, issued no walks, and recorded nine strikeouts during a 3–0 shutout of the Padres on July 24, 1992.

Notable Achievements

- Won 16 games in 1986.
- Compiled ERA under 3.00 five times.
- Posted WHIP under 1.000 once.
- Recorded 200 strikeouts once.
- Threw more than 200 innings three times.

- Led NL pitchers in winning percentage once, fewest hits allowed per nine innings pitched three times, and most strikeouts per nine innings pitched once.
- Ranks third in MLB history in fewest hits allowed per nine innings pitched (6.851).
- Ranks among Mets career leaders in wins (5th), WHIP (4th), strikeouts (5th), shutouts (tied for 8th), innings pitched (5th) and starts (4th).
- Two-time division champion (1986 and 1988).
- 1986 NL champion.
- 1986 world champion.
- October 1, 1989, NL Player of the Week.
- April 1987 NL Pitcher of the Month.
- Two-time NL All-Star selection (1986 and 1987).

31
RON DARLING

A mainstay of the Mets' starting rotation for nearly a decade, Ron Darling spent parts of nine seasons in New York, amassing the fourth-most victories of any pitcher in team annals. The winner of at least 15 games three times, Darling helped the Mets win two division titles, one pennant, and one world championship by also compiling an ERA under 3.00 three times and throwing more than 200 innings on six separate occasions. A onetime NL All-Star who also earned one top-five finish in the Cy Young voting, Darling later received the additional honor of gaining induction into the Mets Hall of Fame.

Born in Honolulu, Hawaii, to a Hawaiian-Chinese mother and a French-Canadian father on August 19, 1960, Ronald Maurice Darling moved with his family at a young age to Millbury, Massachusetts, where he grew up rooting for the Boston Red Sox while enjoying life at home, recalling, "I had an idyllic family life, great parents, three younger brothers who adored me, thought I was the cat's meow."

An excellent all-around athlete, Darling starred in baseball and football at St. John's High School in nearby Shrewsbury, with his proficiency in both sports garnering him interest from Yale University and the University of Connecticut. Ultimately choosing to enroll at Yale, Darling played defensive back on the gridiron and shortstop on the diamond as a freshman, before quitting football prior to the start of his sophomore year to focus exclusively on baseball. Although Darling eventually transitioned to the mound, he agreed to do so only if his coach allowed him to play shortstop or the outfield on his days off. While in college, Darling also spent his summers competing in the Cape Cod Baseball League, earning league MVP honors in 1980 by posting a record of 4-3, while also hitting six homers and batting .336.

Selected by the Texas Rangers with the ninth overall pick of the 1981 MLB Amateur Draft, Darling spent the 1981 season at Double-A Tulsa, winning four of his six decisions and recording 53 strikeouts in 71 innings

Ron Darling recorded the fourth-most wins of any pitcher in franchise history.

of work, but also compiling an ERA of 4.44 and issuing 33 bases on balls. Traded to the Mets along with pitcher Walt Terrell for outfielder Lee Mazzilli at the end of the year, Darling subsequently posted a composite record of 17-18 with their Triple-A affiliate in Tidewater over the course of the next two seasons, before joining the parent club during the latter stages of the 1983 campaign.

After going 1-3 with a 2.80 ERA in his five starts with the Mets in September 1983, Darling became a regular member of their starting rotation the following year. Performing well in his first full big-league season, Darling compiled a record of 12-9, posted an ERA of 3.81, and registered 136 strikeouts in 205⅔ innings pitched. Improving upon those numbers in 1985, Darling gained All-Star recognition for the only time in his career by going 16-6 with a 2.90 ERA and 167 strikeouts in 248 innings of work, while serving as the number two starter in the Mets' rotation behind Dwight Gooden. Darling followed that up with another outstanding season, earning a fifth-place finish in the NL Cy Young voting in 1986 by posting a record of 15-6, ranking among the league leaders with a 2.81

ERA, and striking out 184 batters in 237 innings pitched, before helping the Mets defeat the Red Sox in the World Series by going 1-1 with a 1.53 ERA in his three starts against the team he followed as a youth.

Standing 6'3" and weighing 200 pounds, the right-handed-throwing Darling possessed good velocity on his four-seam fastball, which he mixed in with his slider, curveball, circle-changeup, and splitter to navigate his way through opposing lineups. After struggling with his control early in his career, Darling eventually gained better command of his pitches, walking only 60 batters in 240 innings of work one season. An outstanding fielder as well, Darling, who led all NL hurlers in assists twice and had one of the best pickoff moves among right-handed pitchers, won a Gold Glove during his time in New York. Meanwhile, Darling's athleticism allowed the Mets to occasionally use him as a pinch-runner.

One of the tamer members of a Mets team noted for its raucous behavior, Darling nevertheless ran afoul of the law on July 19, 1986, when police arrested him and teammates Bob Ojeda, Rick Aguilera, and Tim Teufel outside a bar in Houston for fighting with security guards, who turned out to be off-duty police officers. Although Darling and Teufel subsequently pleaded guilty to a misdemeanor charge of resisting arrest and had to each pay a $200 fine, Jeff Pearlman later wrote in his book, *The Bad Guys Won*, that the security guards instigated the fight with an inebriated Teufel, who the other players had been treating to drinks to help him celebrate becoming a father. Yet, while Pearlman also wrote that the four players involved usually carried themselves with far more decorum, the incident tarnished each of their reputations somewhat.

Following a slightly subpar 1987 campaign in which he won 12 of his 20 decisions but posted an ERA of 4.29, Darling rebounded the following year to compile a record of 17-9 and an ERA of 3.25, register 161 strikeouts in 240⅔ innings pitched, and rank among the league leaders with four shutouts. Darling had another solid season in 1989, going 14-14 with a 3.52 ERA and 153 strikeouts, before struggling through a difficult 1990 campaign in which he went just 7-9 with a 4.50 ERA, while splitting his time between starting and relieving.

With the Mets in a period of transition, they completed a trade with the Expos on July 15, 1991, that sent Darling and minor-league pitcher Mike Thomas to Montreal for veteran reliever Tim Burke. Darling, who, during his time in New York, compiled a record of 99-70 and an ERA of 3.50, posted a WHIP of 1.288, threw 25 complete games and 10 shutouts, and struck out 1,148 batters in 1,620 total innings of work, ended up spending just two weeks in Montreal, before being dealt to the Oakland Athletics at the trade deadline. Darling subsequently remained in Oakland until August 15, 1995, when he announced his retirement after being released by the A's. Over parts of 13 big-league seasons, Darling posted a record of 136-116, an ERA of 3.87, and a WHIP of 1.335, tossed 37 complete games and 13 shutouts, and registered 1,590 strikeouts in 2,360⅓ innings pitched.

Following his playing days, Darling began a career in broadcasting, working at various times as a broadcaster for the Oakland Athletics and as an analyst for the YES Network, Fox Sports Net, CSTV, and *The Best Damn Sports Show Period* from 2000 to 2004. Hired by SportsNet New York in 2006 as a color commentator and studio analyst for the Mets, Darling has spent the last 20 years sharing the broadcast booth with play-by-play announcer Gary Cohen and former Mets teammate Keith Hernandez. Darling also works as a color commentator for national baseball coverage on TBS and co-hosts several MLB Network programs.

A survivor of thyroid cancer that forced him to take a one-year leave of absence from broadcasting in 2019, Darling, who founded the Ron Darling Foundation in 2009 to help fund diabetes research after his son Jordan developed the disease as an 11-year-old, is also an accomplished author who has written three books. Darling's third published work, *108 Stitches: Loose Threads, Ripping Yarns, and the Darndest Characters from My Time in the Game*, proved to be his most controversial since it elicited an unfavorable response from former Mets teammate Lenny Dykstra, who sued for defamation of character after the book claimed that he used racial slurs toward Red Sox pitcher Oil Can Boyd during the 1986 World Series. However, the judge assigned to the case ultimately dismissed the lawsuit, ruling that Dykstra's prior reputation made it legally impossible to libel him.

METS CAREER HIGHLIGHTS

Best Season

It could be argued that Darling had his finest season for the Mets in 1988, when, in addition to compiling an ERA of 3.25, registering 161 strikeouts, and throwing 240⅔ innings, he established career-best marks in wins (17), WHIP (1.155), complete games (seven), and shutouts (four). But Darling posted slightly better overall numbers in 1986, when he contributed to the Mets' championship team by going 15-6 with a 2.81 ERA, a WHIP of 1.198, and a career-high 184 strikeouts.

Memorable Moments/Greatest Performances

Darling threw his first career shutout when he allowed just four hits and two walks during a 6–0 win over the Cardinals on June 14, 1984.

Darling tossed another four-hit shutout some three weeks later, when he issued two walks and recorded six strikeouts during a 1–0 win over the Reds on July 6, 1984.

Darling registered a career-high 12 strikeouts during an 8–1 complete-game victory over the Dodgers on May 27, 1986, in which he yielded just five hits and two bases on balls.

Darling threw a complete-game three-hitter on May 8, 1988, surrendering just a double, two singles, and one walk during a 5–1 win over the Reds.

Darling tossed a five-hit shutout against the Dodgers on September 2, 1988, issuing one walk and striking out eight batters during an 8–0 Mets win.

In addition to allowing just one earned run over the first $6\frac{2}{3}$ innings of a 4–2 win over the Phillies on June 24, 1989, Darling hit the first of his two career homers with no one on base.

Darling again reached the seats in his next start six days later, this time homering with two men aboard during an 11–1 win over the Reds in which he allowed just six hits and one run in eight innings of work.

Notable Achievements

- Won at least 15 games three times.
- Compiled ERA under 3.00 three times.
- Threw more than 200 innings six times.
- Led NL pitchers in assists twice.
- Finished third in NL with 2.81 ERA in 1986.
- Ranks among Mets career leaders in wins (4th), winning percentage (tied for 7th), strikeouts (7th), shutouts (tied for 6th), complete games (tied for 9th), innings pitched (4th), and starts (5th).
- Two-time division champion (1986 and 1988).
- 1986 NL champion.
- 1986 world champion.
- June 1984 NL Pitcher of the Month.
- 1989 Gold Glove Award winner.
- Finished fifth in 1986 NL Cy Young voting.
- 1985 NL All-Star selection.
- Inducted into Mets Hall of Fame in 2021.

32
TODD HUNDLEY

A solid defensive catcher who eventually developed into a power threat on offense, Todd Hundley spent parts of nine seasons in New York, helping to bridge the gap from Gary Carter to Mike Piazza. The Mets' primary receiver from 1992 to 1997, the switch-hitting Hundley surpassed 30 homers twice and knocked in more than 100 runs once, earning in the process a pair of All-Star nominations. An outstanding team leader as well, Hundley served as captain of the Mets his last few years in Queens, before being displaced behind the plate by Piazza during the early stages of the 1998 campaign.

Born in Martinsville, Virginia, on May 27, 1969, Todd Randolph Hundley grew up in Illinois, where his father, Randy, spent most of his 14-year major-league career catching for the Chicago Cubs. Developing into an excellent athlete during his teenage years, the younger Hundley starred in baseball and hockey at William Fremd High School in Palatine, Illinois, batting .357 and leading his team in RBIs as a junior.

Following his graduation from William Fremd High, Hundley briefly attended William Rainey Harper College, a community college also located in Palatine, before signing with the Mets after they selected him in the second round of the 1987 MLB Amateur Draft, with the 39th overall pick. The 18-year-old Hundley subsequently spent the next five seasons advancing through New York's farm system, struggling at the plate his first three years in the minors, before gradually turning himself into a decent hitter. Valued more for his defense, Hundley became known for his ability to call a good game and handle a pitching staff, with his proficiency in those areas earning him brief callups to the parent club in both 1990 and 1991.

Joining the Mets for good in 1992 after hitting 14 homers, driving in 66 runs, and batting .273 at Triple-A Tidewater the previous year, Hundley spent his first full season in New York sharing playing time with fellow receivers Charlie O'Brien and Mackey Sasser. Yet even though Hundley remained the team's "catcher of the future" in the eyes of management,

Todd Hundley's 41 homers in 1996 set a new single-season MLB record for catchers.

he hit just seven homers, knocked in only 32 runs, and batted just .209 in 123 games and 390 total plate appearances, later describing himself as "overmatched" during the early stages of his career.

Named the Mets' everyday starting catcher prior to the start of the 1993 season, Hundley performed no better than most of his teammates for much of the year, hitting just 11 homers, driving in only 53 runs, and batting just .228 for a ballclub that ended up finishing last in the NL East with a record of 59-103. However, Hundley posted better numbers during the season's second half, when, after being told by new Mets manager Dallas

Green that he needed to hit better if he wished to remain in the lineup, he began using a bigger bat and pulling the ball more.

Despite being plagued by injuries in each of the next two seasons, Hundley continued to increase his offensive output, concluding the strike-shortened 1994 campaign with 16 homers, 42 RBIs, a .237 batting average, and an OPS of .746, before hitting 15 homers, driving in 51 runs, batting .280, and posting an OPS of .865 in just 90 games and 326 total plate appearances the following year. Taking his game up a notch in 1996, Hundley combined with outfielder Bernard Gilkey to give the Mets a formidable tandem in the middle of their lineup. While Gilkey hit 30 homers, knocked in 117 runs, scored 108 times, and batted .317, Hundley earned All-Star honors by reaching the seats 41 times, driving in 112 runs, batting .259, and posting an OPS of .906, with his 41 homers establishing a new single-season major-league record for catchers.

Hundley, who added more than 20 pounds of bulk onto his lean 5'11", 170-pound frame as his career progressed, possessed good power from both sides of the plate and superior knowledge of the strike zone, leading the Mets in walks once and finishing second two other times, although he also struck out more than 100 times twice. Meanwhile, in addition to being one of the league's better defensive catchers, Hundley gradually emerged as the leader of a rapidly improving Mets team, with ace reliever John Franco saying of his younger teammate during the early stages of the 1997 campaign, "Right now, he's in charge. He kept his mouth shut when he first came up. Now, he's the best captain we've had since Keith Hernandez. All of us watch him and listen to him. He's our leader. People talk about his home runs, but what's really outstanding about him is his defense."

New Mets manager Bobby Valentine added, "He works closely with the pitching staff. He is as much a part of each pitch as the pitcher throwing it. Last year, his offense put him on the map, but you won't find a better all-around catcher."

An All-Star again in 1997, Hundley helped lead the Mets to their first winning record in seven years by hitting 30 homers, driving in 86 runs, scoring 78 times, batting .273, compiling an on-base percentage of .394, and posting a slugging percentage of .549, despite suffering through a late-season slump brought on by injuries to his toe and ribs, and worries over his ailing mother and pregnant wife. Nevertheless, after praising his star catcher earlier in the year, Bobby Valentine found fault with his personal habits as his hitting declined, saying, "I think he doesn't sleep enough. He's a nocturnal person. He needs more rest. He has a really tough time getting to sleep after games. I heard one night he stayed out until 4 o'clock in the morning before he was ready to go to sleep."

Hundley subsequently missed much of the 1998 campaign after undergoing reconstructive elbow surgery during the offseason. And with the Mets acquiring Mike Piazza during his absence, Hundley found himself manning the unfamiliar position of left field when he returned to action in mid-July. Struggling terribly both at the bat and in the field the rest of the year, Hundley hit just three homers, knocked in only 12 runs, and batted just .161 in 53 games and 142 total plate appearances, while also committing five errors in left. Choosing to part ways with Hundley at season's end, the Mets dealt him to the Dodgers on December 1, 1998, as part of a three-team trade that netted them reliever Armando Benítez and outfielder Roger Cedeño in return.

Hundley, who, during his time in New York, hit 124 homers, knocked in 397 runs, scored 340 times, collected 612 hits, 118 doubles, and seven triples, batted .240, compiled an on-base percentage of .323, and posted a slugging percentage of .438, ended up splitting the next five seasons between the Dodgers and Cubs, serving both teams as a part-time player, before announcing his retirement following the conclusion of the 2003 campaign with career totals of 202 homers, 599 RBIs, 495 runs scored, 883 hits, 167 doubles, and seven triples, a .234 batting average, a .320 on-base percentage, and a .443 slugging percentage.

Following his playing days, Hundley returned to Illinois, where he suffered the embarrassment of being named in the Mitchell Report in 2007. With the report revealing that former Mets clubhouse attendant Kirk Radomski told investigators that he sold the PED Deca-Durabolin to Hundley prior to his 1996 record-breaking season, the catcher's offensive accomplishments have since come to be viewed by many in a much different light. Two years earlier, Hundley ran afoul of the law when Lake County, Illinois, police arrested him for endangering the life and health of his two daughters by driving under the influence. Hundley, who attributed his condition to the prescription painkiller Vicodin, later moved with his second wife to San Francisco, where he is currently involved in the gaming business.

METS CAREER HIGHLIGHTS

Best Season

Hundley had his finest all-around season for the Mets in 1996, when, in addition to batting .259 and compiling an OPS of .906, he established career-high marks with 41 homers, 112 RBIs, 85 runs scored, 140 hits, 32 doubles, 297 total bases, 72 assists, and 911 putouts.

Memorable Moments/Greatest Performances

Hundley delivered the decisive blow of a 5–1 win over the Expos on May 4, 1995, when he came off the bench in the top of the 10th inning to hit a pinch-hit grand slam home run.

Hundley led the Mets to a 14–5 victory over the Giants on May 18, 1996, by homering twice and knocking in a career-high seven runs.

Hundley contributed to an 8–3 win over the Braves on June 10, 1996, by going 4-for-4 with two homers and five RBIs.

Hundley set a new single-season home-run record for catchers (since broken) when he homered for the 41st time during a 12-inning, 6–5 win over the Braves on September 14, 1996. Hundley's blast, which came in the bottom of the seventh inning with two men out and two men on, broke Roy Campanella's previous single-season mark of 40 that the Hall of Fame receiver set 43 years earlier.

Hundley provided most of the offensive firepower during a 6–1 win over the Rockies on May 5, 1997, going 4-for-4 with two homers, a double, five RBIs, and three runs scored.

Notable Achievements

- Surpassed 30 home runs twice, topping 40 homers once.
- Knocked in more than 100 runs once.
- Posted slugging percentage over .500 twice.
- Posted OPS over .900 twice.
- May 11, 1997, NL Player of the Week.
- Two-time NL All-Star selection (1996 and 1997).

33
JESSE OROSCO

The only reliever to win three games in a postseason series, Jesse Orosco will always be remembered for recording the final out of both the NLCS and World Series in 1986. Yet even though Orosco's Mets legacy is tied largely to his 1986 postseason performance, he accomplished a great deal more during his 24-year major-league career that included stints with nine different teams. Having most of his finest seasons for the Mets, with whom he made his big-league debut in 1979, the left-handed-throwing Orosco spent most of his eight years in Queens anchoring New York's bullpen, amassing the fifth-most saves of anyone in team annals. The first reliever in franchise history to record as many as 30 saves in a season, Orosco also surpassed 10 victories, compiled an ERA under 2.00, and threw more than 100 innings twice each, earning in the process two All-Star selections and one top-five finish in the NL Cy Young voting. After leaving New York, Orosco continued to pitch for another 16 seasons, ending his career with more mound appearances than any other hurler in MLB history.

Born in Santa Barbara, California, on April 21, 1957, Jesse Russell Orosco grew up with his seven siblings on the Pacific coast. Knowing at an early age that he wanted to pursue a career in baseball, Orosco recalled, "Ever since I was a little tot, my plan was to play in the majors."

The son of a former semipro pitcher and first baseman who chose family life over baseball, Orosco learned how to play the game from his father, remembering, "My dad taught me everything: how to pitch, catch, hit—everything. We would practice afternoons after school and when he got off work."

After getting his start in organized ball at the age of six on a Boys' Club team in his hometown, Orosco developed into a solid all-around player at Santa Barbara High School, before enrolling at Santa Barbara City College, saying, "In junior college, I played outfield and first base, rarely pitched, hit .384, but with no power."

Jesse Orosco appeared in more games than any other pitcher in MLB history.

Selected by the Cardinals in the seventh round of the January phase of the 1977 MLB Amateur Draft, Orosco elected to return to school for one more year, later claiming that he made the right decision when he said, "I was drafted by the Cardinals in the secondary January draft. But they didn't offer me any money. In my second year at the JC, I became a starting pitcher and made All-Conference. Minnesota [which took him in the second round of the draft one year later] signed me and offered me a little money."

However, after Orosco appeared in just 20 games with their minor-league affiliate in Elizabethton, Tennessee, in 1978, the Twins traded him to the Mets on February 7, 1979, to complete an earlier deal that had sent Jerry Koosman from New York to Minnesota. Orosco subsequently spent most of the next three seasons in the minors, during which time he gradually transitioned from a starter into a reliever, recalling years later, "For a few years, I was going back and forth, starter or reliever. They didn't know what they wanted me to be. I never thought I was strong enough to be a starter.

". . . In 1981 at Tidewater, I had about 10 starts. I'd go about four innings and start getting gassed. Bill Monbouquette was our pitching coach. Come July, I told him, 'I can't handle this. I'm not helping us as a starter. I'd like to go back to the bullpen. That's going to be my best opportunity.' Bill said, 'They don't want you to go there, Jess. They want you to be a starter.' I said, 'Tell the Mets I want to go to the bullpen. I'll take my chances there.' He put his job on the line for me and told the Mets what I wanted. The next day he says to me, 'You're now the closer.'"

Promoted to the parent club prior to the start of the 1982 campaign after winning nine games and saving eight others at Triple-A Tidewater the previous year, Orosco soon learned the slider from new Mets manager and former Baltimore Orioles pitching coach George Bamberger, who also helped instill in him a sense of tenacity. Persevering through the loss of his father, who died in a construction accident during the season, Orosco performed well as a middle-inning reliever, compiling an ERA of 2.72, collecting four saves, and striking out 89 batters in 109⅓ innings of work, even though the failures of the Mets as a team relegated him to a record of just 4-10. Assuming the role of closer in 1983, Orosco gained All-Star recognition and earned a third-place finish in the NL Cy Young voting by posting a record of 13-7, compiling an ERA of 1.47 and a WHIP of 1.036, saving 17 games, and registering 84 strikeouts in 110 innings pitched. An All-Star again in 1984, Orosco went 10-6 with an ERA of 2.59 and a WHIP of 1.057, finished third in the league with a career-high 31 saves, and struck out 85 batters in 87 innings of work.

During his peak years, the slender Orosco, who stood 6'2" and weighed barely 180 pounds, relied primarily on a 91–93 mph fastball and a hard slider to retire opposing batters, although his repertoire of pitches also included a sliding changeup. However, as Orosco's career progressed and he lost some of the velocity on his fastball, the slider became his "out" pitch, and he began to throw a split-finger changeup as well. Blessed with a resilient left arm, Orosco needed only 10 pitches to warm up and had the ability to throw four days in a row, once saying, "I never have a sore arm in the morning. I'm just lucky. I never put ice on the arm. Just give me the ball." Totally unflappable on the mound, Orosco also handled the pressure of closing extremely well, stating, "I had nerves a lot of the time, but I embraced the pressure and loved it."

Continuing to perform well for the Mets in 1985, Orosco compiled a record of 8-6 and an ERA of 2.73, collected 17 saves, and registered 68 strikeouts in 79 innings pitched, while sharing closer duties with the right-handed-throwing Roger McDowell. Assuming the same role the following year, Orosco helped lead the Mets to a regular-season record of 108-54 and the division title by going 8-6 with a 2.33 ERA, 21 saves, and 61 strikeouts in 81 innings of work, before serving as one of the key figures in their successful postseason run to the world championship.

Defeating Houston three times in the NLCS, Orosco posted victories in Games 3, 5, and 6, recording the final out of the series by striking out Kevin Bass with two men out and two men on base in the bottom of the 16th inning of a 7–6 Mets win. Orosco subsequently appeared in four games against Boston in the World Series, earning a pair of saves by yielding just two hits and no runs in 5⅔ total innings of work, with the image of him dropping to his knees, tossing his glove high in the air, and thrusting his face toward the heavens after striking out Marty Barrett for the final out remaining one of the most memorable in Mets history.

Recalling that glorious moment years later, Orosco said, "I still remember the strikeout that ended the World Series like it was yesterday. After I saw the swing and miss, it was pure jubilation. I just threw my glove up in the air knowing that the celebration was on. It's also great remembering that I drove in the winning run, something many people forget. Since I wasn't a great hitter, I guess you could say that timing is everything."

Unfortunately, the 1987 campaign brought no such joy to Orosco, who, despite saving 16 games, suffered through a subpar season during which he compiled a record of just 3-9 and an ERA of 4.44. And with Orosco struggling on the mound, he fell into disfavor with manager Davey Johnson and Mets fans, who made him keenly aware of their feelings for him. Finally asking for a trade, Orosco headed for Los Angeles when the Mets dealt him to the Dodgers for three minor-league pitchers on December 11, 1987, as part of a three-way deal that also involved the Oakland Athletics.

Orosco, who left New York with an overall record of 47-47, a composite ERA of 2.73, a WHIP of 1.209, 107 saves, and 506 strikeouts in 595⅔ innings pitched, ended up spending just one season in Los Angeles, before beginning a baseball odyssey in 1989 that took him to the Indians (1989–1991), Brewers (1992–1994), Orioles (1995–1999), Cardinals (2000), Dodgers (2001–2002), Padres (2003), Yankees (2003), and Twins (2003). Assuming the role of a left-handed specialist for virtually all those teams, Orosco never again attained his earlier glory. Nevertheless, he won another 40 games and saved 37 others, giving him a career record of 87-80 and a total of 144 saves. Orosco also compiled a lifetime ERA of 3.16, posted a WHIP of 1.263, struck out 1,179 batters in 1,295⅓ innings pitched, and made a major-league record 1,252 mound appearances, before finally announcing his retirement at the age of 46 following the conclusion of the 2003 campaign.

Following his playing days, Orosco spent several years enjoying a life of leisure, watching his children grow up and playing a lot of golf, before taking a position with the San Diego branch of the Frozen Ropes baseball and softball training centers, close to his home in Carmel Valley. Although no longer affiliated with the Frozen Ropes, Orosco remains active in teaching the art of pitching to youngsters.

In discussing his 24-year big-league career, Orosco says, "I take great pride in the fact that I hold the record for most games pitched. I needed to be ready to take the mound each and every day for my teammates and manager. It's the greatest feeling knowing that I was able to accomplish what I did and leave everything I had out on the field."

METS CAREER HIGHLIGHTS

Best Season

Although Orosco amassed more saves in both 1984 and 1986, he pitched his best ball for the Mets in 1983, when, in addition to saving 17 games and recording 84 strikeouts in 110 innings of work, he held opposing batters to an anemic .269 slugging percentage and posted career-best marks in wins (13), ERA (1.47), and WHIP (1.036), earning in the process his first All-Star selection and a third-place finish in the NL Cy Young voting.

Memorable Moments/Greatest Performances

Orosco won both ends of a doubleheader on July 31, 1983, yielding no runs and just three hits in five total innings of work, in helping the Mets sweep the Pirates 7–6 and 1–0.

Orosco threw 27⅔ consecutive scoreless innings from July 22 to August 27, 1983.

Orosco saved a victory for Dwight Gooden on May 15, 1985, by striking out five of the eight batters he faced in 2⅔ perfect innings of relief during a 5–3 win over the Astros.

Orosco helped the Mets advance to the 1986 World Series by posting victories in Games 3, 5, and 6 of the NLCS, finishing the series with a record of 3-0 and an ERA of 3.38.

Orosco subsequently performed brilliantly in the Fall Classic, saving two games and allowing just two hits and no runs in 5⅔ innings of work, with his two perfect innings of relief in Game 7 earning him a save in the Series finale.

Notable Achievements

- Surpassed 10 victories twice.
- Saved more than 20 games twice, topping 30 saves once.
- Compiled ERA under 3.00 six times, posting mark under 2.00 twice.
- Threw more than 100 innings twice.
- Finished third in NL with 31 saves in 1984.
- Holds MLB record for most pitching appearances (1,252).
- Ranks among Mets career leaders in ERA (3rd), saves (5th), and pitching appearances (6th).
- 1986 division champion.
- 1986 NL champion.
- 1986 world champion.
- Three-time NL Player of the Week.
- August 1983 NL Pitcher of the Month.
- Finished third in 1983 NL Cy Young voting.
- Two-time NL All-Star selection (1983 and 1984).

34
KEVIN MCREYNOLDS

An extremely talented player who performed well for the Mets both at the bat and in the field during his two tours of duty with the club, Kevin McReynolds spent a total of six seasons in New York, starting in left field in five of those. A productive hitter, the righty-swinging McReynolds helped the Mets win one division title and contend for three others by hitting more than 20 homers four times and driving in more than 90 runs twice. An excellent baserunner and outstanding defender as well, McReynolds also stole more than 20 bases once and led all players at his position in assists and fielding percentage twice each, with his outstanding all-around play earning him one top-five finish in the NL MVP voting. Nevertheless, McReynolds failed to earn the favor of Mets fans, who often criticized him for his placid demeanor and lack of intensity on the playing field.

Born in Little Rock, Arkansas, on October 16, 1959, Walter Kevin McReynolds grew up with his sister and two brothers in humble surroundings on the Arkansas National Guard base at which his father worked as a mechanic. Describing his parents' house as "modest, almost shack-like," McReynolds added, "It wasn't much. There was a little kitchen and a little living room and a little hall and a bathroom and three small bedrooms. It wasn't very big at all, but it was very comfortable."

Crediting his parents for instilling in him and his siblings a sense of decency, McReynolds stated, "Our parents taught us to treat people decently. Treat them like human beings."

Acquiring his love of baseball from his father, a veteran of World War II who played the game prior to his enlistment in the military, McReynolds got his start in organized sports in junior high school, where he competed in both baseball and football. Choosing to focus primarily on further developing his skills on the diamond after enrolling at Sylvan High School in nearby Sherwood, McReynolds established himself as one of the finest players in the state, earning Arkansas High School Baseball Player of the

Kevin McReynolds finished third in the 1988 NL MVP voting.

Year honors as a senior by hitting 15 homers, driving in 60 runs, and batting .638.

Selected by the Milwaukee Brewers in the 19th round of the 1978 MLB Amateur Draft following his graduation, McReynolds chose not to turn pro and instead attend the University of Arkansas on a baseball scholarship, remembering, "It wasn't a difficult decision. I didn't come from a wealthy family, and the Brewers offered no money."

McReynolds subsequently spent the next three seasons starring in the outfield for the Razorbacks, earning a pair of All-America and All–Southwest Conference nominations by hitting 33 homers, driving in 121 runs, compiling a batting average of .337, and posting a slugging percentage of .642, which represents the third-highest mark in school history.

In discussing his onetime protégé, former Arkansas head coach Norm DeBriyn said, "He was probably the most talented player I had been around. I mean, he had power, he could hit, he could run. . . . He just had all the tools."

Choosing to forgo his final year of college after the San Diego Padres selected him with the sixth overall pick of the 1981 MLB Amateur Draft, McReynolds recalled, "I think I really got myself on the board when I was a freshman and played in the College World Series. A lot of scouts were there, following us around."

After undergoing surgery to repair a leg injury he sustained during his final year at Arkansas, McReynolds advanced rapidly through San Diego's farm system, joining the parent club during the second half of the 1983 campaign. Appearing in a total of 39 games with the Padres, McReynolds hit four homers, knocked in 14 runs, and batted .221. Named San Diego's starting center fielder prior to the start of the 1984 season, McReynolds helped the Padres capture the NL pennant by hitting 20 homers, driving in 75 runs, batting .278, and posting an OPS of .782. McReynolds continued to start in center for the Padres for two more years, having his finest season as a member of the team in 1986, when he hit 26 homers, knocked in 96 runs, scored 89 times, batted .288, and posted an OPS of .862. Despite his strong showing, though, San Diego GM Jack McKeon elected to include McReynolds in a multi-player trade he completed with the Mets on December 11, 1986, that sent him, relief pitcher Gene Walter, and minor-league infielder Adam Ging to New York for Kevin Mitchell, top prospects Shawn Abner and Stan Jefferson, and minor-league pitchers Kevin Armstrong and Kevin Brown.

Expressing his glee upon learning of the acquisition of McReynolds, Mets manager Davey Johnson said, "We got the guy we need. Immediately, we are a lot stronger than we were. I would hope that our third, fourth, fifth, and sixth hitters are now the best in baseball. And we have the protection for Darryl Strawberry that we were looking for."

McReynolds, on the other hand, felt angry over the trade, recalling, "I was kind of mad at the time. I just had the best season I'd had with San Diego. That really slaps you upside the head, knowing it's a business. It's not just playing."

Moved to left field upon his arrival in New York, McReynolds performed well his first year in Queens, hitting 29 homers, driving in 95 runs, scoring 86 times, stealing 14 bases, batting .276, and posting an OPS of .813. Even better in 1988, McReynolds helped lead the Mets to the NL East title by ranking among the league leaders with 27 homers and 99 RBIs, scoring 82 runs, batting .288, posting an OPS of .832, setting a then-NL record by stealing 21 bases without being caught, and leading all NL outfielders with 18 assists, earning in the process a third-place finish in the league MVP voting.

Nevertheless, while Mets fans accepted the fact that McReynolds's quiet and even-tempered personality set him apart from most of his teammates, they grew increasingly impatient with what they perceived to be his somewhat lackadaisical style of play. A gifted athlete, the solidly built McReynolds, who stood 6-foot and weighed 205 pounds, possessed so much natural ability that he made the game look easy at times. Employing a graceful and seemingly effortless stride, McReynolds often gave others the impression that he did not take the game seriously enough, once saying, "I think it's possible the front office in San Diego didn't know what kind of player I was. I have a fluid motion that makes it seem like I'm loafing."

Yet McReynolds paid little attention to what others thought of him, stating, "I was never trying to play to please anybody in particular. All I was doing was going out to play the best way I knew how. If my style didn't suit them, that's their problem. . . . It wasn't like I was loafing like people said I was. I guess that was my natural gait, or whatever it is. But I was out there to get the job done the best way I know how."

Meanwhile, the media did nothing to change the fans' perception of McReynolds, who preferred not to draw attention to himself and mingle with the press, with Jim Murray of the *Los Angeles Times* writing, "It's not that New York intimidates him: The big city. For him, Tulsa is a big city. Or his native Little Rock. Nor is he a 'Yup, Nope,' type. Kevin will talk, but you better hurry. Your best bet is on the way to the shower. He holds the team record for in and out after a game."

McReynolds briefly endeared himself to Mets fans in Game 1 of the 1988 NLCS, when he scored what proved to be the winning run of a 3–2 victory over the Dodgers in the top of the ninth inning on a mad dash around the bases following a two-out bloop single to center field by Gary Carter. With Carter's pop fly barely eluding a diving John Shelby, McReynolds motored home all the way from first base, driving his left shoulder into catcher Mike Scioscia, a notorious plate blocker, before slapping his left hand on home after the two men crashed to the dirt.

However, whatever goodwill McReynolds created with his jaunt around the basepaths disappeared just a few days later, when, prior to Game 7, he stated that either a win or loss by his team in the series finale would result in a victory for him, since a win would earn his club a berth in the World

Series and a loss would allow him to return to Arkansas sooner so that he could engage in his favorite hobbies of fishing and hunting.

Later attempting to explain his remark, which did not sit well with Mets fans, McReynolds said, "They don't even begin to understand what I was saying. They hear what they want to hear. I was as adamant about winning as anybody. But the consolation for me, if I don't win, a long, grueling season is over. I'm one of nine out there. I cannot carry the load by myself, nor did I ever think I could."

McReynolds had two more solid seasons for the Mets, hitting 22 homers, driving in 85 runs, batting .272, and posting an OPS of .775 in 1989, before reaching the seats 24 times, knocking in 82 runs, batting .269, and compiling an OPS of .808 the following year. But with McReynolds struggling at the plate during the early stages of the 1991 campaign, his relationship with the fans soured even more, prompting him to finally respond to their heckling by telling the local media, "People here like to kick someone when they're down. You more or less expect that in New York. I think a lot of people would like to see me fail."

Although McReynolds rebounded somewhat during the season's second half, he ended up posting disappointing numbers for a Mets team that finished well out of contention, finishing the year with 16 homers, 74 RBIs, a .259 batting average, and an OPS of .738. Dealt to the Royals the following offseason, along with Gregg Jefferies and utility man Keith Miller, for two-time AL Cy Young Award winner Bret Saberhagen and infielder Bill Pecota, McReynolds left New York a scorned man.

Yet following two injury-marred seasons in Kansas City during which he failed to hit more than 13 homers, drive in more than 49 runs, or bat any higher than .247, McReynolds rejoined the Mets when they re-acquired him from the Royals on January 5, 1994, for troubled outfielder Vince Coleman and cash. Claiming that he welcomed a return to New York upon learning of the deal, McReynolds said, "I think that a change of scenery will probably help me. And hopefully my performance dictates that I'm going to be in there every day."

At the same time, McReynolds acknowledged that his emotionless approach to the game and outwardly casual attitude had not pleased many of the fans at Shea Stadium during his first tour of duty with the club, stating, "People say I have a lackadaisical, lazy attitude, and I'm sorry they feel that way. But I'm not going to beat my head up against a wall trying to change it."

Hampered by back problems for much of the season, McReynolds appeared in only 51 games, before the Mets released him in mid-August.

McReynolds subsequently announced his retirement, saying at the time, "I'm ready to turn the page. I've been playing since I was five years old, and I never sat on the bench. I don't want to start at 35."

Over parts of 12 seasons, McReynolds hit 211 homers, knocked in 807 runs, scored 727 times, collected 1,439 hits, 284 doubles, and 35 triples, stole 93 bases, batted .265, compiled an on-base percentage of .328, and posted a slugging percentage of .447. McReynolds's Mets numbers include 122 homers, 456 RBIs, 405 runs scored, 791 hits, 153 doubles, 14 triples, 67 stolen bases, a .272 batting average, a .331 on-base percentage, and a .460 slugging percentage.

Looking back on his time in New York years later, McReynolds said, "Turned out there's a pretty good group of guys in New York. They'd just come off of winning the World Series. It was a lot of fun playing there. It could be tough at times with all the media coverage. . . . For the most part, it was a team with a lot of talent for several years there. We just never were able to completely get to the big show again, but it was a lot of fun. I'm glad I was there."

McReynolds added, "There were always a lot of fans, but they weren't always for you at times. They were always very verbal, and they expected a good product on the field. The fans were just one of the things to look forward to."

Following his playing days, McReynolds returned to his hometown of Little Rock, Arkansas, where he pursued several business interests, including operating a commercial duck hunting club he founded during his playing days. Now fully retired, McReynolds, who still enjoys hunting, fishing, and playing golf, says, "Arkansas has a lot to offer. I'm glad to be where I am. I'm alive and doing fine."

METS CAREER HIGHLIGHTS

Best Season

McReynolds had his finest all-around season as a member of the Mets in 1988, when he earned a third-place finish in the NL MVP balloting by placing near the top of the league rankings with 27 homers, 99 RBIs, and a .496 slugging percentage, batting .288, compiling an on-base percentage of .336, scoring 82 runs, and stealing 21 bases in 21 attempts, while also leading all NL outfielders with 18 assists and five double plays turned.

Memorable Moments/Greatest Performances

McReynolds ended a nearly four-hour marathon on June 4, 1988, when he led off the bottom of the 13th inning with a homer that gave the Mets a 6–5 victory over the Cubs.

McReynolds helped lead the Mets to an 11-inning, 9–8 win over the Braves on July 14, 1988, by going 5-for-6 with a homer, two doubles, four RBIs, and three runs scored.

McReynolds delivered the decisive blow of a 9–6 win over the Cubs on August 11, 1988, when he homered off Rich Gossage in the top of the ninth inning with two men out and the bases loaded.

McReynolds contributed to a 5–1 win over the Dodgers in Game 6 of the 1988 NLCS by going 4-for-4 at the plate with a homer, double, and three RBIs.

McReynolds hit for the cycle during an 11–0 rout of the Cardinals on August 1, 1989, going 4-for-5 with six RBIs and four runs scored.

Just five days later, McReynolds gave the Mets a 2–1 win over the Expos when he led off the bottom of the 14th inning with a homer off right-handed reliever Steve Frey.

McReynolds helped lead the Mets to a 10–9 win over the Giants on August 19, 1990, by homering twice and driving in six runs.

McReynolds gave the Mets a dramatic 8–5 victory over the Expos on June 25, 1991, when he homered with two men out and the bases loaded in the bottom of the ninth inning.

McReynolds led the Mets to a 5–4 win over the Expos on June 12, 1994, by driving in four runs with a triple and a pair of homers.

Notable Achievements

- Hit more than 20 home runs four times.
- Stole more than 20 bases once.
- Hit for the cycle vs St. Louis Cardinals on August 1, 1989.
- Led NL outfielders in assists twice and double plays turned once.
- Led NL left fielders in fielding percentage twice.
- 1988 division champion.
- September 25, 1988, NL Player of the Week.
- September 1988 NL Player of the Month.
- Finished third in 1988 NL MVP voting.
- 1988 *Sporting News* NL All-Star selection.

35
CARLOS DELGADO

One of only six players in MLB history to hit at least 30 home runs in 10 consecutive seasons, Carlos Delgado established himself as one of the most feared sluggers in the game during his 17-year big-league career, most of which he spent with the Toronto Blue Jays. A fixture in the middle of the Blue Jays' lineup for a decade, Delgado earned two All-Star selections, three Silver Sluggers, and a pair of top-five finishes in the AL MVP voting by surpassing 30 homers eight times, 100 RBIs six times, and 100 runs scored on five separate occasions, while also batting over .300 and posting an OPS over 1.000 twice each. Yet even though Delgado did most of his damage in Toronto, he proved to be an extremely productive hitter for the Mets during his relatively brief stint in New York, helping them win one NL East title and finish a close second in the division two other times by hitting more than 30 homers, driving in more than 100 runs, and compiling an OPS over .900 twice each, before succumbing to injuries that eventually forced him to retire.

Born in Aguadilla, Puerto Rico, on June 25, 1972, Carlos Juan Delgado Jr. grew up with his three siblings about two hours west of the capital city of San Juan. The son of a drug and alcohol counselor and a mother who worked as a medical laboratory assistant, Delgado spent much of his youth having his parents stress to him the importance of going to college. Nevertheless, Delgado's mom and dad came to realize before long that a career in baseball likely awaited their son, who, after attending Agustín Stahl Middle School, performed so well on the diamond at José de Diego High School that the Mets, Rangers, Expos, Reds, and Blue Jays all expressed interest in signing him after his junior year. Ultimately choosing to sign with the Blue Jays after they promised to pay for his college education even if he failed to make it to the major leagues, Delgado began his professional career at the tender age of 17.

Originally a catcher, Delgado continued to man that post as he advanced through Toronto's farm system until 1994, when, after a brief

Carlos Delgado surpassed 30 homers and 100 RBIs twice each as a member of the Mets.
Courtesy of Andrew J. Klein

tour of duty with the parent club, he saw some action in the outfield, before gradually transitioning to first base over the course of the next two seasons while at Triple-A Syracuse. Joining the Blue Jays for good in 1996, Delgado gave an early indication of what lay ahead by hitting 25 homers, driving in 92 runs, and batting .270, while serving almost exclusively as a designated hitter.

Although not yet a finished product, the lefty-swinging Delgado, who stood 6'3" and weighed 220 pounds, made an extremely favorable impression on those who witnessed him regularly, with Blue Jays broadcaster Buck Martinez recalling, "He had power that you don't see very often. The first time we saw him, we went, 'Oh my God, this is Carlos Delgado!' We had heard about him."

Named Toronto's starting first baseman in 1997, Delgado had another solid season, hitting 30 homers, driving in 91 runs, and batting .262, before beginning an exceptional six-year run during which he averaged 40 homers, 124 RBIs, and 107 runs scored, batted over .300 twice, and posted an OPS over 1.000 on two separate occasions, earning in the process two All-Star nominations and a pair of top-five finishes in the AL MVP voting. Especially outstanding in 2000 and 2003, Delgado hit 41 homers, knocked in 137 runs, batted .344, and compiled an OPS of 1.134 in the first of those campaigns, before reaching the seats 42 times, batting .302, and leading the league with 145 RBIs and an OPS of 1.109 in the second.

Blessed with tremendous power to all fields, Delgado, who once hit four homers in one game for the Blue Jays, had the ability to reach the seats anywhere in the ballpark. Yet Delgado proved to be more than just a slugger. Although he struck out frequently, fanning well over 100 times in 13 straight seasons, Delgado also hit for a fairly high average and possessed an excellent knowledge of the strike zone, drawing more than 100 bases on balls four times. And even though Delgado built his reputation on his hitting, he did an adequate job in the field, leading all AL first basemen in putouts five times and double plays turned on four separate occasions.

During his time in Toronto, Delgado also became known for publicly expressing his political beliefs, openly opposing the US Navy's use of the island of Vieques, Puerto Rico, as a weapons-testing ground until bombing ceased in 2003. Beltran also protested the US invasion of Iraq in 2003 by remaining in the dugout during the playing of "God Bless America" in the seventh inning of games the following year, claiming that he felt the song had come to be equated with a war in which he did not believe.

Delgado remained in Toronto for one more season, hitting 32 homers, driving in 99 runs, batting .269, and posting an OPS of .907 for the Blue Jays in 2004, before signing with the Florida Marlins for four years and $52 million when he became a free agent at the end of the year. But after earning a sixth-place finish in the NL MVP voting in 2005 by hitting 33 homers, driving in 115 runs, and batting .301, Delgado found himself on the move again when the financially strapped Marlins traded him to the Mets on November 24, 2005, for first baseman Mike Jacobs, pitching prospect Yusmeiro Petit, minor-league infielder Grant Psomas, and $7 million.

While Delgado looked forward to joining a lineup that already included David Wright, José Reyes, and fellow Puerto Rican Carlos Beltrán, he likely lost some of his enthusiasm when Mets ownership asked him to keep his political beliefs to himself. Nevertheless, Delgado agreed to comply with his new employer's wishes, saying during his introductory press conference that he was merely "Employee Number 15" and subsequently agreeing to stand during the singing of "God Bless America." Meanwhile, Mets manager

Willie Randolph stated, "I'd rather have a man who's going to stand up and say what he believes."

Inserted into the cleanup spot in the batting order upon his arrival in New York, Delgado, who spent the year hitting between Carlos Beltrán and David Wright, gave the Mets everything they hoped for in 2006, helping them win their first division title in nearly two decades by hitting 38 homers, driving in 114 runs, scoring 89 times, batting .265, compiling a .361 on-base percentage, and posting a .548 slugging percentage. Somewhat less productive in 2007, Delgado hit 24 homers, knocked in 87 runs, scored 71 times, batted .258, and posted an OPS of .781. But he rebounded the following year to rank among the league leaders with 38 homers and 115 RBIs, score 96 runs, bat .271, and post an OPS of .871, earning in the process a ninth-place finish in the NL MVP voting.

Delgado subsequently got off to a fast start in 2009, hitting four homers, driving in 23 runs, and batting .298 in his first 26 games, before sustaining a hip injury that brought his season to a premature end. After undergoing surgery to remove a bone spur and a torn labrum in his hip, Delgado filed for free agency at the end of the year but experienced a setback while playing winter ball in Puerto Rico. Although Delgado attempted a comeback with the Red Sox in August of 2010, he appeared in just five games with their minor-league affiliate in Pawtucket, before announcing his retirement when he aggravated his hip once again. Over parts of 17 big-league seasons, Delgado hit 473 homers, knocked in 1,512 runs, scored 1,241 times, collected 2,038 hits, 483 doubles, and 18 triples, batted .280, compiled an on-base percentage of .383, and posted a slugging percentage of .546. In his three-plus years with the Mets, Delgado hit 104 homers, knocked in 339 runs, scored 271 times, amassed 468 hits, 99 doubles, and four triples, batted .267, compiled a .351 on-base percentage, and posted a .506 slugging percentage.

Following his playing days, Delgado returned to his hometown of Aguadilla, Puerto Rico, where he currently lives with his wife and two children. Remaining active in the community, Delgado assists Puerto Rico's youth through his nonprofit organization Extra Bases, participates in initiatives to improve the island's public-education system, visits hospitalized children, and donates video-conferencing equipment to the local hospital in Aguadilla.

METS CAREER HIGHLIGHTS

Best Season

Although Delgado compiled extremely comparable numbers two years later, he made his greatest overall impact as a member of the Mets in 2006, when he helped lead them to the NL East title by hitting 38 homers, driving in 114 runs, scoring 89 times, batting .265, and posting an OPS of .909, earning in the process a 12th-place finish in the NL MVP balloting.

Memorable Moments/Greatest Performances

Delgado gave the Mets a 4–3 win over the Pirates on May 3, 2006, when he led off the bottom of the 12th inning with a homer off left-handed reliever Mike Gonzalez.

Delgado provided most of the offensive firepower during a 7–2 win over the Phillies on August 17, 2006, driving in four runs with a triple and a pair of homers.

Delgado led the Mets to an 8–7 victory over the Cardinals on August 22, 2006, by homering twice and knocking in five runs, reaching the seats once with the bases loaded.

Delgado contributed to a 7–2 win over the Marlins on May 26, 2007, by hitting a pair of homers, driving in five runs, and scoring three times.

After homering with one man aboard earlier in the contest, Delgado gave the Mets a dramatic 5–4 victory over the Giants on May 29, 2007, when he reached the seats against Armando Benítez with two men out and no one on base in the bottom of the 12th inning.

Delgado led the Mets to a 15–6 thrashing of the Yankees on June 27, 2008, by homering twice and knocking in nine runs, one of his homers coming with the bases loaded.

After hitting safely in each of his four previous plate appearances, Delgado gave the Mets a 5–4 victory over the Braves on August 21, 2008, when he delivered a game-winning RBI single in the bottom of the ninth inning.

Delgado had another big day at the plate four days later, driving in six runs with a pair of three-run homers during a lopsided 9–1 victory over the Astros on August 25, 2008.

Notable Achievements

- Hit more than 30 home runs twice.
- Knocked in more than 100 runs twice.
- Posted slugging percentage over .500 three times.
- Posted OPS over .900 twice.
- Knocked in nine runs vs Yankees on June 27, 2008.
- Led NL with 10 sacrifice flies in 2006.
- Ranks among Mets career leaders in slugging percentage (4th) and OPS (tied for 6th).
- 2006 division champion.
- 2006 Roberto Clemente Award winner.

36
CLIFF FLOYD

Plagued by injuries throughout his career, Cliff Floyd failed to attain the level of excellence others predicted for him when he first signed with the Montreal Expos in 1991. Yet even though Floyd garnered more than 500 official at-bats in just four of his 17 big-league seasons, he carved out an extremely successful career for himself that included stints with seven different teams. A member of the Mets from 2003 to 2006, Floyd surpassed 30 homers and 90 RBIs once each during his time in New York, while also leading all NL outfielders in assists once. And despite missing a significant amount of playing time his final year in Flushing, Floyd, who ranks among the franchise's career leaders in slugging percentage and OPS, helped the Mets advance to the NLCS by providing veteran leadership to a team in transition.

Born in Chicago, Illinois, on December 5, 1972, Cornelius Clifford Floyd grew up in the small Chicago suburb of Markham, not far from where his father, a former Marine, worked double shifts at a U.S. Steel plant to allow the family to live in a safe and stable neighborhood. Drawing inspiration from his dad, who needed a kidney transplant at a relatively young age, Floyd recalled, "This is a man who, even when he was sick, he always came to my games. There would be days when I was like, 'I know my dad's not coming to the game today,' and there he was at the game. It was mind-boggling. It gives you so much perspective."

A star in multiple sports at Thornwood High School in nearby South Holland, Floyd excelled in baseball, football, and basketball, gaining recognition from the *Chicago Tribune* as the 1991 Athlete of the Year by leading his teams to the Class AA Sectional Playoffs on the hardwood and the state championship on the diamond. Especially outstanding in baseball, Floyd hit seven homers, knocked in 71 runs, and batted .535 as a senior, earning in the process All-State honors for the second straight time.

Heavily recruited by several major college programs as graduation neared, Floyd initially signed a letter of intent to attend Creighton

Cliff Floyd ranks among the Mets' career leaders in both slugging percentage and OPS.

University, whose head baseball coach (and future Chicago Cubs GM) Jim Hendry recalled, "You didn't need to see much to recruit him. I saw him in a workout at St. Xavier College, where he hit a home run into a 40-mile-an-hour wind. And he was a Division I basketball player, no question. We were going to let him play both."

However, Floyd changed his plans and elected to turn pro when the Expos offered him a $300,000 signing bonus after selecting him with the 14th overall pick of the 1991 MLB Amateur Draft. Floyd subsequently spent the next three seasons advancing through Montreal's farm system, establishing himself as one of baseball's top prospects, with one minor-league manager describing the 6'5", 220-pound first baseman/outfielder as a "Willie McCovey-type with speed."

Nevertheless, with the Expos already set at first base and in the outfield, and with Floyd suffering a fracture to his wrist that forced him to miss most of the 1995 campaign, he received a limited amount of playing time in Montreal from 1994 to 1996, prompting him to request a trade to another team. Dealt to the Florida Marlins prior to the start of the 1997 season, Floyd assumed a backup role on the team that won the World Series that year, before having his breakout season in 1998, when, as Florida's starting left fielder, he hit 22 homers, knocked in 90 runs, scored 85 times, amassed 45 doubles, stole 27 bases, batted .282, and posted an OPS of .818.

Unfortunately, the injury bug bit Floyd again in 1999, with torn cartilage in his knee and a damaged Achilles tendon limiting him to just 69 games and 285 total plate appearances. But after hitting 22 homers, driving in 91 runs, batting .300, and posting an OPS of .906 the following year, Floyd had the finest season of his career in 2001, when he earned his lone All-Star nomination by hitting 31 homers, knocking in 103 runs, stealing 18 bases, batting .317, compiling an OPS of .968, and ranking among the league leaders with 123 runs scored and 44 doubles.

With Floyd nearing free agency, the Marlins traded him back to the Expos midway through the 2002 campaign, after which he split the final three months of the season between the Expos and Red Sox, finishing the year with 28 homers, 79 RBIs, 86 runs scored, and a .288 batting average. Subsequently signed by the Mets to a four-year, $26 million contract in January 2003 after receiving offers from just a handful of teams, Floyd said shortly thereafter, "I never thought it would boil down to this, where it was tough to get somebody to want you. And then this [offer] came about. I told my agent, 'You can drop everything else. You get this done.'"

Excited to be joining a team with such a passionate fanbase, Floyd added, "I've been playing for 10 years before crowds of 2,000 . . . 10 years of no adrenaline rush and no one watching us play, so I'm ready for this. . . . I always dreamed of one day playing in New York. Now that dream has finally come true. I couldn't be happier. . . . I enjoy the spotlight. I enjoy it when people see what I'm doing and see me busting my butt out there."

Stating that he eagerly anticipated teaming up with Floyd in the middle of the Mets' lineup upon learning of the signing, Mike Piazza said, "Obviously, Cliff Floyd is one of the few five-tool players in baseball. There's not much he can't do on the field. He's going to really inject some life into the Mets."

Hampered by injuries to his left knee and wrist his first year in New York, Floyd tried to play through the pain, at one point saying, "We ain't doing too well. You just have to suck it up." But after appearing in 108 of the Mets' first 123 games, 94 of which he started in left field, Floyd missed the rest of the season due to an Achilles tendon injury he sustained on August 18.

Commenting on his effort at the end of the year, Floyd, who finished the season with 18 homers, 68 RBIs, 57 runs scored, a .290 batting average, and an OPS of .894, stated, "I've learned a lot about myself this season. I never knew that I could push myself and play through injuries like this."

Meanwhile, Mets manager Art Howe expressed surprise that Floyd made it as far as he did, suggesting that his toughness "shows he's just a special kind of kid."

Plagued by injuries again in 2004, Floyd missed nearly two months of action with an injured elbow and a strained right quadricep. Nevertheless, he managed to put up solid offensive numbers again, concluding the campaign with 18 homers, 63 RBIs, 55 runs scored, a .260 batting average, and an OPS of .814. Healthy for most of 2005, Floyd helped lead the Mets to their first winning record in four years by hitting 34 homers, driving in 98 runs, scoring 85 times, batting .273, compiling a .358 on-base percentage, and posting a .505 slugging percentage.

A powerful left-handed batter who had the ability to hit the ball out of any part of the park, Floyd drove the ball well to all fields, with Mets GM Steve Phillips saying, "Not too many parks can contain this guy."

Commenting on the imposing figure that Floyd presented to opposing pitchers in the batter's box, Baltimore Orioles GM Roland Hemond stated, "He does remind you of Willie [McCovey]. They're both massive; huge. They have so much presence. And they look big. Some guys are big, but when you see them in person, they don't appear that immense. Floyd and McCovey are both immense."

An intelligent hitter, Floyd received high praise for the adjustments he made through the years from Mets pitcher Al Leiter, who commented, "What I've seen from him as a hitter is that now he not only has the ability to hit a ball 500 feet, but he's learned to change his swing with the count. He's thinking with the pitcher. He's a smarter hitter. He can hit for power and average. He's not just hitting solo jacks."

Although Floyd had lost some of the foot speed he possessed earlier in his career by the time he arrived in New York, he also did a solid job defensively, leading all NL left fielders with 15 assists in 2005, while ranking second among players at his position in putouts.

Known through the years for providing leadership and an intangible factor to his teams that helped foster close-knit clubhouses, Floyd contributed to the success of his ballclubs in other ways as well, with Carlos Peña saying of his teammate on the 2008 AL pennant-winning Tampa Bay Rays, "I think his presence was more powerful than we can quantify. He has the quiet confidence that rubs off on people, and soon everyone is believing."

Limited to just 97 games and 376 total plate appearances by a sprained ankle and an injury to his left Achilles tendon in 2006, Floyd hit just 11 homers, knocked in only 44 runs, and batted just .244. Nevertheless, his veteran presence and strong outfield defense proved invaluable to a Mets team that came within one game of advancing to the World Series.

A free agent again at the end of the year, Floyd signed with the Cubs after the Mets chose to pursue Moisés Alou to play left field. Commenting on the decision of Mets GM Omar Minaya, Floyd stated, "He has certain guys on his mind, and he gets them. All I can do is thank him for four years."

Floyd, who, in his four seasons with the Mets, hit 81 homers, knocked in 273 runs, scored 242 times, collected 440 hits, 92 doubles, and five triples, stole 32 bases, batted .268, compiled an on-base percentage of .354, and posted a slugging percentage of .478, ended up spending just one year in Chicago, before splitting his final two seasons between the Tampa Bay Rays and San Diego Padres. Choosing to announce his retirement after being released by the Padres following the conclusion of the 2009 campaign, Floyd ended his career with 233 homers, 865 RBIs, 824 runs scored, 1,479 hits, 340 doubles, 23 triples, 148 stolen bases, a .278 batting average, a .358 on-base percentage, and a .482 slugging percentage.

After retiring as an active player, Floyd began a career in broadcasting that has seen him serve as an analyst for several different stations, including Fox Sports, SNY, Canada-based CTC Sportsnet, Apple TV, and MLB Network. Floyd also started the Cliff Floyd Foundation, which provides scholarships, financial aid, and other opportunities to students with financial hardships, and worked with Pauze Innovation to develop a cap liner designed to protect baseball players hit in the head with batted or thrown balls.

Looking back on his playing career, Floyd, who currently lives in Florida with his wife and three children, said, "I never thought I would play as long as I did. I know I could have been a helluva lot better if my body held up for sure. . . . I dealt with injuries. If there's one thing you hear people say about me, it's, 'I wish he didn't get hurt as much.'"

METS CAREER HIGHLIGHTS

Best Season

Floyd had his best year as a member of the Mets in 2005, when, in addition to hitting a career-high 34 homers, he knocked in 98 runs, scored 85 times, batted .273, posted an OPS of .863, led all NL outfielders with 15 assists, and finished second among NL left fielders with 283 putouts and a .993 fielding percentage.

Memorable Moments/Greatest Performances

Floyd delivered the big blow of a 5–3 win over the Brewers on May 4, 2003, when he homered with the bases loaded in the top of the sixth inning.

Floyd helped lead the Mets to an 8–2 win over the Rangers on June 11, 2003, by going 3-for-4 with a homer and five RBIs.

Floyd led the Mets to a 7–5 win over the Reds on June 29, 2004, by knocking in four runs with a pair of homers.

Floyd hit safely in 20 consecutive games from April 8 to May 4, 2005, a period during which he went 30-for-76 (.395) with seven homers, three doubles, 23 RBIs, and 16 runs scored.

Floyd provided all the scoring in a 2–0 win over the Cardinals on May 13, 2005, with a pair of solo homers.

Floyd gave the Mets a dramatic 5–3 victory over the Angels on June 11, 2005, when he hit a two-out, three-run homer off reliever Brendan Donnelly in the bottom of the 10th inning.

Floyd led the Mets to a 13–7 win over the Cubs on July 16, 2006, by knocking in five runs with a pair of homers, hitting one of his round-trippers with the bases loaded.

Notable Achievements

- Hit more than 30 home runs once.
- Posted slugging percentage over .500 twice.
- Led NL outfielders in assists and double plays turned once each.
- Ranks among Mets career leaders in slugging percentage (9th) and OPS (9th).
- 2006 division champion.

37
JOHN STEARNS

Largely overlooked and underappreciated because he had the misfortune of playing for mostly losing teams, John Stearns spent parts of 10 seasons in New York, serving as the Mets' primary catcher in six of those. A member of the Mets from 1975 to 1984, Stearns proved to be a victim of bad timing, arriving shortly after the organization laid claim to its second NL pennant in 1973 and leaving just prior to the glory days of the mid-to-late 1980s. Nevertheless, Stearns earned the respect of his teammates and opponents with his hard-nosed style of play, which helped him garner four All-Star nominations, before a badly injured elbow brought his career to a premature end.

Born in Denver, Colorado, on August 21, 1951, John Hardin Stearns developed a love for sports at an early age, recalling, "I grew up in a family where sports were just part of our culture." The son of a former college football player who later spent many years coaching at Denver East High School, Stearns excelled in several sports at Thomas Jefferson High School, proving to be especially proficient in baseball and football. Originally an infielder on the diamond, Stearns eventually transitioned to catcher, remembering, "I was an all-league shortstop at high school in Denver. During my senior year, the catcher got kicked off the team, and the coach said, 'It's got to be you, John. You're the best athlete on the team.'"

Offered an athletic scholarship to the University of Colorado, Stearns elected to attend college rather than sign with the Oakland Athletics, who selected him in the 13th round of the 1969 MLB Draft. Continuing to star in both baseball and football at Colorado, Stearns led the NCAA with 15 home runs his senior year, while also setting several school records as a safety and punter on the gridiron, including registering a total of 16 career interceptions. Acquiring the nickname "Bad Dude" while in college, Stearns first became associated with that moniker when, after being asked by *Sports Illustrated* how he would like to be described on the football field, he responded, "as a Bad Dude."

John Stearns earned All-Star honors four times.

Selected by the Buffalo Bills as a defensive back in the 17th round of the 1973 NFL Draft following his graduation, Stearns chose instead to pursue a career in baseball when the Phillies claimed him with the second overall pick of that year's MLB Draft. Stearns subsequently spent most of the next two seasons in the minors, making a brief appearance with the parent club during the latter stages of the 1974 campaign, before being included in a trade with the Mets on December 5, 1974, that sent him, pitcher Mac Scarce, and outfielder Del Unser to New York for reliever Tug McGraw and outfielders Don Hahn and Dave Schneck.

Joining a Mets team less than two years removed from their second World Series appearance, Stearns spent his first season in New York backing up starting receiver Jerry Grote, hitting three homers, driving in 10 runs, scoring 25 times, and batting .189 in 59 games and 169 official at-bats.

Reduced to the role of third-string catcher the following year after getting off to a slow start offensively, Stearns asked to be sent to the minors. Regaining his stroke at Triple-A Tidewater, Stearns batted .310, hit 10 homers, and knocked in 45 runs in 102 games with the Tides, prompting the Mets to recall him in September.

Displacing Grote as the starter behind home plate in 1977, Stearns earned All-Star honors by tying for the team lead with 12 homers, driving in 55 runs, scoring 52 times, batting .251, and posting an OPS of .767, while also finishing second among all NL receivers with 742 putouts. Stearns followed that up with another solid season, concluding the 1978 campaign with 15 homers, 73 RBIs, 65 runs scored, 25 steals, a .264 batting average, and an OPS of .777.

Primarily a line-drive hitter, the right-handed-swinging Stearns, who stood 6 feet and weighed 185 pounds, possessed decent power, drove the ball well to all fields, and knew how to work the count, drawing at least 70 bases on balls in a season twice. Unusually fast for a catcher, Stearns also finished in double digits in steals four times, with his 25 thefts in 1978 representing a single-season franchise record for receivers.

More than anything, though, Stearns became known for his toughness, which he exhibited on June 30, 1978, when, with the Mets holding a 6–5 lead over the Pirates with two men out in the bottom of the ninth inning, he prevented the tying run from scoring by tagging out the much larger Dave Parker, who bowled him over as he approached home plate. Although the 6'5", 235-pound Parker, who suffered a broken cheekbone in the collision, sent him flying, Stearns held on to the ball, recording in the process the final out of the contest.

Stearns also fought with Montreal's Gary Carter following a collision at home plate and set off a bench-clearing brawl with the Expos after pitcher Bill Gullickson sailed an offering over the head of Mets teammate Mike Jorgensen.

Extremely popular with his teammates and the fans of New York for the tenacity he displayed on the playing field, Stearns made a strong impression on Mets manager Joe Torre, who said of his catcher, "He wants so bad to be so good."

Commenting on his batterymate's work ethic and tremendous determination, Jerry Koosman stated, "He's shown as much improvement as any catcher I've known, especially in his aggressiveness and thinking. He still tries to catch pitches in the dirt instead of blocking them."

Continuing to play hard every day even though the Mets' failures as a team often caused Shea Stadium to resemble a morgue, Stearns said years later, "I didn't even notice the crowd. I played for the respect of my peers. I wanted to be one of the best players in the league and a guy who really competed. I think I accomplished that."

Stearns earned his second All-Star nomination in 1979 by hitting nine homers, driving in 66 runs, scoring 58 times, stealing 15 bases, batting .243, and posting an OPS of .667. An All-Star again in 1980, Stearns knocked in 45 runs, batted .285, and posted an OPS of .716 in only 91 games, before missing the final two months of the season with a broken finger.

After being sidelined for the first two weeks of the strike-interrupted 1981 campaign by a twisted ankle, Stearns pinch-hit and spent some time at both first and third base upon his return to action, before resuming his normal catching duties. Appearing in a total of 80 games, Stearns finished the season with just one homer and 24 RBIs, while batting .271 and compiling an OPS of .662. Stearns subsequently gained All-Star recognition for the fourth and final time in 1982 by hitting four homers, driving in 28 runs, scoring 46 times, stealing 17 bases, batting .293, and posting an OPS of .764 despite spending the final two months of the season on the disabled list after injuring his right elbow in early July.

Later revealing that he initially considered his injury to be a minor one, Stearns stated in an article that he wrote for the *New York Times* in 1984, "Every ballplayer has had a sore arm, and I thought that this was nothing to get upset about. By the sixth inning [of a game on July 5, 1982], I was having trouble just tossing the ball to the pitcher. I figured that a couple of days out of the lineup with some therapy and I would be just fine. I wasn't worried."

But even though Stearns worked extensively with doctors and underwent two surgeries on his elbow, he never regained the ability to throw hard. And with Stearns appearing in a total of only 12 games with the Mets the previous two seasons, they released him on November 3, 1984. Recalling his feelings at the time, Stearns said, "I was kind of numb rather than angry. I couldn't admit that it might be over."

Stearns, who, over parts of 10 seasons in New York, hit 46 homers, knocked in 312 runs, scored 334 times, collected 695 hits, 152 doubles, and 10 triples, stole 91 bases, batted .259, compiled an on-base percentage of .341, and posted a slugging percentage of .375, subsequently attempted comebacks with a team in the Puerto Rico Winter League and minor-league affiliates of the Cincinnati Reds and Texas Rangers. But after failing to earn a roster spot with either the Reds or Rangers, he announced his retirement.

Claiming years later that his elbow injury cut his playing career in half, Stearns said, "If you can't throw, you can't be a catcher. I faced the Tommy

John surgery thing. Even with the surgery, they said I might not play again. It was difficult for me. I was 30 years old and thought I could have played another nine, 10 years."

Following his playing days, Stearns remained in baseball for nearly three more decades, serving as a scout for the Milwaukee Brewers, a bullpen coach for the Yankees, a manager in the farm system of the Toronto Blue Jays, and a scout and coach for the Baltimore Orioles, Washington Nationals, and Seattle Mariners, before returning to the Mets, first as a coach under Bobby Valentine and, later, as a scout and minor-league coach. Finally retiring to private life in 2015, Stearns spent his winters at his home in West Palm Beach, Florida, but also tried to spend as much time as possible with his elderly mother in Colorado. Stearns lived until September 15, 2022, when he died at the age of 71 following a long battle with prostate cancer.

Upon learning of his passing, Joe Torre said, "No one played the game harder than John. He never came to the park in a bad mood. All he wanted to do was win."

Former Mets teammate Lee Mazzilli said in a statement, "I am heartbroken. John was just a joy to be around. He loved the game so much."

METS CAREER HIGHLIGHTS

Best Season

Although Stearns failed to gain All-Star recognition in 1978, he had his finest all-around season, establishing career-high marks with 15 homers, 73 RBIs, 65 runs scored, 25 stolen bases, and an OPS of .777, while also batting .264 and ranking second among all NL catchers in both putouts and assists.

Memorable Moments/Greatest Performances

Stearns contributed to an 11–5 victory over the Cubs on September 8, 1976, by going 4-for-5 with a homer, three RBIs, and two runs scored.

Stearns delivered the big blow of a 6–4 win over the Expos on June 1, 1977, when he homered with the bases loaded in the top of the fifth inning.

Stearns had another big day against Montreal on August 9, 1978, going 3-for-4 with a homer, double, walk, stolen base, two RBIs, and three runs scored during a 10–3 Mets win.

Stearns set a new modern-day single-season NL record for catchers when he stole his 24th base during a 9–4 win over the Expos on September 7, 1978.

Stearns contributed to an 8–3 win over the Dodgers on July 18, 1982, by singling twice and stealing a career-high three bases.

Notable Achievements

- Stole 25 bases in 1978.
- Four-time NL All-Star selection (1977, 1979, 1980, and 1982).

38

ROBIN VENTURA

The American League's finest all-around third baseman for much of the 1990s, Robin Ventura spent parts of 10 seasons in Chicago, earning one All-Star nomination and five Gold Gloves by hitting more than 20 homers five times, driving in at least 100 runs twice, and posting an OPS over .800 on six separate occasions, while also leading all players at his position in putouts three times and assists twice. Yet even though Ventura is most closely associated with the White Sox, he made huge contributions to Mets teams that advanced to the NLCS twice and the World Series once during his three years in Flushing. Part of the best infield in franchise history, Ventura hit more than 20 homers three times, knocked in more than 100 runs once, batted over .300 once, and won the last of his six Gold Gloves while manning the hot corner for the Mets, earning in the process one top-10 finish in the NL MVP voting. Nevertheless, Ventura will always be remembered by Mets fans more than anything for delivering one of the biggest hits in team annals.

Born in Santa Maria, California, on July 14, 1967, Robin Mark Ventura grew up with his three brothers near Santa Barbara, where he began playing baseball at an early age, with his mother, Darlene, recalling, "He had to be out there playing. I just told the boys [older brothers, Randy and Rick] 'Just let him play.' They'd say, 'He can't do this or that.' Well, he started to get a lot better. He never feared playing over his head."

Eventually developing into a standout on the diamond at Righetti High School in nearby Orcutt, Ventura performed so well that he received a scholarship to Oklahoma State University. A three-year starter at third base for the Cowboys, Ventura earned three straight All-America nominations by totaling 68 homers, 302 RBIs, 100 runs scored, and 329 hits, while also compiling a .428 batting average and setting an NCAA record that still stands by hitting safely in 58 consecutive games. Named the nation's best amateur player at the end of his junior year after leading Oklahoma State to a school-record 61 wins by hitting 26 homers, driving in 96 runs, and

Robin Ventura will always be remembered by Mets fans for his "Grand Slam Single" against Atlanta in Game 5 of the 1999 NLCS.

batting .391, Ventura declared himself eligible for the 1988 MLB Amateur Draft, where the White Sox selected him in the first round, with the 10th overall pick.

Ventura subsequently spent less than one full season in the minors, before joining the parent club during the latter stages of the 1989 campaign and laying claim to the starting third base job the following year. After posting decent numbers as a rookie, Ventura established himself as one of the top players at his position in 1991 by hitting 23 homers, driving in 100 runs, scoring 92 times, batting .284, and compiling an OPS of .810, while also earning Gold Glove honors for the first of three straight times. Continuing to perform well for the White Sox the next seven seasons, Ventura hit more than 30 homers once, knocked in more than 90 runs five times, batted over

.280 on four separate occasions, and led all AL third sackers in every major defensive category at least once, helping his team win two division titles.

In addition to excelling in the field, Ventura emerged before long as one of Chicago's team leaders, with White Sox pitcher Jack McDowell calling him "the ideal teammate," and adding, "The team is absolutely No. 1 with him . . . He's quiet, but very determined. He's about as even keeled as anyone I've ever come across."

Yet despite his many contributions to the success of the ballclub, the White Sox allowed Ventura to sign a four-year deal with the Mets when he became a free agent at the end of 1998. Making an extremely favorable impression on his new teammates following his arrival in New York, Ventura drew praise from Mike Piazza, who commented, "Robin's very reserved, but he's also very funny. He's a great guy to have on your team. But he's obviously not looking for the spotlight. That's why he fits in very well with this ball club."

Even more enthusiastic, longtime Mets reliever John Franco proclaimed, "I think Robin Ventura is the best free agent signing in the history of this franchise."

Proving to be a huge addition to the Mets his first year in Queens, the left-handed-swinging Ventura, who stood 6'1" and weighed close to 195 pounds, increased the potency of a lineup that also included Piazza, John Olerud, Edgardo Alfonzo, and Rickey Henderson by hitting 32 homers, driving in 120 runs, scoring 88 times, batting .301, and posting an OPS of .908. Meanwhile, Ventura led all NL third basemen in assists and fielding percentage, with his superb all-around play earning him a sixth-place finish in the league MVP voting and helping the Mets compile a record of 97-66 during the regular season that enabled them to advance to the postseason tournament as a wild card after they defeated Cincinnati in a one-game playoff. Ventura also won the sixth Gold Glove of his career, joining first baseman Olerud and shortstop Rey Ordóñez as one of three Mets infielders to be so honored.

Although Ventura subsequently struggled at the plate against Arizona and Atlanta in the playoffs, he earned a permanent place in Mets lore in Game 5 of the NLCS, when, with the bases loaded and the score tied at 3–3 in the bottom of the 15th inning, he hit a home run to right-center field. However, with Todd Pratt, the runner at first base, failing to see the ball leave the park, he rushed back to first and began hugging Ventura, preventing him from circling the bases. Official scorers ended up ruling Ventura's hit an RBI single, leading to the game-winning blow being nicknamed the "Grand Slam Single."

Despite his outstanding performance for the Mets in 1999, Ventura spent the final two months of the campaign playing with an injured right shoulder and torn cartilage in his left knee, both of which required offseason surgery to repair. Returning to the Mets at less than 100 percent the following year, Ventura, who spent part of July on the disabled list with an inflamed shoulder, hit 24 homers and knocked in 84 runs, but batted just .232 and compiled an OPS of only .777. Meanwhile, after committing just nine errors in 160 games at third base the previous season, Ventura made nearly twice as many miscues (17) in 23 fewer games in the field.

Though somewhat healthier by the start of the 2001 season, Ventura continued to struggle at the plate, hitting 21 homers but driving in just 61 runs, batting only .237, and posting an OPS of just .778. Choosing to part ways with Ventura at the end of the year, the Mets traded him to the Yankees for outfielder David Justice on December 7, 2001. Ventura, who, in his three seasons with the Mets, hit 77 homers, knocked in 265 runs, scored 219 times, collected 394 hits, 81 doubles, and one triple, batted .260, compiled an on-base percentage of .360, and posted a slugging percentage of .468, ended up spending a year-and-a-half with the Yankees, earning his second All-Star nomination in 2002 by hitting 27 homers and driving in 93 runs, before being dealt to the Dodgers midway through the ensuing campaign. After assuming a part-time role in Los Angeles through the end of 2004, Ventura announced his retirement, ending his career with 294 homers, 1,182 RBIs, 1,006 runs scored, 1,885 hits, 338 doubles, 14 triples, a .267 batting average, a .362 on-base percentage, a .444 slugging percentage, and 18 grand slams, which ties him with Willie McCovey for fifth place on the all-time list.

Following his playing days, Ventura returned to his home in Arroyo Grande, California, where he spent the first few years of his retirement helping his wife raise their four children, before rejoining the White Sox as a minor-league scout in 2011. Named manager of the Sox the following year, Ventura remained in that post until the end of 2016, when he retired from managing and returned to his home in California, where he currently lives.

METS CAREER HIGHLIGHTS

Best Season

Ventura's first season with the Mets easily proved to be his finest as a member of the team. En route to earning a sixth-place finish in the NL

MVP voting in 1999, Ventura hit 32 homers, scored 88 runs, compiled an on-base percentage of .379, and established career-high marks in batting average (.301), slugging percentage (.529), OPS (.908), RBIs (120), hits (177), doubles (38), and total bases (311), while also serving as a member of an infield that committed the fewest errors of any in baseball history.

Memorable Moments/Greatest Performances

Ventura made history on May 20, 1999, when he became the first player ever to homer with the bases loaded in both ends of a doubleheader, leading the Mets in the process to an 11–10 and 10–1 sweep of the Brewers.

Ventura provided much of the offensive firepower during a 10–4 victory over the Marlins on June 28, 1999, driving in six runs with a pair of three-run homers.

Ventura starred in defeat on July 31, 1999, going 4-for-5 with two homers, a double, and six RBIs during a 17–10 loss to the Cubs.

Ventura experienced his most memorable moment as a member of the Mets in Game 5 of the 1999 NLCS, when he delivered what came to be known as the "Grand Slam Single." With the Mets trailing the Braves 3–1 in the series and the score tied, 3–3, in the bottom of the 15th inning, Ventura drove a pitch thrown by Kevin McGlinchy over the wall in right-center field with the bases loaded. But with Ventura subsequently unable to complete the circuit around the basepaths due to the mayhem that ensued, he ended up being credited with an RBI single that gave the Mets a 4–3 victory.

Ventura helped lead the Mets to a 12–9 win over the Pirates on April 16, 2000, by driving in six runs with a homer, double, and single.

After homering with one man aboard earlier in the contest, Ventura delivered the decisive blow of a 6–4 win over the Braves on April 3, 2001, when he reached the seats again with one man on base in the top of the 10th inning.

Ventura gave the Mets a 4–3 win over the Phillies on July 28, 2001, when he led off the bottom of the ninth inning with a home run off former teammate Turk Wendell.

Notable Achievements

- Hit more than 20 home runs three times, topping 30 homers once.
- Knocked in more than 100 runs once.
- Batted over .300 once.
- Posted slugging percentage over .500 once.

- Posted OPS over .900 once.
- Led NL third basemen in assists once and fielding percentage once.
- Ranks among Mets career leaders in on-base percentage (tied for 9th), slugging percentage (tied for 10th), and OPS (10th).
- 2000 NL champion.
- August 1, 1999, NL Player of the Week.
- 1999 Gold Glove Award winner.
- Finished sixth in 1999 NL MVP voting.

39
FÉLIX MILLÁN

Acquired from the Atlanta Braves in what is generally considered to be one of the better trades in franchise history, Félix Millán spent five seasons in New York, providing the Mets with consistently excellent play at second base. A steady contact hitter who rarely struck out, Millán batted over .280 three times, scored more than 80 runs twice, and fanned fewer times per plate appearance than any other player in the league on three separate occasions, en route to establishing himself as the most difficult man in team annals to strike out. Extremely reliable in the field as well, Millán annually ranked among the top players at his position in putouts and fielding percentage, with his strong all-around play making him a key contributor to the Mets' 1973 pennant-winning ballclub.

Born in Yabucoa, Puerto Rico, on August 21, 1943, Félix Millán grew up in the barrio of El Cerro del Calvario, where he learned how to do without. Often forced to attend school without any shoes, Millán lived in constant fear of his teacher calling him to the front of the classroom, typically hiding his bare feet from the other students by stretching them as far under his seat as possible. Hoping to earn a little money, young Félix worked several odd jobs, including shining shoes and picking grass called coitre, which he sold for 10 cents a bag to people who raised rabbits.

Recalling the poverty of his youth, Millán said, "Yes, growing up was tough, but our faith in God sustained my family and me. I prayed to God that I could make enough money to help my parents."

Adding that he hoped to one day escape his poor upbringing through baseball, Millán stated, "When I was a kid, I always dreamed to be a big leaguer. And I say no matter what happens to me I'm going to try to make it. . . . I never saw him play, but the story of Lou Gehrig was my great inspiration."

After receiving his introduction to the sport as a youngster by batting a ball of string with a guava branch, Millán began playing baseball in grade school in a league sponsored by the Yabucoa police department, before

Félix Millán established himself as the most difficult man to strike out in team annals during his time in New York.

competing for a local amateur team while in high school, remembering, "In Yabucoa, I played 'barrio' baseball . . . I played in high school . . . I played the top caliber of amateur ball with my hometown team. Finally, Kansas City A's scout Felix Delgado signed me to a professional contract in 1964 with Daytona in the Florida State League."

Prior to signing with Kansas City, though, Millán spent two years serving in the US Army, where his unfamiliarity with the English language made him feel lonesome and homesick until he found a sanctuary on his base's baseball team. Then, following his discharge from the military, Millán joined Puerto Rico's Double-A professional league, where Delgado spotted him for the first time.

After signing with the A's, Millán spent a year playing second base for the team's Class A affiliate in the Florida State League, before the Braves claimed him in the 1964 Rule 5 Draft. Advancing rapidly through Atlanta's farm system, Millán joined the parent club in June 1966, batting .275 and scoring 20 runs in 37 games, before being sidelined for the rest of the year by a broken finger.

Millán subsequently split the 1967 campaign between the Braves and their top farm team in Richmond, before arriving in the majors to stay the following year. Praised by new Atlanta skipper Lum Harris, who knew him from their days together in the minors, Millán received the following vote of confidence from his manager during the latter's introductory press conference: "Millán is going to replace Bill Mazeroski as the best second baseman in this league, and I don't mean that as a knock against Maz. But Maz is 31 years old, and Félix already has as much range as Maz ever had."

After laying claim to the starting second base job, Millán performed relatively well in his first full big-league season, batting .289, scoring 49 runs, and finishing third in the league with 14 sacrifice bunts. Improving upon his overall numbers in 1969, Millán gained All-Star recognition for the first of three straight times by hitting a career-high six homers, driving in 57 runs, scoring 98 times, and batting .267, while also winning the first of his two Gold Gloves by leading all players at his position in putouts, assists, and fielding percentage.

Commenting on Millán's stellar all-around play, noted sportswriter Gary Ronberg wrote, "He can hit, he can hit and run, bunt for a hit, sacrifice, and finagle a base on balls. He can run and slide, and he can scramble back up and run some more."

Meanwhile, Lum Harris continued to sing the praises of his young second baseman, saying, "He's the type of player that you never realize is around until the game is over. Then, you look up and he's got two hits, an RBI, a stolen base, and he's been in on two double plays."

Harris added, "The most fantastic thing about him is his quickness. I can name you about five balls hit to him this year that took bad hops at the last possible second. His hands were down there to field the ball—and then suddenly he was jumping in the air, catching the ball above his head."

Remaining one of the league's top second sackers the next two seasons, Millán earned consecutive All-Star nominations by batting .310 and scoring 100 runs in 1970, before posting a mark of .289 and scoring 65 times the following year. But after Millán batted just .257 and scored only 46 runs in 1972, the Braves traded him and left-handed starter George Stone to the Mets for pitchers Gary Gentry and Danny Frisella following the conclusion of the campaign.

Fearing that Millán might be hurt by the team's decision to part ways with him, Braves manager Eddie Mathews tried to break the news to him gently. But Millán remembered thinking to himself, "What's to be sorry about? Doesn't he know how many Puerto Ricans live in New York?"

Millán ended up making a huge impact his first year in Queens, helping the Mets capture the NL East title by leading them in games played (153), runs scored (82), batting average (.290), triples (four), hits (185), and sacrifice hits (18), setting new single-season franchise records in the last two categories. Millán also struck out only 22 times in 699 total plate appearances and 638 official at-bats, making him the most difficult player in the league to strike out for the second of four times. Meanwhile, Millán ranked among the top players at his position in both putouts (410) and fielding percentage (.989), with his outstanding all-around play gaining him recognition from the New York sportswriters as "1973 Met of the Year."

Although the 5'11", 172-pound Millán, who spent most of his career hitting out of the number two spot in the batting order, rarely walked and possessed very little power at the plate, he did an excellent job of moving runners along either by bunting or hitting to the right side of the diamond. A right-handed batter who employed a short, compact swing and choked up on the bat nearly a third of the way, Millán sprayed the ball to all fields, with his ability to make consistent contact making it extremely difficult for him to become engaged in any kind of prolonged slump.

In discussing Millán's hitting style, Braves coach Jim Busby stated, "It's a perfect swing. It's a compact snap, and he's smart enough to control it with a heavy, bottle-handled bat. He's as liable to kick up chalk down the right-field line as he is to drill it inside third base. And he can bunt. Ohhh, is he a beauty."

Meanwhile, Millán described his approach at the plate by saying, "I was simply a contact hitter. I choked up on the bat in a way not regularly seen . . . but it was comfortable for me."

Millán continued to perform well for the Mets the next three seasons, batting .268, leading the NL with 24 sacrifice hits, and striking out only 14 times in more than 500 at-bats in 1974, batting .283, scoring 81 times, and setting new single-season franchise records (since broken) by amassing 191 hits and 37 doubles in 1975, and finishing second among the team's regulars with a .282 batting average in 1976.

But after compiling a batting average of just .248 through the first four months of the 1977 campaign, Millán suffered a devastating injury during an altercation with Pirates catcher Ed Ott at Pittsburgh's Three Rivers Stadium on August 12, 1977, that essentially ended his major-league career. Upset over being bowled over at second base by a hard-sliding Ott, Millán shouted at the Pittsburgh receiver and hit him in the jaw with the ball in his hand. Ott, a former college wrestler, responded by picking up Millán and body-slamming him to the ground, causing him to be carried off the field on a stretcher with a broken clavicle and dislocated shoulder.

Released by the Mets at the end of the year, Millán accepted an offer to play for Japan's Yokohama Taiyo Whales, with whom he spent the next three seasons, compiling a batting average of .346 in 1979 that made him the first foreigner to win the Japanese batting title. Millán subsequently spent one season playing in the Mexican League for the Mexico City Red Devils, before announcing his retirement following the conclusion of the 1981 campaign.

Over parts of 12 big-league seasons, Millán hit 22 homers, knocked in 403 runs, scored 699 times, collected 1,617 hits, 229 doubles, and 38 triples, stole 67 bases, batted .279, compiled a .322 on-base percentage, posted a .343 slugging percentage, and struck out only 242 times in more than 6,300 total plate appearances. As a member of the Mets, Millán hit eight homers, knocked in 182 runs, scored 308 times, amassed 743 hits, 111 doubles, and 12 triples, swiped 11 bags, batted .278, compiled an on-base percentage of .326, posted a slugging percentage of .337, and fanned just 92 times in almost 3,000 total trips to the plate.

Remaining close to the game following his retirement as an active player, Millán worked as an infield instructor for the Mets' rookie league in Port St. Lucie, Florida, during the 1980s, and for a time worked as Latin American coordinator in the team's minor-league system. He also continued to be involved for many years with the Félix Millán Little League that he first established in New York in 1977. Now fully retired, Millán currently resides in his homeland of Puerto Rico.

METS CAREER HIGHLIGHTS

Best Season

Millán had arguably his finest offensive season as a member of the Mets in 1975, when, in addition to becoming the first player in team annals to appear in all 162 games, he set then single-season franchise records for most hits (191) and doubles (37). But Millán also committed 23 errors at second base, giving him a rather mediocre fielding percentage of .972. Meanwhile, Millán not only posted extremely comparable numbers on offense two years earlier, but he also committed just nine errors in the field, recorded a career-high 410 putouts, and finished third among NL second sackers with a .989 fielding percentage, making the 1973 campaign his finest all-around season in New York.

Memorable Moments/Greatest Performances

Millán led the Mets to a 5–2 win over the Reds on July 14, 1973, by scoring twice and driving in three runs with a homer and a pair of singles.

Millán gave the Mets a 1–0 victory over Juan Marichal and the Giants on August 24, 1971, when he drove home the game's only run from second base with a one-out single to right field in the bottom of the 10th inning.

After hitting safely three times and driving in three runs earlier in the contest, Millán knocked in what proved to be the winning run of a 9–8 victory over the Cubs on July 26, 1975, with an RBI single to center field in the top of the 10th inning.

Millán helped lead the Mets to an 11–7 win over the Cardinals on July 28, 1975, by going 4-for-6 at the plate with two doubles, three RBIs, and three runs scored.

Notable Achievements

- Led NL in sacrifice hits once and games played once.
- Holds Mets career record for best at-bat-per-strikeout ratio (29-to-1).
- Ranks fifth in franchise history with 68 sacrifice hits.
- Holds Mets single-season records for most sacrifice hits (24 in 1974), most games played (162 in 1975), and best at-bat-per-strikeout ratio (37-to-1 in 1974).
- 1973 division champion.
- 1973 NL champion.
- June 17, 1973, NL Player of the Week.

40
DAVE KINGMAN

One of the most enigmatic figures in team annals, Dave Kingman spent parts of six seasons in New York, during which time he became known as much for his dour disposition as his mammoth home runs. A member of the Mets from 1975 to 1977, and then again from 1981 to 1983, Kingman displayed extraordinary power at the plate, hitting more than 35 homers in each of the three seasons in which he garnered at least 400 official at-bats. But the towering Kingman, who acquired the nicknames "Kong" and "Sky King" during his time in Gotham, also struck out frequently, rarely walked, failed to hit for much of an average, and struggled terribly in the field. Meanwhile, Kingman's personality, which one teammate likened to that of a tree stump, often caused him to clash with team management and refuse to speak to members of the media.

Born in Pendleton, Oregon, on December 21, 1948, David Arthur Kingman moved with his family to Denver, Colorado, at the age of three, before relocating again to Los Angeles, California, in 1954, and finally to Mount Prospect, Illinois, a few years later. Eventually establishing himself as a star in multiple sports at Prospect High School, Kingman excelled as a center and forward in basketball, a wide receiver and safety in football, and a pitcher in baseball.

Drafted right out of high school by the California Angels in 1967, Kingman chose instead to spend one year at Harper Junior College in Palatine, Illinois, before enrolling at the University of Southern California on a baseball scholarship. Converted into an outfielder while at USC, Kingman helped lead the Trojans to the NCAA championship in 1970 by hitting nine homers, driving in 25 runs, and batting .355, earning in the process All-America honors.

Subsequently selected by the San Francisco Giants with the first overall pick of the 1970 MLB June Draft–Secondary Phase, Kingman spent less than two full seasons in the minors, before joining the parent club four months into the 1971 campaign. After hitting six homers and knocking in

Dave Kingman led the NL with 37 homers in 1982.

24 runs the final two months of the season, Kingman totaled 71 homers in 1,127 official at-bats over the course of the next three seasons, while splitting his time between first base, third base, and the outfield. However, Kingman also posted a composite batting average of just .218, struck out 387 times, and performed erratically in the field wherever he played, prompting the Giants to sell his contract to the Mets for $150,000 on February 28, 1975.

Joining a Mets team that desperately needed a power bat in the middle of their lineup, Kingman provided just that, hitting 36 homers, driving in 88 runs, and posting a slugging percentage of .494 in 1975, despite batting just .231, compiling an on-base percentage of only .284, and striking out 153 times. Concluding the ensuing campaign with extremely similar numbers, Kingman hit 37 homers, knocked in 86 runs, batted .238, compiled an on-base percentage of .286, posted a slugging percentage of .506, and fanned 135 times. Meanwhile, Kingman, who saw a significant amount of action at first base, left field, and right field over the course of those two seasons, continued to struggle with the glove, committing a total of 23 errors, while also often misplaying balls hit to him in the outfield.

Although the right-handed-swinging Kingman proved to be a wildly inconsistent hitter, he became the focal point of the Mets' offense due to his ability to deliver the longball. A streak hitter who tended to hit his home runs in bunches, Kingman, who stood 6'6" and weighed 210 pounds, possessed tremendous power that stemmed more from his lightning-quick swing than from brute strength.

In discussing his teammate, John Stearns said, "Dave is not a muscle hitter. His bat is so quick that he doesn't hit to the opposite field the way Reggie Jackson does. He's the only guy in the league who can pull a ball that's off the plate away from him for a home run."

Capable of hitting the ball as far as anyone in the game, Kingman delivered several tape-measure home runs, one of which came during a 4–3 win over the Houston Astros on June 3, 1975, when he drove a Ken Forsch offering an estimated 480 feet into the Shea Stadium parking lot. Kingman hit another memorable homer during a 6–5 loss to the Cubs on April 14, 1976, when he launched a pitch from Tom Dettore some 540 feet, well over the left field bleachers at Wrigley Field, onto the stoop of a private home two streets down.

Even though Kingman's prodigious slugging often prompted reporters to seek him out after games, he preferred to interact with the media as little as possible. Never one to seek the limelight, Kingman, said John Stearns, "has the personality of a tree trunk. He's not a bad guy, but if you try to talk to him, about all he does is grunt. He's not really the kind of man who wants to be in the public eye, yet here he is, the longest hitter in baseball."

With Kingman remaining very much a mystery to the public, Mets fans sided with management when he tried to renegotiate his contract prior to the start of the 1977 campaign. And as his dispute with the front office grew increasingly contentious, the already shy Kingman became more withdrawn, causing his rift with the media to grow wider.

Finally, with a slumping Kingman having hit just nine homers, driven in only 28 runs, and batted just .209 through the first three months of the season, the Mets traded him to the Padres for utility infielder and future Mets manager Bobby Valentine and minor-league pitcher Paul Siebert on June 15, 1977, as part of the "Midnight Massacre" that also sent Tom Seaver to the Reds.

After splitting the rest of the season between the Padres, Yankees, and Angels, Kingman signed with the Cubs as a free agent at the end of the year. Finding Wrigley Field very much to his liking, Kingman performed extremely well for the Cubs from 1978 to 1980, having the finest season of his career in 1979, when he earned the second of his three All-Star nominations and an 11th-place finish in the NL MVP voting by leading the league with 48 homers, knocking in 115 runs, scoring 97 times, batting .288, and topping the circuit with a .613 slugging percentage and OPS of .956.

Nevertheless, with Kingman having angered many within the Cubs organization by dumping ice water on the head of a reporter and the Mets once again in dire need of a home-run hitter, the two teams completed a trade on February 28, 1981, that sent the slugger back to New York for outfielder Steve Henderson and cash.

Playing mostly first base upon his return to Queens, Kingman hit 22 homers, knocked in 59 runs, batted .221, posted an OPS of .782, and struck out a league-leading 105 times during the strike-interrupted 1981 campaign, before topping the circuit with 37 homers, driving in 99 runs, batting .204, compiling an OPS of .717, and fanning a career-high 156 times the following year. Assuming a somewhat diminished role after the Mets acquired Keith Hernandez from the Cardinals midway through the 1983 season, Kingman appeared in only 100 games, limiting him to just 13 homers and 29 RBIs.

Released by the Mets at the end of the year, Kingman signed as a free agent with the Oakland Athletics, who he spent the next three seasons serving as a full-time designated hitter.

Experiencing a considerable amount of success in Oakland, Kingman hit at least 30 homers and knocked in more than 90 runs three straight times, although he once again drew negative attention to himself by sending a female reporter a package containing a live rat.

A free agent again following the conclusion of the 1986 campaign, Kingman signed a minor-league deal with his original team, the Giants. But after getting off to a poor start at Triple-A Phoenix, Kingman announced his retirement, ending his 16-year major-league career with 442 homers, 1,210 RBIs, 901 runs scored, 1,575 hits, 240 doubles, 25 triples, 85 stolen bases, 608 bases on balls, 1,816 strikeouts, a .236 batting average, a .302 on-base percentage, and a .478 slugging percentage. Over parts of six seasons with the Mets, Kingman hit 154 homers, knocked in 389 runs, scored 302 times, collected 509 hits, 70 doubles, and six triples, stole 29 bases, drew 211 bases on balls, struck out 672 times, batted .219, compiled a .287 on-base percentage, and posted a .453 slugging percentage.

Kingman subsequently remained away from the game for two years, before joining the West Palm Beach Tropics of the Senior Professional Baseball Association in 1989. But after hitting eight homers, driving in 40 runs, and batting .271 for the Tropics, Kingman retired from baseball for good when the league folded at the end of the year. Now 77 years of age, Kingman lives peacefully in the Lake Tahoe area, where he has spent much of his retirement operating a local tennis club.

METS CAREER HIGHLIGHTS

Best Season

Although Kingman led the NL with 37 homers and knocked in 99 runs in 1982, he had his finest season as a member of the Mets in 1976, when, despite missing seven weeks with torn ligaments in his left thumb that he sustained while trying to make a sliding catch in the outfield, he earned All-Star honors by finishing second in the league with 37 homers, driving in 86 runs, scoring 70 times, compiling a slugging percentage of .506, and posting an OPS of .793.

Memorable Moments/Greatest Performances

Kingman led the Mets to a 10–9 win over the Astros on July 20, 1975, by homering twice and driving in six runs.

Kingman gave the Mets a 7–5 win over the Cubs on September 18, 1975, when he homered off left-handed reliever Darold Knowles with two men out and one man on base in the bottom of the ninth inning.

After reaching the seats with one man aboard earlier in the contest, Kingman delivered the decisive blow of a 10–8 win over the Cubs on April 15, 1976, when he hit a three-run homer in the top of the ninth inning.

Kingman again homered twice and knocked in five runs during a 6–2 win over the Padres on May 7, 1976.

Kingman led the Mets to a 6–3 win over the Braves on May 12, 1976, by going 4-for-5 at the plate with a pair of homers, a double, and three RBIs.

Kingman proved to be a one-man wrecking crew on June 4, 1976, hitting three homers and knocking in a career-high eight runs during an 11–0 rout of the Dodgers.

Kingman helped lead the Mets to a 7–6 win over the Pirates on September 19, 1976, by driving in five runs with a pair of homers and a sacrifice fly.

Kingman contributed to a lopsided 9–2 victory over the Padres on April 29, 1977, by hitting a pair of three-run homers.

Kingman provided most of the offensive firepower during a 4–0 win over the Braves on August 18, 1981, going 3-for-4 at the plate with a pair of homers and three RBIs.

Notable Achievements

- Hit more than 30 home runs three times.
- Posted slugging percentage over .500 once.
- Hit three home runs in one game vs Dodgers on June 4, 1976.
- Led NL with 37 home runs in 1982.
- Finished second in NL in home runs twice.
- Ranks sixth in franchise history in home runs.
- Three-time NL Player of the Week.
- July 1975 NL Player of the Month.
- 1976 NL All-Star selection.

41
JOHAN SANTANA

One of the finest pitchers in the game for much of the first decade of the 21st century, Johan Santana won two Cy Young Awards and earned three All-Star nominations as a member of the Minnesota Twins from 2003 to 2007 by leading all AL hurlers in wins once, ERA twice, strikeouts three times, and WHIP on four separate occasions. Continuing to perform at an elite level for the Mets following his arrival in New York in 2008, the lefty-throwing Santana compiled an overall record of 40-25 his first three seasons in Flushing, garnering in the process one All-Star selection and his fifth consecutive top-five finish in the Cy Young voting. However, Santana's period of dominance ended shortly thereafter when he began experiencing arm problems that ultimately brought his career to a premature end. Prior to leaving the game, though, Santana earned a permanent place in Mets lore by becoming the first pitcher in franchise history to throw a no-hitter.

Born in Tovar, Mérida State, Venezuela, on March 13, 1979, Johan Alexander Santana Araque grew up in a small town, where he displayed an early interest in baseball, often playing the game with his father and four brothers. Eventually developing into a star center fielder at Liceo Jose Nucete Sardi High School, Santana performed so well that the Houston Astros signed him as an amateur free agent at only 16 years of age.

Converted into a pitcher shortly after he turned pro, Santana spent three years rising through Houston's farm system, before being selected by the Florida Marlins in the 1999 Rule 5 Draft. Dealt immediately to the Twins, Santana arrived in Minnesota prior to the start of the 2000 campaign, after which he spent the next three seasons working primarily as a middle-inning reliever. While in the bullpen, though, Santana developed his signature changeup, which helped make him a far more effective pitcher.

Promoted to Minnesota's starting rotation midway through the 2003 campaign, Santana finished the season with a record of 12-3, an ERA of 3.07, and 169 strikeouts in 158⅓ innings of work, before beginning an exceptional four-year run during which he compiled an overall record of

Johan Santana made history in 2012, when he became the first Mets pitcher to throw a no-hitter.
Courtesy of Keith Allison

70-32 and led all AL pitchers in ERA twice, strikeouts three times, and WHIP each season, earning in the process three All-Star selections and four straight top-five finishes in the Cy Young balloting, winning the award in both 2004 and 2006. Especially outstanding those two seasons, Santana won his final 13 decisions in 2004, before leading all major-league pitchers in wins, ERA, and strikeouts two years later.

Recognized as the finest southpaw in either league throughout the period, the 6-foot, 210-pound Santana, whose repertoire of pitches included an 88–94 mph fastball, a slider, and a devastating circle changeup, drew widespread acclaim for his ability to dominate the opposition, with Kansas City Royals slugger Mike Sweeney stating, "He's a power pitcher, just like Randy Johnson . . . he's got a parachute changeup . . . he's definitely the best lefty in the league."

Albert Pujols also had high praise for Santana, saying, "He's the best pitcher in the game, he and Roy Oswalt. He's a guy you don't want to get two strikes down against."

Twins coach Al Newman commented, "He definitely has that ace mentality . . . he dominates hitters."

Minnesota first baseman/catcher Matt LeCroy said of his teammate, "He makes the best hitters in the game look silly. . . . He's obviously the most dominant pitcher in the American League right now."

Nevertheless, with Santana nearing free agency, the Twins elected to trade him to the Mets on February 2, 2008, for a package of four players that included promising young outfielder Carlos Gómez, right-handed pitcher Philip Humber, and minor-league hurlers Deolis Guerra and Kevin Mulvey.

Expressing his glee upon acquiring Santana, Mets GM Omar Minaya stated, "I think that Johan Santanas of the world only come around once. Our team last year was a good team, and two years ago we had a good team. Now, the difference between those years and this year? Johan Santana. A front-line guy."

With the Mets subsequently signing the 28-year-old Santana to a six-year, $137 million contract, David Wright looked forward to him anchoring a starting rotation that also included Pedro Martínez and young veterans John Maine, Mike Pelfrey, and Oliver Pérez, saying, "For our younger pitchers to develop under a guy like Pedro, a guy like Johan, you can't ask for any better situation. He's going to go out there, and he's going to give you seven or eight innings every five days, and he's going to get you a win. That's just what it comes down to. I've gotten a chance to get to know him a little bit the past couple years. He seems like a great clubhouse guy. He's going to fit in perfectly with the chemistry that we have."

Excelling in his first season in Flushing, Santana earned a third-place finish in the NL Cy Young voting by compiling a record of 16-7, leading the league with a 2.53 ERA and 234⅓ innings pitched, and finishing second in the circuit with 206 strikeouts. Although somewhat less dominant in 2009, Santana had another outstanding season, gaining All-Star recognition by going 13-9 with a 3.13 ERA and 146 strikeouts in 166⅔ innings pitched, despite missing the final month of the campaign after undergoing arthroscopic surgery to remove bone chips in his left elbow.

Extremely impressed with his first-year teammate, Gary Sheffield stated, "He reminds me of a modern-day Curt Schilling or Randy Johnson."

Although Santana didn't throw quite as hard as either Schilling or Johnson, he struck out batters at nearly the same pace, saying, "I don't try for strikeouts, but batters just swing and miss."

Adding that his breaking ball helped make him such an effective strikeout pitcher, Santana noted, "My changeup looks like a fastball, but one goes straight and the other goes away from the right-handed hitter. Sometimes it cuts by itself, and I don't know where it's going."

Pitching for a mediocre Mets team in 2010, Santana compiled a record of 11-9 and an ERA of 2.98, before once again missing the final few weeks of the season, this time with a torn anterior capsule in his left shoulder that forced him to sit out the entire 2011 campaign as well.

Returning to action in 2012, Santana performed well the first two months of the season, winning three of his five decisions, compiling an ERA of 2.38, and throwing a no-hitter against the Cardinals on June 1. But everything went downhill from that point on, with Santana struggling in his next several starts, before spraining his right ankle and being shut down for the rest of the year in mid-August due to inflammation in his lower back.

Santana, who concluded the 2012 campaign with a record of 6-9 and an ERA of 4.85, rejoined the Mets the following spring but ended up missing the entire season after tearing his shoulder capsule again. The Mets subsequently bought out his 2014 option at the end of the year, making him a free agent. Although Santana later attempted comebacks with minor-league affiliates of the Baltimore Orioles and Toronto Blue Jays, he experienced more bad luck, suffering a torn Achilles tendon and a toe infection that ultimately prompted him to announce his retirement.

Over parts of 12 big-league seasons, Santana compiled a record of 139-78, an ERA of 3.20, and a WHIP of 1.132, threw 15 complete games and 10 shutouts, and struck out 1,988 batters in 2,025⅔ innings pitched. In his four years with the Mets, Santana went 46-34 with a 3.18 ERA, a WHIP of 1.201, nine complete games, six shutouts, and 607 strikeouts in 717 total innings of work.

After retiring from baseball, Santana moved with his wife and three children to Estero, Florida, where he continues to run The Johan Santana Foundation that he founded in 2006 to assist hospitals and help individuals who have lost loved ones to terrorism around the world.

METS CAREER HIGHLIGHTS

Best Season

Santana's first year with the Mets proved to be his finest as a member of the team. In addition to ranking among the NL leaders with 16 victories (against seven losses), 206 strikeouts, two shutouts, and a WHIP of 1.148

in 2008, Santana led the league with a 2.53 ERA and 234⅓ innings pitched, earning in the process a third-place finish in the Cy Young voting.

Memorable Moments/Greatest Performances

Santana dominated Pittsburgh's lineup on August 17, 2008, yielding just three hits, issuing no walks, and recording seven strikeouts during a 4–0 shutout.

Santana tossed another shutout a little over one month later, allowing just three hits, issuing three walks, and striking out nine batters during a 2–0 blanking of the Marlins on September 27, 2008.

Santana punctuated a 3–0, three-hit shutout of the Reds on July 6, 2010, by hitting the only home run of his career.

Santana turned in another dominant performance on August 12, 2010, surrendering just four hits and recording 10 strikeouts during a 4–0 shutout of the Rockies.

Santana tossed another four-hit shutout on May 26, 2012, yielding just four singles and registering seven strikeouts during a 9–0 win over the Padres.

Santana made history in his next start, when, despite issuing five bases on balls during an 8–0 shutout of the Cardinals on June 1, 2012, he became the first Mets pitcher to throw a no-hitter, also recording eight strikeouts during his epic performance.

Notable Achievements

- Won 16 games in 2008.
- Compiled ERA under 3.00 twice.
- Struck out more than 200 batters once.
- Threw more than 200 innings once.
- Threw no-hitter vs St. Louis Cardinals on June 1, 2012.
- Led NL pitchers in ERA once and innings pitched once.
- Finished second in NL in strikeouts once and shutouts twice.
- Two-time NL Player of the Week.
- Two-time NL Pitcher of the Month.
- Finished third in 2008 NL Cy Young voting.
- 2009 NL All-Star selection.

42
JERRY GROTE

An outstanding defensive catcher who became known for his ability to throw out opposing baserunners, call a good game, and handle a pitching staff, Jerry Grote spent parts of 12 seasons in New York, serving as the Mets' primary receiver in 11 of those. A key member of teams that won two pennants and one World Series, Grote, who Lou Brock identified in 1968 as "the toughest catcher in the league to try and steal against," contributed to the success of those ballclubs with his superior defense and fierce competitive spirit. A capable hitter as well, Grote batted over .270 four times, with his solid all-around play earning him two All-Star selections and a place in the Mets Hall of Fame.

Born in San Antonio, Texas, on October 6, 1942, Gerald Wayne Grote grew up in the state's second-largest city, where, at the age of 10, he, his parents, and his two younger sisters survived an F-4 tornado that claimed the life of his grandmother.

Developing into an outstanding all-around athlete during his teenage years, Grote excelled in baseball, track and field, and cross-country at Douglas MacArthur High School, starring as a pitcher and third baseman on the diamond. After turning down an offer to sign with the expansion Houston Colt .45s following his graduation in 1961, Grote enrolled at nearby Trinity University, where former big-league receiver Del Baker tutored him on the finer points of catching. Choosing to turn pro at the end of his freshman year, Grote inked a deal with the Colt .45s, who soon changed their name to the Astros.

After beginning his professional career with the San Antonio Missions of the Texas League in 1963, Grote spent most of the next two seasons shuttling back and forth between the Astros and their top minor-league affiliate in the Pacific Coast League, the Oklahoma City 89ers. Appearing in a total of 103 games with the parent club, Grote hit three homers, knocked in 25 runs, and batted just .182, before being traded to the Mets on October 19, 1965, for pitcher Tom Parsons.

Jerry Grote's superior defense behind the plate made him a key contributor to Mets teams that won two pennants and one World Series.

Recalling his initial impression of Grote, Mets front-office executive Bing Devine stated, "He didn't knock down the fences. But he could really catch and handle a pitcher, call a game, and throw."

Mets manager Wes Westrum also held Grote in high esteem, saying upon completion of the deal, "Jerry Grote, whom we obtained from the Astros, is a hustler and a battler. He backs up plays and keeps both the pitcher and the infield fired up."

Named the Mets' starting catcher upon his arrival in New York, the 23-year-old Grote struggled somewhat in his first full big-league season, batting .237, posting an OPS of .642, and driving in 31 runs, while also committing 11 errors in the field. Although Grote tightened up his defense in 1967, he performed even worse at the plate, batting .195, compiling an OPS of .479, and knocking in 23 runs.

With the help of new Mets manager Gil Hodges, Grote improved himself dramatically as a hitter in 1968, raising his batting average to .282 and his OPS to .706. Recalling the adjustments he made to his approach at the plate under Hodges, Grote said, "Gil changed me completely as a hitter. Gil got me up on the bat and told me all I had to do was make contact, keep the ball in play, and use the whole field."

And with Grote allowing just one passed ball the entire year, throwing out 43 percent of attempted base-stealers, and finishing third among NL receivers with a .994 fielding percentage, he received the first of his two All-Star nominations. Grote subsequently batted .252 for the Mets' 1969 world championship ballclub, before posting marks of .255 and .270 the next two seasons, while leading all NL catchers in putouts both years.

Although the 5'10", 185-pound Grote never developed into anything more than a marginal hitter, typically batting somewhere between .250 and .260, posting an OPS under .700, hitting fewer than five homers, and driving in less than 40 runs, he compensated for his shortcomings on offense with his superb work behind the plate. Widely regarded as one of the finest defensive catchers in the game, Grote received high praise from fellow receiver Johnny Bench, who stated, "If Grote and I were on the same team, I'd be playing third base."

Meanwhile, legendary base-stealer Lou Brock told *Sports Illustrated* in 1974, "Grote's quick out of the box, has a powerful arm, and always seemed to have a sixth sense about me stealing. He would have the ball waiting for me at second base long before I got there."

Grote also did an excellent job of calling pitches and helping young hurlers Tom Seaver, Jerry Koosman, Gary Gentry, and Jon Matlack realize their full potential, with the latter saying of his former batterymate, "He would come out to the mound, and you might have first and second and one out, and whoever you were facing, he'd relay to you exactly what had happened the previous at-bats, pitch-by-pitch, exactly where the guy hit the ball."

At the same time, Matlack suggested that Grote's competitive nature and high expectations for the members of his pitching staff made him an intimidating figure behind home plate, saying that during his rookie season, "Anytime I was pitching, anytime I bounced a ball and there was nobody on base, he would just about clean me off the mound throwing the ball back to me. I was scared to death that I'd bounce a curveball into the dirt and get him mad. You worried about him more than the hitter."

Jerry Koosman recalled an incident that occurred during the early stages of his career, when a dissatisfied Grote rifled the ball back toward his belt buckle. Remembering how he responded to Grote's aggressive act, Koosman said, "I told him, 'If you throw the ball back at me like that one more time, I am going to break your fucking neck.' We had great respect for each other after that."

A self-proclaimed redneck, Grote, wrote sports columnist George Vecsey of the *New York Times*, was "a hard-bitten catcher who would goad his teammates to pitch harder, who could snap at reporters and official scorers."

Revealing that Grote's gruff demeanor rubbed many of his teammates the wrong way, Ron Swoboda claimed that several of them could "barely stand him," adding, "He was a red-ass Texan who loved to fuck with people but who didn't like anyone to fuck with him. It was a one-way street. Grote is Grote."

Plagued by injuries from 1972 to 1974, Grote missed a total of 234 games, although he still managed to earn his second All-Star selection in the last of those campaigns. Despite being hampered by back problems and a strained shoulder in 1975, Grote established career-high marks in batting average (.295) and OPS (.731), while also leading all NL receivers with a .995 fielding percentage. Sharing playing time with Ron Hodges and John Stearns in 1976, Grote started 88 games behind the plate, compiling a batting average of .272, before surrendering the starting job to Stearns the following year. After Grote appeared in only 42 games through the first five months of the 1977 campaign, the Mets traded him to the Dodgers for a pair of minor leaguers on August 31, ending his lengthy association with the organization. Over parts of 12 seasons in New York, Grote hit 35 homers, knocked in 357 runs, scored 314 times, collected 994 hits, 143 doubles, and 18 triples, batted .256, compiled a .321 on-base percentage, and posted a .329 slugging percentage.

After leaving the Mets, Grote assumed a backup role on Dodger teams that won consecutive NL pennants, before announcing his retirement following the conclusion of the 1978 campaign. Choosing to return to the game two years later, Grote appeared in 22 contests with the Kansas City Royals in 1981, before retiring for good at the end of the year with career totals of 39 homers, 404 RBIs, 352 runs scored, 1,092 hits, 160 doubles, and 22 triples, a .252 batting average, an on-base percentage of .316, and a slugging percentage of .326.

Following his playing days, Grote owned and operated several businesses in the San Antonio area, including running a meat market and raising steers on his ranch. Grote lived until April 7, 2024, when he died of respiratory failure at the age of 81 after undergoing a heart procedure at the Texas Cardiac Arrhythmia Institute in Austin, Texas.

Upon learning of his former teammate's passing, Cleon Jones said, "Jerry was a bulldog. He caught one of the greatest pitching staffs in the history of baseball. He was the glue that kept the staff together."

Jerry Koosman stated, "He was the reason for my success. I have the photo in my home of me jumping into his arms after we won in 1969. I am heartbroken. No one was better behind the plate. He really controlled the game."

Jon Matlack added, "He was the best catcher I ever threw to. I don't think I ever shook him off once. I had the pleasure of being his roommate on the road for a few years. It's a sad day."

METS CAREER HIGHLIGHTS

Best Season

It could be argued that Grote had his finest all-around season in 1969, when, despite batting just .252 and compiling an OPS of only .663, he established career-high marks with six homers, 40 RBIs, and 38 runs scored, while also throwing out 56 percent of attempted base-stealers. But Grote posted slightly better overall numbers in 1975, when, in addition to hitting two homers and driving in 39 runs, he batted .295, compiled an OPS of .731, recorded a career-high five triples and 114 hits, and led all NL receivers with a .995 fielding percentage.

Memorable Moments/Greatest Performances

Grote helped lead the Mets to a 3–2 win over the Cubs on May 3, 1971, by going 4-for-5 at the plate with a pair of doubles, one RBI, and one run scored.

Grote led the Mets to a 4–3 win over the Padres on April 27, 1972, by knocking in two runs with a homer and triple.

Grote flexed his muscles again a few weeks later, when he knocked in four runs and homered twice in one game for the only time in his career during an 8–3 win over the Phillies at Veterans Stadium on May 19, 1972.

Grote delivered the big blow of a 7–0 victory over the Padres on August 15, 1973, when he homered with the bases loaded in the top of the fourth inning.

Grote contributed to a 9–2 rout of the Phillies on April 7, 1974, by driving in four runs with a homer and two singles.

Notable Achievements

- Led NL catchers in putouts twice and fielding percentage once.
- Ranks among Mets career leaders in games played (5th), plate appearances (10th), and at-bats (10th).
- Two-time division champion (1969 and 1973).
- Two-time NL champion (1969 and 1973).
- 1969 world champion.
- Two-time NL All-Star selection (1968 and 1974).
- Inducted into Mets Hall of Fame in 1992.

43
BUD HARRELSON

The only man in uniform for the Mets when they won both of their world championships, Bud Harrelson spent nearly a quarter of a century serving the organization in one capacity or another. A light-hitting, slick-fielding shortstop who contributed to the success of two pennant-winning ballclubs primarily with his outstanding glove work, good baserunning, and superior on-field leadership, Harrelson started at short for the Mets from 1967 to 1977, a period during which he earned two NL All-Star selections, one *Sporting News* All-Star nomination, and one Gold Glove. And following the conclusion of his playing career, Harrelson, who split his final three seasons between the Phillies and Texas Rangers, returned to New York, where he spent the next decade serving the Mets at different times as a coach, scout, special instructor, broadcaster, and manager, at both the minor- and major-league levels.

Born in Niles, California, on June 6, 1944, Derrel McKinley Harrelson acquired the nickname "Bud" at an early age from his older brother, Dwayne, who had a difficult time pronouncing his given name. Part of an athletic family that moved to nearby Hayward shortly after he entered the second grade, Harrelson grew up the son of a former football player who dropped out of high school to support his family and a high school track star who supported her children's athletic pursuits.

Following in his parents' footsteps, Harrelson developed into a stellar athlete at Sunset High School, excelling in football, baseball, and basketball despite his smallish frame. Recalling his days on the gridiron, Harrelson, who weighed only 97 pounds at the time, said, "I was all helmet and pads, but I played both ways—halfback and safety."

An outstanding infielder on the diamond and an excellent shooter and defender on the hardwood as well, Harrelson captained Sunset High in all three sports, gaining recognition as East Bay Athlete of the Year in his final season.

Bud Harrelson donned a Mets uniform longer than anyone else in franchise history.

With Harrelson garnering very little interest from pro scouts due to his lack of size, he enrolled at San Francisco State University on a basketball scholarship, although he ended up playing only baseball in college. But after batting .430 in 30 games with the Gators, Harrelson found himself being pursued by several major-league teams, recalling, "We played a top-notch schedule against schools such as Stanford, and soon the pro scouts were putting the rush on me. I decided it was time to take advantage of that and give pro baseball a shot."

After fielding offers from the Yankees, Cardinals, and Cubs, Harrelson elected to sign with the Mets since he believed that they offered him the best opportunity for advancement. Inking his deal with the Mets on June 7, 1963, the day after he celebrated his 19th birthday, Harrelson began his pro career at Class A Salinas, where he struggled at the plate, posting a batting average of just .221 in 136 at-bats, before being hit by a pitch that broke his left arm. Harrelson subsequently split the next two seasons between Salinas and Triple-A Buffalo of the International League, gradually improving his hitting, although he performed somewhat erratically in the field, committing a total of 65 errors. Meanwhile, Harrelson did everything he could to add some much-needed bulk onto his slender frame, including eating a dozen bananas a day.

After making a brief appearance with the parent club late in 1965, the right-handed-swinging Harrelson spent most of the following season learning how to switch-hit while playing for the Jacksonville Suns, the franchise's new International League farm team. Promoted to the majors for good in early August 1966, Harrelson appeared in 33 games, batting just .222, but stealing seven bases and committing just one error in 29 games at short.

Named the Mets' starting shortstop prior to the start of the 1967 campaign after veteran Roy McMillan suffered a career-ending shoulder injury during spring training, Harrelson acquitted himself fairly well in his first full big-league season, batting .254, scoring 59 runs, and hitting the first of his seven career homers, while also ranking among the top players at his position in putouts, assists, and double plays turned. Despite being tutored by Mets coach Yogi Berra, who suggested that he use a heavier bat and try to make better contact at the plate, Harrelson regressed somewhat offensively in 1968, when, plagued by knee problems that forced him to undergo surgery the following offseason, he batted just .219 and posted an OPS of only .524.

After quitting smoking and spending the winter months lifting weights, the 5'11" Harrelson, who previously tipped the scales at somewhere between 150 and 155 pounds, arrived at St. Petersburg in 1969 some 10 pounds heavier. Off to a fast start, Harrelson boasted a batting average of .291 by early June, before the wear-and-tear of the season, which always caused him to lose weight, and his military obligation, which began in July (he served in the National Guard for five years), resulted in a second-half slump. Yet even though Harrelson, who usually batted second against right-handers and slid down to eighth against southpaws in manager Gil Hodges's platoon system, ended up appearing in only 123 contests and batting just .248, he posted a very respectable .341 on-base percentage for the eventual World Series champions.

An All-Star in each of the next two seasons, Harrelson batted .243, stole 23 bases, established career-high marks with 42 RBIs, 72 runs scored, and 95 walks, and led all NL shortstops with 305 putouts in 1970, before batting .252, scoring 55 times, ranking among the league leaders with 28 steals, and earning Gold Glove honors the following year. Injured for much of 1972 and 1973, Harrelson appeared in only 106 games in the second of those campaigns due to a fractured wrist and fractured sternum. Nevertheless, Harrelson made his presence felt during the 1973 NLCS, when he became involved in one of the most memorable brawls in baseball history.

With the series tied at 1–1 after Jon Matlack shut out the heavily favored Cincinnati Reds on just two hits in Game 2, Harrelson told reporters following the contest, "They [the Reds] all look like me hitting."

Angered by Harrelson's remark, Reds second baseman Joe Morgan confronted him during pregame warmups for Game 3 and said, "If you ever say something like that about me again, I'll punch you out! Pete [Rose] is going to use this to get the club fired up. If he has a chance, he is going to come and get you at second."

Rose's opportunity came in the top of the fifth inning of a 9–2 Mets win, when he hit Harrelson with an elbow while sliding hard into second base in trying to break up a double play. Displeased with Rose's overly aggressive act, Harrelson told the near-200-pound outfielder, "That was a cheap (bleeping) shot." After Rose answered, "What did you say?" Harrelson repeated his words, causing that year's NL MVP to grab him and pin him to the ground. A bench-clearing brawl ensued that ultimately led to the fans at Shea Stadium throwing objects at Rose when he returned to his position in left field in the bottom of the inning.

Speaking of the incident afterward, Harrelson said, "I didn't think it [his comment] was all that bad. I was kind of putting myself down a little bit, but I was also putting them down. Then I heard that they were going to come after me and all that, so I figured that was it right there. And when Pete hit me after I'd already thrown the ball, I got mad. And we had the little match. He just kind of lifted me up, laid me down to sleep, and it was over."

And years later, Harrelson wrote in his 2012 memoir, *Turning Two: My Journey to the Top of the World and Back with the New York Mets*, "I have no regrets about going at it with Rose. I did what I had to do to protect myself, and Pete did what he thought he had to do to try to motivate his team. We fought, and that was the end of it."

Harrelson's fiery temperament earned him the respect of his teammates, who also appreciated the many other qualities he brought to the ballclub. Most admired for his outstanding work with the glove, Harrelson drew praise from Jerry Koosman, who said of his longtime teammate, "He was the best shortstop who played behind me—period. I can't tell you how many runs he saved."

Former Mets first baseman Ed Kranepool stated, "He [Harrelson] turned out to be a great shortstop, great defensive player, and he had a great arm, surprisingly, as small as he was. Most of his throws were chest high, and they were easy to catch."

Art Shamsky, his teammate on the 1969 Mets, said, "I just remember how great Buddy was defensively. He was really the glue of the infield."

Close friend and longtime teammate Tom Seaver added, "We simply don't win two pennants without him."

Plagued by injuries to his hands, knees, and back, Harrelson missed almost 300 games from 1974 to 1977, prompting the Mets to trade him to the Phillies for minor-league infielder Fred Andrews and cash prior to the start of the 1978 campaign. Harrelson, who, during his time in New York, hit six homers, knocked in 242 runs, scored 490 times, amassed 1,029 hits, 123 doubles, and 45 triples, stole 115 bases, batted .234, compiled a .324 on-base percentage, and posted a .287 slugging percentage, ended up spending two seasons in the City of Brotherly Love serving the Phillies as a utility infielder, before announcing his retirement after assuming a similar role with the Texas Rangers in 1980.

After spending one year away from the game, Harrelson returned to the Mets as first base coach under manager George Bamberger in 1982, before joining Tim McCarver and Ralph Kiner in the broadcast booth for one season. Returning to the field in 1984, Harrelson spent the next eight years either managing in the Mets' farm system (1984 and 1985), coaching at third base for the parent club (1985–1990), or managing the Mets (1990–1991), before being relieved of his duties after the team posted a record of just 77-84 under him in 1991.

Harrelson, who moved to Long Island in 1969 and never left, co-founded and co-owned the Long Island Ducks of the Atlantic League after he left the Mets organization. Harrelson also remained active in the community until his final years, when he began experiencing memory lapses and difficulty finishing sentences. Diagnosed with Alzheimer's in 2016, Harrelson continued to battle the disease until January 10, 2024, when he died at the age of 79.

Upon learning of his passing, former Mets teammate Ron Swoboda stated, "He looked like he needed shoe weights to keep from blowing away on a windy day. All he proceeded to do was turn himself into all the shortstop you could ever want. You don't win without somebody holding that position down the way he did."

Meanwhile, Art Shamsky said in a phone interview, "We don't win in 1969 without him. A fighter. The heart of the team. He was such a big part of Mets history. He really is a New York Met icon. Player, coach, manager—he's someone that's very, very special."

METS CAREER HIGHLIGHTS

Best Season

Harrelson posted the best overall numbers of his career in 1970, when he earned one of his two NL All-Star nominations by driving in 42 runs, scoring 72 times, collecting eight triples, swiping 23 bags, placing near the top of the league rankings with 95 bases on balls, batting .243, and compiling an on-base percentage of .351, while also leading all players at his position in putouts and setting a since-broken major-league record by going 54 consecutive games at shortstop without committing an error.

Memorable Moments/Greatest Performances

Harrelson accomplished the rare feat of tripling twice in one game during a 5–4 win over the Giants on September 16, 1966.

Harrelson contributed to an 11–5 victory over the Giants on July 26, 1967, by going 4-for-5 with two doubles, two RBIs, and one run scored.

Harrelson hit the first of his seven career homers during a 6–5 victory over the Pirates on August 17, 1967, circling the bases with an inside-the-parker after his line drive eluded right fielder Al Luplow.

Harrelson led the Mets to a 6–0 win over the Phillies on April 17, 1970, by scoring three times and driving in a pair of runs with a homer and triple.

Harrelson had a big day against the Pirates on May 15, 1971, going 4-for-5 with three RBIs and two runs scored during a 9–5 Mets win.

Notable Achievements

- Stole more than 20 bases twice.
- Led NL shortstops in putouts once.
- Ranks among Mets career leaders in hits (7th), triples (3rd), bases on balls (3rd), stolen bases (9th), sacrifice hits (tied for 3rd), games played (4th), plate appearances (4th), and at-bats (4th).

- Two-time division champion (1969 and 1973).
- Two-time NL champion (1969 and 1973).
- 1969 world champion.
- 1971 Gold Glove Award winner.
- Two-time NL All-Star selection (1970 and 1971).
- 1971 *Sporting News* NL All-Star selection.
- Inducted into Mets Hall of Fame in 1986.

44

BRANDON NIMMO

A regular member of the Mets' starting outfield for the last eight seasons, Brandon Nimmo has contributed significantly to teams that have advanced to the playoffs twice with his solid offensive production and strong defensive play. A good left-handed hitter who has exhibited a propensity for reaching base in any number of ways, Nimmo has surpassed 20 homers three times, scored more than 100 runs once, and compiled an on-base percentage over .400 on three separate occasions, while hitting out of various spots in the Mets' batting order. A versatile defender, Nimmo has also performed well at all three outfield positions, excelling in particular in center field in 2022, when he went the entire season without committing a single error. Meanwhile, Nimmo has endeared himself to the hometown fans with his friendly demeanor, strong work ethic, constant hustle, and fierce competitive spirit.

Born in Cheyenne, Wyoming, on March 27, 1993, Brandon Tate Nimmo grew up around sports, recalling, "I was always doing something with a ball, whether it was soccer, whether it was baseball, football, basketball. I always kind of took a liking and leaned towards baseball and football. And I think it was probably because baseball was played in the summer. I just loved going out and getting good weather because in Wyoming, obviously, we don't get as much of that. And, so, from June, late May to August, that was my happy time. I really gravitated towards baseball."

After working on his game year-round in a barn his father built behind the family's house, Nimmo further developed his skills by playing American Legion Baseball while in high school since Wyoming schools do not offer baseball as a sport. Offered an athletic scholarship to the University of Arkansas after hitting 15 home runs, stealing 34 bases, and batting .448 in 70 games in 2010, Nimmo chose instead to sign with the Mets for $2.1 million when they selected him with the 13th overall pick of the 2011 MLB Amateur Draft.

Brandon Nimmo has compiled an on-base percentage over .400 three times.
Courtesy of D. Benjamin Miller

Nimmo subsequently spent most of the next six seasons advancing through New York's farm system, before finally being promoted to the parent club midway through the 2016 campaign after hitting five homers, driving in 37 runs, and batting .328 at Triple-A Las Vegas. Faring relatively well in his first tour of duty at the big-league level, Nimmo homered once, knocked in six runs, and batted .274 in 32 games and 80 total plate appearances. Nevertheless, after straining his right hamstring while playing for Team Italy in the 2017 World Baseball Classic, Nimmo began the ensuing campaign back in the minors.

Rejoining the Mets in mid-June, Nimmo got off to a fast start, compiling a batting average of .350 over his first 24 plate appearances, before a partially collapsed lung forced him to spend three weeks on the disabled list. Returning to action in late July, Nimmo ended up hitting five homers, driving in 21 runs, scoring 26 times, batting .260, and posting an OPS of .797 in 69 games and 215 total plate appearances, while splitting his time between all three outfield positions.

Although not yet a full-time starter in 2018, Nimmo saw a significant amount of action, appearing in 140 games and garnering 535 total plate appearances. Showing increased power at the plate after hitting coaches Kevin Long and Pat Roessler suggested that he try hitting without his front foot striding forward, the 6'3", 205-pound Nimmo finished the season with 17 homers and 47 RBIs, while also scoring 77 runs, drawing 80 bases on balls, batting .263, and posting an OPS of .886.

Troubled by a bulging disc in his neck that limited him to just 69 games in 2019, Nimmo hit just eight homers, knocked in only 29 runs, and batted just .221. With the pandemic subsequently shortening the 2020 campaign to only 60 games and a bruised hand and hamstring strain plaguing him the following year, Nimmo appeared in a total of just 147 contests over the course of those two seasons. Nevertheless, he performed well whenever he took the field, hitting 16 homers, driving in 46 runs, scoring 84 times, drawing 87 bases on balls, and posting a composite batting average of .288, while hitting primarily out of the leadoff spot in the batting order.

Named the Mets' everyday starting center fielder and leadoff hitter prior to the start of the 2022 campaign, Nimmo responded by hitting 16 homers, driving in 64 runs, batting .274, posting an OPS of .800, and ranking among the league leaders with 102 runs scored and a .367 on-base percentage, while also leading all NL outfielders with a perfect 1.000 fielding percentage. Commenting on his role on the ballclub at one point during the season, Nimmo said, "I always aim to be the spark that ignites the team."

Rewarded by the Mets with an eight-year, $162 million contract extension at the end of the year, Nimmo received high praise at the time from manager Buck Showalter, who stated, "The thing about Brandon is that he's gotten better every year. . . . He's always chasing perfection. We all know that it's not gonna happen. There's nothing perfect about a baseball season, but he chases it nonetheless. . . . He's one of the top three leadoff hitters in all of baseball, and he's gotten better every year in some phase of his game."

While Nimmo has always possessed good speed, he worked diligently to improve his ability to track the ball in the outfield, eventually turning himself into one of the league's better defensive center fielders. Nimmo also spends hours in the batting cage tinkering with his stance and approach at the plate, with his hard work and dedication to his profession making him extremely popular with his teammates. Beloved by the hometown fans as well, Nimmo, who has earned a reputation as one of the nicest, most genuine people in all of baseball, often stays late after games to sign autographs in Citi Field's parking lot, participates in several charitable causes, and retains a strong presence in the community.

In discussing his relationship with the fans, Nimmo says, "The fans' energy keeps me going on and off the field."

Nimmo followed up his solid 2022 campaign with another strong showing in 2023, establishing new career highs with 24 homers and 68 RBIs, batting .274, compiling a .363 on-base percentage, posting a .466 slugging percentage, and finishing second among NL outfielders with 352 putouts. Continuing to perform well after being shifted to left field by new Mets manager Carlos Mendoza in 2024, Nimmo hit 23 homers, knocked in 90 runs, scored 88 times, and stole 15 bases, although he batted just .224 and posted an OPS of only .727.

The Mets' starting left fielder again in 2025, Nimmo finished the season with 25 homers, 92 RBIs, 81 runs scored, a .262 batting average, and an OPS of .760. Heading into the 2026 campaign, Nimmo boasts career totals of 135 homers, 463 RBIs, 593 runs scored, 974 hits, 188 doubles, 32 triples, and 54 stolen bases, a lifetime batting average of .262, an on-base percentage of .364, and a slugging percentage of .438.

CAREER HIGHLIGHTS

Best Season

Although Nimmo hit more homers and knocked in more runs in each of the next two seasons, he turned in his finest all-around performance for the Mets in 2022, when, in addition to hitting 16 homers, driving in 64 runs, scoring a career-high 102 times, batting .274, compiling an OPS of .800, and leading the league with seven triples, he played a flawless center field, handling all 308 of his chances without committing a single error.

Memorable Moments/Greatest Performances

Nimmo led the Mets to a 7–2 win over the Reds on September 7, 2017, by going 3-for-4 with two homers, a double, three RBIs, and three runs scored.

Nimmo contributed to a 12–2 rout of the Rockies on June 18, 2018, by hitting safely four times, homering twice, and driving in four runs.

Nimmo gave the Mets a 3–0 win over the Phillies on July 11, 2018, when he hit a two-out, three-run homer off reliever Mark Leiter in the bottom of the 10th inning.

Nimmo helped lead the Mets to a lopsided 16–5 victory over Baltimore on August 15, 2018, by going a perfect 5-for-5 at the plate, with a triple, two doubles, three RBIs, and three runs scored.

Nimmo led the Mets to a 5–3 victory over the Dodgers on April 19, 2023, by going 5-for-5 at the plate with a homer, two RBIs, and two runs scored.

Nimmo helped lead the Mets to an 8–7 win over the Braves on April 8, 2024, by driving in five runs with two homers and a pair of singles.

Nimmo gave the Mets a 4–3 victory over the Braves on May 12, 2024, when he homered with one man aboard in the bottom of the ninth inning off reliever A. J. Minter.

Nimmo led the Mets to a 19–5 rout of the Nationals on April 28, 2025, by going 4-for-6 with two homers, a double, four runs scored, and a career-high nine RBIs, tying in the process the single-game franchise record in the last category.

Nimmo contributed to a 19–9 pasting of the Marlins on August 29, 2025, by going 3-for-4 with a pair of homers, four RBIs, and four runs scored.

Notable Achievements

- Has hit more than 20 home runs three times.
- Has scored more than 100 runs once.
- Has compiled on-base percentage over .400 three times.
- Knocked in nine runs vs Washington on April 28, 2025.
- Led NL with seven triples in 2022.
- Finished second in NL with .404 on-base percentage in 2018.
- Has led NL outfielders in fielding percentage once.
- Ranks among Mets career leaders in home runs (9th), runs scored (6th), triples (5th), doubles (10th), extra-base hits (9th), total bases (10th), bases on balls (5th), on-base percentage (8th), and plate appearances (9th).

45
JEFF MCNEIL

An excellent contact hitter who rarely strikes out and typically hits for a high batting average, Jeff McNeil has spent the last eight seasons in New York providing the Mets with consistent production on offense and solid defense at multiple positions. One of only two players in franchise history to win a batting title, the left-handed-swinging McNeil has batted over .300 four times and slugged more than 20 homers once, earning in the process a pair of All-Star nominations. A strong defender as well, McNeil has done a good job wherever the Mets have put him in the field, with his solid all-around play making him a key contributor to teams that have made two playoff appearances.

Born in Santa Barbara, California, on April 8, 1992, Jeffrey Todd McNeil moved with his family at the age of 13 some 60 miles northwest, to the town of Nipomo, where he excelled in golf, basketball, and baseball at Nipomo High School. Invited to play summer ball for the Santa Barbara Foresters of the California Collegiate League after batting .446 his final year at Nipomo High, McNeil later received high praise from Foresters head coach, Bill Pintard, who recalled, "He didn't act like a high school guy. He was never intimidated. He played full throttle. If you're playing against him, you'd better pay attention, or he's going to show you up."

Offered a baseball scholarship to Cal State Northridge University, McNeil initially signed a letter of intent to play for the Matadors, before changing his commitment to Long Beach State University following the departure of Northridge's head coach. McNeil ended up spending three years starring on the diamond for "The Beach," performing especially well as a junior in 2013, when he earned All–Big West First-Team honors by batting .348 and striking out only 11 times in 221 official at-bats.

Selected by the Mets in the 12th round of the 2013 MLB Amateur Draft, McNeil subsequently spent most of the next six seasons in the minors, during which time he began using an unconventional knob-less bat first presented to him by minor-league hitting coordinator Lamar Johnson.

Jeff McNeil won the NL batting title with a mark of .326 in 2022.
Courtesy of D. Benjamin Miller

Promoted to the parent club in late July 2018 after posting a composite batting average of .342 at Double-A Binghamton and Triple-A Las Vegas, McNeil acquitted himself extremely well the rest of the year, hitting three homers, driving in 19 runs, scoring 35 times, batting .329, and compiling an OPS of .852 in 63 games, most of which he spent at second base.

Employed by the Mets at second, third, and both corner outfield positions in 2019, McNeil had his breakout season, earning All-Star honors by hitting 23 homers, driving in 75 runs, scoring 83 times, ranking among the league leaders with 38 doubles and a .318 batting average, and posting an OPS of .916. Turning in another strong performance during the pandemic-shortened 2020 campaign, McNeil batted .311 and compiled an OPS of .836 in 52 games, becoming in the process the first Mets player since David Wright to bat .300 or better in three straight seasons.

Far less effective on offense in 2021, McNeil hit seven homers, knocked in 35 runs, scored 48 times, batted just .251, and posted an OPS of only .679 in 120 games and 426 total plate appearances. Meanwhile, McNeil, who, despite manning other positions as well, spent most of his time at second base, experienced occasional differences with the Mets' new shortstop, Francisco Lindor, who objected to his double-play partner's failure to align himself properly on defense multiple times. In discussing Lindor's frustration with McNeil, one source said, "He [Lindor] would always try to get him to move, and Jeff would be like, 'Shut up, I got it.' It was building and building."

Things finally boiled over during a 5–4 win over Arizona on May 7, when, after McNeil's poor positioning cost the Mets an out at first base, Lindor confronted him in the tunnel that connects the team's dugout to the clubhouse at Citi Field, grabbed him by the throat, and pinned him against a wall. Fortunately, other Mets players arrived in time to prevent the situation from escalating any further. And Lindor and McNeil provided little fodder to reporters afterward, telling them that they had spotted an animal in the tunnel and were merely arguing over whether it was a rat or a raccoon.

Returning to top form in 2022, McNeil gained All-Star recognition for the second time by hitting nine homers, driving in 62 runs, scoring 73 times, leading the NL with a .326 batting average, and posting an OPS of .836, while once again splitting his time between second base and both corner outfield positions.

Capable of hitting virtually anywhere in the lineup, the 6'1", 195-pound McNeil has enough power to occasionally assume a spot in the middle of the batting order, although his ability to consistently put the ball in play makes him best suited to hit either first or second, with Dodgers batting coach Aaron Bates saying, "He [McNeil] sets the table for everybody else," and adding that the only way to keep him off the bases is to "hope that he hits it at somebody."

Often referred to as a "throwback" player for his high contact rate and low strikeout total, McNeil covers both sides of the plate extremely well and possesses tremendous bat control, which allows him to guide the ball to just about any opening on the field. And even though McNeil lacks elite running speed, he breaks quickly from home to first base, enabling him to get down the line quicker than most other players.

After agreeing to a four-year, $50 million contract extension with the Mets during the offseason, McNeil posted solid numbers in 2023, hitting 10 homers, driving in 55 runs, scoring 75 times, batting .270, and compiling an OPS of .711, despite suffering a partially torn UCL in his right elbow that forced him to miss the final few games of the campaign. McNeil subsequently posted a somewhat less impressive stat-line in 2024, hitting 12 homers, knocking in 44 runs, scoring 57 times, and batting just .238, before being sidelined for the final three weeks of the regular season and the first two rounds of the playoffs with a fractured right wrist he sustained when Reds hurler Brandon Williamson hit him with a pitch on September 6.

Plagued by injuries early in 2025 as well, McNeil began the regular season on the disabled list with a low-grade right oblique strain he suffered during spring training. Posting somewhat subpar numbers following his return to action in late April, McNeil hit 12 homers, knocked in 54 runs, scored 42 times, batted .243, and compiled an OPS of .746, while seeing action at second base and all three outfield positions. McNeil will enter the 2026 campaign with career totals of 80 homers, 367 RBIs, 432 runs scored, 920 hits, 193 doubles, 18 triples, and 37 stolen bases, a lifetime batting average of ,284, an on-base percentage of .351, and a slugging percentage of .428.

Best Season

Although McNeil won the NL batting title with a mark of .326 in 2022, he posted slightly better overall numbers in 2019, when, in addition to placing in the league's top five with a .318 batting average and 38 doubles, he established career highs in homers (23), RBIs (75), runs scored (83), on-base percentage (.384), slugging percentage (.531), and OPS (.916).

Memorable Moments/Greatest Performances

McNeil contributed to an 11–8 victory over the Nationals on March 30, 2019, by going 4-for-5 with a triple, double, two RBIs, and two runs scored.

McNeil homered twice in one game for the first time in his career during a 9–0 rout of the Diamondbacks on September 11, 2019, concluding the contest with three hits, a stolen base, three RBIs, and three runs scored.

McNeil helped lead the Mets to a 7–1 win over the Cardinals on April 18, 2023, by knocking in four runs with a homer and single.

McNeil proved to be the lone bright spot in a 6–4 loss to the Marlins on July 19, 2024, hitting safely three times and driving in three runs with a pair of homers.

McNeil gave the Mets a 3–2 victory over the Braves on July 25, 2024, when he drove home the winning run from second base with a two-out single in the bottom of the 10th inning.

McNeil contributed to a 13–5 rout of the Rockies on June 8, 2025, by going 3-for-5 with two homers, a double, four RBIs, and three runs scored.

McNeil led the Mets to a lopsided 9–2 victory over the Braves on August 23, 2025, by driving in four runs with a pair of homers.

Notable Achievements
- Has hit more than 20 home runs once.
- Has batted over .300 four times.
- Has posted slugging percentage over .500 once.
- Has posted OPS over .900 once.
- Led NL with .326 batting average in 2022.
- Ranks among Mets career leaders in batting average (tied for 9th) and doubles (tied for 8th).
- 2022 Silver Slugger Award winner.
- Two-time NL All-Star selection (2019 and 2022).

46
BOB OJEDA

Acquired from the Boston Red Sox following the conclusion of the 1985 campaign to round out the Mets' starting rotation, Bob Ojeda proved to be a huge addition to an already formidable pitching staff. New York's top hurler during the championship season of 1986, the left-handed-throwing Ojeda posted 18 victories and compiled an ERA of 2.57, earning in the process a fourth-place finish in the NL Cy Young voting. Continuing to excel in the postseason, Ojeda won both his decisions despite pitching with an injured arm that plagued him for the rest of his career. Although not nearly as effective in any of his other four seasons in New York, Ojeda won at least 10 games two other times, before his arm woes prompted the Mets to trade him to the Dodgers.

Born in Los Angeles, California, on December 17, 1957, Robert Michael Ojeda grew up some 170 miles northwest, in the city of Visalia, where he first displayed his pitching prowess at Redwood High School. Although Ojeda continued to perform well on the mound after enrolling at College of the Sequoias, a two-year community college also located in Visalia, he failed to garner much interest from big-league scouts due to his slight build, mediocre fastball, and inability to consistently throw strikes. After no team selected him in the 1978 MLB Amateur Draft, Ojeda worked as a landscaper for his brother-in-law until the Red Sox signed him as an undrafted free agent on the advice of scout Larry Flynn, who remembered him from his high school days.

Ojeda subsequently spent the better part of four years advancing through Boston's farm system, making a brief appearance with the parent club in 1980, before arriving in the majors to stay during the latter stages of the 1981 campaign after learning how to throw the changeup from Red Sox pitching coach Johnny Podres. Experiencing a moderate amount of success over the course of the next five seasons, Ojeda won 12 games twice and posted an ERA under 3.50 once, en route to compiling an overall record of 44-39 and a composite ERA of 4.21. But with the brash and opinionated

Bob Ojeda won 18 games for the Mets' 1986 world championship ballclub.

Ojeda failing to develop a rapport with his Red Sox teammates, and the Mets seeking to add another left-handed starter to a rotation that already included southpaw Sid Fernandez and right-handers Dwight Gooden, Ron Darling, and Rick Aguilera, the two teams completed a trade on November 13, 1985, that sent Ojeda and three minor-league pitchers to New York for relievers Calvin Schiraldi and Wes Gardner and a pair of minor-league outfielders.

In discussing the deal years later, Ojeda revealed that he felt very much out of place in the Red Sox clubhouse, saying, "Let's just say I wasn't their type. I didn't fit the mold."

Expected to be the Mets' fifth starter when he first arrived in New York, Ojeda surprised everyone by establishing himself as the ace of the staff before long. In addition to posting a record of 18-5 that gave him a league-best winning percentage of .783, Ojeda finished second in the NL with a 2.57 ERA, placed third in the circuit with a WHIP of 1.090, and set career-high marks with 148 strikeouts and 217⅓ innings pitched.

Proving to be the perfect complement to the hard throwers that comprised the rest of the Mets' starting rotation, the 6'1", 190-pound Ojeda depended primarily on offspeed pitches to retire opposing batters. However, he also learned how to make better use of his mid-80s fastball after he arrived in Queens, with Gary Carter later saying, "Once Bobby left Boston and came to New York, I really tried to get him to work inside, to throw more fastballs inside. Everyone is so reluctant to throw inside at Fenway Park, because you know if the batter hits a pop-up to left field, it's going to be a home run. What really improved Bobby when he came to the Mets was that he started throwing those inside fastballs, and he had that great changeup, probably the best of anyone I ever caught."

An extremely intelligent pitcher, Ojeda took a cerebral approach to his craft, relying more on guile and deception than sheer physical ability. Once asked if he would like to have the left arm of hard-throwing teammate Randy Myers instead of his own, the always honest Ojeda laughingly responded, "Not if I had to have his brain, too!"

Following his strong showing during the 1986 regular season, Ojeda helped lead the Mets to their second world championship by compiling a record of 2-0 and an ERA of 2.33 in his four postseason starts. After limiting the Astros to just one run on 10 hits during a complete-game 5–1 win in Game 2 of the NLCS, Ojeda returned to the mound for Game 6. Although not as effective, Ojeda, who allowed three runs in five innings of work, kept the Mets within striking distance in a contest they ultimately won in 16 innings, 7–6. Ojeda subsequently won Game 3 of the World Series by yielding just one run and five hits over the first seven innings of a 7–1 victory over the Red Sox, before surrendering two runs on eight hits over the first six innings of the Mets' memorable 6–5 win in Game 6.

Taking special pride in his win over his former team in Game 3 of the Fall Classic, Ojeda later said, "That game was the proudest I'd ever been on a baseball field. Because I didn't like the Red Sox. I had new friends, real friends. I had teammates who would fight and bleed for me. To do something important for my guys was awesome."

However, Ojeda's postseason heroics ended up taking a huge toll on him. After defeating the Astros in Game 2 of the NLCS, Ojeda had to receive a cortisone injection to prepare him for his next start, recalling, "Once I did it, it didn't feel much better. But then when I started to throw in the bullpen in Houston to get loose [for Game 6], it literally felt like sandbags were added in my elbow—like an added product in there, and it took a while to get it out of there. I really couldn't make the ball do what I needed it to do."

Although the pain eventually subsided to the point that Ojeda had the ability to make his next three starts, he knew that complete rest represented the only long-term solution. But with the world championship at stake, Ojeda refused to let himself or his team down, saying, "At that point, it was my dream—it was my father's dream too—and I would have paid that price any day of the week. You could not have kept me out of there. I would have done anything and accepted the consequences. I did them fully conscious of what I was doing and what I was risking, but it was worth the risk—I got a chance to go to the World Series. This was my dream since I was a little guy making up my own uniform because I loved the game so much."

Diagnosed with a chipped bone in his elbow following the conclusion of the Fall Classic, Ojeda later explained, "Most pitchers have debris in there; that's just part of the business and part of what you do. This particular large piece broke off and was scraping the nerve, and that was the problem. That was why the shot alleviated the pain temporarily—allowed me to continue—but when I came back in the spring of '87 . . . a couple of sessions into it, I realized the year was over."

Forced to undergo surgery to reposition the ulnar nerve in his left elbow after making just seven starts, Ojeda spent most of the season on the disabled list, remembering, "It is like being on the outside looking in, and there's a party going on, and they can't see you, they can't hear you, you're invisible, and you feel invisible—and part of you doesn't want to be seen or heard because you're not a part of it. Good, bad or ugly—you're not a part of it. It's an awful place to be. But it actually drives you to get back out there. And the sooner I could go back out there, the better."

Returning to the Mets in 1988, Ojeda went just 10-13, although he pitched much better than his record would seem to indicate, also posting an ERA of 2.88, leading all NL hurlers with a strikeouts-to-walks ratio of 4.030, and ranking among the leaders with a WHIP of 1.004 and five shutouts. But on the same day the Mets clinched the division title, Ojeda severed part of his left middle finger with an electric hedge clipper in a gardening mishap, preventing him from appearing in the postseason and forcing him to undergo microfracture surgery to reattach the digit.

Ojeda remained a regular member of the Mets' starting rotation for one more season, going 13-11 with a 3.47 ERA in 1989, before spending the ensuing campaign assuming the role of a spot-starter/middle-inning reliever. Traded to the Dodgers at the end of the year for former Met Hubie Brooks, Ojeda left New York with a five-season record of 51-40, an ERA of 3.12, a WHIP of 1.182, 17 complete games, nine shutouts, and 459 strikeouts in 764 total innings of work.

Ojeda ended up spending two years in Los Angeles, compiling an overall record of 18-18 for the Dodgers, before signing with the Cleveland Indians as a free agent following the conclusion of the 1992 campaign. But prior to the start of his second season in Cleveland, Ojeda experienced a life-changing event on March 22, 1993, when he survived a boating accident that claimed the lives of teammates Tim Crews and Steve Olin. With the three men returning from a fishing trip in the early evening darkness, their boat crashed into the dock, severely injuring Ojeda and killing his two comrades. Feeling that he needed to isolate himself from everyone (even his own family) following the incident, Ojeda spent nearly the entire year away from the game, before returning to the Indians in September. A free agent again at the end of the year, Ojeda signed with the Yankees, with whom he appeared in two games in 1994, before announcing his retirement following his release in early May. Over parts of 15 big-league seasons, Ojeda compiled a record of 115-98, an ERA of 3.65, and a WHIP of 1.332, threw 41 complete games and 16 shutouts, and struck out 1,128 batters in 1,884⅓ innings pitched.

Following his playing days, Ojeda remained away from baseball until 2001, when he returned to the Mets as a minor-league pitching coach. After serving the organization in that capacity for three years, Ojeda stayed away from the game for another five years, before joining the Mets' Network, SNY, as a postgame commentator, a position he held until the end of the 2014 season.

METS CAREER HIGHLIGHTS

Best Season

Ojeda had easily the finest season of his career in 1986, when he earned a fourth-place finish in the NL Cy Young voting by ranking among the league leaders with 18 victories, an ERA of 2.57, a WHIP of 1.090, seven complete games, and two shutouts, while also topping the circuit with a winning percentage of .783.

Memorable Moments/Greatest Performances

Ojeda earned a 2–1 victory over the Reds on May 9, 1986, by allowing just six hits and one run in eight innings of work, while also recording a career-high 10 strikeouts.

Ojeda helped the Mets post their first victory of the 1986 World Series by allowing just one run on five hits over the first seven innings of a 7–1 win over the Red Sox in Game 3.

Ojeda shut out the Expos on just two hits on April 14, 1988, yielding only a second-inning double by Andres Galarraga and an eighth-inning single by catcher Mike Fitzgerald during a 1–0 Mets win.

Ojeda won another pitchers' duel on July 29, 1988, this time surrendering just three hits and one walk during a 1–0 victory over the Pirates.

Ojeda dominated Montreal's lineup again on September 11, 1988, yielding just five hits and recording eight strikeouts during a 3–0 shutout.

Ojeda hurled another gem on June 17, 1989, surrendering just three hits and one walk during a 1–0 shutout of the Phillies.

Notable Achievements

- Won 18 games in 1986.
- Compiled ERA under 3.00 twice.
- Threw more than 200 innings once.
- Led NL pitchers in winning percentage once and strikeouts-to-walks ratio once.
- Finished second in NL in ERA once.
- Ranks among Mets career leaders in ERA (9th), WHIP (9th), and shutouts (tied for 8th).
- Two-time division champion (1986 and 1988).
- 1986 NL champion.
- 1986 world champion.
- Finished fourth in 1986 NL Cy Young voting.

47
EDWIN DÍAZ

The 2018 *Sporting News* AL Pitcher of the Year, Edwin Díaz earned that honor by performing magnificently for the Seattle Mariners out of the bullpen. Far less proficient as a member of the Mets the following season, Díaz struggled terribly his first year in New York, leaving many to wonder if he lacked the ability to succeed in the Big Apple. Yet even though Díaz has remained wildly inconsistent over the course of the last few seasons, he has been the same dominant pitcher he was in Seattle at times, recording more than 30 saves twice and compiling an ERA under 2.00 three times, en route to earning two All-Star selections and one *Sporting News* NL Pitcher of the Year nomination. And despite being plagued by injuries during his time in Flushing, Díaz has amassed the third-most saves of any reliever in franchise history.

Born in Naguabo, Puerto Rico, on March 22, 1994, Edwin Orlando Díaz grew up on the eastern coast of the island, where he displayed a passion for baseball at a very young age.

Initially an outfielder, Díaz spent his early years playing mostly center field in local leagues, before reluctantly transitioning to the pitching mound as a teenager at the insistence of his father. Eventually developing into an outstanding starter at Caguas Military Academy in nearby Caguas, Díaz performed so well that the Seattle Mariners selected him in the third round of the 2012 MLB Amateur Draft.

Díaz subsequently spent the next four years advancing through Seattle's farm system, during which time he moved to the bullpen. Finally joining the parent club in June 2016, Díaz assumed the role of closer two months later, after which he went on to save 18 games, compile an ERA of 2.79, and strike out 88 batters in 51⅔ innings of work. Equally effective in 2017, Díaz ranked among the AL leaders with 34 saves and posted an ERA of 3.27, before establishing himself as the most dominant closer in the game the following year, when he earned All-Star and *Sporting News* AL Pitcher of the Year honors by leading the majors with 57 saves, compiling an ERA of

Edwin Díaz earned *Sporting News* NL Pitcher of the Year honors in 2022. Courtesy of D. Benjamin Miller

1.96 and a WHIP of 0.791, and registering 124 strikeouts in 73⅓ innings pitched.

Nevertheless, with the Mariners seeking to rid themselves of Robinson Canó's exorbitant contract, they completed a trade with the Mets on December 3, 2018, that sent the aging second baseman, Díaz, and $20 million in cash to New York for veteran outfielder Jay Bruce, pitcher Anthony Swarzak, and minor leaguers Jarred Kelenic, Gerson Bautista, and Justin Dunn. Failing miserably his first year in Queens, Díaz won just two of his nine decisions, pitched to a 5.59 ERA and a 1.379 WHIP, saved only 26 games, and set a single-season major-league record by surrendering 15 ninth-inning home runs.

Vilified by the local media, Díaz himself came to question his ability to perform on the big stage, later saying, "In Seattle, it was not the same. I didn't see the same amount of reporters as here. On social media, things were bigger here. . . . The first year was tough."

Refocusing himself the following offseason, Díaz returned to Puerto Rico, where he reworked his release point and consulted with Hall of Fame pitcher Pedro Martínez, who suggested that he make some minor adjustments to his weight transfer on the mound. Díaz also worked with new Mets pitching coach Jeremy Hefner, who recalled, "I didn't really have to do a lot with him. It was more or less letting his natural abilities come out. It was just one year that was bad."

Rejoining the Mets with a different attitude in 2020, Díaz excelled during the pandemic-shortened campaign, converting six of his 10 save opportunities, compiling a record of 2-1 and an ERA of 1.75, and registering 50 strikeouts in 25⅔ innings pitched. Regressing somewhat in 2021, Díaz went 5-6 with a 3.45 ERA, although he still managed to rank among the league leaders with 32 saves and strike out 89 batters in 62⅔ innings of work. Returning to top form in 2022, Díaz earned All-Star honors and gained recognition as the NL Reliever of the Year and the *Sporting News* NL Pitcher of the Year by going 3-1 with a 1.31 ERA, a WHIP of 0.839, 32 saves, and 118 strikeouts in 62 innings pitched.

Commenting on his outstanding performance following the conclusion of the campaign, Díaz said, "I knew I had the stuff. I got the stuff, and I'm a player that can be one of the best in the game when I am at the top. I flushed everything away, went home, and prepared my body to get back on track in 2020, and everything was going in the right direction."

Rewarded by the Mets at the end of the year with a five-year, $102 million contract that represented the richest deal ever given to a reliever, Díaz later received high praise from teammate Jake Diekman, who stated, "There's a reason why he got, up to that point, the biggest extension ever. He is unbelievable, and he's a commodity that every team needs. You don't worry about the last inning of the game. You worry about, say, innings five through eight, and then, in the ninth, it's over."

The right-handed-throwing Díaz, who stands 6'3" and weighs close to 180 pounds, possesses an arsenal of pitches that includes an upper-90s four-seam fastball on which he relies most heavily. Díaz also throws a slider that averages close to 90 mph on the radar gun and occasionally mixes in a changeup that approaches the plate at just under 92 mph. While Díaz's slider is a good one, it is the movement, velocity, and placement of his fastball that has enabled him to establish himself as an elite strikeout pitcher—one that has averaged almost 15 strikeouts per nine innings pitched over the course of his career.

Unfortunately, just four months after inking his deal with the Mets, Díaz sustained a freak injury when he tore the right patellar tendon in his right knee while celebrating Puerto Rico's victory over the Dominican Republic in the World Baseball Classic. Forced to undergo surgery, Díaz ended up missing the entire 2023 campaign, contributing greatly to the Mets' disappointing fourth-place finish in the NL East.

Showing a considerable amount of rust upon his return to action in 2024, Díaz failed to regain his earlier form for much of the season. Further hampered by a right shoulder impingement that landed him on the disabled list for two weeks, Díaz performed so erratically that he temporarily lost his closer's role. Nevertheless, Brandon Nimmo remained confident that his teammate would eventually right himself, saying at one point during the campaign, "I think you take for granted how playing every day and being in it every day really can help your routine and help you be ready to compete. So, when you take a year off from it, there's definitely a chance for some rust or a lull to happen. But I have confidence that him getting back into it, he'll get that confidence back and execute the pitches and be able to get back to his old form."

Proving Nimmo prophetic, Díaz came up big for the Mets during September, helping them earn a wildcard playoff berth by winning one game and saving six others. Finishing the 2024 season with respectable numbers, Díaz concluded the campaign with a record of 6-4, 20 saves, an ERA of 3.52, a WHIP of 1.043, and 84 strikeouts in 53⅔ innings pitched.

At his very best this past season, Díaz went 6-3 with an ERA of 1.63 and a WHIP of 0.874, recorded 28 saves, and struck out 98 batters in 66⅓ innings of work, earning in the process his second All-Star nomination as a member of the team. Díaz, who will enter the 2026 campaign with a career record of 28-36, 253 saves, and an ERA of 2.82, has posted a mark of 24-22, registered 144 saves, and compiled an ERA of 2.93 during his time in New York.

Best Season

As well as Díaz pitched this past season, he proved to be a bit more dominant in 2022, when he earned *Sporting News* NL Pitcher of the Year honors by compiling a record of 3-1 and an ERA of 1.31, posting a WHIP of 0.839, ranking among the league leaders with 32 saves, and striking out 118 batters in just 62 innings of work.

Memorable Moments/Greatest Performances

Díaz earned a victory over the Yankees on September 3, 2020, by recording four strikeouts and allowing just one walk over the final two frames of a 10-inning, 9–7 Mets win.

Díaz turned in another dominant performance on August 18, 2021, allowing just one batter to reach base on a hit-by-pitch in his two innings of work during a 12-inning, 6–2 win over the Giants.

Díaz struck out all three batters he faced in the ninth inning of a 3–0 win over the Phillies on April 29, 2022, finishing off a combined no-hitter thrown by five Mets pitchers.

Díaz saved a 4–1 victory over the Anaheim Angels on June 12, 2022, by striking out five of the six batters he faced, allowing the sixth man to reach base via a walk.

Díaz earned a victory over the Phillies on August 26, 2025, by working a perfect 1⅔ innings of relief during a 6–5 Mets win, striking out four of the five batters he faced.

Notable Achievements

- Has saved more than 30 games twice.
- Has compiled ERA under 2.00 three times.
- Has posted WHIP under 1.000 twice.
- Has struck out more than 100 batters once.
- Ranks third in franchise history in saves.
- Three-time NL Reliever of the Month.
- 2022 NL Reliever of the Year.
- 2022 *Sporting News* NL Pitcher of the Year.
- 2022 All-MLB First-Team selection.
- 2025 All-MLB Second-Team selection.
- Two-time NL All-Star selection (2022 and 2025).

48
LENNY DYKSTRA

Nicknamed "Nails" for his toughness and all-out style of play, Lenny Dykstra spent parts of five seasons in New York, serving as the Mets' leadoff hitter and primary starter in center field much of that time. Forming with Wally Backman a gritty one-two punch at the top of the lineup, Dykstra did whatever it took to win, including diving for balls and running into outfield walls, taking out infielders on the basepaths, and deriding opponents from the dugout. A strong all-around player, Dykstra, who possessed occasional power at the plate, a keen batting eye, and outstanding speed on the basepaths, helped lead the Mets to two division titles, one pennant, and one world championship by batting over .290 once, posting an OPS over .800 twice, and stealing more than 20 bases three times, while also doing an outstanding job of patrolling center field at Shea Stadium. And after leaving New York, Dykstra developed into an even better player with the Philadelphia Phillies, although he admittedly did so by using performance-enhancing drugs.

Born in Santa Ana, California, on February 10, 1963, Leonard Kyle Dykstra took his last name from his stepfather, Dennis Dykstra, who his mother married after his biological father, Jerry Leswick, deserted the family some years earlier. Raised in the working-class Anaheim suburb of Garden Grove, Dykstra displayed at an early age the feistiness for which he later became so well known, telling anyone willing to listen that his future included a career in major-league baseball, with his older brother, Brian, recalling, "He was always underestimated. People didn't take Lenny seriously because he didn't look all that imposing. But he was a pain in the ass who never took no for an answer."

Far more interested in sports than schoolwork, Dykstra struggled in the classroom but excelled on the ballfield, starring in both baseball and football at Garden Grove High School. After becoming the first and only freshman to play on the school's varsity baseball team three years earlier, Dykstra attended a Mets tryout camp during his senior year, telling a team

Lenny Dykstra's toughness and all-out style of play earned him the nickname "Nails."

employee who questioned his credentials due to his diminutive stature and slight build, "I'm Lenny Dykstra, and I'm the best player you're going to see today."

Ultimately selected by New York in the 13th round of the 1981 MLB Amateur Draft, Dykstra, who had previously committed to play baseball at Arizona State University, decided to sign with the Mets after they agreed to let him bypass rookie ball and begin his pro career at the Class A level. Dykstra subsequently spent the next two seasons with the Shelby Mets of the South Atlantic League, before earning Class A Carolina League MVP honors in 1983 by batting .358, compiling a .472 on-base percentage, and stealing 105 bases for Lynchburg. After one more year in the minors, Dykstra joined the Mets during the early stages of the 1985 campaign.

Platooning with Mookie Wilson in center field the rest of the year, the left-handed-hitting Dykstra homered once, knocked in 19 runs, scored 40 times, stole 15 bases, batted .254, and posted an OPS of .669 in 83 games and 236 official at-bats.

Though not a full-time starter, Dykstra received more playing time in 1986, allowing him to hit eight homers, drive in 45 runs, score 77 times, steal 31 bases, compile a batting average of .295, and post an OPS of .822 for a Mets team that ended up winning the World Series. Continuing his strong play during the postseason, Dykstra batted .304, posted an OPS of .925, and hit a memorable game-winning home run against Houston in the NLCS, before homering twice, knocking in three runs, batting .296, and compiling an OPS of .863 against Boston in the World Series.

The Mets' leadoff hitter for much of the season, Dykstra, who, although officially listed at 5'10" and 160 pounds, stood closer to 5'8" and weighed somewhere in the vicinity of 150 pounds, provided the team with a spark at the top of the batting order, where he used his ability to reach base and outstanding speed to upset opposing pitchers and help set the table for the likes of Keith Hernandez, Gary Carter, and Darryl Strawberry. Meanwhile, Dykstra gave little thought to his welfare in the outfield, often diving for balls and running into fences. Playing just as hard off the field, Dykstra, who Keith Hernandez later characterized in his book, *Pure Baseball*, as being "on the wild and crazy side," fit in perfectly with the rest of the squad, which became famous for its use of drugs and alcohol, chasing women, and partying until all hours of the evening.

Dykstra had another solid season in 1987, hitting 10 homers, driving in 43 runs, scoring 86 times, swiping 27 bases, batting .285, and posting an OPS of .806, before immersing himself in a weight training program the following offseason that helped him add some 10 pounds of muscle onto his frame.

In discussing his additional bulk with reporters during spring training, Dykstra said, "When I was in high school around the batting cages, the Angels were going to draft me. I walked up to Fred Lynn to ask for some advice. I asked him, 'If I get drafted, do you think I should sign?' He looked at me and said, 'It's a strong man's game.'"

Dykstra continued, "I came in with a different idea. I always came into spring training with the idea you have to be ready to swing the bat. I learned that's not true. You have to be physically ready, but when you get out there, you have six weeks to get everything ready. . . . I lifted weights to make me a better ball player. I didn't do it for looks, and I didn't do it to lay out on the beach. It is something to make me a better player."

Not totally convinced that the added muscle would make Dykstra a better player, Mets manager Davey Johnson stated, "He looks bigger. I hope that means better. I just hope when he was working with those weights, he wasn't thinking home runs."

Failing to show any improvement in 1988, Dykstra hit eight homers, knocked in 33 runs, scored 57 times, stole 30 bases, batted .270, and posted an OPS of .706, while again sharing playing time in center with Mookie Wilson. Unhappy over his inability to establish himself as a full-time starter, Dykstra expressed a desire to go elsewhere during the early stages of the 1989 campaign, prompting the Mets to complete a trade with the Phillies on June 18 that sent him and relief pitcher Roger McDowell to Philadelphia for second baseman Juan Samuel.

Dykstra, who, during his time in New York, hit 30 homers, knocked in 153 runs, scored 287 times, collected 469 hits, 104 doubles, and 17 triples, stole 116 bases, batted .278, compiled an on-base percentage of .350, and posted a slugging percentage of .413, subsequently emerged as an elite player in the City of Brotherly Love, earning three All-Star selections, two top-10 finishes in the NL MVP voting, and one Silver Slugger, even though he remained fully healthy in just three of his eight years with the Phillies. Particularly outstanding in 1993, Dykstra helped lead the Phillies to the NL pennant by batting .305 and establishing career-high marks in 10 different offensive categories, including homers (19), RBIs (66), runs scored (143), hits (194), stolen bases (37), and walks (129), earning in the process a runner-up finish to Barry Bonds in the league MVP balloting.

Plagued by injuries in each of the next three seasons, Dykstra appeared in a total of just 186 games, preventing him from performing at the same level. Diagnosed with spinal stenosis in 1996, Dykstra sat out most of the next two seasons, before announcing his retirement during 1998 spring training. Over parts of 12 big-league seasons, Dykstra hit 81 homers, knocked in 404 runs, scored 802 times, collected 1,298 hits, 281 doubles, and 43 triples, stole 285 bases, batted .285, compiled an on-base percentage of .375, and posted a slugging percentage of .419. However, the numbers that he produced during his time in Philadelphia remain tainted in the eyes of many due to his admitted use of steroids.

Nearly a decade after Dykstra left the game, the 2007 Mitchell Report on steroids in baseball revealed that he admitted to the commissioner's office in 2000 that he used performance enhancing drugs during his playing career. In attempting to explain his illicit behavior, Dykstra said, "You gotta understand, there were only 28 people who had my job in the whole world. And thousands of people wanted those jobs, and every year there were guys trying to take my job. So, I needed to do anything I could to protect my job, take care of my family. Do you have any idea how much money was at stake? Do you?"

Unfortunately, Dykstra seems to have failed to follow the letter of the law in retirement as well, with various allegations having been made against him at different times for criminal behavior. The now 63-year-old Dykstra, who suffered a stroke in 2024 that landed him in a Los Angeles hospital, currently lives with his ex-wife, Terri.

METS CAREER HIGHLIGHTS

Best Season

Dykstra had his finest all-around season as a member of the Mets in 1987, when he hit 10 homers, knocked in 43 runs, scored 86 times, stole 27 bases in 34 attempts, ranked among the league leaders with 37 doubles, batted .285, compiled an on-base percentage of .352, and posted a slugging percentage of .455.

Memorable Moments/Greatest Performances

Dykstra hit the first home run of his career in just his second big-league at-bat, reaching the seats with one man aboard off Cincinnati starter Mario Soto in the top of the third inning of a 9–4 win over the Reds on May 3, 1985.

Dykstra experienced his most memorable moment as a member of the Mets in Game 3 of the 1986 NLCS, when he gave them a 6–5 victory over the Astros by hitting a two-run homer off ace reliever Dave Smith with one man out in the bottom of the ninth inning.

Dykstra also came up big for the Mets in Game 3 of the 1986 World Series, leading them to a 7–1 win over the Red Sox by going 4-for-5 at the plate with a homer and two runs scored.

Dykstra starred in defeat on May 23, 1987, homering twice in one game for the first time in his career during a 4–2 loss to the Dodgers.

Dykstra contributed to a 23–10 pasting of the Cubs on August 16, 1987, by going 4-for-7 with a homer, three RBIs, and three runs scored.

Although the Mets lost to the Dodgers in seven games in the 1988 NLCS, Dykstra performed brilliantly, batting .429 (6-for-14), with a homer, three doubles, four walks, three RBIs, six runs scored, and an OPS of 1.457.

Notable Achievements

- Stole more than 20 bases three times, topping 30 thefts twice.
- Led NL center fielders with a .996 fielding percentage in 1988.
- Ranks among Mets career leaders in stolen bases (8th).
- Two-time division champion (1986 and 1988).
- 1986 NL champion.
- 1986 world champion.
- July 13, 1986, NL Player of the Week.

49
WALLY BACKMAN

A scrappy player who combined with his immediate predecessor on this list, Lenny Dykstra, to form a duo that became known as the "Wild Boys," Wally Backman spent parts of nine seasons in New York, serving as one of the Mets' offensive catalysts much of that time. The team's primary starter at second base from 1982 to 1988, Backman did an excellent job of setting the table for middle-of-the-order RBI men Keith Hernandez, Gary Carter, and Darryl Strawberry, batting over .300 three times and stealing more than 30 bases twice. A converted shortstop, Backman also did a solid job in the field, leading all NL second sackers in fielding percentage once, with his strong all-around play making him a key contributor to teams that won two division titles, one pennant, and one World Series.

Born in Hillsboro, Oregon, on September 22, 1959, Walter Wayne Backman grew up with his five siblings in a family that placed a priority on winning, saying, "I was raised to win. I credit my parents for that."

The son of a railroad switchman who spent a few years in the Pittsburgh Pirates farm system, Backman developed into an outstanding player himself at Aloha (Oregon) High School, performing so well his senior year that the Mets selected him with the 16th overall pick of the 1977 MLB Amateur Draft. Backman subsequently spent most of the next five seasons in the minors, although he also made brief appearances with the parent club in both 1980 and 1981. Hitting well wherever he went, Backman compiled batting averages of .326, .302, .282, and .293 at four different levels of New York's farm system from 1977 to 1980, while also posting marks of .323 and .278 during his two stints in New York.

However, even though Backman excelled at the plate, he struggled in the field, committing 30 errors in back-to-back seasons at shortstop. Moved to second base prior to the start of the 1980 campaign, Backman improved his defense dramatically, earning him a late season callup to the big leagues. Performing well during September, Backman batted .323 in 27 games and

Wally Backman batted over .300 for the Mets three times.

110 total plate appearances, while also committing just one error in the field.

Backman subsequently made the major-league roster out of spring training in 1981. But with clubhouse leader and 1980 Gold Glove winner Doug Flynn firmly entrenched at second base, Backman saw very little playing time, prompting the Mets to assign him to Triple-A Tidewater. Upset over his demotion and lack of playing time, Backman initially refused to report, before finally agreeing to accept his assignment after mulling his options for six days. However, after appearing in only 21 games with the Tides, Backman suffered a torn rotator cuff that forced him to miss the rest of the season.

Returning to New York in 1982 after the Mets parted ways with Flynn and starting shortstop Frank Taveras during the offseason, Backman spent much of the year sharing playing time at second with Brian Giles and "super sub" Bob Bailor. Appearing in a total of 96 games before a broken collarbone sustained in a bicycle accident brought his season to a premature end, Backman did a solid job offensively, batting .272, compiling a .387 on-base percentage, and posting an OPS of .759. But his defense left something to be desired, with Backman later saying, "I got labeled that year for a bad glove, and it really bothered me. The season before, I tore my rotator cuff, and in 1982, it still bothered me."

Although fully recovered from his injury by the start of the 1983 season, Backman spent most of the year in the minors, saying upon his demotion on May 17, "I'll go and play hard, but at the end of the season, I hope the Mets trade me or release me. I really need to get away from this organization. There is no place in it for me."

Excelling under Tides manager Davey Johnson in what turned out to be his final year in the minors, Backman batted .316, posted an OPS of .794, scored 69 runs, and stole 37 bases in only 101 games. Later crediting Johnson for much of his success, Backman said, "The best thing that happened to me was having Dave Johnson as a manager last year. Dave put me leadoff to begin the season. He saw what I could do and had confidence in me. That took a lot of pressure off. I could relax and play my game."

Claiming that Johnson also helped him improve himself defensively, Backman added, "In the field, he showed me how to anticipate situations and showed me what I'd been doing wrong on the double play."

With Johnson assuming managerial duties in New York in 1984, he named Backman his starting second baseman. Performing well in his first full big-league season, Backman batted .280, compiled an on-base percentage of .360, posted an OPS of .700, scored 68 runs, and stole 32 bases, while hitting mostly out of the leadoff spot in the batting order. Solid in the field as well, Backman committed just 10 errors, making him one of the league's better all-around players at his position.

Backman had another solid season in 1985, batting .273, posting an on-base percentage of .320 and an OPS of .664, scoring 77 runs, and swiping 30 bags, while also leading all NL second sackers with a .989 fielding percentage. Nevertheless, with the switch-hitting Backman proving to be far more effective from the left side of the plate, the Mets completed a trade with the Minnesota Twins the following offseason that procured the services of the right-handed-swinging Tim Teufel, with whom Backman spent the next few seasons platooning.

Yet even in a somewhat reduced role, Backman made significant contributions to the Mets during their successful run to the 1986 pennant. In addition to leading the team with a .320 batting average, Backman, who spent most of the year hitting second in the Mets' lineup behind either Lenny Dykstra or Mookie Wilson, scored 67 runs, stole 13 bases, compiled an on-base percentage of .376, and posted an OPS of .761.

Standing just 5'9" and weighing only 160 pounds, Backman possessed very little power at the plate. A slap hitter who got many of his hits by going the opposite way, Backman sprayed the ball to all fields and rarely swung at bad pitches, making him extremely difficult to strike out. An excellent bunter, Backman possessed the ability to reach base in that fashion as well.

However, Backman perhaps made his greatest contributions to the Mets with his grit and tremendous determination. The type of player that teammates loved and opponents hated, Backman, who constantly sported a dirty uniform and a chew of tobacco in his mouth, dove for balls, slid hard into bases, and rode the opposition from the bench, with Ron Darling recalling, "He was on a mission every single day he went out there. He was always the smallest guy on the field with the biggest heart. He inspired everybody because, if he could play that hard, why couldn't everyone."

Always one to speak his mind, Backman even had the temerity to challenge his own teammates when he felt they failed to exhibit the same level of passion.

One such instance occurred in 1987, when Backman chastised Darryl Strawberry in the media for claiming that he had a virus and pulling himself out of a crucial game against the Cardinals after he spent the earlier part of the day recording a rap song. Commenting on the often-ill Strawberry's actions, Backman stated, "Nobody I know gets sick 25 times a year."

Upon learning of Backman's remark, an angry Strawberry said, "I'll bust that little redneck in the face."

Plagued by hamstring problems in 1987, Backman batted just .250 and posted an OPS of only .593 in 94 games and 300 official at-bats. Although Backman continued to be platooned at second with Tim Teufel the following year, he rebounded to bat .303 and compile an OPS of .731. But with top prospect Gregg Jefferies waiting in the wings, the Mets traded Backman to the Twins for three minor leaguers on December 7, 1988.

Backman, who left New York with career totals of seven homers, 165 RBIs, 359 runs scored, 670 hits, 95 doubles, 14 triples, and 106 stolen bases, a lifetime batting average of .283, an on-base percentage of .353, and a slugging percentage of .344, ended up spending just one year in Minnesota assuming the role of a part-time player, before splitting the next four seasons between the Pirates, Phillies, and Mariners, serving all three teams in a similar capacity. Released by the Mariners during the early stages of the 1993 campaign, Backman announced his retirement, ending his career with

10 homers, 240 RBIs, 482 runs scored, 893 hits, 138 doubles, 19 triples, 117 stolen bases, a .275 batting average, a .349 on-base percentage, and a .339 slugging percentage.

Transitioning into a career in managing following his playing days, Backman spent several years managing in the farm system of the Chicago White Sox, during which time he became known for his on-field temper tantrums that earned him numerous ejections and suspensions. Once considered the leading candidate for Chicago's vacant managerial job, Backman ended up being bypassed for the post when the organization learned that he had openly rooted against them so that previous skipper Jerry Manuel would be fired. Backman also had a 2004 managerial offer from the Arizona Diamondbacks rescinded when it surfaced that he had pleaded guilty to a 1999 charge of DUI and been arrested in 2001 for a domestic violence incident involving his second wife. Eventually returning to the Mets in 2009, Backman continued to manage in their farm system until 2016, when he received his walking papers for ignoring the organization's demands on how to use a certain player. After also managing in Mexico and the independent Atlantic League, Backman again let his bad temper get the better of him in August 2019, when police arrested him for harassment and criminal mischief after he shoved his girlfriend against a wall, twisted her hand, and stopped her from reporting him to authorities by taking her phone.

METS CAREER HIGHLIGHTS

Best Season

Despite appearing in only 124 games and garnering just 387 official at-bats, Backman made his greatest overall impact on the fortunes of the Mets in 1986, when he helped lead them to the pennant by batting .320, posting an OPS of .761, scoring 67 runs, stealing 13 bases, and finishing third in the league with 14 sacrifice hits.

Memorable Moments/Greatest Performances

Backman hit the first of his 10 career homers with two men aboard in the top of the fifth inning of a 6–4 win over the Braves on May 26, 1982.

Backman gave the Mets a 5–4 victory over the Expos on April 18, 1984, when he knocked in a pair of runs with a two-out, bases loaded double in the bottom of the ninth inning.

Backman delivered the decisive blow of a 2–0 win over the Giants on August 17, 1984, when he homered off Mike Krukow with one man aboard in the top of the 10th inning.

Backman helped lead the Mets to a 6–0 win over the Pirates on April 26, 1985, by going a perfect 5-for-5 at the plate with a double, stolen base, three RBIs, and one run scored.

Backman contributed to a lopsided 13–2 victory over the Astros on July 17, 1986, by going 3-for-6 with a career-high five RBIs.

Notable Achievements

- Batted over .300 three times.
- Stole more than 30 bases twice.
- Led NL with 14 sacrifice hits in 1985.
- Led NL second basemen with a .989 fielding percentage in 1985.
- Ranks among Mets career leaders in stolen bases (10th) and sacrifice hits (10th).
- Two-time division champion (1986 and 1988).
- 1986 NL champion.
- 1986 world champion.

50

DONN CLENDENON

Although Donn Clendenon spent less than three full seasons in New York, the tremendous contributions he made to the Mets' 1969 world championship ballclub earned him the final spot on this list. A solid RBI-man who gave the Mets a powerful bat in the middle of their lineup, Clendenon gained recognition as MVP of the 1969 World Series by homering three times and knocking in four runs against the heavily favored Baltimore Orioles. Remaining the centerpiece of the Mets' offense the following year, Clendenon set a then-single-season franchise record for RBIs, before being released at the end of the ensuing campaign after failing to perform at the same level.

Born in Neosho, Missouri, on July 15, 1935, Donn Alvin Clendenon never knew his father, who died of leukemia at only 32 years of age. Shortly after losing his dad, Clendenon moved with his mother to Atlanta, Georgia, where his mom remarried a few years later, taking as her husband former Negro League baseball player Nish Williams, who became young Donn's athletic mentor.

With his stepfather serving as a coach on nearly every team for which he played, Clendenon eventually developed into an outstanding all-around athlete, lettering in nine different sports at Atlanta's Booker T. Washington High School. Offered several scholarships as graduation neared, Clendenon initially planned to attend UCLA until some coaches from nearby Morehouse College visited his mother and convinced her that he should remain closer to home. Clendenon, who excelled in the classroom as well, ultimately accepted an academic scholarship to Morehouse and became a 12-sport letterman in football, basketball, baseball, and track. While at Morehouse, Clendenon also developed a close relationship with his assigned "big brother," Martin Luther King Jr., who made certain that he did not neglect his studies.

Offered contracts by both the Cleveland Browns and Harlem Globetrotters upon his graduation, Clendenon, who played semipro baseball for

Donn Clendenon earned World Series MVP honors in 1969.

the Atlanta Black Crackers during the summer months while in college, had a difficult decision to make since his mother wanted him to pursue a career in medicine and he wanted to teach. After briefly teaching fourth grade, Clendenon attended a Pittsburgh Pirates tryout camp in Florida at the urging of his stepfather, later saying, "Nish convinced me that I could, in effect, have my cake and eat it too if I went into professional sports. I could have a dozen good years as a professional athlete; make some money; develop a name for myself; and use the off-season to pursue my future plans."

After making a favorable impression on Pirates GM Branch Rickey, Clendenon signed with Pittsburgh as an amateur free agent in late 1956. He subsequently spent the next five years advancing through the team's farm system, before finally being promoted to the majors during the latter stages of the 1961 campaign. Joining the parent club for good the following year, Clendenon spent the 1962 season sharing time at first base with Dick Stuart. Taking over at first full-time in 1963, the right-handed-swinging Clendenon, who stood 6'4" and weighed 215 pounds, soon established himself as one of the NL's more productive hitters, even though he had the misfortune of playing his home games at cavernous Forbes Field. Performing especially well in 1965 and 1966, Clendenon batted .301, hit 14 homers, and knocked in 96 runs in the first of those campaigns, before batting .299 and establishing career-high marks with 28 homers and 98 RBIs in the second. A free swinger who rarely walked, Clendenon fanned more than 100 times in five of his six seasons as a full-time starter, leading the NL in strikeouts twice and placing second in the circuit on two other occasions. Meanwhile, Clendenon displayed superior agility in the field, leading all NL first sackers in putouts and assists three times each.

With top prospect Al Oliver waiting in the wings, the Pirates left the 33-year-old Clendenon unprotected in the 1968 MLB expansion draft, allowing the Montreal Expos to claim him with the 11th overall pick. However, prior to the start of the 1969 season, the Expos traded Clendenon and outfielder Jesús Alou to the Houston Astros for Rusty Staub. But when Houston named former Pirates manager Harry Walker their new skipper, Clendenon refused to report to the Astros, saying that he would rather retire than play for someone who he viewed as a racist.

MLB commissioner Bowie Kuhn eventually interceded, ordering the two teams to rework the deal. Houston settled for two pitchers instead of Clendenon, who remained in Montreal until June 15, 1969, when, after appearing in only 38 games with the Expos, he headed for New York when the Mets acquired him for backup infielder Kevin Collins, three minor leaguers, and a player to be named later.

Joining a Mets team that trailed the first-place Chicago Cubs by nine games in the NL East standings at the time, Clendenon spent most of the second half of the season platooning at first base with the left-handed-swinging Ed Kranepool. Appearing in 72 games with his new ballclub, Clendenon hit 12 homers, knocked in 37 runs, scored 31 times, batted .252, and posted an OPS of .777. But while those numbers might seem relatively modest, Clendenon made an enormous impact following his arrival in New York, with Bud Harrelson later saying, "When we got him [Clendenon], we became a different team. We never had a three-run homer type of guy. He was always humble, never cocky. We were still young kids in that era. He was a veteran that came in and made us better."

Jerry Grote expressed similar sentiments, saying, "Donn made everyone in our lineup better. We all got better pitches to hit because of him."

Cleon Jones also spoke of the effect that Clendenon had on the rest of the team, stating, "Donn gave us the middle of the lineup bat that we were missing. He had such a presence in the clubhouse, too. If we don't get Donn, I don't think we win."

Ron Swoboda also suggested that the Mets would have fallen short without Clendenon, saying, "There is no doubt in my mind that we don't win the World Series without Donn. He was such a heady player. He was like another coach on the field."

Swoboda continued, "In addition to what he did on the field, Donn was such a presence in our clubhouse. Guys listened to him. He was a veteran who already had accomplished so much by the time he came to us. He made things happen in so many different ways."

Art Shamsky further elaborated on the way that Clendenon contributed to team chemistry, stating, "I think Donn's greatest asset, besides having a terrific year and being the MVP in the World Series, is that he was a guy in the locker room that really was a clubhouse lawyer. He was able to get guys going. He would yell things across the locker room. He was a guy that instigated a lot of turmoil, as I like to say, but good turmoil . . . but he had a great year when he did play, and he had the great World Series. Donn was a tremendous asset because we needed some right-handed power, but I think it's a combination of what he did on the field and what he did in the locker room."

After helping the Mets win 38 of their final 49 games during the regular season, Clendenon failed to make an appearance against Atlanta in the NLCS since the Braves started three right-handed pitchers. But with southpaws Mike Cuellar and Dave McNally both starting twice for Baltimore in the World Series, Clendenon made a huge impact on the outcome of the Fall Classic, homering once off Cuellar and twice off McNally, driving in four runs, and batting .357, en route to earning Series MVP honors.

Although the Mets failed to return to the playoffs in 1970, Clendenon continued to perform well in the middle of their lineup, finishing the season with 22 homers, 97 RBIs, a .288 batting average, and an OPS of .863. But after Clendenon slumped to just 11 homers, 37 RBIs, a .247 batting average, and an OPS of .713 in 1971, the Mets released him at the end of the year. Clendenon subsequently signed with the St. Louis Cardinals, for whom he appeared in only 61 games in 1972, before announcing his retirement following his release in early August. Over parts of 12 big-league seasons, Clendenon hit 159 homers, knocked in 682 runs, scored 594 times, collected 1,273 hits, 192 doubles, and 57 triples, stole 90 bases, batted .274, compiled a .328 on-base percentage, and posted a .442 slugging percentage. In his 281 games with the Mets, Clendenon hit 45 homers, knocked in 171 runs, scored 125 times, batted .267, compiled an on-base percentage of .328, and posted a slugging percentage of .469.

Following his retirement from baseball, Clendenon, who held jobs with Mellon National Bank and Trust, the Allegheny District Attorney's Office, and U.S. Steel while playing for the Pirates, ran a successful family-owned restaurant called Donn Clendenon's Supper Club in Atlanta, Georgia, for several years, before earning a JD from Duquesne University in 1978. However, while practicing law in Dayton, Ohio, during the mid-1980s, Clendenon lost almost everything he had when he developed an addiction to cocaine, later telling William C. Rhoden of the *New York Times*, "I was 49 turning 50; that [taking cocaine] was kind of like a birthday present for me. I was hooked immediately."

Forced to resign from the law firm where he worked following an arrest for cocaine possession in 1988, Clendenon sought treatment for drug abuse at a facility in Ogden, Utah, where he learned that he had leukemia. After kicking his drug habit, Clendenon moved to the small city of Sioux Falls, South Dakota, telling Rhoden, "I had to go to a place where I could change my environment, my associates, and everything else."

Establishing himself as a valuable member of the community before long, Clendenon became a certified chemical dependency counselor at the Keystone-Carroll Treatment Center, served as general counsel for the Interstate Audit Corporation in Sioux Falls, and spent several years practicing law at Clendenon, Henney & Hoy. Eventually succumbing to the same disease that killed his father, Clendenon died from leukemia at the age of 70 on September 17, 2005.

METS CAREER HIGHLIGHTS

Best Season

The 1970 campaign proved to be Clendenon's finest in New York. Despite appearing in only 121 games and garnering just 396 official at-bats, Clendenon set a new Mets record by driving in 97 runs, finished second on the team with 22 homers, scored 65 times, batted .288, compiled an on-base percentage of .348, and posted a slugging percentage of .515, earning in the process a 13th-place finish in the NL MVP voting.

Memorable Moments/Greatest Performances

Clendenon delivered the decisive blow of a 3–2 win over the Giants on August 30, 1969, when he homered off Gaylord Perry in the top of the ninth inning with two men out and no one on base.

Clendenon led the Mets to a 5–4 win over the Dodgers on September 2, 1969, by going 3-for-4 with a pair of solo homers off Don Sutton.

Clendenon helped the Mets clinch their first division title by hitting a pair of homers and driving in four runs during a 6–0 victory over the Cardinals on September 24, 1969, with his three-run homer off Steve Carlton in the bottom of the first inning providing the winning margin.

Clendenon earned 1969 World Series MVP honors by hitting three homers, driving in four runs, scoring four times, batting .357, and posting an OPS of 1.509 during the Mets' five-game victory over Baltimore, reaching the seats once each in Games 2, 4, and 5.

Clendenon contributed to a 12–2 rout of the Giants on July 28, 1970, by hitting a pair of three-run homers and driving in a career-high seven runs.

Clendenon gave the Mets a dramatic 6–5 victory over the Phillies on June 19, 1971, when he homered with two men out and no one on base in the bottom of the 15th inning.

Notable Achievements

- Hit more than 20 home runs once.
- Posted slugging percentage over .500 once.
- 1969 division champion.
- 1969 NL champion.
- 1969 world champion.
- 1969 World Series MVP.

SUMMARY

Having identified the 50 greatest players in Mets history, the time has come to select the best of the best. Based on the rankings contained in this book, the members of the Mets all-time team are listed below. Our squad includes the top player at each position, along with a pitching staff that features a five-man starting rotation, a setup man, and a closer. Our starting lineup also includes a designated hitter.

STARTING LINEUP

Player:	Position:
José Reyes	SS
David Wright	3B
Keith Hernandez	1B
Mike Piazza	C
Carlos Beltrán	CF
Darryl Strawberry	RF
Pete Alonso	DH
Edgardo Alfonzo	2B
Cleon Jones	LF

PITCHING STAFF

Tom Seaver	SP
Dwight Gooden	SP
Jacob deGrom	SP
Jerry Koosman	SP
Jon Matlack	SP
John Franco	SU
Billy Wagner	CL

GLOSSARY

ABBREVIATIONS AND STATISTICAL TERMS

1B. First baseman.

2B. Second baseman.

3B. Third baseman or triple.

AVG. Batting average. The number of hits, divided by the number of at-bats.

C. Catcher.

CF. Center fielder.

CG. Complete games pitched.

CL. Closer.

DH. Designated hitter.

ERA. Earned run average. The number of earned runs a pitcher gives up, per nine innings. This does not include runs that scored as a result of errors made in the field and is calculated by dividing the number of runs given up, by the number of innings pitched, and multiplying the result by 9.

HITS. Base hits. Awarded when a runner safely reaches at least first base upon a batted ball, if no error is recorded.

HR. Home runs. Fair ball hit over the fence, or one hit to a spot that allows the batter to circle the bases before the ball is returned to home plate.

IP. Innings pitched.

LF. Left fielder.

OBP. On-base percentage. Hits plus walks plus hit-by-pitches, divided by plate appearance.

OPS. Offensive production statistic—the sum of a player's on-base percentage and slugging percentage.

RBI. Runs batted in. Awarded to the batter when a runner scores upon a safely batted ball, a sacrifice or a walk.

RF. Right fielder.

RUNS. Runs scored by a player.

SB. Stolen bases.

SHO. Shutouts.

SLG. Slugging percentage. The number of total bases earned by all singles, doubles, triples and home runs, divided by the total number of at-bats.

SO. Strikeouts.

SP. Starting pitcher.

SS. Shortstop.

SU. Setup man.

WHIP. The sum of a pitcher's walks and hits divided by the number of innings pitched.

W-L. Won-lost record (for a pitcher).

WINNING PERCENTAGE. A pitcher's number of wins, divided by his number of total decisions (i.e., wins plus losses).

BIBLIOGRAPHY

BOOKS

Cohen, Stanley. *A Magic Summer: The Amazin' Story of the 1969 New York Mets.* New York: Skyhorse Publishing, 2009.

Darling, Ron, and Daniel Paisner. *108 Stitches: Loose Threads, Ripping Yarns, and the Darndest Characters from My Time in the Game.* New York: St. Martin's Press, 2019.

Harrelson, Bud, and Phil Pepe. *Turning Two: My Journey to the Top of the World and Back with the New York Mets.* New York: Thomas Dunne Books, 2012.

Hernandez, Keith, and Mike Bryan. *Pure Baseball.* New York: Harper Perennial, 1995.

James, Bill, and Rob Neyer. *The Neyer/James Guide to Pitchers: An Historical Compendium of Pitching, Pitchers, and Pitches.* New York: Simon & Schuster, 2004.

Keri, Jonah. *Up, Up, and Away: The Kid, the Hawk, Rock, Vladi, Pedro, le Grand Orange, Youppi!, the Crazy Business of Baseball, and the Ill-fated but Unforgettable Montreal Expos.* Canada: Penguin Random House, 2014.

Klapisch, Bob, and John Harper. *The Worst Team Money Could Buy.* Lincoln, NE: Bison Books, 2005.

McGraw, Tug, and Don Yaeger. *Ya Gotta Believe!: My Roller-Coaster Life as a Screwball Pitcher and Part-Time Father, and My Hope-Filled Fight Against Brain Cancer.* New York: Signet, 2005.

Pearlman, Jeff. *The Bad Guys Won: A Season of Brawling, Boozing, Bimbo Chasing, and Championship Baseball with Straw, Doc, Mookie, Nails, the Kid, and the Rest of the 1986 Mets.* New York: Harper Books, 2005.

Pearlman, Jeff. *The Rocket That Fell to Earth: Roger Clemens and the Rage for Baseball Immortality.* New York: Harper Books, 2010.

Robertson, John. *Rusty Staub of the Expos.* Canada: Prentice Hall, 1971.

Shalin, Mike, and Neil Shalin. *Out by a Step: The 100 Best Players Not in the Baseball Hall of Fame.* Lanham, MD: Diamond Communications, Inc., 2002.

Sowell, Mike. *One Pitch Away: The Players' Stories of the 1986 LCS and World Series.* New York: Macmillan Publishing, 1995.

WEBSITES

Bio Project, online at SABR.org
(www.sabr.org/bioproj/person)
The Players, online at Baseball-Almanac.com
(www.baseball-almanac.com/players)
The Players, online at Baseball-Reference.com
(www.baseball-reference.com/players)
The Teams, online at Baseball-Reference.com
(www.baseball-reference.com/teams)

www.ingramcontent.com/pod-product-compliance
Lightning Source LLC
LaVergne TN
LVHW011758060526
838200LV00053B/3628